How to Read a Wedding Dress

Also by Lydia Edwards and also published by Bloomsbury

How to Read a Dress

How to Read a Suit

Lydia Edwards

How to Read a Wedding Dress

A GUIDE TO CHANGING BRIDAL FASHION
FROM THE 18TH TO THE 21ST CENTURY

BLOOMSBURY VISUAL ARTS
LONDON · NEW YORK · OXFORD · NEW DELHI · SYDNEY

BLOOMSBURY VISUAL ARTS
Bloomsbury Publishing Plc, 50 Bedford Square, London, WC1B 3DP, UK
Bloomsbury Publishing Inc, 1359 Broadway, New York, NY 10018, USA
Bloomsbury Publishing Ireland, 29 Earlsfort Terrace, Dublin 2, D02 AY28, Ireland

BLOOMSBURY, BLOOMSBURY VISUAL ARTS and the Diana logo
are trademarks of Bloomsbury Publishing Plc

First published in Great Britain 2026
Copyright © Lydia Edwards, 2026

Lydia Edwards has asserted her right under the Copyright,
Designs and Patents Act, 1988, to be identified as Author of this work.

For legal purposes the Acknowledgments on p. 7 constitute
an extension of this copyright page.

Cover design: Adriana Brioso
Cover image © Dress by Lebanese designer Elie Saab, Spring-Summer 2011
Haute Couture Collection Show (© Bertrand Guay/AFP/Getty Images)

All rights reserved. No part of this publication may be: i) reproduced or
transmitted in any form, electronic or mechanical, including photocopying,
recording or by means of any information storage or retrieval system without prior
permission in writing from the publishers; or ii) used or reproduced in any way for
the training, development or operation of artificial intelligence (AI) technologies,
including generative AI technologies. The rights holders expressly reserve this
publication from the text and data mining exception as per Article 4(3) of the
Digital Single Market Directive (EU) 2019/790.

Bloomsbury Publishing Plc does not have any control over, or responsibility for,
any third-party websites referred to or in this book. All internet addresses given
in this book were correct at the time of going to press. The author and publisher
regret any inconvenience caused if addresses have changed or sites have ceased to
exist, but can accept no responsibility for any such changes.

A catalogue record for this book is available from the British Library.

A catalog record for this book is available from the Library of Congress.

ISBN: HB: 978-1-3502-9304-5
       PB: 978-1-3502-9303-8
       ePDF: 978-1-3502-9305-2
       eBook: 978-1-3502-9306-9

Typeset by Typo·glyphix, Burton-on-Trent, DE14 3HE, UK
Printed and bound in India

For product safety related questions contact productsafety@bloomsbury.com

To find out more about our authors and books
visit www.bloomsbury.com and sign up for our newsletters.

Dedication

This one is for Hannah.

Table of Contents

Acknowledgments 7

Introduction 8

Chapter 1
Before the White Wedding Dress 15

Chapter 2
1720–1789 27

Chapter 3
1790–1836 45

Chapter 4
1837–1869 67

Chapter 5
1870–1889 89

Chapter 6
1890–1916 111

Chapter 7
1918–1929 131

Chapter 8
1930–1946 143

Chapter 9
1947–1959 159

Chapter 10
1960–1979 173

Chapter 11
1980–1999 193

Chapter 12
2000–2023 207

Glossary of Terms 228
Notes 230
Bibliography 243
Image Credits 245
Index 253

Acknowledgments

Every time I sit down to write an acknowledgment it gets harder, because with each *How to Read* comes more advice and support. As ever I must first express gratitude to my wonderful editor Frances Arnold and the team at Bloomsbury. They go above and beyond to make the process smooth, enjoyable, and productive, on both a professional and personal level. My husband Aaron has always been a source of solid support, consistently giving me the space I need to write, and for that I will always be grateful. My parents, Chris and Julia, have believed in my abilities since I wrote my first scrawling stories as a child, buoying me up through both the easy and challenging times.

As ever, I must thank Dr Karin Bohleke of the Fashion Archives and Museum at Shippensburg University. Her support, advice, and friendship mean more than she knows, and some of the beautiful garments and images you'll see in these pages are courtesy of Karin.

Friends can constitute family, becoming even more important when blood family is not close by. I must acknowledge the unfailing support of the following: Nina Levy, Romanie Garcia-Lee, Tina Moss, Claudia Lagos and Rodrigo Tobar, Kristy Juengling, Emilie Maguin, and my fantastic sister-in-law Leanne Feehan.

This book is the culmination of a longstanding fascination with bridal wear, enhanced through past work at a bridal shop. My thanks go to previous proprietor Liz Wootton, who gave me such insight to the workings of the contemporary bridal industry.

I must give particular mention to the following people and institutions for their assistance and generosity: Fashion Museum Riga, Maine Historical Society, Texas Fashion Collection at the University of North Texas, and to designers Curtis Cassell, Chrissy Wai-Ching, Leehwa Studios, Eiko Ueda, and Miranda Bennett Studios. Brides Lauren Joshua, Khadijah Abdul-Aleem, and Rachel Press Frishberg have given their time (and wedding photos) so generously, adding an extra personal and diverse element to the book.

Special thanks to Pattie Boyd for generously sharing her memories of the dress she chose for her 1966 wedding to George Harrison.

My eldest daughter now understands that 'Mummy writes books,' and tells anyone who'll listen. This is probably the biggest accolade and support I could receive, so thank you Holly, and your little sister Hannah – who is showing a promising interest in shoes.

LEFT
Wedding of Romanie Garcia and Danny Lee, Brooklyn, New York, 2012.

Introduction

> White clothing can [also] give that glow, no more so than in bridal wear. Weddings are the privileged moment of heterosexuality, that is, [racial] reproduction, and also of women, since they are glorified on what is seen as their day.[1]

This book is a story of memory. There are few other garments so strongly imbued with the power of remembering, or indeed of forgetting, as a bridal gown. The action of purchasing, making, or inheriting a wedding dress brings with it a raft of emotions: excitement, anticipation, anxiety, and nostalgia for people and places gone by. This encompasses what previous brides wore and, frequently, considers how elements of heritage and legacy can be brought into wedding celebrations through the vessel of a dress. Once the dress has been worn, it is indelibly connected to memories of the day; physical traces of wear are present, and the garment is imbued with all the properties of a valuable souvenir. The dress may be passed on to future brides in the family, it might be sold, it might be repurposed. If the marriage dissolves, the dress frequently becomes a symbol of an unsuccessful union and is not passed down, tinged with superstition and the fear of being tainted. Such emotions and associations are of course universal, but in twenty-first century popular culture they have—for better or worse—become strongly linked to the Western tradition of the white wedding dress. The uncomfortable truth is that in many cases, this complex garment was first introduced to non-Western countries by nineteenth-century missionaries. Belief in Anglo-Saxon superiority, combined with ideals centered around Christian monogamy and purity, resulted in the promotion of the white wedding dress to people who for centuries had been marrying in a myriad of colors. So widespread was this campaign that the adoption of the white dress was often enthusiastically embraced by the very people whose customs were being actively denigrated[2]. In 2003, *Ebony* magazine ran a feature on the ways young women of color were "choosing their own image styles," with white dresses described as "no longer *de rigeour*" and "ethnic" patterning more mainstream.[3] Nevertheless, the resulting spread of images depicted dresses which—although featuring African-inspired trimming and imported fabrics—were all, bar one gold example, in shades of white, cream, and ivory. Almost twenty years on, there are certainly more options within the bridal industry for those who want to incorporate "kitenge" or "Ankara" Nigerian fabric, for example, into an A-line, fit-and-flare, mermaid, ballgown, or one of the countless other styles found in global bridal design. This problematic history should be fully acknowledged, and remembered, as a crucial part of the origin story of this global phenomenon.

RIGHT

This 1912 portrait, entitled "A Fashionable Wedding in Kamerun", depicts a wedding that was highly fashionable in the Western sense. Although traditional marriage ceremonies did survive colonization, this image illustrates the fact that elite families were frequently choosing elaborate European and American practices above those of their own culture.

Today, the white wedding dress is enthusiastically worn worldwide and has become a symbol of marriage for multiple cultures, sometimes alongside or instead of traditional wedding garments. White kimono (*Shiromuku*) with woven decoration have been worn for Japanese Shinto weddings since the Heian period (originally by the daughters of samurai), with the color thought to ward off evil spirits. White is also a traditional mourning color and, within a wedding context, for Japanese brides it can also indicate that a woman has been parted from her birth family as if she were dead.[4] The adoption of Western fashion was first seen during the Meiji-era (1868-1912), when the country opened trade routes with the West and welcomed an influx of sartorial changes. By the 1910s, completely plain white layers of kimono were influenced by the Western bridal gown in a more subtle and sensitive example of cultural fusion.[5] Today, *Uedingu doresu* (white wedding gown) continues to be a popular choice in Japan, where the wearing of traditional wedding kimono also remains paramount—and, as the final chapter will show, many designers successfully blend the two. In India and other South Asian countries, it is not so common to see bridal saris made in white—again, a color of mourning. More often, a bride might choose two garments: both a traditional red sari and a white western gown, particularly if she is marrying a man from a different cultural background. However, as Kavita Ramdya explains, for Indian brides marrying outside India, the wish to assert and celebrate their culture is often inextricably linked to the wearing of a traditional sari. For others wishing to affirm their Americanness or Europeanness, the white wedding dress is a symbol of independence from traditional family involvement; in some cases, even an act of defiance[6]. The latter is expressed neatly in Jhumpa Lahiri's 2003 novel *The Namesake*, in which Moushumi, a Bengali American woman, saves a white wedding dress that she purchased for a wedding with a non-Bengali man that never materialized. Always told not to marry an American, Moushumi spent her childhood being asked "if she planned to get married in a red sari or a white gown."[7] Her subsequent purchase of a white gown, kept hidden in a closet, comes to be a reminder of a previous act of rebellion.

Introduction 9

In China, white is also traditionally the color of mourning. As Daiyun Yue has expressed it, "In China, we often speak of 'red and white happy occasions,' where a red occasion refers to a wedding and a white occasion indicates a funeral."[8] The pull of white bridal wear is put into sharp relief when we consider that the traditional connotations of white are so strong, just mentioning the color raises intense associations of mourning and sadness. Its common adoption for bridal wear among young Chinese women was described in 2010 as a "pragmatic [...] status symbol,"[9] and some will choose three separate dresses to acknowledge differing aspects of heritage and tradition alongside fashion: a patterned *qi pao*, a white western gown, and a long red dress, cut in a Western style.[10] The image on p.11 shows a bridal gown by Taiwanese designer Tsai Meiyue, one of China's top wedding dress designers in the 2010s. With its ivory and gold minidress inspired by *cheongsam*, topped with headdress and shoulder decoration reminiscent of elaborate Ming and Qing dynasty costumes, this outfit almost seems to encompass that tripartite vision. Although research from 2014 reported that the choices of Western celebrities did not affect bridal "dreams" in China, that seems to have shifted in more recent years.[11] "I would like to wear a white fluffy dress. It will make me feel like an elegant princess, just like Kate Middleton, the wife of Prince William," 27-year-old bride-to-be Linda Wang told *China Daily* in 2019.[12] Rather than choosing a white dress to be distinctive, the newspaper continued, modern Chinese brides were more likely to choose traditional dress to stand out.

The gendering of wedding dresses is also a crucial mirror through which to consider this iconic garment. It is a relatively recent, but nevertheless extremely strong, social construct. In the last decade, huge strides have been made to find acceptance in the idea

LEFT
Woodcut of a bride by Utagawa Kuniyoshi, early nineteenth century.

RIGHT
Tsai Meiyue design, 2011.

that wedding dresses, among others, can be worn by all genders for any kind of union and ceremony. The final chapter will discuss the choices made when a wedding includes two brides, and reflect on the ongoing conversation regarding dresses for all, irrespective of gender or sexual orientation. Throughout, the status and philosophy of the white wedding dress will be considered alongside examples of dresses that deviated from it, for socio-economic and aesthetic as well as cultural reasons.

Wedding dresses are big business, with bridal industry revenue of over $44 billion in the USA alone (as of 2023), expected to surpass around $73.2 billion by 2030.[14] There is also a sizeable stake in wedding dress-related entertainment, with smash reality shows including *Say Yes to the Dress* (*SYTTD*), *I Found the Gown*, and *Something Borrowed, Something New* (all via the TLC network) generating multiple spin offs and, in the case of *SYTTD*, garnering an iconic status, along with celebrity for those on screen. Critics have suggested that such shows highlight the worst in privilege and a "first world problems" mentality, with couples spending thousands over budget due to the pressure of finding "the dream dress." Heightened emotions and disproportionate family drama demonstrate the lengths brides will go to procure their fantasy (which was sent up particularly well in the 1996 smash film *Muriel's Wedding*). These exaggerated, romantic connotations no doubt increased tenfold with the rise of commercialization in bridal wear, and with publicity given to royal and celebrity weddings in the press. "It's the most important thing to me", brides frequently explain on reality show *Don't Tell the Bride*, in which the groom must choose every aspect of the wedding—including the clothing. "I don't care about anything else, as long as he gets the dress right." Such intense emotion and scrutiny over this liminal garment again play into the concept of memory. "Making memories" and having the perfect bridal experience is a very real pressure, and previous work in a bridal shop showed me that the "entourage" a bride brings—their opinions and their level of support—are just as much a part of the memory-making as the actual purchase itself. Comedian Margaret Cho summed this up well in 2007:

> Everyone at the bridal boutique was so nice. It was the happiest place on earth: the women trying on gowns, and the women with them on the verge of tears anytime anybody came out of the dressing room. It was the joy that was so seductive.[15]

This is in many respects a new phenomenon, and almost certainly one fueled by the postmodern consumer society. Because of this it is also one that some choose to partially ignore in favor of a less compartmentalized approach (see opposite). At its root, though, is a fierce, powerful, emotional fantasy that has existed at least since the mid-nineteenth century. That is what this book will explore, while dissecting the styles and cultural shifts that sustain it.

RIGHT
At this 2012 wedding, the bride constructed her ensemble from various sources, using a bridal shop, Etsy.com and other small vendors to procure a dreamy, Pre-Raphaelite inspired look.

Chapter 1

Before the White Wedding Dress

For many cultures, the image of a white dress and veil is utterly synonymous with a bride, and this concept is certainly not new. Ancient Greek brides are said to have worn white, carried white flowers and even painted themselves white to symbolize joy and to repel evil spirits.[1] Ancient Hebrew brides typically wore white trimmed with blue. One of the best-known early recorded examples of marrying in white, however, was Philippa of Lancaster (daughter of Henry IV of England), who married Eric of Pomerania on October 26, 1406. She arrived at her wedding in a sumptuous white tunic and mantle trimmed with ermine. A century later, Katherine of Aragon married her first husband, Arthur, Prince of Wales, in white satin embroidered with pearls and gold thread, crowned with a white silk veil. However, it is likely that these choices were down to personal preference rather than any sense of tradition or obligation. The same is true of Mary Queen of Scots who, in 1559, wore a gown of white—simply her favorite color—for her marriage to the Dauphin of France. Blue was a relatively common bridal color in medieval Britain, which may have been related to its association with the Virgin Mary, and hence, fidelity and purity. Red is also cited as a popular choice, although in general there was very little prescriptive advice offered to betrothed women. From the medieval into the early modern period, research suggests that bridal accessories held greater importance than the gown itself; these included, among other items, "wedding girdles," blue garters, and shoes. When the groom was a widower, the bride was sometimes given the finest dress owned by the deceased wife; a symbolic gesture representing a transfer of affection.[2] In terms of procuring a dress to wear on the day itself, those with means to afford it could purchase wedding clothes at "fairs," events made up of gathered communities to acquire and socialize.[3] Husbands and families were under pressure to dress the bride as well as possible, but across Europe sumptuary laws placed significant restrictions on what even the wealthy could wear. Sections of these rules were sometimes relaxed for brides, however. In Venice in 1299, for example, it was decreed that no man or woman "may wear borders of pearls ... except that brides, if they wish, may have borders of pearls on their wedding dress a single time ... they may not place the aforesaid borders on any gown other than the wedding gown." By the time she was married, however, a woman was once again subject to strict laws, which extended to the garments of her early married life: "no bride may carry, or cause to be carried, more than four [new] dresses [in her trousseau]".[4]

In Jewish weddings, Talmudic reference to the bride and groom as a king and queen may lend credence to the notion that wedding dresses should be costly and ornate (although there is no specific stipulation as to garment type). Jewish bridal wear, however, found its own style within different countries, with white westernized dress only adopted by Ashkenazic brides (of Eastern European descent) due to the influence of Christian neighbors.[5] In Sephardic communities bridal clothing tended to be more colorful, also strongly influenced by local style and fashion. As Violet Fenn points out, white is likely to have had roots in ecclesiastical clothing, particularly that of the Roman Catholic Church.[6] It was also worn by some medieval nuns to symbolize the "purity of the Father" in the same manner as their male counterparts. The Cistercian order, meanwhile, founded in 1098, chose white as a way of honoring the Virgin Mary.[7] There are texts that also strongly suggest its importance for other religious or spiritual women, such as *The Book of Margery Kempe*, the earliest English autobiography (*c.*1440). It describes the journey of a spiritual mystic who is bidden by Christ to don white clothing, usually worn by chaste widows and virgins. She gradually adopted the color, and ultimately, it came to represent her full commitment to God and to chastity.

Britain's Elizabethan era witnessed a greater focus on the public aspect of marriage—emphasized through banns, witnesses, and processions, as well as one or more days of celebration and feasting (to the disgust of some religious observers, who found it incompatible with the solemnity of the occasion). The concept of a mutual love marriage was also championed to the public through popular dramatic works, with the obvious example of Shakespeare's Romeo and Juliet, who risk everything to consecrate their love through marriage. Although this might assume a heightened importance in dress to mark the rite of passage, there is little evidence to confirm that bridal clothes themselves were particularly significant. One of the few contemporary accounts to describe wedding clothing is Thomas Deloney's largely fictional *Jack of Newbury* (1597), which recounts the dress of the clothier's bride at his showy second marriage:

> A gowne of sheepes russet, and a kertle of fine woosted, her head attyred with a billiment of gold, and her haire as yellow as gold hanging downe behind her, which was curiously combed and pleated according to the manner in those days.[8]

Gold headdress aside, this account is suggestive of relatively plain attire, albeit made from high quality wool fabrics. This does indicate that, when money was available, a wedding was seen as sufficient excuse to procure a new set of good quality, long-lasting, "best" clothes. For the lower and middle classes, these would go on to form a part of their regular wardrobe for many years to come. For wealthier brides, fabric of all kinds could incorporate embroidery made with spangles ("oes"), small sequin-like ornaments made from silver or silver gilt and would also be kept for subsequent wear.[9]

Given the importance of color symbolism to the Elizabethans, we can speculate on its application to wedding clothes and consider that it may have laid the groundwork for the later connection of white with purity and chastity. Specific colors, Kathleen Oliver explains, were attributed to "abstract attributes", including "obscure gray" for patience, silver for purity, and green for joy, nature, and fertility (making it a popular bridal shade during the 1500s).[10] K. and C. Fehrman have commented that the subsequent shift ("married in green, ashamed to be seen") could link grass stains on a dress as a sign of the loss of virginity.[11]

Into the seventeenth century white and silver remained popular in Britain, as did the structure of a Christian marriage ceremony (an exception was Spain, where Catholic brides took to wearing black silk). Elsewhere in Europe and America, it was imperative that a woman's bridal status be obvious, which was achieved by wearing her hair loose and crowned with a floral or pearl garland—a custom that was followed by brides of all social classes, including Princess Mary (1631-1660) for her marriage to William of Orange in 1641. Her ensemble was described as "White embroidered with Silver, her Hair tyed up with silver Ribbands, not dishevilled about her shoulders as in former Times used, her Head adorned with a Garland of Pendant Pearls."[12] This portrait [Figure 5] depicts the pre-teen bride and groom at the time of their wedding, but here Mary wears a silver court dress rather than the outfit described above. Nevertheless, this sumptuous cloth of silver illustrates the type of fabric most popular with royal brides and grooms; woven with real strands of silver that would glisten and shine magnificently in candlelight.

Our contemporary appreciation of this craftsmanship was furthered in 2014–16, when items from a 1660 shipwreck (off the coast of Texel in the North Sea) were salvaged. Among various luxury goods were two almost intact mid-seventeenth-century gowns. One, believed to have been a wedding dress, is interwoven with pieces of silver, forming a design of love hearts and knotted hearts. These emblems of everlasting affection, confined for four centuries to the seabed, offer a poignant and extraordinarily rare glimpse into the aspirations of a seventeenth-century bride.[13] Impressive and revealing as such artistry is, it represents the experience of only a handful of women. It must also be remembered that during this period, even those more economically buoyant might reject extravagance on religious grounds. Groups such as the Quakers and Puritans eschewed ornate attire in their own nuptials, seeing marriage as a civil contract rather than spiritual sacrament.[14] Though a bride would wear her best dress—made in high quality fabrics where possible—it would be plain and understated in appearance.

Perhaps the most convincing origin of bridal white is Sarah Salih's assertion that the color is in fact representative of *liminality*, intended for people "in carefully defined moments of transition" including marriages, coronations, confirmations, and other rites of passage. These might sometimes simultaneously be "moments of virginity, as in the case of the bride or the novice," but certainly not exclusively.[15] In this case it would make sense that, for various reasons, the liminal status of a wedding was the event for which white remained standard.

RIGHT
William II, Prince of Orange, and his Bride, Mary Stuart by Anthony van Dyck, 1641.

Marco del Buono Giamberti and Apollonio di Giovanni di Tomasco, *The Story of Esther,*

c.1460–70, Metropolitan Museum of Art, New York

This Renaissance panel, which originally graced the front of a cassone (wedding chest), depicts the marriage feast of Esther, the Jewish queen of Ahasuerus (Xerxes). The wedding is represented as if it were taking place in fifteenth-century Florence, and so provides a useful glimpse of what elite brides at this time may have worn on their wedding days.

As well as a gown for the wedding ceremony itself, the family of a wealthy Florentine bride ensured that she had several garments on hand to display her kin's lineage. As well as her dowry (*dote*) and trousseau (*donora*), a woman would also receive additional gifts from her husband-to-be, which could include items of clothing and jewelry.[16]

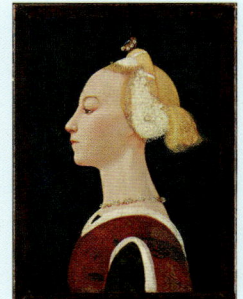

This c.1450s portrait, almost certainly influenced by Paolo Uccello's 1464 *A Young Lady of Fashion*, portrays a similar headdress to that worn by Esther. Sitting far back on the head, both draw attention to a high plucked hairline and are adorned with pearls. In 1490, the bride of the Duke of Milan, Beatrice d'Este, wore a hairstyle ornamented with over 500 pearls.

Brides generally seem to have worn a gown in a fashionably vibrant color to show the wearer's ability to procure expensive dyes. Color could also be a complex topic in mid-fifteenth century Florence. Shades of the same hue were differentiated by specific names, e.g *sbiadato* (smoky gray blue) and *mostanolione* (dark golden yellow), which may be depicted here. In 1469, however, Clarice Orsini wore a gown of white and gold brocade for her marriage to Lorenzo de' Medici—but this was in line with the fashion for combining striking shades with contrasting colors.[17]

Esther is shown wearing an overgown (*cioppa*) with sewn hanging sleeves, probably made from a patterned silk.

Ornamentation included embroidery, pearls, silver buttons, and topaz, which was believed to ward off impure love (and quell desire). So decorated would bridal dresses be, that they could cost up to 400 florins.[19]

For special occasions, women's dress usually sported a long train. These attracted criticism from some, including Saint Bernardine (1380–1444), who was a frequent disparager of female fashion in general. He commented that long trains made women look like animals: "muddy in winter, dusty in summer."[18]

Abraham Bosse, Branle,

c.1650–59, New York Public Library Digital Collections

◆

This engraving, by renowned printmaker Abraham Bosse (1604–1676), portrays dancing at a village wedding sometime during the 1650s. It is likely that the figures shown here are the bride and groom, since it was customary until the end of the century for a woman to wear her hair loose at the ceremony—a symbol of virginity. John Webster refers to this practice in his 1612 play *The White Devil*: "And let them dangle loose as a bride's hair."[20]

Veils were not unheard of in the seventeenth century, but they were rare. The main adornment for a bride's hair would commonly be a wreath of fresh flowers, seen here. In Protestant parts of France, this would be principally composed of orange blossom or jasmine, sometimes decorated further with silk stars.[21]

Instead of real jewelry, lower-class brides sometimes wore clothing embroidered with imitations, particularly across the decolletage. Here, however, the rows of beads appear to be real, if not necessarily precious.

Abraham Bosse depicted the fashion and customs of his native France, but given the great disparities between region and social class at this time, it is difficult to gauge exactly what part of the country is being shown. Certainly, a "best dress" chosen by the bride as her wedding gown would usually be brightly colored, with scarlet favored by some peasant communities and crimson, purple, or silver by the upper classes.[22]

Patterned fabrics displaying floral emblems were fashionable, and therefore desirable for weddings. This design ties into the great importance of flowers, from aforementioned headwear to the path of flowers strewn on the ground where the bride walked into church.

It is well known that poorer seventeenth-century brides did not, in general, buy new clothes for their wedding. In records indicating rare occasions this had not been the case, note of the purchase is usually accompanied by reports of fathers being "exceeding angry" due to perceived vanity of the bride. Moral as well as financial censure therefore contributed to the far more common practice of bride, bridegroom, and guests choosing to accentuate their clothing with new bunches or loops of ribbons, a popular fashion accessory.[23]

Re-use of ribbon was also recorded on some occasions when, the morning following the celebration, the newlyweds would "perambulate the streets ... each wearing two bits of narrow ribbon, about two inches in length ... which are pinned crossways upon the breast. These ... originally formed the garters of the bride and bridegroom ... divided ... the moment the happy pair had been formally installed in the bridal bed."[24]

During the 1600s and 1700s, garters were an important part of both the bride and groom's ensemble.

Garters on the leg of a male wedding guest.

Jean-Baptist Vanmour, *Fille Armenienne, que l'on conduit à l'eglise pour la marier*, 1714,

New York Public Library Digital Collections

◆

This image, made in the early eighteenth century, depicts Armenian bridal dress from the end of the seventeenth. During the 1600s and 1700s, Persia and Turkey battled over the Caucasus, resulting in the destruction of parts of Armenia.[25] The east was dominated by Persia and the west by Turkey; consequently, overlaps could be found in clothing. This image is therefore an important record of distinct sartorial wedding customs that were often written about, but rarely understood, by Western European travellers. In 1896 one English writer asserted that the veil was "a sign of her subjection … [it] is often kept on until her first baby is born." This simply meant that the veil was worn daily until the birth of a son, taking its symbolism beyond the confines of the wedding and into the bride's life as a married woman and mother.[26]

This early eighteenth-century painting depicts an Armenian wedding procession, with the bride again in red. It is possible to discern small differences in the way garments were worn and accessorized depending on region and time period. Members of the bridal party wear green, which alongside red holds distinct significance in Armenian marriage tradition. In the twenty-first century diaspora this has not changed, with grooms who engage in a traditional ceremony wearing two ribbons across the chest to symbolize life (green) and sacrifice (red).

In 1798, Lady Mary Wortley Montagu recorded that "The bride is carried to church with a cap on her head in the fashion of a large trencher, and over it a red silken veil which covers her all over to her feet."[27] The flat-topped "trencher" style can be compared to an academic mortar board, and also had roots in the ecclesiastical *biretta* worn by Roman Catholic clergy.

Beneath the outer crimson veil the bride would wear an additional, shorter linen variety over her face. Some reports also mention the use of "tinsel or gold sheets" as a third layer.[28]

This whole-body covering is often referred to as a "duvack" or "duvak," a term which seems to have been used to describe similar marriage garments across central and eastern Europe. In some places (for example Serbia) this meant a transparent red silk hair kerchief worn by brides up until the First World War.[29]

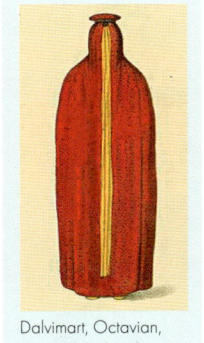

Dalvimart, Octavian, *A Turkish lady in her wedding dress*, 1802, New York Public Library

RIGHT
Meester van de Heilige Elisabeth-Panelen. Wedding Feast of Saint Elizabeth of Hungary and Louis of Thuringia in the Wartburg, inner left wing of an altarpiece made for the Grote Kerk in Dordrecht, c. 1490–1495. Rijksmuseum, Amsterdam. Purchased with the support of the Vereniging Rembrandt.

Marco del Buono Giamberti and Apollonio di Giovanni di Tomasco, *The Story of Esther*, c.1460–70, Metropolitan Museum of Art.

Chapter 1: Before the White Wedding Dress 25

Chapter 2
1720–1789

LEFT
Scotin after Hogarth, *A Marriage Negotiation*, 1745.

E ighteenth century bridal gowns are among the most diverse in this book, largely because there was no set standard for a bride. All but the very wealthiest women usually married in their best clothing, which could be anything from a wool gown to a silk caraco jacket and petticoat. While we know that brides wanted, where possible, to look their best on their wedding days, the basic concept of marriage was very different during the eighteenth century, despite Enlightenment tropes that espoused freedom, liberty, and love.[1] At its core was the joining of two families as well as two people (with, ideally, a significant economic investment), resulting in a legal and moral contract that was very hard to break. Therefore, as Diana O'Hara has put it, marriage was something of a "social drama."[2] On many occasions, the couple barely knew each other before their wedding, and this is reflected in writings of the period. Eliza Haywood's periodical *The Female Spectator*, written by women for women, spoke candidly about love and marriage. References to bridal gowns are rare but, when they appear, often linked to feelings of apprehension, resignation, or even doom: "My wedding cloaths [sic] are making, (would to God it were my winding-sheet) and I must, in a few days, be forced into a bridal bed, by far more dreadful to me than the grave."[3] "Love" does not often enter into such discourse and was generally seen more as a bonus than a requirement (although it was acknowledged that love in marriage was likely to result in more offspring). It is also important

28 How to Read a Wedding Dress

not to oversimplify the complex and varied factors that lead, in any age, to two people making such a commitment.

While the ceremony itself was fairly rigidly prescribed (even, as Rebecca Probert has discussed, prior to the Marriage Act of 1753), what a bride should wear was not, particularly in the first half of the century. Records show that elite brides and grooms favored white trimmed with silver (such light colored, impractical fabrics were the province only of the wealthy) but this was certainly not prescribed: one wealthy English woman in 1714, for example, chose blue satin over a rose-colored petticoat trimmed in silver.[4] The future wife of George Washington, Martha Dandridge Custis, wore a golden yellow damask gown of Spitalfields silk for her first wedding in 1750.[5] Since wedding dresses would so often be worn again after the ceremony, and since so little documentation exists that can point with certainty to a garment being "bridal," there is inevitably a lot of conjecture. Often, dresses in museum collections rely on family lore to determine whether a dress was made explicitly for a wedding or "special occasion." The quality of fabric is usually a good indicator, with either highly fashionable *or* imported and richly embroidered silks immediately denoting that the material was purchased (or kept in the family) for such a purpose.

Dress for many brides may have been relatively open in terms of style and color, but in some parts of the world there were significant restrictions. Under Peter the Great, a Europeanization of the Russian Empire began to take place, and this extended to dress. From 1700, strict sumptuary laws forbade the use of traditional Muscovite clothing and customs, including bridal. Instead, brides were forced to adopt fashionable German and Austrian styles, with French wigs and fashionable low-cut gowns for weddings of the upper classes. Peter's wedding to Catherine in 1712 was a very public spectacle, partly staged to instruct the people about this new Western-style modernity.[6]

Any discussion of marriage in the eighteenth century must mention clandestine weddings (or 'Fleet weddings') that took place without banns or license, and away from the bride and groom's home parish. Fascination around the secrecy and assumed romance of these unions has made them a popular eighteenth-century trope, although they were certainly not without risk, including the possibility of forced marriage or bigamy. Unsurprisingly, there is scant information relating to what clandestine brides wore for their weddings. However, Samuel Richardson's *Clarissa* (1748) made sure to describe the clothes his fictional heroine wore to elope. Though not an intentional wedding garment, this was certainly a fine ensemble that suggested she was dressing for the possibility of a marriage: "Her morning gown was a pale primrose-coloured paduasoy … embroidered … in a running pattern of violets and their leaves … Her apron a flowered lawn. Her coat white sattin, quilted: blue sattin her shoes … Her hands … uncovered the freer to be grasped by those of her adorer." [7]

Another area largely bereft of evidence is the weddings of the lower and lower middle classes. For men and women who were employed, a wedding would often take place on a weekday morning, with the newlyweds returning to work in the afternoon.[8] In many parts of Europe bridal clothes were recorded in marriage contracts and sometimes formed part of the dowry, depending on the wealth of the families. However, because these garments would certainly be worn post-ceremony, and were often remodeled or cut up to make clothes for children, they never survived as intact bridal gowns. Bizarrely, in rare cases, a bride could even arrive at her wedding without any dress at all—the so-called "smock," "shift" or even "naked" wedding. This little-known practice (mostly recorded in Britain and the United States) was borne out of the idea that if a bride was married wearing only her shift, her new husband would not be responsible for any debts she brought with her to the union.

Toward the end of the century there was an increased use of cotton and linen for fashionable clothing. While silk was still first choice for dresses of the wealthiest brides, many other women were choosing to wear simpler and plainer fabrics for their wedding days: even if they could afford more luxurious materials. This was in part due to the broader influence of, in France, "Anglomania" (the use of natural fabrics and colors in the manner of English country society) which grew as the teachings of Rousseau took hold. In England, the relaxed "chemise" dress of Marie Antoinette was simultaneously popularized by the fashionable Duchess of Devonshire, who herself was married in an extravagant white and gold *robe à la française* in 1774.

William Hogarth, *The Wedding of Stephen Beckingham and Mary Cox*,
1729, Metropolitan Museum of Art, New York

This painting is an early example of one of Hogarth's "conversation pieces," fashionable group portraits depicting events in English society. Although a little solemn for the artist's more vibrant tastes (he described such commissions as a "kind of drudgery"), it skilfully and tenderly portrays the moment that this handsome young couple were married.[9] Her dress is very representative of early eighteenth-century bridal attire of the elite: a typical fashionable billowing silhouette in silver with gold accents, and a lace lappet cap. It represents a transitional period between the seventeenth-century mantua and robe à la française, which would dominate for much of the eighteenth.

The groom in this image was a member of the landed gentry, so his bride would not have had a budget. For those of more moderate income, patterned wedding dresses were a popular alternative. During this period, bizarre silk—figured with large-scale patterns, in the example below made to resemble lace—provided a striking bridal gown that had the potential to be worn for many years to come.

Pearl parures (matching sets) of jewelry were popular wedding gifts in the early to mid-eighteenth century, frequently by a groom to his bride. Other fashionable choices at this date included emeralds, rubies, opals, and amethysts.[12]

Folding fans were fashionable and necessary accessories throughout the century, and "betrothal" or "wedding" fans were often given as gifts to the bride. They would usually be painted with scenes depicting romantic love, famous historical weddings, or references to classical love stories. So great was the demand for fans of all types, that during the 1720s fan makers were forced to produce cheaper printed fans in bulk to appease demand.[13]

Dress, British, c.1725, Metropolitan Museum of Art

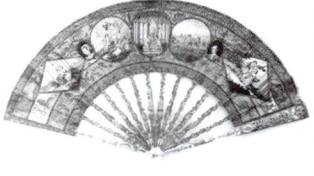

Wedding or betrothal fan, c.1770–90, German, Metropolitan Museum of Art

This gown's silver and gold color scheme suggests significant wealth, as well as an awareness of shifting fashion trends. In England, white trimmed with gold or silver was popular for both bride and groom, and up until the middle of the century some women chose colors such as blue, lilac, and rose for the main body of their gown.[10] In 1734, Princess Anne wore a gown of silver tissue when she married William IV, Prince of Orange.[11]

Chapter 2: 1720–1789

Elizabeth Bull's wedding dress,

1735, Revolutionary Spaces, Boston

◆

This dress bears all the hallmarks of a fashionable 1830s dress, but it was worn as a bridal gown one hundred years earlier, in April 1735. The bride was nineteen-year-old British citizen Elizabeth Bull (1717–80), daughter of Atlantic merchant John Bull and a member of the Boston colonial elite. She married Reverend Roger Price (c.1694–1764) in this sumptuously embroidered bodice and petticoat that display an Asian as well as European aesthetic. This suggests a "global consciousness" on the part of the young woman, and we can speculate that she would have approved of the long life her bridal gown enjoyed after she died. It was passed from her daughter to granddaughter, eventually becoming part of the Revolutionary Spaces collection in 1910.[14]

The silk thread for this sumptuous embroidery (known as crewel work, which was usually done in wool on domestic items) also came from China.[15] With it, the bride herself created vibrant tulips, carnations, and trawling vines across the expanse of the skirt. When Bull first started this piece it was not intended to be her bridal gown; rather, a suitable project for a teenage girl in polite society. Once she became betrothed, several years later, she chose to wear her handiwork, but by the day of the wedding—as seen in this detail—some portions of the design remained unfinished. However, these sections would have been covered by the gown; an incomplete secret hidden from public view. While the embroidery was created by Bull, given her societal status it is likely that the dress itself was made by one of Boston's dress or mantua makers.[16]

This silk overlay was a conservation addition in 2012, and recreates the fashionable balloon-shaped sleeve of the early 1830s.

The dress is made from imported Chinese silk in a celadon (or "sea") green, which over time has faded to a cream color. The term "celadon" is thought to relate to a character of that name from a seventeenth-century French comedy, whose green costume reminded European viewers of Chinese pottery glazed in a distinctive jade green color.[18]

These two dresses, from the Rijksmuseum and the Metropolitan Museum of Art, illustrate the two distinct silhouettes of the gown's lifetime. On the left is a wedding dress, c.1835, with similarly puffed sleeves and waisted bodice. On the right is another intricately embroidered petticoat worn with a casaquin jacket, c.1725–40, showing the dome-shaped skirt, sleeve flounces and long bodice so reminiscent of the period.

In Christian iconography the carnation symbolizes betrothal, commitment, and love. Red specifically indicates true love, marriage, and passion, and pink varieties, both seen in Bull's embroidery, indicate fidelity, young love, and maternal love.[17] We can also see a Tudor rose, lilies, strawberries, and forget-me-nots.

Dress of Spitalfields silk, with pink satin quilted petticoat,

c.1730–50, artist unknown. The Print Collector/Heritage Images

◆

This brocaded silk dress is representative of fashionable bridal fabrics worn throughout the century. Its fabric was purchased at London's Spitalfields, an East London silk weaving district whose value would be shown in 1765, when Queen Charlotte required her court to wear only silk from Spitalfields. Overseas and particularly in America, if brides had bolts of silk or garments already made from this fabric, it was common for them to choose these as their bridal wear.

....

Brides would invariably wear some kind of hat, bonnet, or cap for the wedding in this period, often trimmed with lace "falls."

This *bergère* hat illustrates a popular fashion that first appeared in the 1730s, and can be seen in the fourth of Hogarth's *Marriage A-la-Mode* series, *The Toilette* (1743).

The edges of these sleeves' pleated robings are scalloped, a popular detail sometimes mirrored on bodice and skirt openings.

This dress shows signs of alteration, suggesting wear over a considerable period of time. The shape of the bodice and sleeves conform to the first half of the century, particularly the 1730s, but modifications appear to have been made to the neckline and bodice closure at a later date. However, the draped arrangement at the front of the skirt is not common for any decade of the century, and may have been for the purposes of display only.

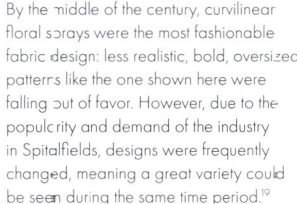

By the middle of the century, curvilinear floral sprays were the most fashionable fabric design: less realistic, bold, oversized patterns like the one shown here were falling out of favor. However, due to the popularity and demand of the industry in Spitalfields, designs were frequently changed, meaning a great variety could be seen during the same time period.[19]

The motifs shown here are a mix of the fantastical and exotic, including both the natural and the manmade. Houses, fences, ducks, along with poppies, ferns, and possibly sprigs of myrtle adorn the material. The latter is broadly associated with everlasting love, and it has long held a role in the marriage ceremony and preparations. During the eighteenth century, a superstition persisted that if bridesmaids planted myrtle in the garden of a newlywed couple (and it took root), the bridesmaids themselves would have happy marriages. The well-known tradition of catching the bride's bouquet existed at this period, too, but the woman who caught it would marry soon only if the myrtle within successfully bloomed.[20]

The luxuriousness of a fabric was often a solid indicator of whether the dress had been made expressly for a wedding or other special occasion. Also in 1742, another American bride, Elizabeth Pitkin, wore a silk brocade with flowers and foliage in rose, blue, and yellow on a white and green ground. The fabric was probably imported from either England or Holland, and its design was typical of the 1730s which suggests that it had been kept aside for this special purpose.[21]

Wedding dress (Robe à l'Anglaise),

1747, altered 1770s, British. Metropolitan Museum of Art, New York

◆

This ivory silk faille dress is believed to have been originally worn as a wedding dress in 1747. Stylistically it now dates to the 1770s, indicating significant alteration—but there is no documentation to suggest it was worn as a bridal gown a second time. It is a good illustration of both a wealthy bride's choice in the 1740s, and of the practice—even among society's elite—of re-working an old style into a new.

....

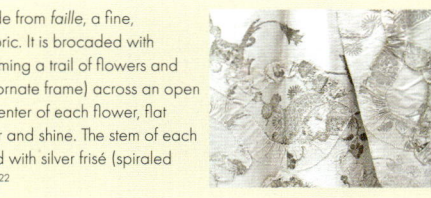

This 1740 illustration for Samuel Richardson's Pamela shows a bridal gown in the shape of an early robe à l'anglaise or "English" gown which, with its broad skirt and meticulously fitted back, would go on to become the quintessential look of the second half of the century. It gives an idea of how this dress might have been worn and accessorized.

This dress is made from *faille*, a fine, cross-ribbed fabric. It is brocaded with silver thread, forming a trail of flowers and cartouches (an ornate frame) across an open ground. At the center of each flower, flat silver strips glitter and shine. The stem of each bloom is created with silver frisé (spiraled metallic thread).[22]

The hoop petticoat was at its widest during the 1740s. By the 1770s, this dress—in its new altered shape—would have been worn over hip pads rather than paniers.

Self-fabric ruffles or "robings" are placed in a serpentine curve across the front of the skirt. This type of trimming was most popular in the Rococo period, which corresponds with the original date of this gown.

The design bears similarities to the patterns of Anna Maria Garthwaite, whose silks depicted sprays of flowers set on a white background. The branch "meandered back and forth across the width of the fabric", as seen in this example.

Dress (Mantua) with train, The Netherlands,
1759, Rijksmuseum, Amsterdam

This imposing mantua (a seventeenth- and eighteenth-century style of gown that was draped and pleated on the body) was worn by Helena Slicher at her wedding to Aelbrecht, Baron van Slingelandt on September 4, 1759. At around the time of the marriage, the word "mantua" was largely discarded in favor of the term "night gown", used to describe a dress worn in the evening, or for a special occasion such as a wedding.[23] The couple married at the Kloosterkerk in the Hague,[24] and Helena must have been an imposing sight as she walked down the aisle in this two-meter-wide skirt.

In England and some other parts of Europe, white trimmed with silver was a common combination for wealthy brides and grooms. By the 1770s, many younger brides were showing a preference for white with very little additional color. Here, Helena Slicher combines various elements, but since her gown was essentially court dress (which could be created in a wide combination of colors and trimmings) it is possible it was not made expressly for the purpose of her wedding.

Low necklines were fashionable, sometimes filled in with a fichu during the day. As one nineteenth-century account of "the eighteenth-century woman" put it, a wealthy bride wore "nuptial low-neck," with "patches, rouge and orange blossoms" drawing attention to her face and hair.[25]

Circular lead weights, encased in linen, sit in the sleeve lining at the elbow. This serves to both hold the sleeve in place, and encourage the bride to hold her arms in a slightly bent position.[26]

The dress is hand-embroidered in silk and portrays a dizzying array of flora. Among them are carnations, clematis, primroses, and lilies, bordered with prized pineapples and entwined in serpentine bands of embroidery. Despite the sumptuousness on display here, the most expensive aspect of a bridal costume at this time was the fabric, costing hundreds of florins (rather than the cost of construction or embellishment). National Museums Scotland have estimated that the cost of a similar fabric would be approximately £5,000 today ($5,995 USD).[27] Therefore, the flawless light-blue silk on which these flowers are embroidered would have been just as much a mark of Helena Slicher's—and her family's—status and worth.

Unusually, this English-style mantua contains an element more commonly seen in continental Europe: a long, detached train.

Chapter 2: 1720–1789

"Second day wedding dress,"

1765, The National Museum of Finland, Helsinki

This skirt and jacket were worn by Anna Kristina Stillman for the second day of her wedding in Vaasa, Finland, in 1765. Wedding celebrations that lasted more than a single day were common in Nordic countries, and if the bride could afford it, might involve the wearing of a special dress to mark that phase of the celebration. In this sense it is still a "wedding" dress, though not worn for the ceremony itself. This is clear in the degree of relaxation suggested by the caraco jacket, a style derived from the shortgown of working-class women. While a popular daywear option, it would not have been acceptable ceremonial wear for upper-class brides.

Green, blue, yellow, and pink knotted tassels on a trim of silk floss (later known as "fly fringe") edges the pleated robings on bodice and sleeves. Such trimming was very fashionable between c.1750s and 1780s.

The same trimming technique is seen here on another wedding dress, c.1760 (Metropolitan Museum of Art).

A choker adorns the neck of this young wife in W. Proud's *The Pleasures of the Married State*, c.1780.

A quilted petticoat like this was a hugely skilled and labor-intensive endeavor. The flower vine along the hem is exquisitely embroidered in multi-colored silk with chevron, stem and knot stitches.[28] It was fairly standard to include ornamental stitching on the bottom third of a quilted petticoat, but the intricacy and detail would vary depending on the wearer's finances and the intended purpose of the garment.[29] This petticoat demonstrates additional luxury in its application of a more complex design than simple lozenge, diamond, or scallop configurations on the top two thirds of the garment.[30]

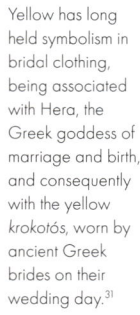

This example of another yellow quilted petticoat, from around the middle of the century, shows a depiction of Cupid with his bow. This leads us to the speculation that it was worn for a marriage.
(Five Colleges and Historic Deerfield Museum Consortium, 1750)

Caraco jackets either fastened at the front with lacing or pins, or a stomacher was inserted into the space between the bodice openings. Here, decorative ribbon bows (*échelle*) cover a row of lacing.

Choker-style necklaces could be as simple as a length of velvet ribbon tied around the neck, as seen here.

Yellow has long held symbolism in bridal clothing, being associated with Hera, the Greek goddess of marriage and birth, and consequently with the yellow *krokotós*, worn by ancient Greek brides on their wedding day.[31]

Wedding dress of Princess Sofia Magdalena,

1766, The Royal Armoury, Stockholm

This sumptuous wedding dress was worn by Sofia Magdalena of Denmark at her wedding to Sweden's Crown Prince Gustav on November 4, 1766. As was common for royal European brides at this time, the gown is in the style of a court dress or "robe de cour/grand habit," a design first implemented in 1680s France. Worn exclusively for the most formal of court occasions, including presentations and balls, it was an appropriate choice for a bride of Sofia Magdalena's standing. As was customary, the couple had two wedding ceremonies, one in Denmark and one in Sweden, and the dress was described after the first in Stockholm's Post Tidningar as "A rather precious dress, made of silver fabric, and on her head she wore a gold crown richly adorned with jewels. Her train was carried by Lady-in-Waiting Miss von Trolle and Miss v. Rabe."[32]

The neckline of the court gown was typically wide and low, sitting right at the edge of the shoulders. The feature was highly favored by Sun King Louis XIV, who instigated this style of dress for ladies of the French court in the late seventeenth century. He was particularly fond of similarly constructed bodices of the 1660s, despite his ladies' great preference for the newer, looser, shoulder-covering mantua.

The sleeves of court dress are one of its most notable features, comprising layers of pleated ruffles arranged with the ends pointed both upwards and downwards. They have sometimes been known as sabot sleeves, named after their shape - similar to a sabot shoe (clog), fitted to smoothly envelop the curve of the elbow.

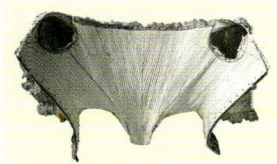

Unlike ordinary dresses of this era, the *robe de cour* was not worn over stays. Instead, the bodice was heavily boned and this provided sufficient support.

The extreme "grand panier" worn under this dress served an obvious purpose; to show off the gown's luxurious fabric to its best advantage. Although the silhouette of the gown was outdated by the late 1760s, the fabric design is right on trend. Floral emblems are set within diagonally-set squares edged with lace-like bands. This incorporation of lace with natural motifs was popular during the decade (which also saw depictions of materials such as ribbon and fur), and demonstrated the skill of weavers as well as developing technology.[33]

Two rows of eyelets at the back are concealed by overlapping fabric, and point to another unusual feature for the time: a back-fastening bodice.

The length of a train denoted rank. The bride's two attendants carried her train at the Danish ceremony while she was still unmarried, whereas her mother-in-law, Queen Ulrika, had her train carried by four ladies-in-waiting.[34]

Wedding dress,

c.1760s, England, Collection of Mary D. Doering

Little is known about the identity of the bride who wore this dress, except that she married in the west of England in around 1760. Given its almost pristine state, this champagne-colored dress was probably worn only for the wedding, and therefore offers a rarely immaculate example of bridal fashions in the middle of the eighteenth century.

This *compère* stomacher with decorative buttons is a later addition for display purposes; however, similar examples can be seen on bridal and other formal gowns in the second half of the century. Two vertical lines of pleated robings are edged with floss trim.

Self-fabric ruching on the petticoat, cuffs, and bodice sport a serrated (pinked) edge, created with a sharp tool—made from iron or steel—that cut through fabric when hit with a mallet.[35] This delicate punchwork pattern of three holes would have been made using an awl and a sharp rolling wheel.[36]

Close-fitting pleats with an *en fourreau* back ("as a sheath," in which the skirt and a section of the bodice are cut from a continuous length of fabric) characterize the fashionable robe à l'anglaise.

A similar floss trim is seen here on the compere stomacher of another gown, c.1775.

To the twenty-first century eye, this dress looks decidedly "bridal"—and although shades of white were not viewed as such in the eighteenth century, there are instances of the color being directly associated with weddings. After a small, private ceremony in 1773, actress Mary Darby Robinson changed into "white muslin" and was greeted by an acquaintance, unaware of her wedding, who said that she was "dressed like a bride." The observation, Robinson continued, "overwhelmed her with confusion."[37]

Sack-back open robe and petticoat,

c.1770–75, England, Hampshire Cultural Trust

◆

As with many formal eighteenth-century dresses, we cannot say for certain that this was specifically made as a wedding dress—though its ornateness suggests that it was very likely worn as one, coupled with the donor's belief that it was worn by their great-great-great aunt. This light-colored silk with floral pattern corresponds to fashions worn by the gentry and middle classes; with white and silver still preferred by aristocratic brides.

There is a drawstring inserted at the neckline and also around the waist of the petticoat, allowing the bride to adjust the fit.

By 1770–5, it was more common to see bodices that closed at the center, rather than being pinned to the sides of a stomacher.

The sleeve cuffs—engageantes—are weighed down with lead, helping to keep their shape intact.

Popular floral motifs often found their way onto bridal silks. The flowers brocaded on this gown look similar to thistles, which could represent a Scottish connection on the part of the bride or groom or the common associations with chivalry, royalty, and pride. The light blue of the flowers is reminiscent of forget-me-nots, which have long been a symbol of love and remembrance. One version of a German legend tells the story of a bridegroom who wanted to decorate his bride's hair with these tiny blue flowers, growing on the banks of the Danube. However, they were pulled away by the waves, which engulfed the groom, his last words to his bride being "forget me not."

The silk is probably from Spitalfields in London, suggested partly by the presence of blue stripes in the selvedge (self-finished edge) of the fabric. Three blue threads were woven into the selvedge in order to distinguish the fabric as British-made, rather than an import.[39]

There is evidence of the outer skirt having originally been looped up with ties, into the "polonaise" style so fashionable in the 1770s. This could have been added after the wedding for subsequent wear.

The size and position of these rear pleats, which create the "Watteau back" so connected with the sack-back (robe à la française) are a good indicator of the gown's date of c.1770s. By this decade they were narrower, moving closer to the center back: as is clear here. However, the pleats on this dress are sewn down several inches from the neckline, which was a less common construction technique as the decade progressed.

Feather sprays and tassels of fly fringe adorn the petticoat and skirt of this robe. Feathers enjoyed something of a craze in the mid-1770s, with an entire industry built around preparing them for use on gowns, interior decoration, and for the military. Popular plumes included ostrich, egret, heron, peacock, and swansdown, and—as likely the case here—they were often dyed to match the shade of the dress.[38]

Wedding dress,

c.1779–1780, Norway, National Museum, Oslo

This robe à la française was worn as a wedding dress in c.1779–80 in Norway. Silver and white were popular bridal colors among the elite throughout the century, but this gown introduces another popular shade: blue. In Europe and the United States, silks in blue as well as cream, pink, and white were increasingly fashionable for brides during the 1770s and 1780s.[40] In Norway, similar preference dominated, since the majority of silk and trimming was imported from England and France.[41]

The construction of sack gowns remained largely unchanged across the century, but one way to date the passing of time is through the placement of the rear pleats. By the 1770s, this section of fabric was slimmer and moving closer to the center of the bodice. This example, therefore, is outdated in that respect. Traits that place it within the attributed date range include double-layered cuffs and an increasingly close fit to the body.

A robe and petticoat could require upwards of 25 yards of silk or satin to create, the cost of which would be far beyond the means of most people.[42] However, even the poorest Norwegians would aim to procure imported fabrics despite the country's healthy domestic production of wool, flax, and hemp.[43]

Blue braid *guimpe* (gimp) *passementerie* edges the gown's robings, cuffs, and neckline. The wife of English sculptor Joseph Nollekens wore, for her wedding day in 1772, a sacque dress with a stomacher which "was exquisitely gimped."[44]

These sections of puffed trim would have been stuffed with wool batting to create a consistent shape. The technique become demode as the 1780s progressed, with dress in general becoming simpler.

A single bow made from silk, edged in the same blue braid, sits at the top of the stomacher. It was more common to see a series of bows descending the stomacher, in a style known as *échelle* or *eschelle*, as shown on this contemporaneous bodice.

While wealthier, urban brides would emulate the latest London and Paris fashions, working-class rural women would usually choose to marry in traditional dress. Known since the twentieth century as *bunad*, a bride would wear this woolen skirt, linen shirt, waistcoat, shawl, and apron with a silver crown. This, along with a bib, are two aspects of the costume that have remained almost unchanged for centuries.

Bridal crown, nineteenth century, Norway, Metropolitan Museum of Art

Linen copperplate-printed wedding gown,

1780s, Historic New England, Massachusetts

It is highly likely that this dress was worn by Deborah Sampson Gannett (1760–1827), the daughter of farmers in Plympton, Massachusetts, for her wedding in the late 1780s– early 1790s. Deborah's life was an extraordinary one for a woman of her era. After working as a servant during her childhood and adolescence, she enlisted in the Continental Army as a man, going under the names Timothy Thayer and Robert Shurtleff for nearly three years. She was wounded and later contracted yellow fever, receiving an honorable discharge in 1792. She published her story in 1797, and went on tour to talk about her experiences. "Our Heroine leaped from the masculine, to the feminine sphere," her memoirs concluded. "Throwing off her martial attire, she once more hid her form with the dishabille of Flora, renounced her former occupation; and I know not, that she found difficulty in its performance."[45]

The dress was originally made in c.1770 as an open robe, worn over a visible petticoat. When Deborah Sampson wore it for her wedding in the early 1790s it was in the form seen here; that of the "round gown." In this construction, the skirt is fully closed across the front and represents growing simplicity in dress.

This fichu is a reproduction but represents the type of neck covering that was probably worn. It was common during the century for brides to wear nosegays, small bunches of flowers often tucked into the decolletage.

It was common for brides to wear nosegays, small bunches of flowers tucked into the decolletage. One example from a wedding in 1772 was described: "wherein [the beauty of her bosom], confined by a large bow, was a bouquet of rosebuds, the delicacy of which were imperceptibly blended with the transparency of her complexion."[49]

These white sleeve ruffles are reproductions for display purposes. The dress originally featured self-fabric ruffles on the sleeves, which were ironed out and pieced into the skirt during its 1790s alterations.[46]

This indigo design was created using copperplate printing, which had been in existence since the seventeenth century. A colorfast technique was not successfully developed until the mid-eighteenth century.[47]

The fabric design includes floral sprays and, in among the flowers, seashells.

Shells had a significant artistic hold in the eighteenth century, with their spiral shape influencing Rococo's extravagant depictions of natural forms. They were fashionable among the European elite, from shell grottoes in country houses to a growing interest in natural science. One of the most famous examples of shell artistry, the "Sharpham Shellwork," is a mahogany tripod stand with a representation of Venus's temple worked in shells from the West Indies. It was commissioned in 1762 for the marriage of Captain Philemon Pownall to Jane Majendie, and was allegedly used as a banqueting centerpiece for their marriage celebrations.[50]

There are various leaves, flowers, and buds depicted on the fabric, including roses and what appear to be snowdrops. In 1788, an heiress's bridesmaids were recorded dressed in white, with "snowdrops and myrtle for adornments."[48]

Chapter 2: 1720–1789 41

Dress (mantua) with train, c.1750–1760, Rijksmuseum (rear view detail).

Fabric detail from a robe à la française, worn by the wife of English sculptor Joseph Nollekens, for her wedding day in 1772.

Chapter 3
1790–1836

By the close of the century, white was becoming more and more cemented as an expected and "traditional" bridal color. This was partly because of its general modishness (based on neoclassical aesthetics, even though the idea that ancient clothing was usually white was misguided), partly because of the washability of popular fabrics like muslin, sarsenet and cambric, and partly because the aristocracy's fondness for bridal white and silver grew in the second half of the 1700s.[1] The latter reason would not, of course, have been a concern in the case of the dress that opens this chapter. The print in question hails from a seismic shift in European politics and attitudes, the French Revolution, and was made in the same year the Tuileries Palace was stormed and the monarchy finally abolished. It depicts ordinary, if fashionable, day dress with a small posy of flowers offering the only clue that this is the outfit of a bride. Unsurprisingly, the upheaval of this era affected domestic textile manufacture, particularly that of silk. In France, the subsequent fashion for simpler modes was partly fueled by this demise, and it was not until Napoleon's influence (1799–1815) that luxury fabrics were given a boost and made an appearance more frequently in bridalwear. However, when Napoleon married Josephine in 1796 she reputedly wore a simple muslin dress: lavish display was reserved for her magnificent gemstone-studded, silver and gold embroidered silk gown at the couples' 1804 coronation.[2] Among the wealthy, accessories such as wigs seem to have made up more of the bridal trousseau than dresses: in c.1801, Suzanne Le Peletier de Saint-Fargeau, who wore her hair in the fashionable short "à la sacrifiée" style, had twelve blonde wigs in her wedding trousseau.[3]

LEFT
John Lewis Krimmel, *Country Wedding, Bishop White Officiating*, c. 1814.

Meanwhile, Britain was experiencing a period of economic growth and industrial development. Here, most middle-class women could afford quality evening or ball gowns and would often wear their best example as a bridal gown. However, at the start of the century these would rarely be ostentatious, and ordinary women of reasonable means who expended finances on lavish or "one-off" bridal wear were damned in contemporary commentary. The showy and pretentious nature of Jane Austen's Mrs. Elton, the vicar's wife in *Emma* (1815), is made manifest through the way she discusses her wedding clothes: "A bride, you know, must appear like a bride, but my natural taste is all for simplicity; a simple style of dress is so infinitely preferable to finery. But I am quite in the minority, I believe."[4] Her later criticism of Emma's plain wedding gown demonstrates the insecurity of the mercantile middle class, exacerbating the fashionable perception that true elegance lay in restraint. During this period, it is therefore rare to find fashion plates that explicitly mention or show "wedding" attire, and even descriptions of royal weddings focused more on a bride's jewelry and accessories than her dress.

In the 1820s, this began to slowly change. The decade is generally regarded as the time when bridal white became a "tradition," although this would not be firmly solidified until Queen Victoria's 1840 wedding. However, as an 1820 example in this chapter shows, there was far greater attention paid to wedding clothes in journals, magazines, and periodicals, with plates clearly labelled as such. The symbolic importance of the wedding itself was part of this shift in attitude, and in Britain and the United States, this was shown through increasingly popular bridal trips or "tours." Overseas trips were undertaken exclusively by the wealthy at this time, comprising both sightseeing and visiting relatives who could not attend the wedding festivities. However, the custom started to become widespread among the middle classes too, as Julia Ann Tevis remembered in 1878 of her 1824 wedding:

> My wedding-dress was an India muslin robe, made in the prevailing style ... and severely plain in every respect. I did expect to take a trip, but I should need neither a traveling dress nor a large trunk. A pair of common saddle-bags would carry all I wanted.[5]

This frugal bride clearly reveled in the simplicity of her trousseau, her autobiography revealing the increasingly expected accoutrements that she was doing without, including "no chaplet of orange flowers gleaming with pearls; no rich laces, no ornaments of any kind, not even a veil".

Wealthy brides would only purchase custom-made bridal gowns, whereas the middle classes might consult a "warehouse," where families could buy not only garments for the trousseau, but also dress fabric, household linens and other items a bride would need in her early married life. One such establishment in London described its diverse range in 1818: "caps, scarfs, habit-shirts ... magnificent wedding-dresses, plain and exquisitely worked

Cambric Handkerchiefs, an enormous variety of bordered Morning and Evening Dresses, now so fashionable."[6] This variety of wares is what *Pride and Prejudice*'s Mrs. Bennet was referring to when she lamented that her eloped daughter Lydia should "not give any directions about her clothes, till she has seen me, for she does not know which are the best warehouses."[7]

As fashions in general became more and more ornate, however, the expectations of brides altered to fit, and some degree of lavishness was wished for, if not always obtainable. The concept of nobody present "outshining" the bride can also be seen at this time, "To give the bride an opportunity of shining singly, [the three bridesmaids] had come habited all in green." The bride, meanwhile, "stood at the altar in vestments white and candid as her thoughts, a sacrificial whiteness."[8] Such symbolism became deep rooted thanks to the influence of romantic poets and novelists of the period, who promoted the image of a veiled virgin bride dressed head to toe in white. *Redmond's Bride*, published in 1824, extols the ideal of "white rob'd virtue" and a bride who is:

> A lilly in her virgin pride…
> A long deep veil of vestal white;
> She rather seems as one of light.[9]

Alongside these virtuous and modest connotations, commercial fashion magazines devoted whole columns to bridal styles alone, and by the 1830s a veil was almost always shown as part of a "bridal costume," as it was increasingly called. By this point, women who could afford it were far more likely to purchase a gown specifically for their wedding day. They were also likely to choose dresses adhering to new trends *for* bridal gowns, described in detail in fashion columns and magazines:

> A dress of spotted tulle, over white satin, with two flounces, elegantly finished at the edges with figured gauze ribbon … The corsage is à la Marie Stuart … the sleeves are full, and have mancherons formed of two scallops, on each shoulder, of white satin, edged with blond … The hair is arranged à la Grecque [worn with] a light, short plume of white feathers … The ear-pendants and necklace are of fine pearls (La Belle Assemblée, 1828).[10]

Even if the dress was commissioned especially for a wedding, it would usually be worn again as a woman's "best dress" (especially given the popularity of white for evening wear), but this specific purchase marks an important new phase in the journey of the white wedding dress. In other parts of the world, wearing a new dress especially for the wedding was the norm. North African Jewish women, for example, had for centuries worn specialized ceremonial dress based on the style of their region or even town. Known as the "great costume" in Morocco,

RIGHT
Eugène Delacrcix, *Saada, the Wife of Abraham Ben-Chimol, and Préciada, One of Their Daughters*, 1832.

these distinct garments were, sadly, phased out when the Western wedding dress later became popular.¹¹ During the 1830s, Eugène Delacroix (whose approach has been fairly criticized by Edward Saïd and others) published artworks and a journal relating to Jewish weddings in Tangiers, which illustrated the richness of bridal attire (see image above). In the context of the white Western dress, this demonstrates the universality of having a special, traditional, one-off garment that would be worn in a modified fashion after the wedding itself.

Republican marriage,

1792, engraving, France, Musée Carnavalet – Histoire de Paris

◆

Following the tumultuous years of the French Revolution, weddings became far more practical, civil affairs. Ceremonies were short and pragmatic, and this simplicity is shown through the "everyday" nature of the bride's clothing in this engraving. In addition to the speed and ease of weddings, divorces also became far easier to obtain during this period, meaning that marriage was increasingly viewed as a short-term state. It was not until Napoleon allocated around 4 million for the restoration of churches that the institution of marriage regained its solemnity.[12]

. . . .

Women's dress at this time continued the 1780s line, consisting of two-piece ensembles made from plain silks and cottons. Before the universal introduction of the high-waisted empire silhouette the waistline was still low and dipped at center front, but increasing attention was given to the top of the body through voluminous neckerchiefs and, as seen here, a fichu with the ends crossed in front and tied behind.

During this decade women's hats became tall and conical, but still heavily and ornately trimmed as in the 1780s: this bride appears to be wearing ribbons and feathers in her bridal hat. Ribbons were frequently seen in abundance at late eighteenth century weddings; according to one eyewitness of an Irish "Village Wedding" in 1793: "The bride most glaringly [bedizened with ribbands] ... white, red, and every other colour, were conspicuous about her gown and hat."[14]

It appears that the bride may be wearing an apron. Long, delicate, purely decorative aprons were fashionable and could well have been part of a wedding ensemble. Several variations of this item were included on a trousseau list from around this date that was published in Robert Southey's *Common Place Book* (1850): "A laced cambrick [sic] apron, a spotted cambrick apron, A plain cambrick apron, a lawn apron."[15]

The custom of holding a bridal bouquet probably became standard sometime in the eighteenth century. It was usual for the bouquet itself to be small, as shown here, and similar bunches were sometimes handed out to guests by the bride's parents. These could be substituted for bunches of ribbon.[13]

This 1792 fashion plate shows a similar fichu, with the ends crossed in front and tied behind.

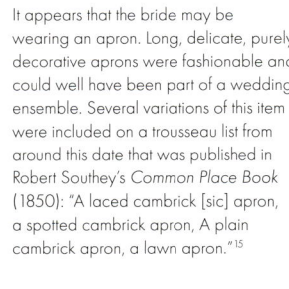

An example of an apron from the early 1790s is seen worn over this round gown; a highly decorative, sheer example that had little practical use.

The groom (and quite possibly the bride also, as this was a unisex fashion) wears stockings with "clocks"—embroidered patterns at the ankle, extending to around mid-calf.

50   How to Read a Wedding Dress

Bridal gown,

c.1797, National Museum of Denmark, Copenhagen

This round gown is constructed in "nettle cloth," a fabric made from—as the name suggests—fibers of the nettle plant. This was first commercialized in Germany in the 1720s, but in Denmark, examples of the cloth have been found dating from the Bronze Age. It was cultivated and produced there until the nineteenth century and produced a soft, glossy linen.[16] This made it the perfect fabric for a "chemise" wedding dress; rich, smooth, and lustrous. The dress was probably worn by Baroness Eleonora Sophie Rantzau when she married Viscount Preben Bille-Brahe at Hvedholm Castle, Faaborg, in 1797.

Pleated bodice sections at the front cross over the shoulders and meet at center back, creating a slightly raised collar.

There are two rows of whitework embroidery, the top featuring vines of slender leaves that cross and join a lower level of stylized leaves and flora. Danish whitework, particularly in the form of pulled thread, was allegedly so delicate and admired that it competed with domestically made lace across Europe.[17]

So precious was this fabric, that it was very commonly re-used after the wedding for another rite of passage: baptism. Research into surviving examples of Danish christening robes has frequently revealed fabric from the mother's bridal clothes, and sometimes, material from older sartorial heirlooms. It is therefore always surprising when these bridal gowns survive intact; especially in this case since we know that the bride had at least two children.[18]

The bodice features a crossover front, which was a popular neckline in the last decade of the century. Internal lacing at the front helps to fit and shape the dress to the wearer's liking, and is tied at the right hand side.

We do not know how Baroness Rantzau accessorized this dress. However, an American account of a wedding in the early 1790s described the bride wearing a bonnet with "curtain," presumably a veil, and this ties in with commonly recorded marriage customs from c.1790.[19] Although lace trimming was largely out of favor, it was fashionable to wear veils of lace for eveningwear, and some brides followed suit. The presence of a veil would enhance the long, classical lines that were becoming a staple of female fashion.

The skirt is edged at the hem with a 7mm wide band, which both stabilizes and decorates.

Chapter 3: 1790–1836 51

Wedding dress, American,

c.1799, USA, Museum of Fine Arts, Boston

◆

This dress was worn by bride Eunice Cooper at her wedding to her cousin, John Hooper, in Massachusetts. Her two-piece dress is comprised of an Indian "mull" muslin petticoat and satin overdress or "open robe," a popular style that documents the transition between eighteenth century and Regency styling.

....

Fashion plates of the era show huge variety in sleeve trimming, and two similar examples are shown above. In keeping with neoclassical themes, the bands and drapery are meant to mimic ancient Greek and Roman dress.

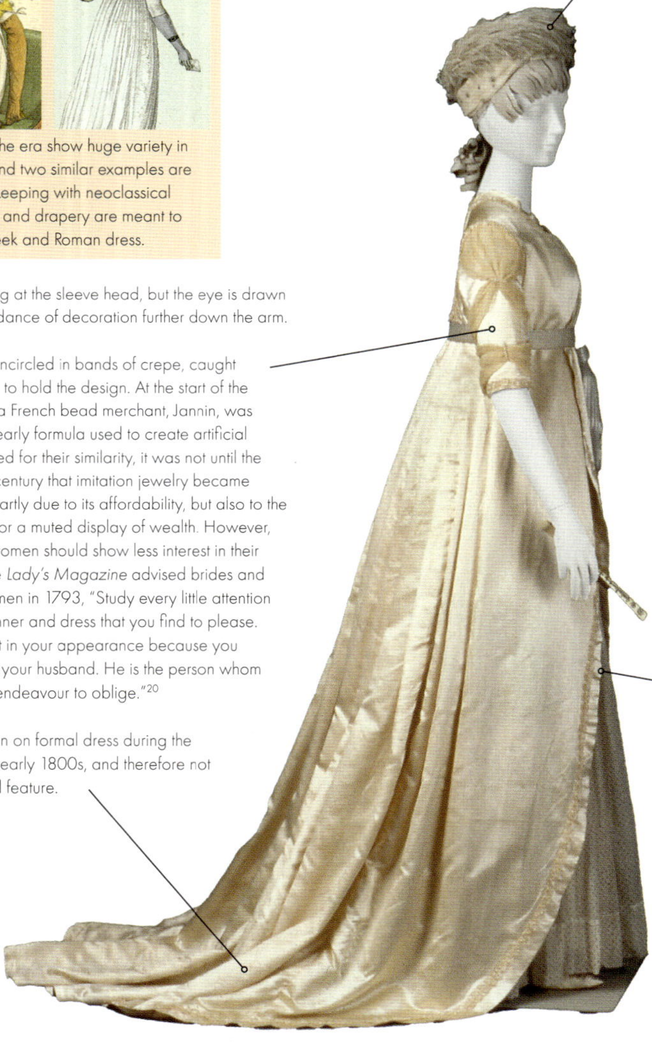

There is no gathering at the sleeve head, but the eye is drawn instead to an abundance of decoration further down the arm.

These sleeves are encircled in bands of crepe, caught with artificial pearls to hold the design. At the start of the eighteenth century a French bead merchant, Jannin, was responsible for an early formula used to create artificial pearls. While praised for their similarity, it was not until the second half of the century that imitation jewelry became popular. This was partly due to its affordability, but also to the growing proclivity for a muted display of wealth. However, this did not mean women should show less interest in their appearance: as the *Lady's Magazine* advised brides and young married women in 1793, "Study every little attention in your person, manner and dress that you find to please. Never be negligent in your appearance because you expect nobody but your husband. He is the person whom you should chiefly endeavour to oblige."[20]

Trains were common on formal dress during the 1790s and into the early 1800s, and therefore not a specifically bridal feature.

Turban-style headdresses made an appearance thanks to the influence of *Turquerie* (or *Turquoiserie*), the European interpolation of Turkish fashion. This one is accessorized with a crown of ostrich feathers.

The (once white) satin of this robe is reminiscent of the heavy, stately styles of the previous years of the century, but it is worn with a petticoat of extremely thin and delicate embroidered "mull" muslin. This was the ideal fabric for the slim, ethereal gowns that were now in fashion. In December 1798 Jane Austen wrote to her sister Cassandra, expressing this desirability: "I am full of Joy ... that you should meditate the purchase of a new muslin Gown ... I am determined to buy a handsome one whenever I can."[21] In this example the bride pairs old and new to present a conflicting, but effective, design in one of the most rapidly changing eras of fashion.

A report of a wedding in 1796 describes the bride wearing "a light slate colored silk gown," but that the girls and younger women in her party all dressed in "white muslins, cut square in the neck, and short sleeves."[22] It seems likely that more mature brides chose silk for their gowns, and Eunice Cooper was over the age of 30 when she married (and therefore, by contemporary standards, not young). By contrast, Bathsheba Walker Goldsbury, a bride in her mid-20s, wore a lightweight calico gown made in Massachusetts for her ceremony in 1794.[23]

The robe openings and cuffs are trimmed with *robings*, gathered strips of fabric used in previous decades.

An example of trimmed robings on a robe a la Francaise from 1750 (Los Angeles County Museum of Art).

Indian muslin wedding dress,

c.1806, England, Manchester Art Gallery

◆

This delicate muslin dress was worn by Charlotte Margaret Martin at her marriage to John Edwards on December 2, 1806. The Lancaster Gazette noted the union: "John Edwards, of Great Ness, Esq. to Miss Martin, only daughter of the Rev. George Martin."[24] It is likely that this dress was made with bobbin lace from the East Midlands, more accessible and cheaper than its Lille counterpart, and known for the simplicity of its designs.

The bodice fastens at the back with a drawstring across neck and waist. At the front is another drawstring that adjusts the fit, covered with bands of drawn threadwork.

Square necklines were fashionably youthful in general, but reports exist of their specific use at weddings. In 1796, young members of an American bridal party wore "new white muslins, cut square in the neck, and short sleeves."[26]

The spotted embroidery covering most of the skirt is made using tambour work, which was created using a chain stitch on fabric stretched tightly over a frame. This was available ready-made, to be taken to a seamstress or constructed into a gown by the bride. In 1801 London's Morning Post advertised "some very handsome tambours a yard and half wide, at 4s. 6d. per yard."[25] A formal dress such as this would typically require around 6–8 yards (5–7 meters).

White-on-white embroidery worked onto net was a hugely popular choice, and for brides was often worn over a thin silk underdress. Diarist Eugenia Wynne wrote of her bridal ensemble in 1806: "My bridal array consisted of a white satin underdress and a patent net over it, with a long veil."[27] It is highly likely that Eugenia's dress featured similar embroidery.

From around 1805, this style of dress lost its train for all but the most formal occasions.

The central panel of embroidery is made in tambour and knot work, and features a lattice, scrolls, and a plant which could represent a type of thistle or dandelion. Meanwhile, along the hem, bunches of flowers hang below sheaves of wheat. Since the Middle Ages, grains such as wheat were common wedding flora, symbolizing growth, abundance, and fertility.

This 1806 "wedding portrait" depicts Emilie and Johann Philipp Petersen of Hamburg. Although this gown may not be the sitter's actual wedding dress, it presents a similar shape to Miss Martin's, and illustrates alternate ways the style could be worn: here with a chemisette (required for daytime church ceremonies) featuring standing ruffed collar, and worn with a vibrant red shawl (Deutsches Historisches Museum Berlin).

Quaker wedding dress,

1809, Philadelphia Museum of Art, Pennsylvania

◆

This fashionable but unadorned dress was worn by Lydia Poultney at her wedding to James B. Thompson in 1809. Although Quakers promoted plainness in dress, this usually meant a lack of trimmings and muted colors: not necessarily an avoidance of the fashionable line. This gown, with its raised waistline, short, puffed sleeves and low rounded neckline, illustrates a typical silhouette of the first decade of the nineteenth century. Because Quaker weddings were, and still are, relatively informal affairs conducted by the Friends and not clergy, it is unusual that a dress specifically designed for the purpose has survived.

Although the silver-gray shade of this dress fits within what was described in 1853 as "drab" or "Quaker colors" (i.e. dull/light-brown, and initially a name inspired by undyed, homespun wool), it aligns with the pale color scheme chosen by many Regency brides.[28]

It was common for necklines to be tightened and shaped via a drawstring, and the visible gathers suggest that this technique was employed here.

These sleeves are gathered at the back and the cuff, creating fullness towards the rear. This volume was often supported and maintained through an additional lining made from coarser muslin.

Until c.1810, it was common for sleeves to be set far back into the bodice, as seen in this evening dress from the same year (Metropolitan Museum of Art).

When the neo-classical line became fashionable in Pennsylvania in the early years of the nineteenth century, some Quakers "discarded their old-fashioned dress and turned to this style, although much more modestly." The simple structure and plain line of these gowns suited the Friends' aesthetic, and a prescribed lack of ornament allowed Quaker women to practice simplicity by avoiding excess. Nevertheless, a lack of prohibition on costly fabrics meant that rich materials like the silk satin seen here were permissible wedding wear. On the day itself, however, the bridal gown would have been accessorized with a veiled bonnet, and a fichu covering neck and shoulders to ensure modesty.[29] The image above illustrates Quaker daywear during this era:

Muslin remained the most popular fabric for both day and evening gowns, although by c.1809 stiffer materials like silk were gaining prominence for formal clothing. Here, the sturdiness of silk satin emphasizes the line of the slightly flared skirt, which—on non-Quaker bridal gowns—could be enhanced by the addition of trimmings including frills at the hemline. It is possible to make out the addition of triangular side gores (popular from around this date onwards) to increase the width of the hem.

By 1809, trains had largely disappeared on daywear. Quakers, with their wish to avoid waste and excess, would have been unlikely to use trains, even on bridal wear.

Wedding gown,

1812, The Netherlands, Rijksmuseum, Amsterdam

◆

Margaretha Johanna Weddik Wende wore this silk crepe dress at her marriage to Baron Hieronymus Nicolaas van Slingelandt on November 25, 1812.[30] Their wedding probably took place at the fifteenth century Nieuwe Kerk in Amsterdam, an imposing building in which a bride would wish to make a memorable entrance. The dress shows a classic silhouette of the era, trimmed with puffs of tulle, and fashionable rose embellishments. Its shades of pink, blue, and creamy white adhere to the most fashionable bridal colors at this date.

From c.1811, ribbon skirt decoration was frequently seen in fashion plates depicting ball and evening gowns. Given the prevalence of these dresses for bridal wear, we can assume such trimming was seen on many wedding gowns too.

Delicate, gauzy puffs of silk tulle embellish the neckline, cuffs, and hem. Machine-made tulle was first commercially available c.1810, though an earlier version was produced in Nottingham, England, in 1768.[31]

Drawstrings at the neckline adjust to fit, fastening in a bow at the back.

The same technique is seen in this wedding dress from the same year (Metropolitan Museum of Art).

Roses dominate descriptions of fashionable dress during the decade, from fabric embellishment to hair ornamentation. They were usually—as seen here—naturalistic rather than abstract representations, aligning with the nineteenth-century fondness for "refuge within nature" at a time of increasing industrialization.[32] Here, silk roses are arranged in rosette shapes with trails of single petals emanating from each flower. Rows of gathered green ribbon emulate stalks and also provide a trim for the tulle flounce.

Trains were most popular on evening wear towards the very beginning of the century. After this time, evening styles sometimes featured a shorter "demi-train," as did wedding gowns—as this English 1812 newspaper described: "[A] crape [sic] dress over white sarsenet, trimmed with pearl or white beads, with a demi-train."[33]

Rouleaux (stuffed tubes of fabric) were an especially popular method of skirt ornamentation in the later teens and into the 1820s, making this a rare early example of the trend.

Princess Charlotte's wedding dress,

1816, Photo by Museum of London/Heritage Images/Getty Images

Princess Charlotte of Wales wore this silver ensemble for her wedding to Prince Leopold Saxe-Coburg in May 1816. It was created for her in London by dressmaker Mrs. Triaud who, strangely, does not appear in any trade directories or other sources from the era.[34] In an account written that same year, it was described as made of "a most magnificent silver lama (sic) ... over a rich silver tissue slip ... the body and sleeves trimmed with most beautiful Brussels point lace ... the manteau of rich silver tissue ... fastened in front with a most brilliant and tasteful ornament of diamonds. The whole of the dress surpassed all conception, particularly in the brilliancy and richness of its effect."[35] This amount of detail and discussion was unusual for the time but befits the status of the wearer. Brides who could afford it often wore white—but the use of silver was an indication of extreme wealth, and this is further emphasized in records that the Princess had at least fifteen other dresses made "for the occasion."[36]

Wide, low, uncovered necklines were popular for formal wear during the 1810s.

These layered sleeves are reminiscent of the frilled, elbow-length variety seen on the formal *robe de cour* or "grand habit" (court dress), which remained until c. 1820. Unsurprisingly for an aristocratic bride, other elements of this gown conform to expected norms of court dress, too, particularly the extensive use of metallic embroidery.

It is well documented that the Princess herself preferred simpler modes of dress, although she still had a keen eye for fashion. In the words of her and Leopold's physician Baron Stockmar, "I have never yet seen her in any dress which was not both simple and in good taste."[37] Contemporary images of Charlotte support this preference and are testament to the fact that for those in the public eye, the choice of a wedding gown was far less about personal taste than about convention and expectation.

Marie Antoinette: The Queen of Fashion: Court Lady in a Robe de cour (detail), Pietro Antonio Martini, after Jean Michel Moreau, 1789

The bodice is ornamented with abalone, the shell of marine snails which has an interior layer of shimmering nacre (mother-of-pearl).

During the mid-1810s, waistlines reached their highest point; in July 1816 *Ackerman's Repository* reported that "waistlines have now attained a very becoming length" and this fashionable feature is emphasized through corresponding ornamentation on the waistband.[39]

Rich metallic embroidery including sequins, spangles, and silver thread were hugely prized during this period. Not surprisingly, such ornamentation would have glittered and gleamed under candlelight, and this prompted Lord Byron—on seeing his cousin in a spangled dress in 1814—to comment that she "walks in Beauty, like the Night."[40]

Brussels point lace was already popular at the time of Charlotte's nuptials (and was worn at another high-profile wedding; that of heiress Catherine Tylney-Long to William Wesley-Pole in 1812).[41] After the ceremony Charlotte changed into a dress also trimmed with Brussels, a surprising choice given her well-documented support of domestic textile manufacture.

Princess Charlotte and Prince Leopold after their wedding on 2 May, 1816. (Photo by Museum of London/Heritage Images/Getty Images)

As with the "apron" overskirt, due to inconsistencies in trimming and design, it is highly likely that this train was also a later replacement—especially considering that it was described contemporaneously as being "two and a half yards long."[38]

This draped "apron" front with rounded edges is entirely atypical of the era, not becoming fashionable until the late nineteenth century. This, coupled with the fact that it does not appear in artistic renderings of the day, suggests that it must have been a later addition: possibly for display purposes and to reuse the original edging of the train or "manteau."

Wedding dress,

1818, Philadelphia Museum of Art, Pennsylvania

◆

The short, puffed sleeves and low neckline of this gown bear the hallmarks of evening rather than bridal dress. If, as was usual, this bride had a morning wedding ceremony, it is unlikely she would have worn this dress without some kind of covering. Alternatively, she may have worn it later in the day or for another event related to the union.

Very short, puffed sleeves are decorated with satin *languettes*, arranged to suggest the petals of a flower. They are edged in self-piping, and a covered button punctuates the center of the floral design.

The dress is composed of figured silk, featuring vertical rows of two alternating exotic floral designs. These include depictions of pineapples, a symbol of wealth and luxury and a highly fashionable emblem during the era. Other representations include berries, daisies, and leaves that appear to be acanthus—a plant symbolizing life and rebirth.

At the hem, the pattern also shows small *potentilla recta*, a species of cinquefoil flower which, heraldically, symbolizes attributes including honor and loyalty. This makes it an eminently suitable emblem for a wedding gown.

Fashion plate showing a front-fastening crossover or 'surplice' style bodice.

It is likely this crossover (or "surplice") style bodice was front fastening, to allow a smooth back view to the dress. The design was seen from the middle of the 1810s onwards, and examples can often be seen in fashion plates (above). Nevertheless, obvious contemporary terms to describe it do not appear to exist.

This dress is relatively restrained compared to such stylish examples, seen in this fashion plate from the same year. In the case of this wedding dress, focus is placed instead on the sumptuousness of the fabric and its rich patterning.

Brides would often wear slippers redolent of evening or ball styles, made from silk and/or leather and with strong classical influences (sometimes referred to contemporaneously as "Grecian" or "Roman" slippers or sandals).[42]

By the late teens, elaborate hem trimmings—sometimes described as "hem sculptures" due to their dimensions and complexity—were becoming very fashionable.

William Greatbach,

1848, *The Penny Wedding*, after David Wilkie, 1818, New York Public Library

In 1818 this work was commissioned by George IV, the Prince Regent, and later displayed at the Royal Academy. It depicts the festivities of a "penny wedding," a Scottish tradition whereby each guest paid a penny towards expenses, with remaining money contributing to the newlyweds' home (for this reason, such weddings were sometimes arranged for serving staff by their employers). The bride, seen here on the arm of her new husband, is being lead, somewhat hesitantly, to dance. Penny weddings could be rambunctious and associated strongly with rural communities. The two other types of wedding common in Scotland at this time were the "free"—private and with a few paid-for guests—and "dinner," at which a meal was provided.[43] The necessary financial focus of a penny wedding, and the fact that they were sometimes called "beggars' weddings"' confirms the status of the brides and grooms who sought one, and leads us to consider this bride's costume as unpretentious, inexpensive, but nevertheless her best.

Unmarried lowland women were less inclined to cover their heads than their Highland counterparts, for whom it was deemed socially necessary. This newly married bride's cap was customary for all wives, regardless of geographical location. It corresponds to the Lowland preference for a white bonnet decorated with ribbons, worn close to the head.[44]

By the early 1820s, most Lowland women once more wore their waistlines at a more natural position.

The costume in *The Penny Wedding* is not specific to any particular Scottish region. However, certain elements of the bride's dress do suggest a Lowland (between the Firth of Forth and Aberdeen) connection; a location that Wilkie had depicted in earlier works. Examples seen here include low-heeled shoes, sleeves cut relatively full to the elbow and finished in a tight-fitting cuff, and a dark ribbon tied at the waist (with a bow in back) to emphasize the empire line.[45]

Wedding celebrations typically lasted from Thursday to Sunday, on which day the bride was "kirked": seen for the first time at church as a married woman.[46]

Shawls were commonly worn by Lowland women, sometimes in a plaid, paisley, or striped design (until later in the century, tartan was more exclusively the reserve of Highlanders). Lower classes in general, particularly working women, wore a shawl (or fichu) over her shoulders and neckline, and in Scotland, this would often be crossed and tied in front.[47] The Penny bride's shawl is tied loosely at her throat and seems to be more for decoration than modesty or practicality, since we can see evidence of another shawl—or possibly chemisette—worn under her bodice.

Aprons were worn for practical reasons by most working, lower-class women, but had long been appropriated as decorative accessories by the upper class. Its presence here, however, is probably simply as part of the bride's usual wardrobe. Other possibilities arise from an old saying, recorded in one 1860s history of marriage, "that all children under the mother's girdle or apron-string at the time of her marriage are legitimate."[48]

Wedding dress,

1820, France, Metropolitan Museum of Art, New York

This fashion plate is from *Journal des Dames et des Modes* (The Journal of Ladies and Fashion), a prolific French fashion magazine published between 1797 and 1839. Although fashion plates do not necessarily represent what "most" women wore, this one does give a good idea of how brides styled themselves in the decade where "full" white dress as a marriage staple started to become commonplace. Like most fashion plates, accompanying text for this one gives scant information about the dress itself, focusing far more on hairstyle and accessories.

The bride wears "a crescent of orange blossoms and tuberose in her hair" in a style executed by one "Mr Plaisir." Orange blossom was a relatively new addition to the bridal ensemble in 1820, but tube roses were more established. Images of roses, with leafy fronds encircling them, decorate the hem of the veil and skirt.

Decorative piping at center front pulls the neckline into a demi-cœur shape.

This overskirt is made either entirely of lace or, as was more likely, embroidered net with an embroidered or lace scalloped trim. The underskirt is of satin with a rouleau beneath, a precursor to the heavily padded and trimmed hems of the later 1820s and 1830s.

For a morning ceremony (which was usual at this date), a bride with short sleeves would wear elbow-length gloves.

This rich lace veil, with its trim matching the design on the skirt, is described as specifically 'English'. This may refer to the particular style, or indicate that veils were not standard bridal wear in France before this date. However, depictions and descriptions of lace veils on French brides do exist—for example, in the *velatio nuptialis* part of a Roman Catholic marriage ceremony, in which two clerics or witnesses hold a white veil over a kneeling groom and (additionally veiled) bride.

Good quality bridal lace was renowned for its expense, but this luxury item was often made by women who would never be able to wear it themselves. An 1890s history of lacemaking records that in 1820, an Irish rector's wife taught her servant to make lace. This led to other local classes designed to provide employment. "It is scarcely possible to conceive", the author wrote, "how these beautiful laces come so clean and dainty for bridal array from such poor homes".[49]

Heart-shaped cutouts, probably indicating heart-shaped leaves, sit in each scalloped edge. A similar design is seen in this piece of late eighteenth-century Flemish bobbin lace (Metropolitan Museum of Art).

Chapter 3: 1790–1836

Batiste wedding dress,

1825, Fashion Archives and Museum, Shippensburg University, Pennsylvania

This dainty dress was worn by Louisa Stokes (1802–1886) on the occasion of her marriage to John Sager Cash (c. 1803–1885) on November 17, 1825. Scandalously for the time, the couple had a child out of wedlock in 1817, when Louisa was 15 and John 14. It seems that the child, a boy, did not survive infancy, but the couple had six further children between 1826 and 1842 and, by all accounts, a successful union. Commonly for the era, the dress was worn again after the wedding and—in contrast to the previous dress—is relatively plain and restrained in terms of its surface decoration.

This 1823 engraving shows a low neckline filled in with a chemisette or fichu.

If the wedding took place during the day (a morning ceremony was common), it is likely that the neck would have been covered. Where it was not, the ceremony probably took place in the privacy of the home.

Sleeves *en gigot* were a permanent feature by 1826. These demi examples foretell the style with soft gathering at the shoulders, tapering to the elbow and a close fit around the wrist.

The dress fastens at center back. The white cotton lining is pinned first, with drawstrings at the waist and neckline adjusting the fit of the outer layer. The close-fitting bodice has two darts, which also shape the fabric to the body.

The waistline is slowly starting to drop, sitting considerably closer to the natural waist as neoclassical fashion makes way for oncoming Victoriana.

A band of 'Swiss lace' adorns the hem. Popular until the 1860s, this time-consuming but simple technique involved a design drawn onto muslin, which was then basted onto one layer of net and one of cotton. A layer of oilcloth (*toile cirée*) temporarily supported the garment and prevented warping while it was being embroidered. Next, the muslin layer was cut away to reveal solid areas of the pattern against a sheer net background.[51]

Narrow tucking of the fabric was a fashionable and accessible decorative technique, particularly for morning gowns. It is relatively plain compared to the fashionable 'hem sculpture' that persisted throughout the decade, and was still recommended as a key feature for bridal gowns by 1829: especially when made in an 'uncommon breadth' above a padded band at the hem known as *rouleau*.[50]

An example of elaborate, complex hem sculpture can be seen in this 1824 wedding dress from the Metropolitan Museum of Art, which features puffed, swagged and piped sections of fabric to add depth and volume.

The leaf motifs show similarities to oak and maple varieties. Both carry strong symbolic connotations of longevity, wisdom, strength, and balance.

In the United States during this period, wedding dresses were often referred to as bridal 'frocks' rather than 'gowns'. The term 'frock' usually suggested that the dress did not have a train, a feature which was generally rare except for court dress.[52]

Silk gauze and lace wedding dress,

1829, Costumes Parisiens, and pale gold silk wedding dress, 1829, Maine Historical Society

◆

This analysis compares two wedding dresses from the same year: one, an idealized fashion plate displaying the height of silken bridal sophistication with full bishop oversleeves and exquisite lace. The other is also made from silk but is relatively unadorned, relying on its simple but stylish silhouette to make an impression. It is associated with the marriage of Arcy Cary to Richmond Bradford on September 3, 1829 in the town of Turner, Maine.

Fashionable 1830s hairstyles were notoriously complex, and the same was true for bridal. Flowered hair ornaments were particularly popular, and fronds could be nestled among the high plaited sections of hair.

This dress has a neckline en demi-cœur, creating a soft sweetheart dip in the center. A flat pleat along the neckline and bust emphasizes this shaping. Arcy Cary's dress features a higher, demurer neckline with vertical gathers extending down the bodice front.

The voluminous gigot sleeve had not yet reached its peak size in 1829, but this dress displays the closest fashionable aesthetic of the two. Its long oversleeve sits below a puffed band, which adds breadth and, on the comparative example, is replaced by a simple row of piping. A more elaborate version of this sleeve arrangement for a wedding dress is described in Ackermann's Repository of Fashion from December 1829: "Long sleeves à l'imbecille cover the manche à la béret of the slip."[53]

While fabric is gathered in a single vertical fold across the fashion plate bodice, here it is drawn in to create a soft fullness around the chest. Jane Loudon's Stories of a Bride (1829) described a similar effect: "Her chemise ... reached in small pleats to her throat, where it was finished by a band."[55] Small gathers also provide shape at the rear of the bodice.

An increasingly fashionable nipped-in waist is highlighted by a wide silk belt with gold buckle on the left, and a simple waistline on the right. Evidence of prior stitching inside this dress indicates that the waist was lowered at some point. This suggests that the gown may have had a previous life before its use as a wedding dress and was altered to bring it more in line with changing fashions.

This 1828 fashion plate illustrates a similar style, but in this case the sheer oversleeves are caught up into another popular 1820s trend; *mameluke*, in which sections of the fabric are divided into puffs.

This lace is described as "dentelle d'Angleterre," but at this date Madras was a hugely fashionable alternative. A sheer bobbin lace produced in India, it was often made to imitate Maltese patterns. It was created at a school established in the late 1800s, and was among the costliest lace available to brides. The dominant floral design on this dress is dog roses (rosa canina or "Briar rose"), the most common wild rose that is native to Britain and Europe. In 1838, the *Rose Fancier's Manual* wrote that dog roses could be found "in all woods and hedges," making them an accessible bouquet flower for brides of all social classes.[54]

Rather than using lace frills to edge the cuffs, this dress features a net option. Net and gauze were popular alternatives, especially after the introduction of a machine patent in 1808.

This skirt is narrower than that of the lace example but would have been worn over stiffened petticoats to create the required volume.

Printed cotton wedding dress,

1834, Hereford, Herefordshire Museum, UK

◆

This dress was worn, and probably made by, smock maker Mary Bufton for her marriage in 1834. Its modish shape, particularly the voluminous gigot sleeves, shows an awareness of fashion and the status of this garment as a "special occasion" piece. However, other elements clearly illustrate its non-elite origins, and we can be sure that wearing such a gown would not be an everyday experience for this bride.

....

The dress was probably worn with a pelerine (a small, lightweight cape) or fichu to cover neck and shoulders. In 1834–36, "double-layered" pelerines like this one were especially fashionable.

By the 1830s, significant advances had been made in textile printing. These are evident in this vibrant fabric, which was a fashionable everyday choice and meant that little other ornamentation was required. This fashion plate from 1831 shows a similar fabric used on a highly fashionable gown.

The bodice is not boned; possibly a cost and labor-saving decision, but more likely because it was simply not a common feature of construction until c.1835.

The size and shape of these sleeves was maintained through stiffened lining, padding or, on occasion, wire or crin (horsehair) supports.

The pintuck around the hem was let down at least once in the dress's history.[56] By the date of this wedding, fashionable skirts could be worn at ankle-length, so this alteration suggests that Mary wore her wedding gown again in the years after her nuptials.

Existing reports mentioning other "provincial" English brides also discuss the use of cotton gowns in the first half of the nineteenth century. However, those with extended means would often choose glazed ("polished") cotton, which immediately denoted higher quality. Wealthy women would often use this fabric as a lining on their wedding dresses.

62 How to Read a Wedding Dress

Wedding dress,

1835, Rijksmuseum, Amsterdam

◆

This sumptuous gown was worn by a member of the prestigious van Slingelandt family for her wedding in 1835. It is an extremely fashionable design, illustrating the apex of sleeve width that was so prized throughout the decade. For those brides who could afford a new dress, lace was especially popular, but this example is made from woven silk that only imitates the presence of lace. This adds a point of difference to the highly modish silhouette.

....

For daywear, sleeves were usually full to the elbow and from there, tight-fitting to the wrist. These, ending at the elbow with a self-fabric ruffle, mirror those of evening dress, and of the introduction in 1835 of a round, full, tightly pleated sleeve. Indeed, aside from the presence of a veil, for private ceremonies there was often little to distinguish bridal gowns from ordinary white evening wear.[57] The following year, sleeves would start to significantly diminish in size.

This fashion plate from 1832 shows a bridal gown with a silk sash, echoing this example. The plate also demonstrates how veils were generally worn throughout the decade; fastened to the back of the head below ornate hair ornaments. A historian in 1893 commented that, in 1835, "bonnets do not seem to have been worn by fashionable brides,"[58] and certainly they are rarely seen in fashion plates.

Skirts had reached their widest by mid-decade. In 1837 one fashion column lamented that "The skirts of dresses are not likely to undergo any diminution of their enormous width."[59]

Lace was worn by several high-profile brides in the 1830s, including Queen Louise Marie of Belgium, a champion of the country's famous domestic lace industry. As Queen Victoria chose to do eight years later, it is likely that Louise Marie made a very public nod to this industry with her bridal gown in 1832:

The fact that this dress eschews lace is, then, interesting and suggests a strong personal preference. In August 1834, *The World of Fashion* made an early mention of "a printed imitation of lace on a cotton ground; we presume that the same representation of lace can be printed on muslin or silk dresses." The article credits "Mr. Lloyd, of Newmarket-buildings, Manchester" for this invention.[60]

Additional threads were added to the tulle ground to create this floral pattern. The technique was described in an 1829 edition of *The Young Lady's Book*: "Where the material is sufficiently transparent, a paper pattern is placed underneath; the outline is run in white thread." For court and ball gowns, this would usually be further "worked in gold thread satin stitch, or at the tambour. [It is] also worked in silver thread." In this bridal example, the color of the design matches the rest of the gown.[61]

Princess Charlotte's wedding dress, 1816. White silk net embroidered in silver strip with a spotted ground and borders.

Edging, Flemish, late 18th century (detail), Metropolitan Museum of Art.

Chapter 4

1837–1869

No discussion of the white wedding dress would be complete without mentioning Queen Victoria's cream satin and Honiton lace bridal gown. However, it is not featured individually in this chapter purely because of such intense exposure and debate ever since it was worn in 1840. It is frequently labelled as the dress that "started it all" for the white bridal gown, and though the tradition undeniably solidified soon after Victoria's wedding, she was not the first. What her choice probably did, though, was to imbue a sentiment and importance that had not been there previously. Victoria and Albert's relationship was famous for its deep passion and genuine affection, which could be another reason why her choice of dress sparked such acceptance of a standardized wedding outfit. The era also saw changes in the way marriage was perceived both legally and socially, which may have had some influence on its sartorial representation. In Britain, the institution had been strengthened and equalized by the Marriage Act of 1836, which allowed marriages to be legally registered in buildings of diverse religious groups.

LEFT
Portrait of a Bride,
c. 1864–65.

RIGHT
Wedding stereoview,
c. 1859, USA.

For those not adhering to Anglican, Jewish, or Quaker beliefs, this gave meaning to the ceremony and, for some, meaning to the associated rituals and clothing. Conversely, 1857 saw the implementation of divorce by decree of the civil courts, which gave women the means to request dissolution of a union.[1] This was a watershed moment for female marriage reformers, whose voices were increasing in strength and number. It is especially interesting that despite vociferous protest, dress reform activist Lydia Sayer Hasbrouck (1827-1910) chose a reform wedding outfit (a short dress worn over trousers)—but, allegedly, all in white.[2] Queens and social reformers are, however, few. In any discussion of dress, it is always crucial to acknowledge that these elite and unusual examples were worn by a miniscule fraction of the population. Most women during the 1840s and 50s would have continued to wear their best dress for their wedding but sometimes incorporating a longer train than was fashionable for daywear. This chapter showcases two brown silk dresses, both modestly trimmed with fringe, to represent what the "best dress" of rural brides might have looked like. Even among poorer women, though, there were certain customs that continued whatever the economic circumstances. In Germany, brides wore the *Brautkranz* (bridal garland or wreath), often made from allspice (pimento), which should be fresh, not wilted since "a wilted wreath causes premature wilting [of the marriage]." The groom should also wind ears of corn into the wreath, which would then be preserved and displayed in the house after the wedding.[3] It was this accessory, rather than the dress, that therefore held sentimental ties. In communities where there was no access to (or desire for) fashionable Parisian wedding styles, the bridal dress would often be black, decorated with—at most—ribbons and/or flowers.

Linking the white wedding dress to notions of sexual purity is pervasively cited as starting with Victoria's wedding but is, in fact, a much more recent construct. In the nineteenth century, as in the eighteenth, white continued to be a symbol of wealth (most fitting for the dress of a queen), and this maintained its status as an elite choice, keeping a white dress out of the reach of most of the population until the later advent of synthetic fabrics and industrialized production. The chapter explores an extraordinary exception in the dress of Sarah Tate, an African American woman enslaved until 1865, who was married during this period. Unusually, her dress was procured for her by her mistress, but what makes her story so poignant is the way the gown was cared for or "curated" by Tate herself. Her modest heirlooms, including this dress, speak to various landmarks in an individual life, but also narrate an experience of slavery and separation from loved ones. So important was this dress that when she was emancipated, Tate's first garment as a free woman was based closely on her bridal style.

There was some freedom implicit in the standardization of white, cream, ivory, and other light shades. Brides were at liberty to focus instead on the personalization of cut, decoration, and accessories, and by the 1860s there was plenty to choose from (although, following Victoria's nuptials, orange blossom was expected). A burgeoning bridal market now included specific caterers, photographers, stationery, and floral arrangements. The concept of fashions specifically for wedding dresses was becoming more common, with women's magazines and newspapers devoting ever larger sections to styles and options. Because of the prevailing fashion for bodices and skirts to be constructed separately, however, many still took the opportunity to re-use one or the other as part of a non-bridal outfit, and this was widely encouraged. Accounts of "real" weddings in newspapers contained more and more detailed overviews of what the bride and bridesmaids wore, and this provided realistic inspiration for brides-to-be. Etiquette guides advised proper behavior for both bride and groom, and promoted the idea of the bride as "an object of supreme attention," and her wedding day as being "The Happy Day"[4]—although one 1859 manual was sanguine enough to admit that "it is not always the case. The cup is seldom filled with happiness;—many bitter ingredients are intermixed."[5]

Two examples in this chapter discuss gowns worn for weddings during the American Civil War (1861–65), a period in which ordinary families had to engineer incredible resourcefulness to put a wedding trousseau together. One contemporary, Mary Chestnut, described the creativity she and her friends employed to create a bridesmaid's dress:

> Kate remembers some [material] she had in the house for curtains bought before the war and laid aside as not needed now. The stuff was white and sheer, if a little coarse, but we covered it with no end of beautiful lace. It made a beautiful dress.[6]

Such an approach was seen in subsequent popular fiction about the war, most famously Scarlett O'Hara's curtain dress in the film adaptation of *Gone with the Wind* (1939). This invented scene was, quite clearly, based on fact, and similar repurposing must have been used by scores of Civil War brides in pinched circumstances. Others were forced to wear their relatives' dresses, and Chestnut records a particularly distressing instance of a bride wearing "white satin and point d'Alençon", an exquisite dress that had been worn by her recently widowed sister – who, 'swathed in weeds for her young husband … came rapidly up the aisle alone. She dropped upon her knees in the front pew. And there remained, motionless, during the whole ceremony—a mass of black crape and a dead weight on my heart."[7] Brides in mourning is a repeated theme throughout this book, and indeed, death and marriage often went hand in hand. On some occasions, new brides of a recent widower would even go into mourning for their predecessor. Nevertheless, overall, weddings during this period were relatively colorful affairs, with bridesmaids in soft shades, and even gentlemen were encouraged to don coats in colors other than black or gray.

In the final years of the decade, the focus of skirts started moving toward the back, in preparation for the impending bustle. In support of this, layering became common, with peplums ("basqued" bodices) and overskirts providing the necessary distinction. In 1867 an extraordinary wedding dress was described in *The Queen* (London) that adhered to these changes, all for the hefty price of £500:

> The skirt was cut round the edge in large scollops; the scollops were bordered with two cross-cut bands of satin … The bodice was a sort of peplum, which formed a double skirt very short at the front and long at the back.[8]

For most women bridal gowns took a simpler tone, but for those who could afford to move with the fashions, skirts were made with a "small rounded apron," still trimmed with flounces "cut on the cross and gathered," and finished in a "full and ample" train.[9] By the end of this period, such a richly trimmed bridal gown might be worn again by the bride at her first ball or evening function as a married woman.

Wedding dress,

1837, Indianapolis Museum of Art, and 1839, Fashion Archives and Museum, Shippensburg

◆

This pink French silk damask wedding dress was worn by Martha Ann Bush of Brunswick, Maine, probably for her marriage to prominent Boston attorney Peleg Whitman Chandler. The pale green gown was worn by Amanda Grove Grim (1816–1841), probably as her bridal gown: its styling is commensurate with Grim's recorded 1839 wedding date.

Both are beautiful examples of the early Victorian "Gothic" silhouette, with a lengthening waistline and low, sloping shoulders leading into the latest version of gigot sleeves with volume set above the elbow, rather than near the shoulder.

Amanda Grim, portrayed at around the time of her wedding.

On both dresses, bands of pleated silk create a "bertha" across the front of the bodice, drawing attention to the low-set sleeves and, on the 1837 example, a corresponding point with the waistline.

While the hem of the skirt is ornamented with French motifs, including a basket of flowers and a vase, the remainder of the brocade depicts a Chinese meander intertwined with eight Buddhist symbols: wheel of the law, lotus blossom, conch shell, umbrella, canopy, vase, pair of fish, and endless knot (shown below). Chinese silk was particularly fashionable, but these motifs, particularly the endless knot, have been used at weddings across the globe—even as part of the ceremony itself.

Grim's dress is made from pale green silk; a shade promoted by *The Court Magazine and Monthly Critic* in July 1838 as being among the "newest modes of Paris" alongside "several shades of grey and lavender."[10] Wherever possible, wedding dresses would be made from fabric of the most fashionable hue. The dusty pink silk, with its mix of Western and Eastern-style patterning, creates an interesting variation. Although white, cream, and ivory shades were fast becoming the ultimate bridal hues, fashion papers in the 1830s did on occasion recommend that brides add a splash of color. In August 1834, *World of Fashion* described a similar silk dress with an overlay in light fabric, lined in a "rose color" which was picked up in a "girdle [made from] ... a wide rose color satin ribbon."[11]

During this era the length of a skirt was adjusted at the waist rather than the hem. This was achieved by turning down fabric to create a skirt that was shorter at center front and longer in the back. On the Grim dress, conservators discovered two separate turn-down lines, which suggest that previous alterations had been made to the dress. This reinforces the common practice of altering an existing dress for bridal use, even among women who could afford a new gown for the occasion.

Both skirts are unadorned, allowing their surface detail to shine through—despite various fashion columns' claims in mid-late 1837 that "flounces have become almost indispensible! [sic]"[12]

Wedding dress,

c.1844, Metropolitan Museum of Art, New York

From around c.1844, wedding attire in the style of an afternoon dress—generally featuring a high neckline and long sleeves—replaced the previously popular evening silhouette, which comprised short sleeves and a low, sometimes off-the-shoulder neckline. Like Queen Victoria, this bride may have worn a floral wreath with a veil attached. Embroidered net was a common way of displaying lace in the first decades of the century, with Rococo-style floral scrolls as popular designs.[13] Some brides were obliged to create their own, and *The Ladies' Work-table Book* (1843) recommends "a honeycomb netting, with two meshes" as being appropriate for a veil.[14] These factors suggest that the dress sits within the last period of popularity for the evening-style bridal gown.

For young women, wide and shallow necklines during the day were appropriate for dressier occasions such as a wedding.

Given the huge popularity of lace following Victoria's 1840 wedding, it is likely that this dress once featured lace, although its minimalist self-trim is in keeping with the general aesthetic of the decade. The only other applied trimming is a row of hanging fabric balls, encased in net, on the outer side of each sleeve.

This dress follows the line of fashionable evening dress during the decade. Both feature short, narrow sleeves (a prominent style of the decade after c.1842), a low neckline and increasingly wide, plain skirts (Metropolitan Museum of Art, 1840-2).

There were many silk options available to brides. At around the middle of the decade, lightweight woven silk warp and worsted weft blends (such as challis) were popular.[15] They were described by prominent dye manufacturer, Michael Stark, as "certainly the neatest and most elegant silk and worsted article ever manufactured."[16]

Mittens or short gloves were often worn for bridal or evening wear, and these might be made from lace, silk, or net. This fashion plate shows a dress with a similar bodice and sleeves, worn with short white gloves and bracelets on each wrist (Metropolitan Museum of Art).

Wedding dress,

c.1845, USA, The Witte Museum, Texas

This dress was worn by Sarah Tate, a slave who was brought to De Witt County, Texas, by the Edgar family. It is believed that it was made for Sarah by her mistress and treasured by her until her death at nearly 100 years of age. The dress is a rare relic of this period of history, but most importantly, it is a tangible reminder of the individual lives—and loves—of people of color who were enslaved. Sarah Tate was emancipated in June 1865, and one of her first acts as a free woman was to purchase fabric to make a dress of entirely her own choosing. This garment is also held by the museum, along with a red dress worn by her baby daughter who died in infancy.[17]

The "fan-fronted" bodice is gathered across both shoulders, tapering to a shirred "V" at the waist. This popular technique added interest to the bodice, and helped to highlight a small waist and fashionable dropped torso.

Plain-woven homespun cotton was not expensive, but nor was it at all similar to the coarse "Negro cloth" that enslaved people usually wore. This indicates the importance that Tate's mistress attributed to the garment.

In May 1845, *Blackwood's Edinburgh Magazine* observed with relief that: "Those abominable gigot sleeves, so well named from our old familiar family-joint—they were utter abominations; and those bishop's sleeves—they were foolish caricatures. Ladies are doing much better now; either, in the evening, they trust to nature herself to set off their arms as she pleases, or else, in the morning, they envelope them in a covering that hardly destroys the beauty of their form."[20] Since most weddings took place on a weekday morning, this description aligns with the sleeve style shown here.

This nineteenth-century woodcut depicts a marriage between two slaves. Based on the clothing shown, the wedding probably took place in the 1830s–1840s, and the bride wears similarly long, loose sleeves. The circumstances under which such ceremonies took place, and the formality of the occasion, varied greatly. Charles Lyle described a slave wedding he witnessed in Charleston in the 1840s, which was performed by an Episcopal minister, with the bride in white and attended by bridesmaids.[18] Other reports describe unions taking place in the plantation chapel, with only the couple and white guests permitted into the house afterwards for a low-key celebration. In general, planters tried to promote slave marriages as a way to produce offspring and elicit compliance from the enslaved. However, it was uncommon for the acknowledgment of the new family unit to continue once children had been born.[19]

There is one two-inch wide tuck, located about six inches above a plain hemline. Tate expanded on this fashionable feature when she made her emancipation dress, which had a row of decorative tucks around the skirt and a very deep hem. This feature continued throughout the decade, even when more elaborate flounces grew in popularity. "Ladies who do not like wearing flounces," reported *The Politician* in October 1846, "or who wish for a light and simple dress made with tucks ... the number of five or seven, according to the height of the skirt [is suggested]."[21]

This detail from an 1845 French fashion plate shows a bridesmaid wearing no less than eight tucks across the skirt (Metropolitan Museum of Art).

Silk wedding dress,

1848, Wales, Amgueddfa Cymru—Museum Wales, Cardiff

This brown silk dress was worn by Miss Mary Jones of Colfa, Radnorshire, for her wedding on 27 April 1848. Colfa is a village in the rural county of Radnorshire, now Powys, on the English border. The 1840s had not been kind to rural Wales economically, and largely due to land-hunger, Radnorshire's population fell by three percent during the decade.[22] It is safe to assume that although this is a silk dress, its owner was probably of ordinary, relatively modest means.

This dipped rounded neckline may have been worn with a collar, though bridal fashion plates from the period do show similar styles without. *Le Moniteur de la Mode*, 1849, Metropolitan Museum of Art.

Decorative "jockey" oversleeves often covered structural details, such as pleats and repairs. They were also a fashionable feature, sometimes appearing on designated "bridal" dresses well into the following decade. One example was described in *The New Monthly Belle Assemblée*, 1857: "... a jockey of white moire antique, falling on the head of the second flounce."[24]

Due to its practical nature, brown was not an uncommon bridal color at this time, even when a dress was chosen specifically for the occasion. As seen in Mary Elizabeth Braddon's *The Doctor's Wife* (1865) set in the early 1850s, the protagonist Isabel Sleaford wears "a sombre brown-silk dress, which had been chosen by [her fiancé] George himself because of its homely merit of usefulness, rather than for any special beauty or elegance."[25] Other brides felt more positive about the shade, and where possible, bridal gowns—if not white—would always be made from the most fashionable colors. One newspaper reported from Paris in 1849 that "Fashionable Colours are now of dark rich hues, such as damson, claret, brown, violet ... many being relieved and intermixed by shades of lighter hues."[26] This is applied here in the use of a rust-brown fringe trim, which is applied across the bodice and sleeves. Evidence of former stitch holes below the waist suggests that the skirt could have been let down, or once had additional applied decoration—possibly of the same lighter-brown fringe.

The dress was probably accessorized with a bonnet, and the bride may have carried a handkerchief as a good luck charm. This tradition was especially popular among rural women—relating not only to the idea that, if she cried at her wedding, a bride would not cry again during her married life—but also that tears on that day would bring rain for the crops. The bride may or may not have carried a bouquet: in the countryside, it was more common for unmarried village girls to spread wildflowers on the bride's path.[23]

This 1849 fashion plate depicts the new fashionable ideal of a white wedding dress. Like the Welsh example, its delicate silk fringe adorns bodice and sleeves but also the skirt, showing how fringe might have been placed if (as suggested above) the skirt of Mary Jones's dress was once trimmed

Magasin des Demoiselles, March 1849, Metropolitan Museum of Art, New York

Chapter 4: 1837–1869

Wedding dress,

1850, England, National Gallery of Victoria, Melbourne

◆

This elegant gown was worn by Mary Pearce for her wedding to Ephraim Pearce in 1850 and was one of the treasured items brought to Australia when the couple emigrated three years later. The dress is a beautiful example of the transition between the long-waisted, drooping styles of the 1840s and the newly fashionable wide skirt and sleeves of the 1850s.[27]

Mary Pearce probably accessorized this dress with a lace veil (perhaps Honiton or Brussels), worn behind a wreath of orange blossom. As shown in this French fashion plate from 1850, the fashionable accompanying hairstyle was a center parting, smoothed over the ears and caught in a chignon.[28]

High, round necklines—often finished off with a lace collar—were very common for daywear.

These sham buttons are wrapped in a bright aquamarine colored thread, which matches the floral emblems on the dress. They are purely decorative and sit in between the deep pleats that form a "fan front," a particularly fashionable feature in the previous decade.

Frayed silk and puffed trim brings attention to newly fashionable flared "pagoda" sleeves. These would be at their widest in c.1857.

The skirt is flat pleated at the front and cartridge or "organ" pleated at the back; by this time a very typical pleating method.

In an 1850 edition of literary annual *The Keepsake*, a story entitled *The Government Appointment* describes the wedding of a young woman who, because there had been "no time to procure a trousseau ... was attired in the identical green silk dress" that she wore as her Sunday best. Despite this not being a planned wedding outfit, the fictional bride was up to date with her color choice.[29] *Blackwood's Lady's Magazine and Gazette of the Fashionable World* mentioned, in January 1850, that light green predominated (particularly for evening wear) "more than ever."[30] An 1851 fashion column reporting from Paris sang the praises of "Chambord green ... somewhat blue, and slightly resembles two shades already very much in fashion - Sea green and Islay green."[31] This dual hue echoes what is seen here, suggesting a bride who could afford to be significantly fashion-conscious for her wedding day.

Metropolitan Museum of Art

This figured silk taffeta features a variety of flowers, including chrysanthemums, daisies, and roses. By the early 1850s, machines such as the Jacquard Loom were enabling the cheaper and swifter production of "fancy or figured silks to an extraordinary extent."[32] Such silks were not only the province of the bride, however: an etiquette guide from 1850 declared that, in upper class weddings when the bride wears a veil, "the groom must appear in ... a white or figured-silk waistcoat" like the one shown right from 1860.[33]

White tarlatan wedding dress,

1854, Stockholm, The Nordic Museum

Svea Beata Myhrman (1819-1910) wore this fashionable gown for her wedding on August 19, 1854, to mill owner Gustaf Myhrman. At 35, she was considered a relatively mature bride, but the use of white was by now fashionable for all first-time brides. In 1851, the Home Circle recommended that brides getting married in the afternoon or evening should wear "white satin with lace flounces" rather than the simpler "plain white muslin or net, or white damask silk with plain sleeves" for morning. Therefore, it is a possibility that Svea Beata was married at a ceremony later in the day.[34]

This bridal crown was worn by Svea Beata on her wedding day. The Swedish tradition of wearing a crown dates back to the medieval era, and remained common until the early twentieth century. This one is made of thin steel wire, thread, and myrtle sprigs, and embellished with a bunch of wax flowers. Myrtle, an evergreen plant, has been a symbol of love and virginity since ancient times, and is still a popular part of bridal bouquets—including, since c.1850, that of many royal brides in England.

The ribbon sash and trimmings feature pinked or "scalloped" edges.

Sheer fabric, gathered into a "fan front," sits across the shoulders, chest, and back. It leads fluidly into transparent sleeves.

Sashes or belts (sometimes referred to by the French *ceinture* in fashion press), tied with a bow in front, were popular and sometimes seen on bridal ensembles. It was fashionable for, as *The Lady's Newspaper* put it in 1854, "the long ends [to flow] nearly to the bottom of the skirt," and that effect is also seen here.[35]

Lightweight fabrics teamed perfectly with the increasingly voluminous skirts. This dress is made from tarlatan, a stiffened, open-weave cotton that created a sheer overlay. It was especially popular for dancing, used on ball gowns.

Flounced, layered skirts were incredibly fashionable during this decade. For bridal gowns, their popularity was heightened further when Queen Victoria's eldest daughter, the Princess Royal, married Crown Prince Friedrich Wilhelm of Prussia in January 1858. Her dress was described as "rich white moire antique; the dress of exquisite Honiton guipure, consisting of three flounces, the body being to match."[36]

By 1859, the extremes to which this trend could reach were being lampooned in the press. "Robes are generally made with five or seven flounces" wrote *Le Follet* in September 1859. "Husbands, with incomes under GBP 300 a year, will be delighted to learn that the number is so limited." Here, the flounces are exaggerated further by the use of trimming à disposition; in this case, two rows of silk ribbon placed at the edge of each flounce.[37]

Wedding dress,

c.1855–1905, Quirindi & District Historical Society, Wollombi, New South Wales

This is a rare, documented example of a wedding dress worn by brides across multiple generations. It demonstrates the great emotional pull of this garment, which has the power to override contemporary fashion preferences. It is a good example of the trends in style at the date of the first wedding and does not appear to have been altered for the subsequent ceremonies.

Although wearing the same dress as a relative was a money-saver, it was not done for reasons of thrift alone. Even among the wealthy, this was common practice, and reports exist throughout the century of the dresses being given further life not only as bridal gowns, but ball dresses and even fancy-dress costumes.

In 1858, shades of purple became extremely fashionable following the wedding of Queen Victoria's eldest daughter. The mother of the bride's mauve dress received almost as much attention as the wedding gown, leading to great interest in various shades of the color.[39]

The Queen's aunt, the Duchess of Cambridge, also wore a lilac dress featuring the highly fashionable double skirt and trimmed with tulle and Honiton lace.[40]

The dress was worn first by bride Mary Ann Porter in 1855, then by her daughter Isabella in 1883, and finally by Isabella's granddaughter, Mary Ann Schofield, in 1905.[38] The image above shows descendant Venn Porter wearing the gown, which was donated to the historical society in the 1970s. While men were often less enthusiastic to wear "something borrowed" on their wedding day, for women it was a meaningful (not to mention practical) way of expressing family attachment across the generations.

These layers of silk fringe at the cuff recall the highly fashionable double frill. In July 1853 one Australian newspaper declared that "nothing can be prettier than this style, especially on robes of taffetas."[41] The application of fringe seen here simulates this layered effect but uses less fabric, demonstrating how ordinary brides achieved fashionable trends within a modest budget.

This daguerreotype of an 1851 bride, made by masters of the craft Southworth and Hawes, shows those fashionable trends played out in multiple rich layers of delicate silk fringe.

In 1885 the dress was worn by Isabella, daughter of the original bride Mary Ann Porter. She purchased a matching parasol to carry on her wedding day, a decision aided by numerous fashion advice columns. "Fashionable ladies have a parasol for each dress," South London Observer explained in 1881. "The colour and material of the handle are considered with especial regard to their suitability to those of the dress."[42] In 1885, several columns made special mention of a parasol recommended "as a gift for the bride" which was made from "plaited tulle" with a scent-bottle or "bonhommière" contained in the handle, which was further "encrusted with precious stones."[43]

Wedding dress,

c.1860, Manning Valley Historical Society, New South Wales

This shot silk taffeta dress was handmade in rural eastern Australia by Mary Halpin, a young Irish Catholic migrant. As with so many garments worn by non-wealthy owners, it is not certain that this was used as a wedding dress, but the idea is maintained by the family. If it is the case, the gown is a hugely valuable example of a modest wedding dress that was worn for nuptials between a man and a woman of different faiths, a situation that would have caused considerable heartache and difficulty in the mid-nineteenth century. Furthermore, it is possible that the bride was pregnant at the time of her wedding, and examination of the inner structure of the bodice reveals that the dress was later altered to accommodate breastfeeding.[44]

The structure of this dress is simple, but it does present a recognizably late 1850s/early 1860s silhouette, particularly evident through the low, sloping shoulders, high rounded neckline and centered row of buttons.

The 2cm wide gold fringe trimming bodice and cuffs are very representative of the preceding decade, a simple but effective method of ornamentation. One American newspaper commented in November 1855 that "everything is trimmed [and] we have a most bewildering variety ... velvet [...] fringe, ribbon and lace."[46]

A dress with similar features is documented here on this bridal gown c.1860, though clearly a more complex and probably professionally made piece, worn with undergarments to provide the sought-after fashionable shape.

The dress was worn with this velvet and lace bonnet. It provides a slight nod to high fashion in the form of an accessory: as various fashion columns reported, the year 1860 saw white and cream-colored velvet becoming an increasingly popular fabric for wedding dresses.[47]

If worn as a "Sunday best" dress after the wedding (or even if this was the gown's sole purpose), its coffee-brown shade would be highly practical. However, as a shot silk taffeta, it has a subtle, changeable royal blue tone which features in the popular "something borrowed, something blue" rhyme.[45]

From around the early 1850s, clothing patterns became mass-marketed, and the bride would have had access to various designs via newspapers and magazines. This resulted in more women making their own dresses—even those who could easily afford a dressmaker. Particularly for public garments such as wedding and ball gowns, displaying her own handiwork allowed a woman to show off both her acquisition of skills and knowledge of current fashions.

Silk taffeta wedding dress,

c.1860, South Canterbury Museum

◆

This distinctive dress was made with two bodices: one for daywear, and one for evening. This "two-in-one" approach was not uncommon for a "special" outfit, and brides often married in their "Sunday best" to combine practical considerations with aesthetic preference. This approach was economic and allowed years of varied use, long after bride and groom had said "I do".

....

Gold purl (bullion) thread edged with black chenille makes up this frogged, military-style ornamentation. In between, sham buttons cover the true hook-and-eye front fastening beneath.

The pattern on this silk is composed of scattered black diamond shapes with a yellow rosebud in the center of each. Diamond motifs on clothing were seen throughout the decade, often as part of a trim design (à la disposition) or on a larger scale to heighten the effect of a crinoline skirt. One fashion column from 1861 described a particularly opulent effect:[48] In each diamond formed by the trimming was a small jet hanging ornament.

As the decade progressed and "separates" became even more popular, fashion writers praised the variety and practicality of this approach: "One dress has frequently two bodices, and two paletots, and with different sashes and trimmings, with one skirt. A variety of costumes is obtained."[49]

If a wedding took place in the evening (usually in a private, at-home ceremony), it is possible that this low-necked second bodice could be worn. Below, a late 1850s example shows that effect on a white bridal gown:

This bridal fashion plate from May 1861 depicts sleeves that are similarly structured, but lavishly and generously trimmed. Those shown in this New Zealand example are edged with the same braid that adorns the bodice front. From c.1864, wide pagoda or funnel-shaped sleeves would more or less disappear. This dress, probably made in the late 1850s, retains a feature that was at its widest c.1857–8.

A slim length of gold trim edges the hem. The look was specifically referenced in an edition of *New Peterson Magazine* in 1860; the dress in question also trimmed with gold or colored braid.[50]

Quaker wedding dress,

1863, Gettysburg, Fashion Archives and Museum, Shippensburg University, Pennsylvania

An unverified story goes that Maria Griest, married to Charles John Tyson two months before the Battle of Gettysburg, nearly lost her gown to Confederate soldiers. She begged them not to steal it and thankfully they relented, leaving this dress to posterity. The gray silk taffeta is not worn due to mourning; rather to fit within the couples' religious sensibilities. A gray "plain" dress was the accepted standard for a Quaker bride, although increasing general interest in the simple aesthetic of Quaker style led to a new influence on contemporary dress. In 1870, Godey's Lady's Book praised the use of percales (cotton) in "écru buff, pearl, gray, dove and soft Quaker drabs."[51]

The 1850s and 60s saw great changes in the way Quakers presented themselves to the world. In England and Ireland, an 1860 Act of Parliament made it easier for Friends to "marry out" of their religion. This prompted a greater reform and consideration of what it meant to be a contemporary Quaker, and dress was the most visible manifestation of such change. Brides now felt freer to dress as they pleased, often in white, with lavish trimming and accessories.[52] Nevertheless, the simplistic aesthetic persisted in the general mindset, including in relation to weddings. Louisa May Alcott's *Work: A Story of Experience* (1873), set in the Civil War years, describes protagonist Christie "looking very like a Quaker bride in her gray gown with no ornament but delicate frills at neck and wrist, and the roses in her bosom."[53] She eschews white in order to "consecrate my uniform as you do yours by being married in it. Isn't it fitter for a soldier's wife than lace and silk at a time like this?" There is an irony in that despite the Quakers' pacifist stance, here their simple style of dress is linked to military support and solemn patriotism.

In keeping with Quaker style, ornamentation is sparse. It comprises this white collar and a band of satin running from the shoulders across the breast, finishing at a point at the center back waistline. Reports exist of some brides choosing white but keeping to traditional roots by keeping their dress free of trim.[54]

Light gray, in general, was not out of place for a bride. In 1863, *The Habits of Good Society* commented that for older brides, "nothing is so becoming as moiré silk, either white or silver grey."[55]

This Quaker bonnet from c.1860 displays characteristic deep pleats and is suggestive of the type of headwear that Maria Griest might have worn.

The dress was re-modelled for wear in the years following the wedding. Fullness has been moved to the back of the skirt to allow for the fashionable elliptical shape of the late 1860s

Wedding dress,

1865, The Hallwyl Museum, Stockholm

This elaborately trimmed gown was worn by Wilhelmina Kempe at her marriage to Count Walther von Hallwyl in 1865. Made from white silk moiré, the dress took a month to make and features fashionable military-style surface decoration and an imposing front-tied sash. It was worn with a myrtle wreath headdress, veil, taffeta ribbon garters and white silk pumps. The bride carried a bouquet of myrtle, white lilies, roses and golden brush.[56]

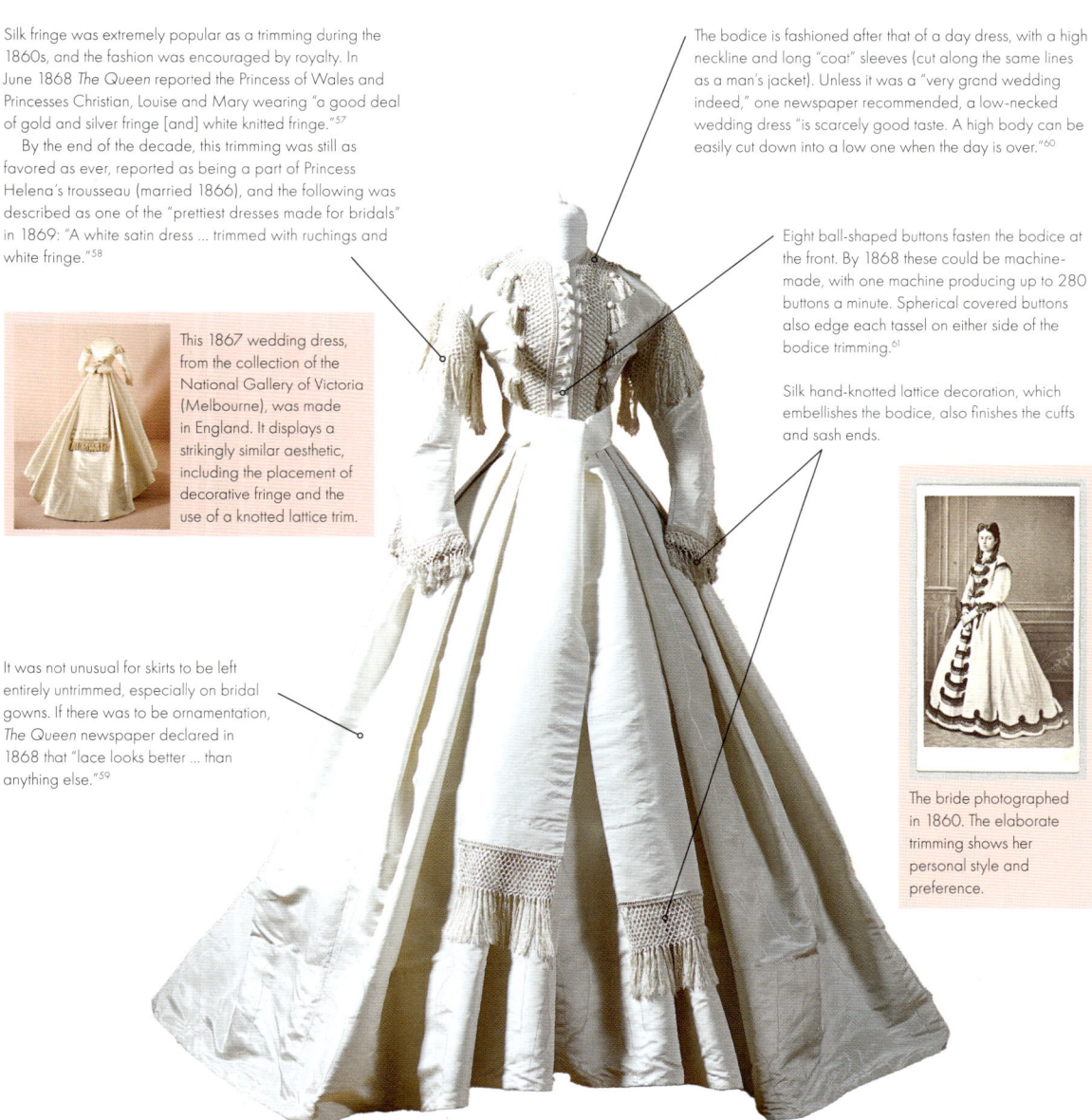

Silk fringe was extremely popular as a trimming during the 1860s, and the fashion was encouraged by royalty. In June 1868 *The Queen* reported the Princess of Wales and Princesses Christian, Louise and Mary wearing "a good deal of gold and silver fringe [and] white knitted fringe."[57]

By the end of the decade, this trimming was still as favored as ever, reported as being a part of Princess Helena's trousseau (married 1866), and the following was described as one of the "prettiest dresses made for bridals" in 1869: "A white satin dress ... trimmed with ruchings and white fringe."[58]

This 1867 wedding dress, from the collection of the National Gallery of Victoria (Melbourne), was made in England. It displays a strikingly similar aesthetic, including the placement of decorative fringe and the use of a knotted lattice trim.

It was not unusual for skirts to be left entirely untrimmed, especially on bridal gowns. If there was to be ornamentation, *The Queen* newspaper declared in 1868 that "lace looks better ... than anything else."[59]

The bodice is fashioned after that of a day dress, with a high neckline and long "coat" sleeves (cut along the same lines as a man's jacket). Unless it was a "very grand wedding indeed," one newspaper recommended, a low-necked wedding dress "is scarcely good taste. A high body can be easily cut down into a low one when the day is over."[60]

Eight ball-shaped buttons fasten the bodice at the front. By 1868 these could be machine-made, with one machine producing up to 280 buttons a minute. Spherical covered buttons also edge each tassel on either side of the bodice trimming.[61]

Silk hand-knotted lattice decoration, which embellishes the bodice, also finishes the cuffs and sash ends.

The bride photographed in 1860. The elaborate trimming shows her personal style and preference.

Wedding ensemble, USA,

1868, Metropolitan Museum of Art, New York

This dress, in half-mourning colors of gray and black, represents patriotic grief rather than individual loss. The bride, Amelia Jane Carley, did not lose immediate family during the Civil War (1861–65) and nor did her husband, William Edward Chess—although he did serve in the Union Army along with Amelia's brother. It was custom to trim one's dress with black to honor wartime deaths, but to choose a bridal gown entirely in half-mourning colors suggests a deeper personal sense of social responsibility.[62] The dress is representative of late 1860s fashions, with emphasis moving toward the bustle, peplum, and overskirt, and with the use of a separate basqued bodice.

No bridal jewelry is shown here, but polished jet jewelry, along with gold or glass beads, was deemed the most appropriate for mourning wear.[63]

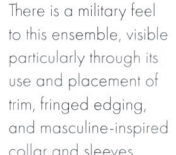

The dress is made from a gray silk wool poplin. A similar but heavier fabric, bengaline, was a cheaper alternative that became more widely used in the following decades. "Bengaline is nice," wrote *The Bazaar, The Exchange and Mart* in 1891, "it is softer-looking than faille, and you can soften it still further ... by festooned flounce ... or other draperies."[66]

The popularity of fringe as a bridal trimming is illustrated in this 1867 fashion plate, from *Peterson's Magazine* (Metropolitan Museum of Art).

For half mourning, shades of purple (particularly lavender) were also an option and one that many brides took advantage of. Whichever color was chosen, however, women were encouraged to buy "the best materials when making up mourning ... a cheaper article will wear miserably; there is no greater error in economy than purchasing cheap mourning."[64]

There is a military feel to this ensemble, visible particularly through its use and placement of trim, fringed edging, and masculine-inspired collar and sleeves.

Etiquette guides throughout the century were stringent on what was deemed "appropriate" for a bride in mourning, with dizzying rules on dress color, trim, accessories, and personal deportment. However, from the middle of the century in America—particularly after such a seismic shift as war—there appeared guides which were far more sanguine. Sarah Hales's *Manners: Or, Happy Homes and Good Society All the Year Round* (1868) gently decreed that "With regard to marriage ... it is impossible to give rules, as practice must ever vary with circumstances ... With regard to dress, the same rule exists; therefore no allusion is made to it."[65]

The bride wore these laced boots as part of her wedding ensemble.

Slave Marriage Ceremony, a wedding ceremony. Woodcut, 19th century.

Silk taffeta wedding dress, 1860, (front view)

Wedding dress, 1837, (fabric detail)

Chapter 5

1870–1889

By the 1870s, the tradition of bridal white with orange blossom (especially wax flowers) seems to have been firmly established, at least in the United States. For those choosing a colored wedding dress over pure white, this period ushered in more frequent examples of what have been termed "hybrid" costumes—for example, a dark dress—even black—worn with a white veil and wreath or sprig of orange blossom. This was a compromise that made the bride's identity obvious, something that was ever more important as couples were able to photographically document their unions. Cunningham and Lab (1993) suggest that this may also have been influenced by Queen Victoria, who, since the death of Albert in 1861, consistently wore black widow's weeds with a white lace veil.[1] In another technological advance, some women rushed to marry in one of the exciting new chemical aniline dyes (at least two documented examples, in bronze and claret, survive in the United Kingdom) but this was not a conventional choice.[2] In 1878, a comedic column in *Arthur's Illustrated Home Magazine* cynically outlined the highly practical reasons for choosing a dyed wedding dress:

LEFT
Bride and groom, late 1870s.

[Dark gray cashmere] could be dyed into half a dozen new dresses before it was wore out. When she was tired of gray, she could take some of the Aniline Dye and make it slate color…then light brown, then dark brown, then plum, then navy blue.[3]

The almost universal dominance of white was aptly shown at a "breach of promise" court case in 1871, in which the young woman in question's main allegation was that her fiancé had "even suggested that her wedding dress should be violet instead of white, as the color would be more useful afterwards." According to a report by a London newspaper at the time, this was more than enough to convince the jury, who awarded damages of £20.[4]

The decade saw further expansion in the availability of associated bridal items, including lingerie—which, by this time, was attaining what has been described as "the new underwear fetish," with popular magazines openly discussing the titillation of such garments.[5] These were not necessarily marketed as separate trousseau items, but rather as "bridal sets," a term first instigated by Moritz Goldenson (who is often credited with the "invention" of the bridal nightgown). A nightgown was included in Goldenson's "set"; apparently inspired by those worn by brides of Austro-Hungarian royalty.[6] Other manufacturers followed suit, and by the end of the decade some items of wedding lingerie were even displayed publicly to customers. Those living away from the urban centers were also catered to with mail-order catalogs, offering a variety of items aimed at couples planning to marry. This shows the development of a separate industry, although, as Vicki Howard has emphasized, in the United States neither urban nor rural brides were yet part of a defined market segment.[7]

In terms of the dress itself, high-fashion examples would always be white, trained, and often styled like an evening dress. The wedding of Princess Louise, Queen Victoria's fourth daughter, in 1871, unsurprisingly spurred a great deal of interest. Her dress, described as "a rich white satin covered with a deep flounce of Honiton point lace, trimmed with cordons of orange blossoms, white heather and myrtle, and a train of white satin trimmed to correspond with the dress"[8] mirrored all the burgeoning bridal ideals. It also recalled elements of her mother's dress thirty years before, particularly with its use of Honiton lace—a trimming revived by all the Queen's daughters at their weddings. Such nostalgia and a nod to generational tradition is a mindset seen increasingly throughout the final decades of the nineteenth century, often in sharp contrast to the voices of social reformers who felt that bridal extravagance was immoral. Margaret Doake's *May Darling* (1881) illustrates these new ideas around the wedding dress as not only souvenir, but heirloom:

"I think a wedding-dress should be kept sacred instead of being cut up for anybody else. I might have thought so, too, when I was your age; and when you are mine you will find it will be every bit as sacred if your daughter wears it."[9]

LEFT
Satin wedding dress with orange blossom, 1879, Poland.

92 How to Read a Wedding Dress

At the same time, dissenting voices declared such sentiments as: "To my mind, wedding-dresses should always be made with an eye to the future. The days for preserving them in order to show them to one's great grandchildren are happily gone by." (1882)[10] Such conflicting feelings are still firmly in place today, and ironically, sentimentality has only grown in the wake of mass-produced dresses and "off the rack" styles. [11]

The 1880s marked a ground-breaking change in the way bridal gowns were procured. For the first time, women could purchase wedding dresses ready or partially made from mail order catalogues and department stores. These could not provide the perfect fit and finish of a custom-made gown, so middle-class brides might find themselves refitting a dress or, if they could afford it, employing the services of a seamstress to get a more exacting result. Economy was obviously the main reason for such purchases, but there are examples of the aforementioned ethical considerations too. In early 1880s New York, Kate Field founded the short-lived Co-operative Dress Association, which was created to "abandon the extravagancies of the past" and instill self-respect amid notions of dress reform. "They keep ready made dresses at the Cooperative", a newspaper reported in 1881, "and you can find almost anything from a bridal trousseau to a complete baby's outfit, cradle and all." [12] The general popularity of ready-made wedding dresses during the 1880s is, however, shown in the sheer number of companies advertising their "specialty" in this area. One, a firm in Tunbridge Wells, England, declared in 1886 that it possessed "unsurpassed … value and excellence" in wedding and mourning orders, for which "special attention" was given.[13]

As had been the case for some time, pattern companies also supplied patterns and instructions for bridal wear, and numerous options existed for brides to "mix and match" by purchasing a ready-made skirt, for example (usually kept in stock continuously), but making the bodice themselves. *The Sydney Mail* advised in April 1880 that decorated plastrons for bodice fronts could be purchased "ready-made in the shops, to be placed on any dress."[14] The most desirable bridal gowns were, however, far from simple in terms of either construction or embellishment. As examples in this chapter show, fashionable dresses were silken layers of armor, ornamented with complex pleats, sculptural drapery, shirring and panels of different textures. Even when advances in machinery meant that such elaborate trimming was available to more sections of society, other small but vocal communities were quick to reject it. These reform, aesthetic, and rational dress movements expressed their distaste for excess, championing healthy, unrestrictive garments for both sexes. Vanishingly few brides married in a "true" reform dress, though, with some paying lip service by displaying aesthetic elements they admired—but still worn over the obligatory corset, boned bodice, and layers of petticoats. An exception to this will be discussed later in the book, showing the strength of some "reform" brides' convictions as time elapsed and their philosophy became more widespread.

By the end of the decade, so universal was the use of a veil that a significant portion of fashion columns were devoted to the purchasing and arranging of one. As seen with the procurement of wedding dresses, it was acknowledged that not all brides could afford elite services, and that many would rely on help from family and friends. "You cannot buy a veil by the yard," advised the *Ladies' Home Journal* in 1889, "you cannot tell how much you need; the proper way is to have the shopkeeper send a piece of tulle and then drape it on the bride's head." Once the veil is bought, the writer continued, brides not residing in large cities (and therefore, allegedly, without access to hair-dressers), should remember that "while it is as light as air it still must be firmly pinned in position, and the orange blossoms well in place, so that when the front part is thrown back they will present a perfectly well arranged appearance." [15]

"It is in excellent taste for the bride to wear a travelling dress and bonnet at the marriage ceremony," "A Perplexed Subscriber" wrote to *The Delineator* in 1880.[16] This was in response to some disagreement, at the end of the previous decade, regarding the suitability of tailored travelling costume as the main wedding dress. As the popularity of leaving for the honeymoon on the same day grew, however, many women began to consider the option of combining two-in-one. This was also partly due to the increased popularity of afternoon marriage ceremonies (in England, thanks to changing canonical hours—the times during which a marriage may lawfully be celebrated), which meant that the couple would leave immediately afterwards for their honeymoon.[17] Other women chose to make their honeymoon journey in their bridal gown, which many fashion columns staunchly advised against. Rather, the bride should change into a new travelling ensemble but remove any suggestion that she was coming to the journey immediately from her wedding, a disconcerting idea that suggests additional social concerns around propriety. As Kate Hill discusses, these concepts had been developing throughout the early part of the century as travel became more accessible, and mixed reactions to the wedding party depicted in William Powell Frith's painting *The Railway Station* in 1862 speak to some confusion over where and how a newlywed bride should be publicly seen.[18]

RIGHT
Travelling ensemble worn as a wedding gown in 1887.

Silk taffeta wedding dress,

1872, Salem, Massachusetts, Peabody Essex Museum

"Something blue" is the old adage, suggesting that a bride needs to wear an accessory of that shade in order to ensure a happy marriage. Blue also implied fidelity, but it is unlikely that these superstitions dictated this bride's choice of a soft sky blue. Along with the deeper, richer new aniline dyes available during the decade, lighter tones were still regarded as elegant and fashionable, and recommended for the trousseau of brides wearing white. The "wedding wardrobe" of Italian Donna Anna Maria Torlonia, which cost £10,000 in 1873, included a light blue "velvet visiting dress … a pale blue silk evening dress … and a blue faille."[19]

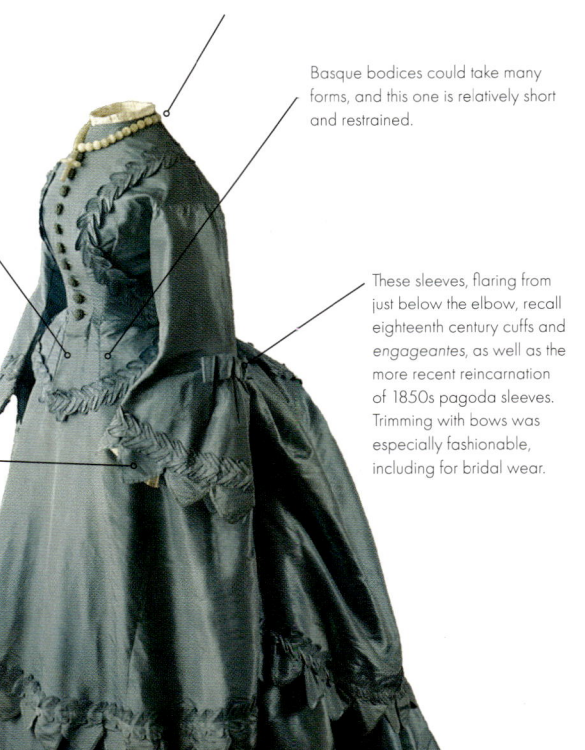

This dress is a beautiful example of the new bustle silhouette, whilst still retaining some late 1860s style features. The coat-like basque bodice, with deep waistline and flared sleeves, is very representative of the era. At the same time its row of floral applique trim around the shoulders seems to simulate a bolero jacket, especially popular during the previous decade.

The same trim is repeated elsewhere on the dress, bordering bold triangular Vandyke edging. Along with "scallops," this had made a return to favor, *Arthur's Lady's Home Magazine* advised brides in 1872. It further suggested that women should trim the front of their bridal skirt "according to taste" but, if made of heavy fabric, is "exceedingly elegant made perfectly plain." This egalitarian publication also assured brides that although white satin and lace were conventional, they "are expensive [and] should only be adopted when strictly in keeping with the circumstances of the bride and bridegroom, and their future prospects."[20]

"Any great display of jewellery is in bad taste" wrote etiquette author Eliza Cheadle in 1872, "and the little that may be allowed should not be florid or elaborate. A set of pearls looks well, or something of the same plain and simple character."[21]

Basque bodices could take many forms, and this one is relatively short and restrained.

These sleeves, flaring from just below the elbow, recall eighteenth century cuffs and *engageantes*, as well as the more recent reincarnation of 1850s pagoda sleeves. Trimming with bows was especially fashionable, including for bridal wear.

Skirt fullness has been entirely swept to the rear, with a draped overskirt. It was common to have a demi-train in a less formal ceremony, although reports do exist of luxurious ensembles featuring one. In September 1870, a British newspaper reported "a very rich demi train of white satin, (trimmed) elegantly with lace and orange blossoms."[22]

This image shows a very similar bodice design from the very start of the decade.

By 1872 brides could also select a longer, tunic-like construction, as seen in this fashion plate from the same year.

Wedding dress,

c.1872–1876, maker unknown, Agnes Etherington Art Centre, Queen's University, Ontario

This dress is a dynamic example of two forces at play in 1870s fashion: eighteenth-century and military detailing. Both are incorporated through self-trimming in a vivid chestnut shade, with a pop of unexpected color appearing in the form of a bright white triple layered collar.

A standing collar of white satin guides the eye to the bride's face. It also provides a further historical nod, this time to the standing ruffs of the sixteenth and seventeenth centuries.

This high-necked panel provides modesty through an illusion of multiple layers, as well as the surrounding ruffles which would usually serve that purpose.

An asymmetric bodice opening was not common during the decade—although asymmetry elsewhere, particularly on skirt drapery and trimming, was. Aligning with other masculine influences in this gown, it is more akin to the sharply angled "University Coat" that was in fashion for young men during the early 1870s.[23]

Structural stitching was by this era mostly machine-produced, leaving time for more elaborate and extensive decorative detailing. Although *The Young Lady's Journal* recommended in 1873 that bridal skirts should be made "without an atom of trimming," most women chose to honor the general fashion for ruffles, puffs, and swags on their wedding day.[24]

This distinctive sleeve detail is taken from a naval influence, the "mariner's cuff" or *cuff à la marinière* which was made from a vent outside the sleeve, fastened with a flap and sometimes edged with braid. This interpretation features the common sham buttonholes and is edged with ribbon to highlight the shape.

Similar decorative features were found on the sleeves of men's coats in the eighteenth century, as seen in this 1780s example:

National Gallery of Victoria, Melbourne

Rust-colored crochet lace edges the collar, bodice hem, and bias flounces on the skirt. Following the 1870 Education Act and broader levels of literacy in society, crochet patterns and books became more cheaply available.[25] Crochet lace was also the fastest to hand-produce, with inexpensive tools and thread. By 1877 it was being described as "more fashionable than embroidery." This enabled brides to trim their gowns in increasingly varied and individual ways.[26]

This drawing of Marie Antoinette, c. 1780–1781, illustrates many of the influences seen in the bridal gown. The billowing skirt of the *robe à la polonaise* was a prime model for the first bustle phase of the 1870s, and the puffed and ruched sections of fabric across each skirt hem complement this aesthetic. (Metropolitan Museum of Art)

Chapter 5: 1870–1889

Plaid wedding dress,

1873, New York, Fashion Archives and Museum, Shippensburg University, Pennsylvania

◆

Ellen Sawyer of Allegany County, New York, wore this bright plaid dress for her wedding to Philetus Cartwright in 1873. This was Philetus's second marriage, and unfortunately it would not be a long one: Ellen died in 1875, possibly due to complications in childbirth at the end of the previous year. Her dress is another example of the common practice of choosing a practical, yet attractive fabric that could be used long after the wedding. The silhouette is fashionable, with its basqued bodice and flared sleeves, and the skirt—though made to fit over a bustle—lacks the overskirt and layering that had been especially popular from the late 1860s onwards. Ellen's choice of bold velvet trimming in place of this is probably a good example of her personal taste and preference.[27]

Peterson's Magazine, November 1870, Metropolitan Museum of Art

It was quite usual for high necklines to be worn for the wedding ceremony, and for daywear, a high, round neck with front button fastening was common. This combination can frequently be seen in idealized fashion plates as well as "real" surviving examples.

A similar vertical skirt trim is seen on this dress worn by Pauline Princesse de Metternich, in 1864. (The J. Paul Getty Museum, Los Angeles)

Styles from the 1850s made a re-appearance in 1870s fashion, including the basque bodice with wide pagoda sleeves. Though more modest than their predecessors twenty years earlier, these were referred to by the same name in the fashionable press and seem to have been popular for all types of bridal wear. One report from *The Queen* in 1872 described a style seen at some of the "leading houses" in Paris: "The bodices of brides' dresses are cut with a point, which is always becoming ... with the pagoda sleeve."[32]

This detail from an 1872 fashion plate shows the most modish way for a bride to wear pagoda sleeves: with a split at the back, as seen here, but (as with fashionable skirts) ruffled and ornamented with bows and lace "à la Louis XV."[33] *Journal des Dames et des Demoiselles*, November 15, 1872, Rijksmuseum, Amsterdam

Plaids, checks, and tartans were popular during this period, tying in to the general trend for a combination of bright colors and patterns. One 1870s "Prairie bride" in Illinois made herself a gown from black-and-white plaid silk trimmed with black velvet ribbon with which she was "delighted."[28] We also hear of patterns such as gingham being representative of a "sensible" bride; as an 1870 Unitarian series of *Lectures to Young Men* pointed out:

"For Heaven's sake get a sensible one, and not a fashionable woman to be your help-meet ... It is hard to find one who is willing to wear a gingham dress instead of a silk one."[29]

There seems to have been a place more broadly for plaid in formal wear, too. *Our Lady's Letter* from London commented in December 1875 that "bodices and tabliers of plaid velvet will be much worn for full dress."[30] By 1878, the red and black color scheme seen here was described as "the most fashionable plaid."[31]

Wedding dress,

1878, England, Fashion Archives and Museum, Shippensburg University, Pennsylvania

This dress was purchased from Halling, Pearce and Stone, a business described as "the handsome general drapery establishment" on Cockspur Street, London.[34] It was worn by Beatrice Marcia Carlisle for her marriage to Thomas Cave on October 16, 1878.

The skirt and bodice are made from Ottoman silk. During the nineteenth century, a rise in domestic cotton production (which became a prime focus over silk for many manufacturers) meant that silks made in Bursa were less commonly seen. For Ottoman brides, bright colors such as red were especially popular, and had been for centuries. From the 1870s, however, European styles were becoming increasingly fashionable. This resulted in two-piece dresses with a train, made from silk in pastel shades and embellished with lace, pearls, and sequins. They would sometimes be worn under a fur-lined kaftan.[35]

It is documented that the bride wore a floor-length veil. This was a common accessory for women who could afford it, and its use was declared necessary at evening church weddings. A well-known "manual of politeness" wrote in 1876 that the bride should wear "A veil, falling from her head to her feet, fastened to the hair by a coiffure of orange flowers."[37]

A substantial part of the skirt's surface decoration is composed of fabric loops and tassels. *Le Follet* commented in September 1873 that "What are technically called self-trimmings—i.e., ornaments made of the same material as the dress—are very much used for all classes and toilettes."[38]

The gown was given a second life as the wedding dress of descendant Ann Barclay on July 17, 1948. The practice of re-using family dresses was common during and after the war years. In 1943 one Californian bride was recorded as wearing "her grandmother's wedding gown ... [a] quaint grey and blue taffeta gown ... styled in the mode of [1880] with a lace yolk [sic] and collar, lace trimming the sleeves and tiers of ruffles on the skirt which fell into a long train."[36]

Construction details at the side of the bodice show that, despite the simulation produced by rows of piping, this is a one-piece gown.

The dramatic "crenelated" cut of this hem is inspired by history. In the early to mid-years of the decade, when such designs began to be more frequently seen, one fashion column commented that "Our garments at present borrow strange names; we have Cuirasses, coats of mail [...] crenelated trimmings, chatelaines, &c ..." This encourages, the article continued, thoughts of medieval and Renaissance fashions.[39]

Wedding dress,

c.1879, Hampshire Cultural Trust

This dress, with its swansdown trimming and shimmering cream silk panels, creates a perfect winter bridal ensemble. The presence of swansdown alone indicates the bride's status: it was very expensive and used by exclusive couturiers such as Charles Worth, whose designs could only be purchased by society's elite.[40] Newspaper fashion columns and marriage reports give an indication of how swansdown trimming might be accessorized: "The bride was ... attired [in] a dress of white satin, trimmed with swansdown, veil of Brussels net, and a wreath of orange blossoms."[41]

....

Swansdown was an indicator of luxury, but even wealthy brides would expect to wear their wedding dress more than once. 1870 manual *The Art of Dressing Well* gave thorough directions for cleaning both heavily and slightly soiled swansdown to "look as well as new," enabling many years of use.[44]

Peachy pink taffeta bows are arranged across the entire front panel of the dress, from neck to hem. Inspiration for this detail may have been taken from the wedding gown of Princess Louise Margaret of Prussia, who married Queen Victoria's son Arthur, Duke of Connaught on March 13, 1879. Her dress was described by one fashion correspondent in May that year as "white satin [and lace] ... Bows of the same lace are placed on the front in a spiral pattern."[42]

Horizontal gathered silk panels were a common decorative and structural feature of the era. The same effect can be seen on this bridal fashion plate from the same year. (*Illustrierte Frauen-Zeitung*, 14 April 1879)

An oversized bow of silk moiré cascades down the back of the dress towards the train. This was a popular point of interest in ordinary daywear too; described by *Demorest's Monthly Magazine* in 1880 as "especially graceful and stylish ... an enormous bow just below the waist line [falls] plainly below."[45]

Silk was—and remains—a consistently popular bridal choice. However, newspapers in the winter of 1879 cited velvet as the prized material, for both bride and guests. At one fashionable London wedding "there was scarcely anything but this costly fabric used in the toilets" including the bride, who wore a "ruby red ... travelling costume."[43]

Silk wedding dress,

1880, USA, Metropolitan Museum of Art, New York

◆

This incredibly ornate gown employs multiple decorative techniques to make a statement. No information survives pertaining to the identity of the bride, but the opulence of the gown strongly suggests that she was from a wealthy family, and therefore this dress was probably a commissioned design.

Wedding dresses—along with other day styles—would almost always be high necked. This example sports a standing collar with fronts that extend down to the bust, terminating at a large ribbon bow. The open space at the bride's chest is filled with ruffles of lace that overlap, but may have been worn with an additional chemisette or "modesty panel," as shown in the fashion plate to the right.

This dress is a prime example of the svelte princess line, an uncompromising, figure-hugging design that remained until the appearance of the "second" bustle phase from c.1883 to 1889.

Fashionable three-quarter-length sleeves are finished with lace flounces and vertical bands of satin. Further up the arm, the sleeves display a similar technique to one seen on a wedding dress by Charles Frederick Worth, c.1878, in which knotted cream satin bands create a "slashed" effect over the net foundation. Here, triangular beaded appliques sit over a sheer net underlay.

Puffed and shirred bands of fabric mirror popular trimmings on day dress, highly reminiscent of eighteenth-century styling.

To match the pearl fringe, scattered pearl beads can be seen across the whole dress, embellishing the sleeves, cuffs, and lace trimmings. In 1881 a "lady well known in the society circles of San Francisco" wore a bridal gown "embroidered with pearl beads, edged with pearl lace ... [a] square neck [is trimmed with] an elegant pearl fringe."[46]

Rows of beaded fringe, each strand threaded with pearl beads, border an asymmetrical panel at the front of the skirt. This border curves around the left-hand side to create an ornamental feature, and a similar fringed effect is seen in this 1879 fashion plate (above) (Les Modes Parisiennes, Peterson's Magazine).

Coquillé (shell-shaped) layers of crisp triple-pleated silk edge the hem of this substantial train. By 1882 it was being described as "the most fashionable trimming" for the bottom of a formal skirt.[47]

Two-piece wedding dress,

c.1882–85, Fashion Archives and Museum, Shippensburg University, Pennsylvania

◆

This burgundy silk ensemble was worn by rural bride Mary Ellen Mackey for her wedding to Martin Luther Rosenberry on September 29, 1882 in Chambersburg, Pennsylvania. The couple settled in the small community of Freestone in Horse Valley and had eleven children.[48]

In June 1888, *New Peterson Magazine* remarked that "There has been a very decided change in the styles of wedding-dresses. Plain materials—such as white faille, or corded silk, or satin—are no longer in vogue. Fashion now decrees heavy brocades, the pattern large leaves and flowers in satin on a faille ground or a very rich silk in wide alternate stripes of corded silk and satin."[49] This dress would almost certainly have been the bride's "best," rather than a designated "wedding" outfit, but its fabric is unintentionally ahead of its time in terms of specific bridal fashions. However, while the above quote mentions floral designs, the pattern seen here is abstract and geometric.

The dress may have been accessorized with orange blossoms, as was so popular following Queen Victoria's nuptials. This was seen with colored as well as white gowns: in January 1882, the *Sacramento Daily Union* reported a bride wearing "a wine colored satin dress, trimmed with orange blossoms, ornaments, diamonds."[50] This color was also popular with brides wearing "travelling suits" for their wedding; a practical option for those heading straight to a honeymoon after the ceremony and breakfast.

We know that this bride came from a poor background, and the dress shows signs of extensive wear post-wedding. An example can be seen in this patch of discolored fabric under one arm.

This broad claret-colored trim extends from the front of the bodice and falls into a bustled arrangement in back.

These rows of knife pleats may appear complex and time-consuming to produce, but the invention of pleating or "kilting" machines changed everything, pressing fabric to make it ready-pleated and greatly saving labor cost and time.

 Carved metal buttons, wrote one fashion column in 1883, could be "shaded and coloured to match any tone required" as can be seen in the reddish hue of these examples.[51]

 This c.1885 wedding dress from Melbourne's National Gallery of Victoria displays very similar design traits within a much grander, more traditional bridal ensemble. The pointed waist, high neckline, front buttoned fastening, close-fitting sleeves, and layers of frills and pleats on the skirt, represents just how closely specific bridal design mirrored the fashionable line.

Floral wedding dress,

c.1875–1885, The Queensland Women's Historical Association

This dress has a wide date range attributed, reflecting the reality of how slowly fashions evolved, and how long-lived a dress could be for a woman of modest income. Considering several details, it was probably made at the very start of the 1880s. Despite the incessant advice for brides to wear silk and satin, more egalitarian voices could be heard in the popular press. One fashion column in 1881 urged that "There is a latent desire to improve the present state of things. One gentleman...not being in affluent circumstances, insisted that his daughter...united to a rich bridegroom, should wear nothing more than a cotton dress..."[52]

Small-patterned floral prints were especially popular during the 1870s and were often used for both adult and children's clothes, making them a sensible choice for less wealthy brides planning for family life. By 1880, the concept of wearing fabrics other than silk and satin—even for wealthy brides—was slowly becoming acceptable. One fashion column reported in November 1879 that: "The traditional satin and silk ... bids fair to lose something of its transmitted orthodoxy. Brides are beginning to think the ceremony might be equally valid if they (mix) white corduroy [...] with white taffetas or Indian muslin for wedding attire; white Irish poplin is also occasionally worn."[53]

However, an elitist stain still fell across the use of florals, and indeed on any dress that was not white. In 1884, John Addington Symonds's *New Italian Sketches* described a woman whose "bridal dress of sprigged grey silk ... reduced her to the level of a *bourgeoise*."[54]

Fashion columns occasionally mentioned floral-sprigged silk brocade, which, though almost certainly all in one shade (as shown in this late 1880s bridal portrait), nevertheless demonstrates its charm and effectiveness across society. It was also viewed as a more sophisticated option, as expressed in the American serial *Patty's Literary Experiences* (1884) in which the protagonist causes great offense by describing a friend's party dress as "sprigged" rather than "brocaded."[55]

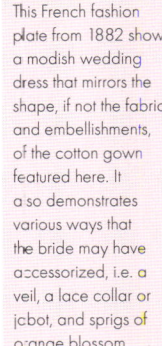

This French fashion plate from 1882 shows a modish wedding dress that mirrors the shape, if not the fabric and embellishments, of the cotton gown featured here. It also demonstrates various ways that the bride may have accessorized, i.e. a veil, a lace collar or jabot, and sprigs of orange blossom.

There were high profile precedents for floral bridal gowns, including fictional ones in the form of Eppie from George Eliot's *Silas Marner* (1861), who wore a white cotton dress "with the tiniest pink sprig at wide intervals."[56] This sprigged violet dress, c.1866–75, is a possible bridal gown. The fabric is cotton warp and alpaca wool weft, a combination that was perfected and broadly produced in Britain from the late 1830s. (Manchester Art Gallery)

Mrs. Daniel Reese Wolfe in her wedding dress,

1884, J.C. Strauss Studio, Missouri Historical Society

This mounted photograph depicts a bride posed in her wedding dress, probably taken after her marriage. She stands with confidence and contentment to show off her bridal costume, presenting a somewhat rare view of a young woman who does not embody the typical "willowy" proportions shown in fashion plates. Indeed, as one "stout woman" complained in 1887, "fashion newspapers and magazines print no plates that give fleshy women any satisfaction."[57] However, the New York Sun pointed out, "American women, especially those who have the means to dress in accordance with fashion's decrees, are inclined; to decided plumpness."[58] This is therefore both a fashionable and realistic depiction of what many brides of means would have looked like in the early 1880s.

Jabots were relatively inexpensive and could be made at home, although in 1880 *The Delineator* advised women to buy ready-made "unless a lady has some fine lace which she desires to use for the purpose."[59] When seen on fashion plates and elite examples of bridal dress, jabots often waterfalled down the entire front of a bodice, making Mrs. Wolfe's seem fairly restrained.

Another example of a jabot can be seen in this fashion plate from *Revue de la Mode, Gazette de la Famille*, October 18, 1885 Rijksmuseum, Amsterdam.

This relatively narrow underskirt is typical of what has become known as the "second" bustle era. Circular clusters of beaded tassels form the dominant ornamentation on the front of the skirt, with narrow rows of gauging (pleating) separating the decorated panels.

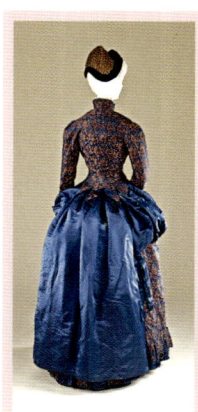

We cannot see the back of the bodice and skirt, but the rear construction is probably not dissimilar to this dress from the early 1880s (Los Angeles County Museum of Art). Here, a panier-style overskirt is drawn around the hips and pulled up over the shelf-like bustle, above which rests an elaborately pleated peplum. In Mrs. Wolfe's case, the skirt falls gracefully into a substantial train.

A fashion commentator described a similar bodice in 1884: "I beheld the very loveliest bridal-dress I have ever seen ... a jabot of Brussels lace greatly added to the effect in front. The elbow sleeves were finished with a ... little lace frill:"[60] Elbow length sleeves were a common feature of afternoon dress in this period.

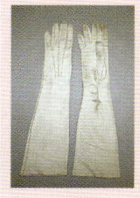

For brides who chose them, the look would be accessorized with long satin or kid gloves such as this pair from the Metropolitan Museum of Art, 1887.

Soutache braid is most often discussed in fashion columns when the outfit in question is a travelling or walking dress. In the 1880s, these could often double as a wedding dress when the ceremony was a small one. In 1884, *Arthur's Home Magazine* commented that, for such a bridal gown, the braid (usually the only ornamentation) would be applied directly by a tailor or dressmaker. For women who wished to apply it themselves, dress patterns "already braided" would be purchased, "and then made up to order."[61] Here, the use of soutache braid among other decorative elements suggests strong personal taste.

The *balayeuse*, translated as "sweeper" and also known as a dust ruffle, was a removeable length of flounced fabric that attached to the underside of the skirt hem. It was used to protect the garment from dirt and dust and ensure the train did not touch the floor. These were occasionally mentioned in the press if a bride had used an especially fine fabric for her *balayeuse*, rather than a sturdy but cheaper option. An example from April 1884 described "a balayeuse of rich silk Brussels point lace" at a society wedding in Sydney."[62]

Cotton batiste and lace wedding dress,

1885, Fashion Archives and Museum, Shippensburg University, Pennsylvania

◆

This gown is a rare example of a beautifully preserved cotton batiste garment. Batiste is a fine, sheer fabric, originally made from linen and named after French weaver Jean Baptiste in the thirteenth century.[63] By the date of this dress, it was made from combed cotton plain weave fabric, and was a fashionable choice, described in one 1889 fashion column as being "much in favour with French dressmakers."[64] Its delicate texture made it the ideal fabric for Ellen Vermillion Clagett, a relatively moneyed bride from Maryland who married Walter Worthington Bowie on September 23, 1885. Her gown creates a soft, frothy, feminine outline and indicates the ability to afford a dress that would not withstand multiple wears and washes.

The bodice was made in a pleated cross-over with a V-neck, which was filled in to the throat with cream gauzy material. A similar effect on another bridal gown in 1887 was described as "light and pretty."[65] The following year, another fashion column described several such designs "crossing to the left side at the waist line, and finished there with a rosette or flowing bow of ribbon"—as seen here.[66]

"The dress is always made high to the throat," wrote the *Adelaide Observer* in 1888, "and with sleeves below the elbow; and the bride does not, therefore, run the risk of catching a severe cold on her wedding day."[68]

Strips of lace insertion alternate between rows of tucked batiste. This also frames and supports the lace on the skirt and overskirt hems.

Three-quarter length-sleeves became fashionable after around 1883 and would often—as here—be edged with lace frills. Frills at the neck and bodice front were also popular, although by the end of 1887 some fashion columns declared that "ladies of highly fashionable tastes wear gowns having neither frilling nor collar at the neck."[69]

Ribbon ornamentation was extremely popular throughout the decade, and loops or bows would often be arranged in a side cascade and, as seen here, a focal point to emphasize the skirt drapery.

This 1882 fashion plate demonstrates that the crossover bodice was not new, shown here teamed with a similar draped overskirt. It is, however, made from the common choice of heavy silk or satin (*Revue de la Mode, Gazette de la Famille*, Rijksmuseum, Amsterdam).

This apron-style overskirt is layered and busy, made up of irregularly shaped panels. The effect was aptly described by a Californian newspaper in July 1887 as giving "an idea of being totally unlike on both sides."[67]

Ruffles and frills soften the severe "shelf" bustle fashionable in the second half of the decade.

Two-piece wedding dress,

c.1887, MAAS Museum, Sydney

◆

This silk taffeta dress was worn by Janet McDonald, an Australian Indigenous woman, for her marriage in around 1887. It reflects European and American trends and not those of Mrs. McDonald's own community and background. One of few contemporary accounts of marriages between Aboriginal couples described a "traditional" wedding dress in 1888 as follows: "A brown winsey (sic) skirt, hanging from one shoulder, stockings of pipeclay, and the ornaments—a necklace and earrings of glass beads."[70] In this way, the dress is representative of the lack of autonomy given to Aboriginal people, and the decisions made on their behalf by missionaries and reserve managers. For these marriages, brides would often wear hand-me-downs, which could well be the case here.

Panels of applied braid adorn the skirt, bodice, and sleeve cuffs. This could be seen throughout the decade and was a recommended technique for the home dressmaker: as one Australian newspaper put it in 1889, "Braiding, put on *applique* fashion ... while most effective is very easy to do."[71] We know that this dress was well-worn and subsequently altered, with some fabric removed for re-use, so it is possible that these braided sections were removed and re-attached more than once over the garment's lifespan.

This illustration from 1885 shows a similar bodice with "a long garland of blossoms" crossing the chest.[72] Such an arrangement would not have been replicated for Janet McDonald, but the trellises of floral-inspired braid on her bodice create a bold—and sustainable—bridal trimming.

Gilt buttons were popular for a bridegroom's jacket, and the influence was seen on tailored, masculine-inspired bodices like this one.

Contemporary wedding reports specifically mentioned brides marrying in varying shades of purple, from "bright purple and white" to a deeper purple velvet "with bonnet to match" (1888).[73] In Western tradition, the color purple is said to symbolize attributes including royalty and piety. In Australian Aboriginal cultures, the significance of colors generally derives from their place in the natural world; "on country." Purple, however, has a more specific link to major life changes for Yirritja and Dhuwa people. A silvery dark mauve ochre pigment, Radjpa, is painted on the bodies of young men to signify their entry into manhood.[74]

This image from 1873 depicts the marriage of an Aboriginal couple under English ceremony and law. It is far removed from Aboriginal practice and belief, which were diverse and saw marriage preparations and negotiations conclude over the course of several days. Sometimes there was no single "ceremony," but rather a particular act (for example, a campfire) that recognized the new union. Marriage was not viewed as a "contract" in the European sense.[75] Despite white writers' claims to the contrary (one witness to a group wedding in 1868 remarked that "a desire for proper [European] matrimonial relations is growing among the blacks"), on rare occasions, songs and speeches in Aboriginal languages were incorporated into Western-style weddings.[76]

Silk faille wedding dress,

1889, USA, Museum of Fine Arts, Boston

◆

This gown was worn by Ellen Nichols Wood for her marriage to Harry S. Hall in 1889. This sumptuous gown embodies the "happy medium" described by Table Talk magazine, in which "sweeping court trains and robe-fronts of rare lace, or pearl-embroidered silk, combine both grace and beauty."[77]

For the fashion-conscious bride, high necks and standing collars such as this were not necessarily mandatory. "If the bride has handsome shoulders she is very apt to have her bodice cut accordingly"—in the manner of evening and dinner gowns.[78]

This luxurious Tiffany & Co. fan is composed of sixteen mother-of-pearl sticks, with the body made from white ostrich plumes. The popularity of bridal feathers was probably heightened by Louise, Princess of Wales's ostrich-trimmed sunshade, used at her wedding the same year. This bride also carried a bunch of artificial orange blossoms made of cloth and wire, arranged in a conical mass.[79]

The Princess of Wales, along with Ellen Nichols Wood, wore dresses with pearl-embroidered net or lace for their weddings. The Princess's trousseau also contained a gown much spoken of in the press, which incorporated "white net studded closely with pearls, which are wrought in a pretty star-like design."[80] The effect was a popular one in the 1880s and 1890s and is seen here on another bridal gown from 1892 (Metropolitan Museum of Art).

Bridal slippers, with a low heel, are made from cream-colored corded silk. This material was noted among the trousseau of a bride who was said to have an impressive one hundred pairs of shoes.[85]

These striking, architectural sleeves seem to have been a feature at the end of the 1880s and early 1890s. A similar effect is seen in the fashion plate to the right, and its construction was described in an 1889 issue of *The Delineator*: "A shaped stay of coarse net [is] placed at the top of the plaits (sic: pleats) to give firmness and produce the slightly raised effect visible at the shoulders."[81]

The ends of the sash are caught up in two thick, pearl-studded rings. A similar accessory was described as a "steel buckle or slide" arranged "in the loopings" of a sash to keep it in place and add visual interest.[82]

By 1889 the bustle was diminishing, but some volume was retained using hip padding or a very small bustle frame. "The tournure is ... effected by its seeming absence; but all the same, every dress sent out of a fashionable costumier's establishment has a small [indispensable] cushion bustle and two steels at the back of the skirt."[83]

This plate shows fashionable wedding guest attire of July 1889. Several similarities are shown, including ribbon detail at the waist, fringe trimming, and ornately pleated bodice and sleeves (Metropolitan Museum of Art)

"The most stylish sashes are ... finished with handsome fringes" *The Australian Journal* declared in 1889. The use of fringe extended to homemade wedding favors, too, as one newspaper instructed in 1887: "small white banners ... of white satin or silk ... trim[med] with white silk fringe about half an inch in width."[84]

Woman's dress England, c. 1885, Los Angeles County Museum of Art (rear view detail)

Wedding dress, Department Store Fox, 1892, (detail), Metropolitan Museum of Art

Chapter 6
1890–1916

Bridal gowns increased their simplicity during the 1890s, including a growing popularity of formal daywear for the bride. This was largely a result of fashionable changes in general, with a focus on plain skirts after the intense intricacy of late 1880s designs. At the close of 1889, the *Ladies' Home Journal* commented that "The bride's gown is made in a very simple fashion; the front of it [is] almost plain … [a] graceful train is of plain white cloth."[1] By the close of the decade, this preference had not abated, as a Californian fashion column observed in March 1899:

> Wedding gowns are never profusely trimmed, as the effect always aimed at is dignity and gracefulness, and these are better secured by long, flowing lines than by the choppy, broken lines produced by lavish drapery and decoration.[2]

Paradoxically, however, wedding ceremonies and receptions themselves (at least among the wealthy) were becoming increasingly elaborate, far removed from the small, intimate, at-home celebrations of previous decades. Events associated with the wedding itself, such as the bridal shower, in turn became more commonplace. Particularly in Scandinavia, these parties involved games where guests would cross-dress and play the part of a wooing suitor.[3] More universally, gifting at bridal showers was increasingly expected, and widespread by the 1930s.[4] The cake we now associate with weddings, comprising sponge or fruit cake layered with marzipan and icing, was also a product of the very late nineteenth century, as was the accessibility of engagement and wedding bands: jewelers capitalized on developing traditions to make versions available at a variety of budgets.[5] Meanwhile, commercial photography firms were there to capture it all, including engagement or pre-nuptial portraits, where the bride would often wear her chosen gown. This decade also saw the growth of the large wedding portrait, often taken outside, which would include extended family and sometimes friends as well as the happy couple. As Jayne Shrimpton has observed, this "lent an air of grandeur" and allowed the costumes of not only the bride, but also her mother and other female relatives, to be recorded for posterity.[6] This all contributes to the development of the twenty-first century concept of a wedding being "the bride's day," with the focus squarely on her: bridesmaids no longer wore veils, and it was rarer for them to be dressed all in white (during the 1890s the phrase "white wedding" was often employed on occasions when the bridesmaids *did* wear white, with the bride choosing a softly tinted pastel dress).[7]

By the close of the 1890s, "specialization" of female clothing seemed to have reached its apex. For middle-class brides, knowing what to wear (and when) became synonymous with knowing how, and where, to shop appropriately.[8] The layout of department stores aided this, although the psychology of consumerism and tantalizing window dressing had not quite taken hold. Consequently, most stores aimed at impressing shoppers with the sheer volume of their wares, presenting the luxury of choice.[9] Department store catalogs, however, did hold a certain persuasion, and have been cited in France as a key player in the continued dominance of white as *the* bridal color.[10]

Elsewhere, white became a major player on the world bridal stage. In Turkey (then the Ottoman Empire), Naime Sultan, the daughter of Abdulhamid II (1876–1909), broke with tradition by wearing a white wedding dress, eschewing the usual red dress and veil (a symbol of eternity and happiness).[11] Her choice is even more pertinent when we consider that Ottoman women did not generally wear richly made or ornately decorated dresses until their wedding day. The dress therefore signified not only the institution of marriage, but also the transition of childhood to maturity. Western style and cut had been slowly integrated into fashion since *c.*1870s, but Naime's wedding solidified this preference and, by the 1920s, the red bridal gown had in many instances been entirely replaced by the white. This shift could also be seen in the dress of brides with both Chinese and Western heritage, particularly in Australia, where sources show China and Australian-born couples who were, as Sophie Couchman has expressed it, "not simply assimilating into established Western, Christian cultural practices [but] building something new—the global phenomenon of the modern white wedding."[12] Bride Teresa Sue Yek is shown below at her wedding to storekeeper James "Jimmy" Ung Yumm in Rockhampton, Queensland, in 1900. She wears the typical white high-necked, long-sleeved gown, probably made from silk, and worn with a floor-length veil.[13] This choice was not unusual for couples from the merchant elite, of which Yek's family were a part— and for her new husband, who received his naturalization certificate the following year, a "white wedding" may have represented integration and acceptance in more ways than one.

RIGHT
Chinese-Australian bridal party, Rockhampton, Queensland, c. 1900.

Chapter 6: 1890–1916   113

1905 marked an important egalitarian turning point in the way wedding dresses were produced and marketed. Department stores played a large part in the promotion of the so-called "lingerie" dress; a versatile, lightweight, ready-to-wear style that could be made and ordered in a variety of fabrics. It spanned social and economic divides through the fact that subtle differences—principally the quality of fabric used, and mastery of cut and construction—were all that differentiated a high-end example from a more accessible one. A bride could of course opt to display wealth through surface decoration, with extensive and elaborate trimming that incorporated lace, embroidery, and ribbon. Nevertheless, the "blank slate" of these white or pastel-colored gowns was ideal for self-trimming and decoration, including pintucking and shirring, or modest lace appliques. These dresses were often worn with picture hats rather than a veil (or sometimes alongside one), although there seems to have been a short-lived trend in Britain in which the bride and her maids swapped places: "the former appears in a hat, the latter in veils. Whether the bride in a hat has come to stay remains to be seen."[14]

Into the 1910s, specific manufacturers of wedding dresses began to establish themselves (including still-running Ellis Bridal in 1912), and their designs were sold through department stores and private bridal salons. The first bridal salon in America appeared at St Joseph's on Fifth Avenue, New York City, in 1912.[15] A 1911 Scottish store-bought gown will feature in this chapter as an example of what one of these well-made, often highly ornamented garments looked like. Ironically, at a time when female suffrage was at its height, this increase of store-bought bridal gowns helped to demolish a female economy of dressmaking. In rural communities, a lack of space and time was often responsible for the lack of a "proper" wedding dress. As one American farming bride wrote in 1912, "Well, there was no time to make wedding clothes, so I had to "do up" what I did have. Isn't it queer how sometimes, do what you can, work will keep getting in the way until you can't get anything done? That is how it was with me those few days before the wedding."[16]

The advent of war in 1914 did not necessarily create restrictions everywhere; in the US, for example, Congress decreed that wedding dresses should be exempt from government clothing rationing. This permitted American brides to maintain some element of luxury in their bridal dress and trousseau, allowing a temporary sense of escapism from world events. Elsewhere, however, women were forced to be more creative. If time and resources allowed, the idealized white gown might still be chosen but, even then, the dark political circumstances prompted reserve and humility. As Nina Edwards has pointed out, the new, pared-down wartime silhouette required significantly less fabric and dresses were simpler to construct, meaning that a certain amount of economy and restraint was present even for the most fashion-conscious bride.[17] Others attended their wedding in service uniform, a necessary (and sometimes, proudly displayed) consequence of hurried nuptials. By 1916, female dress had shifted somewhat into a softer, sheerer, broader silhouette, and this was quickly reflected in available dress sewing patterns and accessories. However, on some occasions brides chose to offset this with, as *Vanity Fair* recorded of one wedding in early 1916, "a rather straight frock – the skirt not narrow by any means, but built to produce a rather slender silhouette which the ruffled, flower-like frocks of her maids set off to advantage."[18]

Ribbed silk wedding dress,

1890, USA, Fashion Archives and Museum, Shippensburg University, Pennsylvania

This striking dress was worn by Maria V. Demorest for her wedding to Edwin Pratt Veldran in 1890. Its gold-green shade, twinned with pink, would not have been a popular choice for superstitious brides; according to the rhyme frequently quoted in late-nineteenth-century literature: "Married in green, ashamed to be seen ... Married in pink, your spirits will sink." However, this belief did not hold true everywhere: Italian brides commonly wore green and yellow, and in parts of France green trimmed with silver was the norm.[19]

"It should always be remembered", wrote the *Ladies' Home Journal* in 1889 (and republished in an Australian journal in 1892), "that no matter how beautiful the neck and arms of a bride are, she is sinning against good form who does not have a high neck and long-sleeved bodice ... [in her frock] there should be an expression of her knowledge of that which she is undertaking."[20]

These cascading pink ribbons match the ruffled trim at the bodice center, which runs from the neckline to the waistline. Beneath it (not visible in these images) is an interior layer of green silk, and thirty released directional knife pleats border this opening on the lower portion of the bodice. This impressively rendered—though relatively restrained—ornamentation is in line with recommendations of the time: "The trimming employed should not be too elaborate—simplicity in this department of dress is the mark of good taste."[21]

Twenty handsewn released directional knife pleats adorn each wrist, creating a close-fitting cuff. The style was also popular with bridesmaids and fit especially well with a quaint trend introduced in the early 1890s: "floral wedding handcuffs" to link the bridesmaids together. "The maids on the left side have their right wrists connected," wrote *The Florist's Exchange* in 1890, "the [floral] chains are long enough to curve gracefully from wrist to wrist."[22]

Skirt and bodice are made from a fine ribbed faille silk, described by a textiles dictionary in 1892 as a "changeable term," but one which "at present indicates a popular variety of soft, ribbed silk distinguished by a prominent grain or cord extending from side to side of the fabric."[23] It was a favored textile and could be used either for the entirety of the bridal gown, or, as was reported at an Australian wedding in 1891, as a trimming: "folds of white faille ... crossing from the right shoulder and fastened to the left side."[24]

At the back of the skirt, the pleats are larger and less numerous than those at the front, where decoration is chiefly made up of 38 released directional knife pleats. This type of detail is mentioned in wedding reports throughout the decade, with a bride described as wearing "one of the new knife-pleated skirts" in December 1899.[25]

This fashion drawing from Philadelphia's *The Peterson* magazine of July 1890 shows two bridal gowns with a similar focus on pleating. The dress on the right illustrates methods of further adornment that highlight the pleats' presence and placement (New York Public Library).

Wedding dress,

1893, Metropolitan Museum of Art, New York

◆

This understated wedding dress was made by Irish dressmaker Alice Bergen Coady, who emigrated to the USA in the 1860s. She established a successful career in Brooklyn, New York and used frequent trips to Europe to inspire her creations. This gown was commissioned by Luigia Castruccio for her marriage to Enrico Pensa in January 1893. The bengaline silk, in a muted gray-purple shade, was purchased from the Frederick Loeser department store and then taken to Coacy's shop at 23 Elm Street, Brooklyn.[26]

By the date of this dress, collars were often high and close-fitting, usually supported by lengths of boning. Since most weddings took place during the day, bodices were usually high-necked rather than decollete. In 1892, one "Manual of Politeness" recommended that wedding dresses should be made "high and the arms covered. No jewelry should be worn save pearls or diamonds." The writer praises the "simplicity of bridal toilettes" in continental Europe, which, he concludes, "is more commendable than that of England and America, where [it is] made as expensive and heavy with rich and costly lace as it can possibly be made."[27]

This gown is made from silk bengaline, a rayon and cotton mix which saw special popularity in the 1880s and 1890s. It was also cited as a suitable bridal fabric, as *The Ladies' Home Journal* told home dressmakers in May 1893: "You need a wedding gown of bengaline, satin or crepe."[28]

From around 1893 to 1895, fashion columns made frequent mention of the "return" of lace collars and cuffs, sometimes extravagantly layered. Those seen here are relatively modest and may have been made from a small amount of "old lace" kept in the family for such occasions.[29]

In 1986 the Brookly Blue Bank advertised Coady as supplying 'tailor made gowns' as well as 'exclusive novelties for debutantes and bridesmaids' gowns, with 'mourning orders complete in ten hours'.

Bold, circular motifs comprise the skirt and bodice trimming. The design of the same pattern is inverted on the *plastron* (central panel) of the bodice and edged with borders of darker gray velvet. Its placement around the sleeves simulates a bolero, a style revived in the 1890s following its initial popularity during the 1860s.

This French dress from 1895 demonstrates a similar bolero style.

National Gallery of Victoria, Melbourne

This fairly conservative skirt and bodice demonstrate features of afternoon dress, including long sleeves, a high neckline and a degree of restrained elaboration. Since weddings commonly took place in the afternoon, it became usual to see such styles doubling as bridal gowns. Afternoon dresses were also usually colored, and this gown reflects that trend also. There is no evidence to suggest that this bride was a widow or in mourning at the time of her marriage, but the shade of her dress was redolent with mourning etiquette. Gray, soft lilac and, as one fashion column suggested, "cerulean blue" was commonly chosen by brides in mourning.[30]

Wedding dress,

1894, Wales, Museum of New Zealand Te Papa Tongarewa, Wellington

◆

This striking blue dress was worn for a wedding in Wales, UK, in 1894 and was later brought to New Zealand with the wearer in 1907. It is a beautiful example of the still-regular trend for wearing a "best" colored dress for a wedding, and of the fashion for bold aniline dyes that developed from the mid-nineteenth century onwards. Blue was a popular choice for daywear, and consequently often seen in daytime weddings as well (the popular rhyme referenced elsewhere in this book sanctioned that "Married in blue, he'll always be true"), and this was nothing new in the 1890s. A San Francisco newspaper reported an "Afternoon wedding" in June 1899 at which "the bride was gowned in a silk dress of blue—the same one used by her mother at her wedding." The difference with this Te Papa example, of course, is in the vibrancy of the artificial dye, creating a shade of "electric" blue that seems to have been chosen more commonly for bridesmaids: particularly when the bride was attired in a more subdued blue.[31]

....

These leg-of-mutton or "gigot" sleeves are entirely on trend for 1894. Their full, drooping puff was designed to mirror the width of the skirt and heighten the effect of a fashionably small waist in the middle. Various methods were recommended for home dressmakers to keep such sleeves in shape, including interlinings of organdie or crinoline.[32] In 1894, advertisements appeared for "fibre chamois," claiming that "puffed sleeves will not set as they should unless supported by it."[33]

In records of 1890s New Zealand and Australian weddings, brides were often reported wearing electric or navy blue "travelling costumes" as their "going-away outfit" following the ceremony and reception. Indeed, such outfits of similar practicality were sometimes worn as the bridal gown itself, as the *Ladies' Home Journal* discussed in 1891:

– "What would you do yourself if you were going to be married and felt that you couldn't have satin and tulle, had to choose a gown in which to travel, wanted it to be pretty ... and refined?"

– "My dear girl [it should be smart and simple] ... the wearer will never be distinguished as a bride by her gown, and in selecting it she will obtain a costume from which much wear could be obtained."[34]

The dress shown here was probably made, worn and brought to New Zealand with exactly this thought in mind. In 1894, the Journal suggested that "bright blue—mistral or royal" as a "church or visiting costume," should be included as part of the bridal outfit or trousseau.

Glass buttons provided an impression of luxury, although, as one fashion writer commented, "some call them crystal, but this is a forced politeness, for they really do not rise to the dignity of crystal."[35]

This bow is lightly stitched into place to form an additional feature. This was a fashionable touch in 1894—that same year, it was reported that "Whatever else a girl doesn't have this spring, she must have a bow."[36]

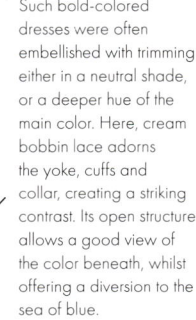

Such bold-colored dresses were often embellished with trimming either in a neutral shade, or a deeper hue of the main color. Here, cream bobbin lace adorns the yoke, cuffs and collar, creating a striking contrast. Its open structure allows a good view of the color beneath, whilst offering a diversion to the sea of blue.

Stripes of a darker blue adorn this silk. The use of stripes was incredibly fashionable during the decade and was recommended for short and/or "stout" brides in one fashion column from 1892 because "you are well aware that stripes give height to the figure."[37]

Although fashion plates usually showed wedding dresses with trains, this was by no means a staple, especially when the dress was made in a more practical shade and was intended for future wear post-wedding.

118 How to Read a Wedding Dress

Wedding and graduation gown,

1894, Pennsylvania, Daughters of the American Revolution, Washington D.C.

This dress, worn by Eva Brawley Dickson, in 1894 as both a graduation and wedding gown, serves as a powerful illustration of women's expanding roles in late-nineteenth-century American society. It is a rare example of a dress worn for that most liberating and emancipating of events—a graduation—and of an ancient and traditionally unequal rite of passage: marriage. Its light shade corresponds with increasingly set-in-stone color recommendations, as well as a fashion writer's observation in 1896 that "There is but little change in the regulation of wedding costume from season to season. The most approved styles are quite plain."[38]

The dress corresponds closely to a recommendation from a New York writer in 1894 that, for graduations, "cream-colored China silk" was optimal, the bodice "confined by a wide surah sash tying behind with ends reaching to the bottom of the skirt ... The sleeves reach only to the elbow."[39] The benefit of this style, as with so many bridal gowns, was its suitability as an evening or dinner dress in the future.

Flat ribbon bows cover each sleeve head. These had been popular for formal and evening wear at various points from the seventeenth century, and in the 1890s could be seen on one or both sides. It was also a fashionable decoration for ribbons to extend down across the chest, sometimes crossing and fastening in a bow at the side.

Sashes were fashionable, but also a clever way to enhance an outfit. "Nothing does more to smarten up an old dress than a pretty sash," one Australian fashion column commented, continuing to advise that: "The virtue of the sash lies in the fact that if you have one white summer dress of washing material and half a dozen sashes, each of a different shade, you are for all practical purposes the proud possessor of the same number of separate toilettes."[40]

By 1890, some providers of graduation gowns had begun to advertise their product in a similar tone to that of bridal, advising early and careful selection: "It may be a month before you are ready for the new graduation dress, but it is none too soon to see what there is to see, and be turning the matter over in your mind. Our stock was never larger or fresher."[41]

White was a common color for dresses of all occasions during the decade, particularly—with its associations of youth and innocence—weddings and graduations. This generally meant white throughout the entire dress, as one etiquette manual from 1896 explained: "It is to be hoped that the custom of using pure white in the composition of the toilet will not be superseded by any passing freak of Dame Fashion's for softly tinted shades."[42] This even included trimmings, a custom gently poked fun at in one newspaper's short story, in which a bride declares: "I never wore white but once before; that was on graduation day. It will be only the second time to-morrow. Oh, yes!" she recalls, "I wore white, too, when I went to a ball once; and I wore it at a concert, and at the theatre. But those times don't count, because it was all trimmed with blue."[43] This acknowledges the contradictions, and indeed confusion, present in much advice of the time.

This portrait of graduate Octavia C. Long in 1909 shows the continuing trend of white dresses worn for the occasion. Collection of the Smithsonian National Museum of African American History and Culture, Gift of Naomi Long Madgett.

Reform wedding dress,

c.1900–04, National Museum of Denmark, Copenhagen

◆

This wedding dress was made in Denmark and purchased from a store or dressmaker in Rosenvænget, an avant-garde neighborhood in the Østerbro district of Copenhagen. The rational dress movement, which called for the abolition of cumbersome, restrictive clothing for women, founded a Society in London in 1881. Its tenets were adopted across Europe, promoted particularly strongly in Scandinavia through the Swedish Dress Reform Society, which in turn influenced Danish women's rights group Dansk Kvindesamfund.[44] In 1888, the group exhibited five "rational" dresses at an industrial exhibition in Copenhagen. Given the small numbers of women who had the interest or opportunity to engage in the movement, there are extremely few surviving examples of bridal dress made on these principles. To choose such a garment as a wedding dress would suggest fervent enthusiasm for the cause. The bride who wore this dress, Olga Elise Sophie Rasmussen, married doctor Mads Jørgensen Lund in 1904 and chose this "new empire" design with strong medieval influences.[45] This is testament to its designer's non-conformist leanings and speaks to the late Victorian and early Edwardian penchant for romanticism and chivalry: eminently appropriate connotations for a bridal garment.

This wedding portrait was taken in New Zealand in 1894. It shows dress reform advocates Kate Walker and James Wilkinson (center back), with bride and bridesmaids all attired in "knickers, not too full, long vest, and slightly longer coat, with revers worn open."[47] This is an extremely rare example of female rational dress taken to its extreme, resulting in highly principled and brave wedding outfits. In 1900, newspapers reported the engagement of "eccentric octogenarian" Susan Fowler of New Jersey, an "apostle of women's dress reform" for sixty years, to a man forty years her junior. She had prepared her trousseau, the article continued, herself, with "a new pair of trousers made by herself."

Sections of cream-colored silk are used to create curved ornamentation around the neck, waistline, and vertically along each upper sleeve. This is emphasized through gimp braid trimming, a popular decoration on bridal dresses more generally. Wedding reports of the era mentioned gimp in shades of white, silver, oyster, and pearl.

The skirt falls softly from beneath a simulated waistband. This same treatment extends to the sleeves, which are gathered into a broad silk cuff.

For the most fastidious dress reformists, one of the problems with modern dress was its inherent hazards: particularly long trains with their propensity to harbor dirt and, potentially, disease. That concern is not apparent here, with an attractive train in place for the occasion. Its presence also suggests that the bride was more of the "aesthetic" school of thought. While sympathetic to reform principles, this movement espoused simplicity of design, natural colors, and fabrics, and was heavily influenced by history—particularly the medieval period and the inspiration drawn by members of the Pre-Raphaelite Brotherhood in the mid-nineteenth century.

The looseness and softness of this dress recall the informal wrapper or tea gown, often constructed in a style known as the "Mother Hubbard." One fashion column described this in 1883: "As a balloon it is all right enough ... but as a dress, it is a ... failure ... a reproach to the boasted culture of the Nineteenth Century."[46] Simultaneously, dress reform designers were inspired by an aesthetic based on early Italian Renaissance art; spearheaded by the Pre-Raphaelite Brotherhood in the middle of the century. The parallels are clear in this painting by Rossetti, *The Salutation of Beatrice* (1880–1882, Toledo Museum of Art).

Wedding dress,

1903, Pennsylvania, Author's collection

◆

This two-piece wedding gown was made by its original owner for her 1903 wedding ceremony and was subsequently worn by two more generations. It is highly representative of the popular "lingerie" or "lawn" style of dress, made from lightweight fabrics with lace and tucks as chief forms of decoration. This example is made from a sheer batiste (an extremely fine grade cotton or linen) and was worn over cotton petticoats, although contemporary records of weddings often describe batiste dresses being worn over satin or taffeta. This is indicative of the varying means and status of American brides in the early twentieth century, and this bride chose to display a hint of luxurious silk through the use of a long, wide sash.

A contemporary illustration of the "bishop" sleeve, also mirroring the line of the neck and shoulders, is seen in the Charles Dana Gibson illustration above (1903).

This is an early example of the "bishop" sleeve, which reached the height of its popularity between 1903–06. All the 1890s upper volume has disappeared and shifted to the other end of the sleeve, flaring out below the elbow into a gentle bell shape which is gathered into a cuff.

The fashionable "mono-bosom" or "pigeon breast" silhouette was at its height when this dress was made, and is clearly in evidence here. The blouse is made with an abundance of fabric at the waist, and tight gathers below the yoke, with the resulting volume arranged in a blouson effect above the sash.

Narrow bands break up these rows of delicate lace on yoke and sleeves. "The yoke," wrote an English newspaper in 1904, "is generally formed of bands of the stuff the blouse is composed."[48]

Vertical tucks on this skirt accentuate the fashionable "trumpet" shape, flaring out from just below the knee.

Satin was frequently suggested as the "ideal" bridal fabric, but fashion columns in newspapers and magazines were realistic—and enthusiastic—about cheaper, lightweight alternatives such as the sheer batiste seen here. Such fabrics were also far more in keeping with this style, known as "lingerie" or "lawn" dresses— or sometimes, simply as "whites." In May 1903 one Californian newspaper wrote that "Chiffon cloth ... is in great favor and is a handsome change from [satin] ... [it] is the most frequent choice for young brides ... because so generally becoming. Fine veiling is also worn and forms a very pretty and less expensive gown than the fabrics just mentioned."[49]

Floral lace appliques mark the end of the vertical tucks on the skirt and are mirrored on the bodice.

Trains were swiftly losing popularity on daywear, but longer versions could still be seen for more formal occasions, especially weddings. This one contains a small hole, allegedly ripped by the bride's heel on the day of her wedding. Rather than being viewed as a blemish, such details offer a humanizing glimpse into the woman who wore this dress and allow us to piece together a narrative around her "big day."

Chapter 6: 1890–1916

Wool wedding dress,

c.1906, USA, Fashion Archives and Museum, Shippensburg University, Pennsylvania

◆

This striking outfit was worn in around 1906 by Lucy Dent Carrico at her wedding to Joseph Benjamin Burch in Maryland. It illustrates several fashionable features and changing silhouette. However, its woolen fabric and tailored appearance bring to mind more practical suits and walking costumes, despite the elaborate braiding. This could be seen to be in keeping with commentary from *Harper's Bazaar* of that year, suggesting that more and more women were choosing the independence of single life over an expectation of marriage.[50] The use of wool suggests a less formal affair, and wedding reports at the time often mentioned a woolen dress in conjunction with "home" and "quiet" weddings. It is quite possible that this dress may have doubled as a "going-away" outfit after the reception, or at least as a broader part of the bridal trousseau.

....

"Scroll" or "Grecian" designs were popular trimming for a variety of outfits. They were described in one 1906 fashion column as designs that "seem well to the eye and the industry of the worker."[51]

Sleeves have long jockeys that end about 6 inches above the wrist. They are edged in ball trimming, sometimes referred to as ball fringe.

One-piece dresses were usually constructed in the princess style between c.1900–1907, with the bodice and skirt cut as one.[52] Here, the long central panel creates a fluid line at the front, but the presence of a separate skirt is simulated by this hip-length bodice.

"The bridal gown is nowadays cut with a medium train" wrote the Californian *Chico Record* in March 1906, "the extremely long or court train being considered somewhat passé. The skirt must just barely touch the ground all around on the front and sides, leaving free passage (or the foot, for the bride to stumble on her way to or from the altar is the extreme of bad luck, according to the old superstition)."[53]

Soutache, sometimes known as "Russian braid," is a flat narrow braid or galloon, used to trim and decorate items of clothing. Its effect was impressive, but it could be procured relatively inexpensively, as one American newspaper assured brides in 1908: "Silk soutache trimming, will not add more than $5 to the expense [of the wedding gown]."[54]

At around this date, the waistline of fashionable dresses shifted slightly to just above the waist, with the back raised higher than the front. Here, the braiding that signals the position of the waistline rises to a slight curve in back, and graduates to a dip at center front, either side of the panel. This emphasizes the S-bend silhouette still in vogue during the period.

Buttons fashioned from the same braid adorn the back of the bodice, and can be seen scattered among the decoration on the front. Buttons or "button effects" crafted in this way were reported as being vastly prominent in 1907, particularly for travelling "auto styles." These were "buttonlike molds covered with soutache braid or cord ... these may fasten with looped cords ... or they may be placed with simulated buttonholes."[55]

From hip to floor, the skirt is arranged in directional knife pleats. A fashion editor wrote in 1906 that there was no excuse for any woman to wear a skirt "unsuited to her figure," since there existed such a range of equally fashionable options including "flounced, shirred, tucked, pleated, gored, and circular" among others.[56] The pleated style does seem to be especially frequently mentioned in fashion reports from 1905 and 1906, however: in September 1905 one fashion column described a broadcloth plum-colored visiting costume with "a long pleated skirt and correspondingly long tabs in front," and another broadcloth ensemble, this time for a wedding, which was "elaborately trimmed with soutache braid ... and a pleated skirt."[57]

Black wedding dress,

1906, Fashion Archives and Museum, Shippensburg University, Pennsylvania

◆

The original owner of this dress, Lydia Luella Conn, was married previously in July 1893. For that first wedding she wore a light floral printed silk dress, also owned by this museum, which shows signs of continued wear after the ceremony. Tragically, the marriage ended three years later when Lydia's husband Fred Parlin, a police officer, was fatally shot. After a decade living as a widow Lydia became engaged to Canadian Robert Ireton and wore this black silk dress for the wedding in March 1906. This dress, composed of high-quality taffeta and dotted net, is representative both of the fashionable silhouette at the date of the wedding, and of the options available to second-time brides, who faced something of a dilemma in terms of the etiquette of remarrying after a death.

....

Although it was perfectly acceptable for a previously bereaved bride to wear black, white, or half-mourning colors (such as purple and gray) were more common. "Once a widow remarries, she should not wear a bridal veil—and orange blossoms never—and most authorities decide against her having bridesmaids. She may wear a light-colored silk or other dress, but not white."[58]

The volume of these sleeves corresponds to a brief resurgence of the 1890s gigot or "leg of mutton" shape, that took place between c. 1905–1907. During this period, many newspaper wedding notices mention elbow-length puffed sleeves finished with frills—and this can be seen here, albeit with a wrist-length sleeve added underneath.

Not all brides could afford high-quality silk, as was used in this example. It was common for early twentieth-century silk manufacturers to overweigh their fabrics with metal salts (the most common being tin salts such as stannic or stannous chloride) which made them heavier—and consequently give the impression of a higher-grade silk. Because fabrics were sold by weight, this of course resulted in significant profits for some manufacturers.[59] However, corrupt manufacturing techniques resulted in silks that did not last, and some even began to split and shatter within a year of purchase.

Self-colored dots on the netted overlay correspond to a broader trend of the era. This subtle decoration was described by one fashion column in 1904 as being "the ultra thing."[60]

A yoke is created through bands of shirring at the hips. "The close effect around the waist and hips [is] made by shirring," wrote one American fashion column in May 1905, describing a similar skirt that is also finished with "wide tucks on the skirt [to] complete the picture."[61]

The sleeves end in black silk ribbon ornamented with French knots (decorative stitches used to create one or more small knots) and lace trim. French knots were a popular decoration on more conventional bridal gowns too, with soft pastel colors often featuring on skirts between c. 1906 and 1908.

Lydia Conn wore this green/gray gown for her first wedding in 1893. The portrait to the right shows her posing in the black outfit as a second-time bride fourteen years later. (Fashion Archives and Museum Shippensburg University).

Cotton wedding dress, London,

c.1910, Museum of London

◆

This soft lilac dress was worn by Londoner Minnie Beatrice Long for her marriage to a railway worker in Leytonstone, September 1910. Although she could not afford the ideal white silk or satin, her dress was elegant, fashionable, and professionally made by a local dressmaker.

High-necked and long-sleeved dresses were generally worn at daytime functions, especially weddings. One etiquette guide suggested that sleeves should be "long or elbow length as may be fashionable at the time. Gloves will, of course, meet short sleeves."[62]

Additional detail and shaping is created by rows of pintucks on the bodice and sleeves. This was both a popular home sewing technique, and one employed by couture dressmakers, as illustrated in one Australian wedding report from July 1910: "The bride … looked charming … in a dress of white Japanese silk, over skirt trimmed with pin tucks and silk embroidery bodice, yoke of tucked Paris net … finished with silk braid and ribbon, with tucked belt."[63]

Purple was a prominent feature in this period, with "amethyst, violet, lilac and heliotrope shades" fashionable in 1910,[64] and in 1913 a bride was reported arriving in "a lavender silk dress, with hat and feathers to match."[65] Even on occasions where full white or cream were worn, lilac could often be seen in bridal trimmings or accessories. In August 1908 "a bridal gown of white silk, handsomely embroidered with wreaths of roses, lilac and forget-me-nots"[66] was worn in Buckinghamshire, England, and from the very start of the decade these light purple tones seem to have been a popular shade for bridesmaids. Etiquette guides and household manuals, which so often dictated the strict wearing of white, were now offering advice on protocol "*if* white is worn" [emphasis added], suggesting that alternatives were increasingly accepted.[67]

Although etiquette and fashion columns suggested that wedding dresses should be made "en train," this was the ideal, not the practical choice, especially if a bride planned to re-use the dress. A "train" could instead be created through the wearing of a long, floor-length veil.

De Gracieuse, by Doucet, 1908 Metropolitan Museum of Art.

This fashion plate from 1908 depicts a bridal design by Doucet, illustrating many of these elements that were to remain highly popular for the next few years. It also demonstrates the attention paid to such images by professional dressmakers. At the same time, as the *Bulletin of the Bureau of Labor Statistics* pointed out in 1915, "the dressmaker who caters to the middle and lower classes is much less bound by Parisian decrees, and as a result has a longer and more regular season."[68]

Time and again, fashion columns and marriage notices in 1910 describe the bride wearing "a princess robe," a dress made "en princesse," "an Empire princess gown." This dress is cut in the fashionable style for c.1908–1912, featuring the long, lean princess line, high neckline, circular yoke, vertical pleats across shoulder and torso, and simulation tunic or overskirt.

"Lingerie" wedding dress,

c.1909–12, USA, Author's collection

"Lingerie" dresses, also known as "whites," were popular throughout the mid-1900s and early 1910s, including for use as wedding gowns. From c.1905 urban department stores started to advertise these ready-to-wear designs, always made from a light fabric, and particularly popular for middle-to-lower-class summer brides with a more limited income.[69] As the Dundee Evening Telegraph pointed out in 1909, "Every bride naturally longs to be married in white, and the June bride is fortunate in having a choice among less formidably costly fabrics than the conventional white satin."[70] Like any other wedding dress, they could be accessorized in multiple ways; here shown with a silk sash that could be tied either in back or to the front of the skirt.

Insertions of delicate bobbin lace adorn the bodice, sleeves, and skirt, arranged in different configurations for a striking effect. As one British newspaper pointed out, over fifty varieties exist, but they are all based on three foundation stitches.[71] Although this lace could be machine-made, crafty brides could try their hand at home production with the use of publications such as Louisa and Rosa Tebbs' *The Art of Bobbin Lace* (1907–1911). This book recommends smaller projects for brides to attempt, including veil trimming and a skirt "flounce, which is 6 inches deep ... worked in size 3 thread ... [and] requires on an average nine pairs of bobbins."[72]

This 1912 fashion illustration shows a wedding dress with several similar elements, including a broad sash and deep yoke forming a pointed front. The drawing also demonstrates how the dress might be veiled, but many simpler options were available, including—according to one fashion column from 1911—"A plain tulle veil [that] is fashioned into a cap with a soft frill that folds over the hair."[73]

Although bridal gowns with lower necks were gaining acceptance, it was still common to see dresses with yokes and high necks. This one is made from a light dotted net. Such a design was even more striking on a black background, a choice sometimes seen on wedding guests at prominent ceremonies.

If a young bride could not afford to have her whole dress made from silk or satin, a smaller accessory—such as a sash—could add that touch of luxury and sheen. Popular shades during this period were pastel pink and blue. For older women getting married, "voile, lansdowne or crepe de chine" would, *Talks on Successful Gowning* advised in 1910, look becoming.[74]

A detachable silk bow is included in the ensemble, giving the bride an additional element of choice. "If the figure can stand the thickness," one fashion column suggested in 1912, "[a] broad bow is fastened in the back or at the side."[75]

Wedding dress,

c.1911–13, Scotland, Author's collection

◆

This dress was purchased from Daly's department store in Glasgow, Scotland. Located on Sauchiehall Street, the business was established in 1846 and gained a reputation as a high-class, high fashion establishment. This silk crepe and satin wedding gown illustrates the relatively simple cut of the period, with striking trimming and decorative techniques providing a level of complexity and interest.

The bride wore these shoes, decorated with silk roses and matching, amber-studded net.

Often referred to as a "V decolletage" in fashion columns, crossover or "surplice" necklines were also popular. Either way, "[the dress] must be high-necked always ... [it] may show a transparent yoke but a decollette effect will be in very bad taste."[76]

Tiny black-silver bugle beads are scattered diagonally across these front and back panels, broken up by two horizontally arranged rows.

Delicate net oversleeves, edged with satin, create the tiered sleeve that was so fashionable c.1908–12. This net is studded with amber-colored beads, and the same embellished netting can be seen on the overskirt hem and side slits, and as a filler for the triangular Van Dyck sections.

These triangular "Van Dyck" edgings were a common fashionable feature, a historical detail named for the works of painter Antony Van Dyck, who particularly admired this decorative element of fashionable seventeenth-century dress. Here, they are a clear and sharply defined design, but some brides chose a softer effect, as reported in Australia in 1913/14:

"The bride ... wore a handsome gown of ivory embroidered China silk, finished with Van dycked guipure edged soft frills."[77]

During this period, it was fashionable for dresses to incorporate a "tunic" or over-skirt which, as in this example, could be made with slits at side or front. Here, two side slits present the opportunity to showcase additional studded net trim.

Stuffed silk spheres, covered in the studded net, hang from strips of satin to create decorative baubles. This "ball" or "bobble trimming" was a common addition during the nineteenth and early twentieth centuries, often used to accentuate and balance the silhouette, including on bridal wear, as one newspaper column described in June 1911: "The bride will wear a dainty one-piece dress of embroidered Swiss trimmed in Irish lace and ball trimming, and carry a shower bouquet of bride roses."[78] Ball trimming was also favored by designers including Paul Poiret and Jeanne Paquin, who drew on prevailing "orientalist" trends by incorporating influences from Leon Bakst and the Ballet Ruses.

Similar ball trimming seen on the sleeve of an embroidered cotton dress, c.1910–15, author's collection.

Close-set tucks form the main decoration on the lower sleeves, V-neckline, collar, and modesty panel.

Highly fashionable bridal gowns often featured significant trains, but it was quite common (and acceptable) for ordinary brides to sport a modest version, or none, as seen here. Whatever the length, it was fashionable by this date for trains to be "quite unadorned," as one Scottish newspaper expressed it in April 1910.[79]

Cotton batiste wedding dress,

1915, Fashion Archives and Museum, Shippensburg University, Pennsylvania

◆

This pretty dress was worn by Olive Side for her wedding to Fred Side in 1915. Its light, summery appearance aligns with one fashion column's assertion that "Not all brides wear white satin—there are exquisite voiles and batistes and French lawns as sheer as cobwebs which make lovely wedding gowns."[80]

"The bride no longer swathes her throat in high Puritanical collar," the *San Luis Obispo Daily Telegram* declared in May 1916. "The low neck once banned to brides is now very proper, unless to be sure the ceremony takes place in the early morning."[81] This oval neckline adheres to such advice, with its modest dip meeting a dainty scalloped closure.

A similar upstanding collar is seen on this dress from the same year, purchased from the Hirsch & Cie department store in Amsterdam.

Delicate daisy embroidery covers the bodice. Daisies, long a symbol of innocence and joy, were used in weddings from the Victorian period onwards. One bride in 1915 featured daisies as a prominent part of her ensemble; her "veil, which was arranged in cap effect ... was caught with daisy blossoms, and the bride carried a shower bouquet of daisies."[82] In 1919 *The Delineator* recommended field daisies for home wedding decorations "with fascinating results."[83]

The bride's lace collar was accessorized on the day as a standing ('Medici') collar, fashionable during the era and stiffened using wire or starch. This striking but accessible effect made it a popular finish for bridal gowns, particularly ones with a crossover front. In August 1915 an Australian newspaper's "Wardrobe" column suggested that a wedding dress "might have an upstanding collar ... [made] of ivory net or lace."[86]

Most skirts of this period measured between 0.7 and 3 yards, but brides who could afford it would have allowed enough fabric for a "flare skirt" measuring as much as five yards circumference at the hem.[84] This vogue for wider skirts, which took effect during 1915, is shown to good effect here in the broad scalloped hem. Scallops were a distinctive feature that lent itself well to the increasing popularity for shorter, tiered skirts. A wedding report from August 1916 described this effect well: "The skirt was bouffant, cut short and trimmed with scalloped ruffles from the hem to the girdle, each of the little frills being edged with white satin." Like Olive, this bride wore a feathered picture hat and sash to accentuate the waist.[85]

The dress fastens with pressure snaps at center front and waistline. These were first patented in 1885 but became especially popular during the war years. "The dress that answers the purpose of the energetic and much-occupied woman," wrote one magazine in 1915, "is essentially neat, and must be easy to get into and out of to suit her requirements ... [on one model] ... just three snap fastenings comprised the whole duty attendant upon putting the dress on."[87] This sense of ease and unfussiness was, as shown here, transferred to bridal wear also.

Fashion-conscious women generally wore their waistlines around 2 inches above the natural point, a feature which was enhanced through use of a sash or cummerbund, seen in this photo of the bride.

Wedding dress by Lucile,

1916, Chicago History Museum, and Wedding Dress, 1791, National Gallery of Victoria

Lucy Christiana, Lady Duff-Gordon (1863–1935) was a famed British fashion designer and couturier, who worked under the name Lucile. A high-profile survivor of the Titanic, she was a prime choice for brides without a budget, providing gowns, bridesmaid dresses, and elaborate trousseaux. This unusual silk satin dress has significant historical parallels, which, for a garment made during a period of turbulent conflict, suggests poignant nostalgic escapism. The dress was made for Katherine Keith, daughter of a prominent Chicago family, when she married architect David Adler on June 1, 1916. Its historical leanings are not surprising when we consider that the Adlers were artistic and academic, with author Katherine a member of the "Scribblers"—a women's literary group that sometimes hosted costume parties based on specific historical periods.[88] This 1791 wedding dress and petticoat is strikingly similar and helps to confirm Lucile's historical inspiration for the gown. However, further interest is raised when we consider that this dress, made in the early 1790s, is itself channeling styles that would soon become unfashionable.

On her wedding day the bride wore a close-fitting cap, fastened under the chin with a sheer strap, which was reminiscent of the increasingly fashionable "medieval" style.

This deep, square-shaped bodice has two historical precedents: first, the mid-late eighteenth century, and second, the revival of the style in the 1870s. It, and the sleeve cuffs, are edged with pleated sections of fabric referred to as "robings"—another eighteenth-century conception which found its way into mid nineteenth-century fashion.

Sleeves of this length were popular during the 1910s. Their use here does recall eighteenth-century fashions, particularly earlier examples edged with robings and frilly *engageantes*. They do not fit the arm as closely as these early 1790s examples, which became increasingly tight and tubular during the decade.

In the last quarter of the eighteenth century, it was fashionable to pair a dress with a brightly colored sash around the waist. It can be seen here on this *robe à l'anglaise*, here matching a beribboned hat in Vigée Le Brun's 1789 portrait of the Comtesse de la Châtre (Metropolitan Museum of Art).

These deep, pointed waistlines are almost identical in shape. Neither were the height of fashion in their time: in the case of the 1790s gown, the point illustrates fashions of the 1770s and 1780s, which would soon make way for the round gown and developing empire line. Similarly, the styles of 1915–16 more often showed a higher waistline, which here is perhaps indicated by the presence of the sash.

Katherine Adler's skirt was stiffened with whale bone to create volume reminiscent of the late eighteenth-century. It also foretells the reincarnation of eighteenth-century paniers in the 1920s, worn as part of the briefly fashionable *robe de style*. This 1791 example would have been worn with hip pads (known as a "bum roll") to provide shaping around the hips.

The petticoat is made from "pussy willow silk." Pussy Willow was the trade name for a silk created by H. R. Mallinson & co., a fine, plain weave "radium" fabric that was described by one 1914 advertisement as "delightfully soft and lustrous."[89]

RIGHT
Wedding dress with standing collar by Hirsch & Cie., Amsterdam, 1915, Rijksmuseum. Gift of the heirs of Van Reenen.

Chapter 7
1918–1929

This period saw the production of more long-standing designers and producers of bridal gowns, including Spain's Pronovias in 1922. Wedding dresses, now more often bought distinctly for the purpose, were imbued with a new significance and would (where possible) follow the latest fashions, making them a useful indicator of changing style. Pre-war wedding splendor did not, of course, return overnight: even for those who could afford it. In Britain, this was largely due to the "melancholy fact that the public purse has touched bottom," as *Hull Daily Mail* lamented in September 1919. The author empathized with the plight of the post-war British bride:

> Poor little bride of to-day! Whatever be her rank or condition, and whether she be marrying a duke's son or a cook's son, her life, unless she has the good luck to be the daughter or the bride of a war profiteer, will be utterly unlike what it would have been in pre-war days.[1]

Advising engaged and newly married couples to "Pay ready-money for everything you buy," this tone could not be further removed from that of the American *Delineator* earlier that year, which stated that now there is a new home, a trousseau, and most importantly a returned fiancée, the bride "can go to the altar like a medieval princess in satin and pearls or silver brocade."[2] Such potent language suggested new horizons far beyond the wedding day; the image of a shimmering bride offering hopes of a bright and prosperous future ahead. American beauty companies were not slow to monopolize these associations for their marketing, powerfully implying that women became brides in the first place largely thanks to a brand of soap, perfume, mouthwash etc.[3] Colgate were one such company and referenced a "real" wedding incident in which a guest complimented the bride on her teeth. As Daniel Dellis-Hill has observed, however, to an early-1920s female reader, this message would be less powerful than the accompanying imagery of the ad, which also promoted a fashionable headdress, gown and floral bouquet. "Colgate knew," he remarks, "that the image of this bride … would linger in women's minds"; a vision subliminally associated with something as mundane as toothpaste.

The comparatively rapid rise of hemlines and dropping of waists during the 1920s was, perhaps, partly thanks to a new generation shaking off the constraints of an uncertain, straitened wartime childhood. To whatever extent this is true, the spirit of emancipation also affected traditionally conservative bridal fashions, perhaps in part ignited by the formal removal of "obey" from marriage vows. In addition, the late 1920s ushered in the practice of grooms—not just brides—receiving a wedding band at the altar. This would not become standard until the 1940s, and even then, not for all men—but its inception did spark the potential of more equal wedding traditions for both genders.

In this spirit, for the first time, bare arms started to become acceptable even for church weddings—though this was not met without criticism. Even by the end of the decade it was still a topic of discussion, but fashion columns insisted that "Sleeveless dresses in themselves do not constitute indecency, and they are at the moment the dictate of fashion for certain wear."[4] By this time, it was increasingly popular to wear an evening dress as bridal gown; styles that were invariably sleeveless and more revealing. Interestingly, these were particularly worn among older brides and those marrying for the second time, a practical as well as cost-saving initiative. Nevertheless, debates around modesty were especially rife following the well-publicized actions of an Australian Roman Catholic priest, who demanded that two sleeveless bridesmaids "attire or retire" when they arrived at the wedding in short frocks and bare arms.[5] The conversation extended to headwear too. Even for church weddings, bolder brides were reported with no veil or headdress for an evening ceremony—and one even asked her female guests not to wear a hat.[6] More commonly, however, the 1920s bride is recognizable for her elaborate headdress. This often comprised a band worn low on the forehead, with the veil itself fitted closely around the head. However, a myriad of designs was available; among them the "Juliet cap, a medieval headdress, a lace coronet or tiara of the Russian or Oriental type ... [but] must, of course, be of the same theme as the gown."[7] Historical references were rife and illustrated in this chapter with a "medieval" wedding dress by celebrated couturier Jeanne Lanvin.

RIGHT
A colorful wedding dress worn in Wales, (detail) 1926.

Chapter 7: 1918–1929

As in the previous century much inspiration was taken from royal weddings, particularly the unprecedented levels of press and public interest in the wedding of George V's daughter Princess Mary to Henry, Viscount Lascelles in February 1922. Sketches of the dress, designed by royal favorite Reville and Rossiter and made from Indian silk, were available to the public and covered extensively in *Vogue*—the first royal wedding to feature in a fashion magazine. "The wedding of Princess Mary will have a more far-reaching influence on fashion than a casual observer imagines," another magazine, *The Sphere,* observed in 1922—although the simple, tubular construction of 1920s dresses did welcome a far more egalitarian approach to bridal fashion.[8] Wealth was indicated by the quality of fabric and the amount and costliness of ornamentation, but a skilled seamstress making her own gown could create an outfit that, in silhouette at least, closely mirrored that of the high society wedding.

The influence of the previously discussed loose, easy wearing "flapper" style would come to dominate, and not only in Europe. After the establishment of the Turkish republic in 1923, the secular "civil code" within marriage took effect, which allowed both men and women equal rights. Wedding dresses reflected this transitional phase in the country, with white gowns and veils replacing traditional red ensembles. Nevertheless, as Adanir, Goknur and Kueli emphasize, this did not mean that previous Turkish culture was completely abandoned: subtle, but unmistakable links remained with the use of "silver tinsels and red ribbon tying around the waist before the ceremony"—although this was rarely shown in accompanying wedding photographs.[9]

As a new decade dawned, hemlines changed once again. While the low waist remained, the skirt was edging nearer to the ground, particularly at the back of the skirt. In 1929 this feature was noted as an "unusual" bridal choice, negating the need for a separate train: "The skirts were inlet with godets and trimmed with flared panels of uneven length, which extended at the back into a long train."[10] This paved the way for the feminine, screen siren-inspired bridal gowns of the following decade, sometimes incorporating the short-lived *robe de style,* a fuller-skirted gown instigated by designer Jeanne Lanvin. In order to illustrate the diversity and contrast of this post-war period, this chapter explores a range of bridal styles and circumstances, from the "costume" of an Italian refugee in 1918 to a luscious lace confection worn by an American socialite.

Refugee bride and groom separated at time of enemy's invasion of Udine, finally united at Rome,

1918, Library of Congress, Washington D.C.

◆

Apart from the modest posy, there is little evidence that the woman in this image (Elisa Pasqualis) is, in fact, a bride. She is dressed fashionably, but without the traditional bridal trappings of white or light-colored dress with veil. This was not unusual for the time, as even at more conventional weddings, wearing a travelling suit was popular. Reports describe examples in blue, gray, brown and rust, though the ideal was "some pretty light color ... gray, champagne, tan, or biscuit,"[14] often made from silk or mole (cotton with a brushed surface). However, this bride's choice is also likely to do with the realities of her and her husband's situation. As refugees of Italy's so-called "Fourth War of Independence," their wedding also marked their reunion. The photograph was taken as they left the Hall of Marriages on Rome's Piazza del Campidoglio, accompanied only by three close relatives.[11]

This hat contains design features seen throughout 1914–18, particularly on winter styles like this, from *The Delineator*. The height and breadth of the crown creates a striking impression, with ruching contributing to a delicate softness. Given the popularity for brimless hats around 1917, this hat was probably made during that year. "Hats with ... puffy tops ... and next to brimless are offered this autumn," wrote an Australian *Sunday Times* fashion column in March 1917.[12]

The Delineator November 1917

The fashionably wide revers help to date this garment to around 1916–18.

The bride carries a silk purse and fur stole over her arm. Stoles and muffs were recommended as suitable gifts for a bride, but during the war years fabric versions—velvet, satin or chiffon, lined in silk—were deemed an appropriate substitute.[13]

Even at more conventional weddings, the pre-War option of wearing a travelling suit was popular. As with tailored bridal costumes, reports describe travelling suits in blue, gray, brown, sand, and rust, often made from mole (a densely woven cotton cloth with a brushed surface) or various silks, especially watered. Although the ideal travelling suit shade was touted as "some pretty light color ... light gray, champagne, tan, or biscuit color,"[14] the reality was that many wartime and post-war brides wore whatever was available.

This colorized version of the original image gives an idea of how the bride may have looked on her wedding day. The deep blue purple of her suit, and the copper brown of her hat, correspond to the fashionable colors quoted here.

By the end of the First World War, women's tailoring reflected the multiple ways that female lives (and corresponding style choices) had changed during the period. Wearing a wedding suit or two-piece "costume," instead of a luxurious white silk gown, also denoted a suitable degree of levity in the aftermath of such horror and devastation. Even press-reported "fashionable weddings" in 1918 frequently mention a bridal "suit"—though these would often be in lighter shades, composed of silk or satin. The example shown here is probably wool, with curlicued embroidery on lapels and waistband. It is interesting to note the similarity in cut between both bride and groom's coats.

Chapter 7: 1918–1929

Wedding dress,

1920, Dunedin, Museum of New Zealand Te Papa Tongarewa, Wellington

This silk georgette dress was worn by Tui McKinnon for her wedding to Harold Mein Preston on June 9, 1920. It was purchased from the Drapery Supply Association (DSA), a Dunedin department store that offered a made-to-measure clothing service. This means that the bride would have had a considerable input to the design of her gown, and the result is a very contemporary confection trimmed with ostrich feathers and metallic thread.[15]

Soft, filmy ostrich feathers line the neck, waist, and cuffs. Spring 1920 was described as "a season of feathers" by one fashion column.[16]

Metallic ribbon emphasizes the neckline and waist, picking up on the embroidery, which depicts bronze spheres and leaf fronds.

Silk georgette was perfectly suited to the soft, dreamy impression this dress evokes, and was often cited in descriptions of high society weddings. However, the use of sheer fabrics was not always deemed appropriate for bridal wear. In New Orleans in 1920, an Italian bride was refused entry to her wedding at St Louis Cathedral because her dress's bodice consisted of "nothing more than a piece of gauze." The Archbishop of Melbourne followed up with a hope that brides would "steadfastly set your faces against the scanty dress which so many women ... are now wearing."[17] The transparency of this dress is demonstrated through the visibility of pink silk fabric flowers at the neckline, which adorn the net lining beneath.

Two rectangular lengths of georgette give the impression of sash ends, featuring corresponding embroidery.

The wedding was described by the *Otago Witness* as "very pretty and quiet ... The bride looked charming in a very dainty dress of white georgette, with train lined with pink satin."[19] This was either removed to make the dress wearable at a later date or made as a detachable train (at this date, these often hung from the shoulders). Bridesmaids were attired in pink to match, and the attention to detail recalls a poignant statement on "post-war weddings" from March, 1920: "In violent reaction to the hurried detail of the war wedding, marriage ceremonies are now becoming more and more elaborate ... embroidered Georgette is worn ... with a long pointed or square train hanging from the shoulders."[20]

Empire waistlines were hugely fashionable during the Directoire revival of the 1910s. For a very brief period at the beginning of the following decade they were revived, though one Australian fashion column from April 1920 bemoaned the frequency of change: "Among the many new models we shall see ... the tight waistline, the high waist and the low, as well as no waistline at all."[18]

Tiered skirts were very fashionable in the early years of the decade, and these seven layers present an ideal illustration of the trend.

136 How to Read a Wedding Dress

Wedding dress,

1921, Liverpool, England, Brighton Historical Society, Victoria

◆

Elizabeth Goodwin married Horace Book in a ceremony described by Melbourne's *Table Talk* as "charmingly arranged."[21] Her dress was made in Liverpool, UK from a Butterick's pattern; one of 600–800 new styles per year produced by the company during the decade. This made them among the most popular for brides wishing to make their own dresses or commission a seamstress.[22] The dress was made from Chinese silk, purchased there by the father of the bride, a ship's captain. Until the 1920s, Japanese silk was a more common Australian import, making this dress an interesting mix of the commercial and the unique.

A newspaper account of the wedding reports Elizabeth wearing a veil which—though long—may not have been substantial. The 1920s saw fashions change quickly for bridal headwear, as Lillian Eichler noted in 1921: "Not so long ago, the veil was of tulle ... and fell over [a bride's] shoulders, completely enveloping her to the very tips of her toes. This ... is no longer considered good form. In its place, is the very charming veil that is gathered into a becoming, flower-trimmed crown at the back of her head, falling gracefully to the hem of the dress, leaving the face entirely uncovered."[23]

Limerick lace is set onto a machine-made net base, making it something of a hybrid technique. It was especially popular for wedding dresses during the nineteenth century, and during the 1920s was often referenced as an example of "family" or "heirloom" lace, re-used by a bride in her outfit.

The newspaper report offers a full description of the ensemble, including an indication of how it was accessorized:
"The bridal frock was of ivory corded silk, with accordion pleated panels back and front, while the cross-over bodice was finished with long sleeves of Limerick lace, which was also effectively draped on the gown ... She carried a bouquet of hyacinths, camellias, freesias and maidenhair fern, and wore a cameo ring and ivory bangle ... gifts of the bridegroom."[24]

A penchant for large decorative bows was noticeable during the 1920s, particularly during the earlier years of the decade. These were popularly made from ribbon, though as one fashion column pointed out in 1923, "Ribbon has always been expensive, and some of the better kinds are now priced at many shillings a yard." As a solution they suggest what is seen here; a bow fashioned from "self material, [which will] do very well hereby."[25]

Floating side panels, here made from the same Limerick lace as sleeves and bodice, were a common feature of early-mid 1920s bridal gowns. They broke up the straight, tubular shape of these dresses and added a light feminine touch to the ensemble. On some examples, these would be floor-length to form a double train.

The creamy ivory tone of this dress is in keeping with bridal trends at the start of the decade. "Pure white is very seldom worn for a wedding dress," wrote one Australian fashion column in August 1921. "In most cases an ivory tinted silk or a pale cream is more becoming and many brides nowadays like an even warmer touch of color, and line the train with faint pink material."[26]

Silk crepe wedding dress by Jeanne Lanvin,

1924, France, Chicago History Museum

Janet Lawrence wore this theatrical dress at her wedding to Robert McCormick Adams on May 3, 1924 at St. James Episcopal Church in Chicago.[27] It was designed anc made in Paris by renowned couturier Jeanne Lanvin (1867–1946), known for a youthful elegance and ingenuity. Her creations (such as the eighteenth-century inspired robe de style), often embodied historicism and this wedding dress is no exception, with its strong medieval overtones.

A slim lace collar, still a fashionable accessory, adorns this wide neckline. Those without the funds for a Lanvin gown could, *Good Housekeeping* suggested in 1924, re-work an "old-fashioned" wedding gown to include such details in a modern design. "The shape of the one-time Duchess lace bertha, yoke, and collar will assume new character without injury of any kind." A couple of years later lace was not viewed quite so favorably, as fictional bride-to-be Marjorie Ferrar noted in Galsworthy's *The Silver Spoon* when asked if she would like lace as a wedding present: "Oh! No, please, dear. Nobody's wearing lace."[28]

Pearls edge almost every seam: from the waistline to the alternating crepe and net panels on each sleeve, to panels stretching across the width of the overskirt. This use of pearls as extensive decoration was an haute couture favorite in the middle of the decade.

Medieval design was frequently referenced throughout the decade in relation to bridal style. Any hint of historicism was declared "romantic" and encouraged for bridalwear despite the intense keenness for "modernity" in other aspects of fashion and life. In 1928, one fashion column expressed this desire particularly well:

Fashion cannot kill romance in the toilette chosen by the present-day bride. In fact, she returns to the most romantic of days for the design of her bridal gown. On her wedding day at least, she drops all trappings of the modern girl and goes back to the medieval tradition.[29]

The "medieval" aspects of this dress are based more on fantasy than historical fact. This is shown through popular discussion of "medieval" fashion being mentioned in the same breath as "Renaissance" and "Shakespearean," suggesting a greater interest in the general flavor of a distant past than rigorous accuracy. However, it is easy to see the inspiration for the most dominant feature of this wedding dress. Strips of fabric extend from each shoulder, fastening to the cuffs to create the effect of a hanging sleeve. These were particularly prevalent in the eleventh to thirteenth century bliaut, a unisex, floor-length, slim-fitting robe with extremely long, square-edged sleeves.

Strips of luxurious gold lamé back these "hanging sleeve" panels. This costly fabric was often used as lining or to accent one part of a gown, as seen here. If a bride wished to purchase a dress made entirely of lamé, it would cost the equivalent of around £500 in the late 1920s.[30]

Overskirts and forms of overdress found popularity during the 1920s. As seen here, they would often dip to form a small train in back.

Bridal ensemble,

c.1926, Daughters of the American Revolution, Washington D.C.

This spectacular flapper-style gown is right on trend with its intricate beading and knee-length skirt, a feature which became extremely fashionable from 1925. It was made in New York, and legend has it that the bride, Marguerite Dotter Hogan, travelled to the city for a fitting on August 30, 1926, the day of Rudolph Valentino's funeral. The streets were thronged with distraught female fans, and, as one newspaper described it, "500 policemen" were needed to control the crowds.[31]

Just like the bride in this image, Marguerite's bouquet included cascading ribbons that reached almost to the floor. This was a popular form of decoration, creating a focal point in the ensemble.

Heart-shaped necklines were not widely fashionable until the late 1930s. Here, it sits below a round neck to aid in breaking up the long, tubular silhouette. Beaded circular motifs adorn the top half of the bodice, while the mid-section is of beaded satin. Floral shapes represented include lilies, tulips, and roses.

This wealthy and connected bride was able to afford enough lace to create long, close-fitting sleeves. Not all were so lucky; as one newspaper reported in 1929: "Her lovely gown was sleeveless because it was impossible to get any more of the Limerick lace of which it was made, though Miss Drew badly wanted long, tight lace sleeves."[32]

This ensemble features not only a long train, but a floor-length veil as well. Since the short dresses of this era often omitted a train, veils sometimes took on that role. A short alternative arrangement, also worn with a train attached at the shoulders, is seen in this illustration from *Le Petit Écho de la Mode*, December 1926.

Seed beads in a darker shade edge the hem, waistline, yoke, and selected floral motifs picked up from the pattern on the lace. This beadwork is applied directly to the delicate lace, used to outline a design. Various manuals throughout the early years of the decade advised sewing each bead twice, to ensure no "wobbling." Despite the beautiful beadwork seen here, there is substantially less than was fashionable a few years previously. As in this example, interest and texture was now provided with different fabrics, shades of color, tucking, and shirring.

Long trains on a short dress needed to be attached either from the shoulders or waist. This 10.5-foot-long example hung from the shoulders, a choice recommended for "the bride of stature and dignified bearing."[33] Its square edge had been fashionable since the beginning of the decade, seen particularly in bridal wear in the second half. One fashion column described the square finish as "adding dignity," suggesting a grown-up sophistication.[34] The sheer volume of fabric here is a good indicator of wealth and social status.

Silk crepe wedding dress,

1928, Pennsylvania, USA, Author's collection

◆

This dress was worn in Verona, Pennsylvania, by bride Mary at her marriage to Ralph Tremba on July 28, 1928. The couple had three daughters, and Ralph went on to become Mayor of Verona. If the bride, commented *Weddings: Modes, Manners & Customs of Weddings* in 1927, "is a very modern-minded person with a very modern taste … she will probably choose a smart modern day or evening mode, exemplified or embellished to suit her taste."[35] At the same time, as discussed here, rigid etiquette dictated that such "modern" styles, worn without veil and train, also denoted an "informal" wedding that would probably have taken place in the home.[36]

Beading was hugely popular during the decade, with designs often covering the entire garment. This example is relatively restrained with its lattice design and floral outlines.

In 1929, one newspaper, discussing the best way to use beads in dressmaking, told the story of *Armand's Bride*, in which a prince vowed to marry the first lady he saw whose gown was trimmed differently. This he found in Clothilde, who, in order to impress him, gathered up "all the dewdrops [that had] turned into little, hard balls … fairies had turned them into mirrors for their toilets." These were sewn onto her gown and the following day she was married to Armand. "That," the story concludes, "is how beads began!" The idea of bridal wear being a first use for beads, albeit in the form of a fairy story, reinforces the superiority of this type of decoration.[37]

Diamond-shaped motifs were popular during the 1920s, often used as panels to hold sections of the skirt together. Here, however, they are purely decorative and ornamented with beads.

This beaded shape outlines a simplified fleur-de-lis. The ancient chivalric symbol had long been used in bridal imagery, but in November 1926, it was given fresh relevance in the wedding of Princess Astrid of Sweden to Prince Leopold of Belgium. Her "magnificent" white satin brocade gown was worked with fleur-de-lis, a prominent feature that was discussed in the press descriptions.[38]

"Pleats, pleats and again pleats," *Tatler* declared in 1927, a feature that "the great dressmakers demand … in soft materials … as today it offends the canons of good taste to rustle."[39] This combination is shown to good effect here, with soft billowy folds breaking up flat panels of fabric around the skirt.

The bride wore a picture hat as part of her ensemble, a style that competed with the popular cloche until the end of the decade. For brides, these were often frothy tulle concoctions worn with a small veil.

According to some contemporary etiquette guides, her lack of veil and train made this an "informal" bridal choice. In 1927, *Weddings; modes, manners and customs of weddings* even stated that if a woman chose an "informal" dress of crepe satin or silk crepe, she was readjusting "her plans to wear the dress of a 'real bride.'"[40]

Chiffon wedding dress with silver tissue overlay,

1928, MAAS Museum, Sydney

◆

This locally made dress was worn by Margaret Elizabeth Hamilton at her wedding to Ernest Harold Cowled in New South Wales, Australia, on February 28, 1928.[41] It is a stunning example of the seismic shift in women's fashion that occurred between the end of the First World War and the start of the Second. Even at a rural Australian wedding, the emphasis on a more androgynous figure is reflected in this light, knee-length, sleeveless bridal choice. Nevertheless, for all its modernity this dress takes significant inspiration from the past in its adoption of paniers, an interpretation of eighteenth-century design known as the robe de style, popularized in Paris.

Metallic threads are woven into the lace. Silver lace over a base of silver tissue, was described by the *Ladies' Home Journal* in 1920 as being "one of the loveliest" foundations for a wedding gown.[42] The hugely influential wedding of Princess Mary six years earlier undoubtedly influenced this bridal fabric choice, although by the end of the decade the accessibility of artificial silk tissue meant that it was no longer exclusive.

Shirring was a popular and simple way of providing definition and shape at the waist, and would be applied to either the edge of the bodice or top of the skirt where it met the waistline.

Silver lace over silver tissue makes up most of the bodice, with flared side panels of the same. "Skirts are often made in separate panels which are cut with a flare and then gathered," advised *The West Australian* newspaper in 1928.[43] Uneven hemlines were also fashionable at this date, particularly when skirts were made with panels or inserts; however, in this case the different sections of skirt appear relatively uniform.

An interest in fashion history during this decade went beyond the nineteenth century. The costume collection at London's Victoria & Albert Museum was cited as a significant bridal influence in 1927, as the *Westminster Gazette* remarked: "The bride and her mother mount the staircase to the showcases containing the fashions of the centuries, and there proceed to ransack these treasures for new ideas."[44] So fervent was this "fancy dress" inspiration, some expressed concern that the seriousness of marriage, and of the ceremony itself, would be forgotten.

These 'panniers' or 'side hoops' acted as skirt supports for eighteenth-century sack dresses. Their wide shape is clearly referenced in this 1920s design.

Panniers c. 1750, Metropolitan Museum of Art

Although this skirt's silhouette is most reminiscent of the eighteenth century, a newspaper account of the event describes Margaret wearing "a dainty early Victorian frock of ivory georgette and silver lace."[45] The term "Victorian" seems to have been used liberally throughout the 1920s to describe various "feminine" attributes in dress, including—as seen here—"crinolined frills and furbelows," overskirts, lace overlays, and a relatively fitted bodice. Many other wedding descriptions reference the "early Victorian posy," meaning a hand-tied bouquet with flowers arranged in concentric rings around a central bloom. It lost favor to the cascading bouquet introduced in the early twentieth century, but enjoyed a brief revival during the 1920s.

Chapter 8
1930–1946

The 1930s bridal aesthetic can best be characterized as diverse—garden party dresses in light, summery, often floral fabrics were in vogue at the start of the decade, particularly in the United Kingdom. Brides sometimes opted for a small straw hat over a veil and headdress, worn with minimal jewelry and modest flowers. Later, the marriage of Wallis Simpson to the Duke of Windsor in 1937 resulted in the creation of copies of her conservative, pale blue, Mainbocher-designed dress (allegedly made in a cornflower hue to match her eyes) and wedding reports for several years following mention the use of "Wallis blue" for either a bride or her maids. More broadly, Simpson's choice exacerbated the acceptability of color in bridal wear, a trend which was borne from necessity in the United States. The Great Depression forced many brides to revert to what their foremothers had done for their big day: simply wear their best frock as a wedding dress. A necessary knack for frugality meant that by the end of the 1930s, women had learned how to budget fiercely to get what they wanted. One woman married at the close of the Depression remembered the exact cost of her dress and accessories: "I made my own wedding dress … the cost [of the fabric] was $5.35 and the veil plus crescent head piece brought the total to nearly ten dollars. White satin sandals at $3.95 were my extravagance."[1] The publication of the first bridal magazine in 1934, *Bride's* (originally titled *So You're Going to be Married*) by Wells Drorbaugh, was launched during this era. Though

LEFT
Wedding portrait of Lollaretta Pemberton and Grover Allen, 1939. Collection of the Smithsonian National Museum of African American History and Culture, Gift of Rita C. Organ and Pemberton Family.

RIGHT
Wedding in uniform at St. George's Cathedral on June 3, 1942.

originally aimed at affluent women, it enjoyed large enough profits to survive into the post-Depression period: partly due to its ability to reflect changing customs and expectations.[2] For those who could afford specially made bridal wear, art deco detailing, such as chevron-shaped panels, was inserted into the gown to accentuate the developing hourglass silhouette. Silk and crepe de chine were the ideal fabrics to display this new clinging, svelte ideal that was championed in Hollywood by stars such as Carole Lombard and Jean Harlow.

Across the globe, this era saw the development of new ways of celebrating and staging nuptials. Derived largely from Japanese expressions of Western culture, Korean *sinsik* merged aspects of a Christian wedding to include a focus on the couple rather than extended family; wedding halls, banquets, and—of course—a white wedding dress, which would often be rented rather than bought (now a popular option in Japan and Israel as well as in Korea). This formed the public display of marriage, whereas a more private at-home ceremony could still involve the wearing of traditional bridal *hanbok*.³ Just as Japanese brides adopted white kimono, white hanbok could be seen more and more frequently from the start of the country's colonial period (1910–1945). The procurement of Western dress of all kinds was aided by the opening of Unjwaok, Korea's first store for Western women's clothing, in 1937. The following year, women wishing to create their own dress could enroll at the International Clothing School and receive technical training that "usher[ed] in a new era of Westernization in women's clothing."⁴ In China, modern young 1940s brides would commonly get married in a floral *qi pao*, accessorized with a long tulle veil.⁵

By the early 1930s, many American and European department stores began hiring bridal specialists who provided ready-to-wear styles. This signaled a huge shift in the way bridal fashions were produced and consumed, and from the late 1940s onwards, ready-to-wear and ready-to-order wedding dresses were available at all price points. Globally renowned and still-running company Justin Alexander was established in 1946 as T&G Bridal, and its mid-twentieth-century origins have remained, described in 2022 as the ideal brand for "the nostalgic bride who seeks an Old Hollywood vibe."⁶

Naturally, the advent of another world war disrupted any new developments that might have occurred in the world of bridal wear. Yet, war did not diminish the importance of marriage and the clothing worn to celebrate it: if anything, that clothing was made more pertinent by its absence. This chapter explores gowns borne out of necessity and circumstance, including dresses worn by Holocaust victims and survivors, gowns made from military silk, and outfits without an original bridal intent. Underlying many of these examples lies the knowledge that clothing was rationed to various extents in Britain, Ireland, Germany, The Soviet Union, the USA, Australia, New Zealand, and Germany, among others. In the USA, the Association of Bridal Manufacturers persuaded Congress to exempt makers of wedding clothes from fabric restrictions. This victory made a very public statement about the importance of wedding clothing and its role in national morale. Elsewhere, rationing meant that there existed a global push to re-think bridalwear and, for some, to re-evaluate its importance. Nevertheless, in Britain women were strongly encouraged to keep up appearances, which the government believed was crucial in sustaining morale across the population. The necessity of hastily arranged "service marriages," however, presented significant challenges. For women who were in the forces, the problem was sometimes averted by both bride and groom wearing uniform (see p145. In the USA there was often no other choice, as service personnel were not given civilian clothing coupons). Even when the bride was not in the military, she sometimes coordinated aspects of her outfit to match her husband's uniform. One British bride, Audrey Stokes, wore a dress, jacket, and veiled skull cap in Air Force blue for her marriage to Hugh Verity in 1940—although as Hugh later confessed, he was "disappointed" not to see her in a traditional wedding dress.⁷ Some wedding reports even mention Land Army brides wearing their uniform of green jersey, brown breeches or dungarees, with brown felt hats—but no mention of the groom's suit or uniform. Women with no existing bridal gown or alternative uniform had to be more ingenious, and the period saw increasing numbers wearing or repurposing their mother's gown, or that worn by another close relative. Newspapers also made special mention of those who "defied superstition" by choosing green or pink dresses against the advice of the ancient rhyme: "married in green, ashamed to be seen / married in pink, your spirits will sink" (As the *Manchester Evening News* sagely remarked in 1942, however, "the bride's dream of a white dress had to fade before practical considerations."[8] Although the well-known story of brides using parachute silk is not a myth (an example features in this chapter), it was not common. Those who did marry in white, or at least in formal dresses, more often took advantage of developments in synthetic, high-sheen fabrics. In the USA, these included Celanese rayon (its name deriving from the words "celluloid" and "ease"), a relatively cheap, easy to care for silk alternative.[9] In terms of general style, 1940s wedding gowns tended to follow the path of evening wear, featuring fitted bodices and long sleeves with gathered heads.[10] Skirts were invariably A-line, although more options unsurprisingly popped up in the closing years of the decade. Fashion columns mentioned one design known as the "loop line," in which fabric was "looped up at the hem, giving a rounded effect to a straight skirt."[11] Volume procured by loops, gathering, layers and, as described in one 1947 report, "a cascading bustle"[12] was largely the result of the hugely influential New Look, examples of which will be explored in the following chapter.

RIGHT
Bride in a floral wedding gown. Canada, 1936.

Wedding dress,

1930, Perth, Western Australia, Author's collection

◆

Although the fashion for short skirts was waning by the late 1920s, this dress (with a certified wedding date of 1930) illustrates the reality that not all brides could afford to be up to date. Other elements, however, portray a burgeoning early 1930s aesthetic, with the sheer fabric clinging to this bride's very svelte frame.

....

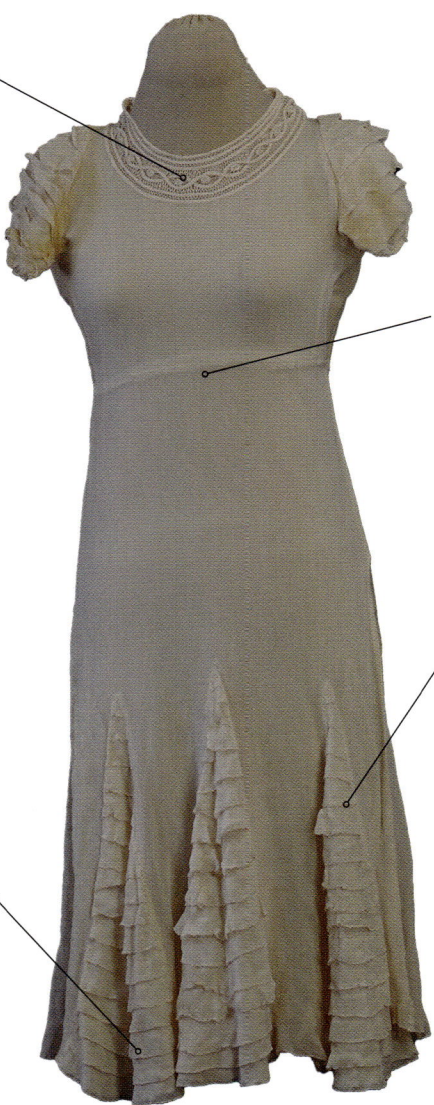

This collar effect is made from a twisted inversion stitch, known at the time as "faggot stitching." This is a simple form of point lace featuring herring-boning with strips of folded material tacked onto the surface. According to *The Australian Woman's Mirror* in December 1930, this resulted in "narrow collar effects built into the frock and shaped to set flatly on the figure." In relation to wedding and "special occasion" dresses, it advised that "Beautiful hand work on frocks has never been so popular as it is today, and much of it is far beyond the reach of the average purse: but no girl with a few hours to spare need be without it, for it is all very simple to do."[13]

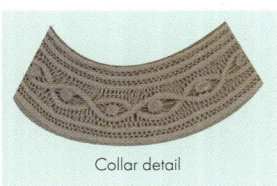

Collar detail

This hem ends at around mid-calf length. Towards the end of the 1920s, there was also a resurgence of bridal gowns with ankle-length skirts. Although brief, it seems to have been significant enough for one marriage report to point out that, for the bride in question, her short dress was "a departure from the long style of dress, worn by many recent brides."[14]

Similar layered, ruffled sleeves are seen on this evening gown. The more exaggerated frills were made popular later in the decade through the dress worn by Joan Crawford in *Letty Lynton* (1932). These were widely copied for evening and formal daywear, seen in this fashion plate.

Towards the end of the 1920s, the waistline started to creep back to its natural position. One fashion column compared this new look to the Directoire line revival of the 1910s, along with a trend for longer skirts which was also gaining significant traction by the early 1930s.[15]

Between 1929 and 1930, there was a transitional period when the attention was simultaneously on both a higher waistline and detail on the hips and thighs.[16] This split focus can be seen here, with a strong nod to the incoming 1930s aesthetic in this skirt's detailing. Fluted godets (triangular inserts to give extra volume and movement) provide a swing to the skirt, which is further emphasized with these overlapping bands of fabric that mirror the design of the sleeves. They also form the fashionable uneven hemline, popular from c.1927 in evening and other formal dresses.

Elopement outfit,

1935, Fashion Archives and Museum, Shippensburg University, Pennsylvania

◆

This ensemble is something of an outlier, since it was not made to be worn as a bridal outfit. However, it is an important illustration of the fact that—sometimes due to circumstances beyond a couples' control—seemingly "ordinary" clothes can become imbued with special significance. The bride, Carol Kessler, knitted the skirt and blouse herself. She recalled that: "When I knitted this dress in the spring of '35 I had no intention of being married in it. But I was."[17]

A single mother-of-pearl button fastens the blouse at the back. Bridal gifts and accessories made from mother-of-pearl were popular during the 1930s, but were particularly prized since Bakelite had replaced so many natural materials.

Although white was still the prime bridal choice, Carol Kessler may have been closer on trend than she realized. Other colors—including yellow—were linked to brides throughout the decade. "Brides are choosing wedding dresses with touches of maize yellow, blush pink and even pale green. What a change from the famous wedding dresses of history" wrote Adelaide's *Chronicle* in 1934.[19] That same year, a wedding was described in which the bride wore "yellow crepe romaine"[20] and, three years later, another newspaper report mentioned "satin of the softest yellow for the bridal frock."[21]

Elopement was not viewed favorably by large portions of society, and the bride's own mother was so incensed by her daughter's actions that she never spoke to her again. We do not know the reasons for elopement in this case over a conventional ceremony, but a 1930s justice of the peace in Maryland (home to Elkton, the "elopement capital" of the eastern United States), commented that in his experience, the driving force was usually financial. Carol Kessler and her fiancé simply told her parents one day that they were going to the grocery store—they returned home a married couple.[18]

Less frequently seen was a knitted wedding dress. Knitting was, however, a hugely popular pastime and many women created their own clothes in this way. Therefore, since this dress was not planned as bridal wear, it is not surprising to see an accomplished homemade piece being used. The blouse is made with a lace and cable stitch, the latter described in 1939 as a knitting stitch that "the clever girls are doing."[22] Two-piece knitted garments were fashionable; "If you do not have at least one knitted costume in your wardrobe today, something is wrong. If you can hold your head up with pride and brag that you knitted a dress yourself, then you are indeed a woman of achievement. Knitting is the order of the time, and smart women are accomplished with their knitting needles."[23]

The importance and integration of knitting into women's lives—both publicly and privately—is illustrated in this photograph from 1938: "Without dropping a stitch, Mrs. Leon Henderson, wife of the Secretary of the Monopoly Committee, nonchalantly continues her knitting as she listened to testimony at the Committee hearing today." (Washington, D.C., Library of Congress)

Satin and lace wedding dress,

1936, Pennsylvania, Author's collection

◆

This gown was worn by Helen Rose Hawbaker for her marriage to Roy George Shaull on Saturday, June 13, 1936. A handwritten account of "The Trousseau" described the ensemble as "white satin and lace made along Princess lines." Her veil of white lace was "bound in small white Pearls with a small brim over the face". Her shoes were of white satin, with a bridal bouquet of "white roses and white Baby Breath."

．．

With its smart wired lace collar, this bodice presents a more formal version of the shirtwaist style that grew in popularity during the decade. "Shirtwaist" wedding dresses—which often simply meant the inclusion of a collar and long buttoned sleeves—were described by a fashion writer in 1935 as "beguilingly youthful" with a "captivating simplicity."[24] Furthermore, some brides enjoyed a practical two-in-one construction whereby "the shirtwaist and train are built in one and worn over a sleeveless evening gown of the identical satin."[25]

Gathered shells of satin are arranged in "rouleau" style trim across the yoke and neckline.

A similar dress was described in 1930 as being "fashioned with yoke and tight-fitting sleeves formed entirely of lace."[26] Yokes in this material were extremely popular, including for bridal negligée designs, which sometimes featured appliqué lace on net.

As seen in the photo of bride and groom below, the wired collar is shaped upright, reaching the jawline.

Buttons and loops were often described as a gown's main "trimming," especially when they adorned sleeve cuffs as well as the bodice. Here they are self-covered, which was a popular technique: but wedding reports from the era mention variations including wooden buttons with braid loops, pearl buttons, and ball buttons.

This upwardly curved seam slims the waist and adds a soft fullness to the chest.

By the 1930s, many bridal gowns were being made with shorter trains. However, even when more substantial, the tradition and ceremony of having a train carried was becoming less of a requirement. "It should be dropped at the entrance to the church," wrote Brisbane's *The Week* in May 1934, "and left to sweep along the ground as the bride walks up the aisle."[27]

Cream silk wedding dress,

c.1936, Berlin, United States Holocaust Memorial Museum

This dress was worn by Alice Lubranitsky at her wedding to Robert Plocki, a fashion entrepreneur in Berlin, at the Fasanenstrasse Synagogue on Sunday, August 16, 1936. With plans to emigrate to the USA, German-Jewish Alice shipped her wedding dress to New York ahead of her intended departure. Tragically, however, she and her husband were murdered at the Riga ghetto in 1941. The dress therefore survives not only as a personal memento, but as a symbol of hope, perseverance, and resourcefulness in one of humanity's darkest eras.

Throughout the decade, descriptions of weddings included mentions of long, full raglan sleeves (a one-piece sleeve extending to the collar). As seen here, these were often made in the full "bishop" style—extremely popular from c.1931—and caught at the wrist in a close-fitting cuff. Their fullness was markedly on-trend, too, as one Scottish newspaper described a month before the Plockis' wedding: "It is almost impossible to wear a tightfitting sleeve this autumn and still be in the fashion news. All the new sleeves have fullness somewhere."[28]

Cuff detail

Although bright white bridalwear was reigning supreme in high society, many other brides opted for more muted shades such as this cream. Other fashionable choices included fawn, pale blue, and soft pink.[29]

Between the high, rounded neckline and round yoke is a fold in the fabric that creates a layered drape. Like many 1930s dresses, this achieves decorative interest without any additional ornamentation.

The buttons are purely decorative. There is a vertical opening on the left side of the waist with eleven metal snaps. Until the end of the decade, when zips became lighter and more delicate, snap fastenings were generally preferred for bridal and occasion wear.

A marriage notice from the *Jüdische Rundschau* noted the date, year, and time of Alice and Robert's ceremony. They were married at the Fasanenstrasse Synagogue in Berlin, which was closed by the Nazis that same year, burned during the Kristallnacht in 1938, and finally destroyed by Allied bombing in 1943.[30]

The sleeves, buttons, and train are made from the reverse sheen side of the fabric. The material used here could be charmeuse, which has a matte and a satin side (either are suitable as a garment's "right" side), and was popular with film stars due to its sumptuous sheer and seductive cling.[31]

The long train is inset at a diagonal on the lower half of the skirt. Like the sleeves it is made from the reverse side of the fabric to create variation in the design.

Chapter 8: 1930–1946   151

Wedding outfit,

1937, UK, John Bright Collection

This dress and cloak were made by the bride, Constance Kingcombe, for her marriage to Henry Ordewer at the West London Synagogue, May 23, 1937. Similarly to Christian convention, Jewish marriage tradition favored the use of white, long-sleeved dresses worn with veils, so this choice is a bright, bold statement of individuality.

The cloak fastens at the neck with a turquoise-studded clasp. Both soft and vivid shades of turquoise were fashionable during the decade, and the stone was often chosen as a bride's "something blue"—which could be the case here.

Cloaks, too, were a departure from tradition for bridal wear. When used, they were often worn in the place of a veil, with a hood covering the bride's hair. During the mid–late 1930s cloaks were popular evening wear, leading some brides to choose an evening dress as their "going away" outfit, teaming it with their wedding cloak. Here, Constance combined both as her bridal ensemble.

Wedding gowns sometimes incorporated lamé as a trimming or as part of an accessory, but it was unusual to find an entire dress made from this material. Another rare example was seen at a 1938 wedding in Dundee, Scotland, for which the bride wore a "stately wedding gown of gleaming gold satin lamé [with] ... high cowl neckline, full sleeve tops and Venetian Blind ruching on the bodice and skirt."[32]

Along with the cloak, other more subtle elements suggest the fashionable medieval influence of the decade. These include this close-fitting skirt that accentuates the hips, with a now-missing jeweled clasp reminiscent of fourteenth-century girdles worn around the hips. In 1931, serial author Cecile V. Sayer described an imagined, perfect version of such a dress in her story *Fate's Intervention*: "The bride was dressed in a gown of cloth of gold, cut in the Plantagenet style, with a full long-trained skirt and a jewelled girdle about the hips. She wore a long velvet cloak, fur lined, over her dress."[33]

The halter neck is given extra support through a bar of fabric running down in between the shoulder blades. This was also a popular decorative device for evening and other formal wear, seen in the comparative image below right. Halter necks were often seen on bridal wear during the 1930s and again into the 1950s, and a soft, "draped" version, gently accentuating the bust, seems to have been especially popular during the late 1930s.

Back view of a green evening dress, with a similar halter neck with extra support through the back, 1934.

Parachute silk wedding dress,

c.1945, UK, Author's collection

◆

Bridal gowns made from the repurposed silk of parachutes have become a favorite Second World War fashion anecdote, and were certainly not common—but, when available, they were a genuine choice for brides wanting that sought-after "real silk" effect. Until the end of the war in 1945 it was extremely difficult to obtain parachute silk (by either legal or illegal means), so it is most likely that this dress was made in or just after 1945. The restrictions placed on luxury fabrics meant that women had to be both highly inventive and highly practical. After rationing was implemented in June 1941, Make Do and Mend classes across the country taught skills such as pattern cutting and more complex sewing techniques. Books and manuals such as Joanna Chase's *Sew and Save* also offered economic, technical, and aesthetic advice to the home dressmaker, and the original maker/owner of this dress would probably have made use of such resources.

This gathered bust creates something of an empire line effect, and presents a silhouette in keeping with wedding fashions that continued into the mid-late 1940s. Shirring, a gathering technique similar to smocking, was commonly used to decorate and fit bodices. In a dress like the one shown here, it would be applied in panels either to the bust or the waist to create a long, narrow silhouette. This aligns closely with one Australian description of a bridal gown from April 1948: "The V-necked bodice was trimmed with rows of shirring at shoulders and bust."[34]

Californian bride Helen Rothschild's wedding gown was made by dressmaker Ulva Hartman from a "condemned parachute" in 1941. It contained several of the design elements seen in the dress under discussion, including a shallow V-neck, lightly gathered sleeve heads, gathered cuffs, and a wide sash with a relatively high waistline.[35]

Small silk-covered pads widen the shoulders, with gathered sleeve heads adding volume.

The sash ends extend from a panel of fabric built into the front of the dress, just below the bustline shirring. It can be adjusted to fit according to the wearer's size and preference.

Long sleeves finish with slight bell cuffs and are lightly gathered into a slim band with adjustable ties.

A similar silhouette is seen in this Finnish wedding dress, early-mid 1940s, Valokuvaaja.

The frilled hem adds a touch of luxury, since it uses unnecessary fabric to create one of the few decorative aspects of the dress. Rationing was still in effect in the years after the war, but in countries where its effects were less severe, fashion columns and wedding descriptions frequently mentioned brides applying multiple frills to bridal skirts—as in this 1946 Australian description: "Lines of frilling ran from the waist to the hem of the bride's gown."[36]

Chapter 8: 1930–1946

Wedding dress by Norman Norell,

1946, Newfields, Indiana

◆

This unique gown was worn by Bonnie Birnbaum for her wedding on November 14, 1946, in New York City. It was designed by Norman Norell, a man credited as the "father of American high fashion"—a designer who helped to establish the USA's fashion industry. He would not found his own label until 1960, so this dress was made whilst Norell was partnered with fellow designer Anthony Traina.[37] His approach was typically sophisticated yet relaxed, combining French couture details with burgeoning American style.[38] This dress harks back to his early career as a costume designer, with its various historical references that combine to create a luxurious, fantastical mix of influences.

....

This gathered neckline is another nod towards "peasant" style, which had come in and out of fashion since the 1920s. Use of a drawstring at the neck was mentioned in one bridal fashion column during the war years, suggested as a simple way to bring an older, borrowed wedding dress "up to date."[39]

The front lacing recalls a decorative version seen on late eighteenth century bodices, a style borne of "peasant" or "milkmaid" dress that so infamously influenced Marie Antoinette. The effect was seen especially frequently towards the end of the 1940s; one example being "laced in front from the deep V neckline to the waist where the lacing finished in a soft bow."[40]

Corset-style bodice detail.

This corset-style bodice, with its pointed waistline and cinched-in waist, is remarkably similar to a corselet (sometimes known as a "Swiss waist" or "Swiss belt") that was hugely popular during the 1860s. These were often worn over a blouse or shirtwaist, creating a similar effect to that seen here. It is a style that made a resurgence during the 1930s, usually described as a "corselet".

A 1931 "corselet" worn with puffed sleeves.

The long, full skirt foreshadows Dior's New Look of 1947, with its focus on luxury following the austerity of the war years. In c.1946 a trend started to be seen for padding the hips to create a more voluptuous figure, sometimes incorporating stiffened petticoats or paniers under the skirt to create volume. For brides concerned about the cost of this extra fabric, fashion columns recommended wearing a dress with a circle skirt, which would create a "swirling skirt ... an attractive and easy-to-wear current fashion."[43]

Puffed sleeves have appeared in many phases of fashion history, but these can be most closely linked to the balloon shape popular in the early–mid 1830s. This link was made often by fashion writers, sometimes very explicitly: "Fashion will show coats with enormously wide 1830 shoulders."[41]

Indeed, the overall silhouette of the 1830s wedding dress, shown opposite, with its low neckline, puffed sleeves and gathered skirt, creates a strong parallel with the gown in question. Another design with all these elements combined was mentioned in a description of a wedding in California in September 1946: "[The wedding gown] will be made with a low neck, short puff sleeves, tight bodice and gathered skirt."[42]

Woman's wedding gown with veil, United States, 1830–1833, Los Angeles County Museum of Art

Wedding dress shipped to the United States by a German Jewish woman murdered at Riga, 1936, (sleeve detail).

Wedding dress by Norman Norell, 1946, Newfields (front view detail).

Chapter 9

1947–1959

In recent years, 1950s-style wedding dresses have made a big impact on the bridal scene. This is partly due to the rose-tinted nostalgia that "vintage" represents. The very word often seems to be associated with the perceived glamour and luxury of a bygone age— and an assumption that most women were able to use fashion to "keep their spirits up" at a harrowing time, none more so than the bride. An element of provocativeness—particularly in 1950s-inspired clothing—can work to hypersexualize the clothing of women who often lived in continued post-war rationing and anxiety. (Owen Hatherley describes this as the "semi-ironic sexualized style usually called 'burlesque'".[1]) At the same time, the vintage movement is tied up with a resurgence in crafts, particularly knitting and sewing. The "make do and mend" approach of wartime and postwar, embraced by (mainly) women because they had no choice, is now part of the wider aesthetic of vintage and has resurrected an interest in "slow" fashion, recycling, thrift, and cautious consumption at a time when it is direly needed. Some twenty-first-century brides choose original 1940s and 1950s dresses for their big day, partly for the reasons mentioned and partly as an attempt to evoke a note of uniqueness. For most brides in the late 1940s and early 1950s, however, uniqueness was not necessarily a selling point. The white wedding was hugely commercialized and, in the USA, sold as a key part of the "American Dream." Bridal shows and magazines promoted a conformity that must have been attractive following years of austerity, "making do," and hurried, shotgun weddings. At the same time, the luxury and femininity presented by Dior's pioneering New Look in 1947 underpinned almost all bridal designs, offering the layers of fabric and perfect fit that suggested a brighter sartorial future after years of rationing. Britain was subject to clothes rationing regulations until May 1949, and once this was relaxed newspapers were keen to emphasize that "designers of wedding dresses can afford the luxury of sweeping

LEFT
A British wedding reception in July 1947, showing the bride in a plain suit decorated with a small corsage of fresh flowers.

trains."² The same could not be said for the ordinary bride, for although fabric was more accessible, the funds to purchase a ready-made dress or fashion a "dream wedding" were not. Women continued to make their own wedding gowns well into the 1950s, often out of necessity rather than preference. This was not the case in the United States, where social middle-class pressure to conform to the commercialized white wedding (well-illustrated in the immensely popular film *Father of the Bride* in 1950) demonstrated different priorities (illustrated well through the launch of the second American bridal magazine, *Modern Bride*, in 1949). Meanwhile, different priorities (and very different pressures) faced Russian brides during this era. From the 1930s onwards, wedding dresses had been largely considered "anti-Soviet" due to their association with bourgeois ideals of wealth and luxury. In any case, drab municipal Communist wedding venues did not provide an appropriate backdrop for an elaborate bridal gown, and due to a lack of demand, such designs disappeared altogether from fashion magazines. They would return after Stalin's death in 1953, along with a focus on the fashionable silhouette but also on the straightened circumstances of most readers. In the end, lingering disassociation and a desperate economic situation meant that the white bridal gown was frequently omitted well into the 1960s.³

This chapter features examples of wedding dresses by popular designers Alfred Angelo and Priscilla of Boston, which could be purchased "off the rack" and altered to fit where necessary. Such styles would have been chosen with the assistance of a bridal consultant, a role that encompassed more than fashion: as *LIFE* magazine described it in 1952, the consultant was ready to equip the bride with everything she needed "from gowns, garters, and garlands, to souvenir ashtrays, honeymoon budgets, and even custom-written wedding odes."⁴ In the world of haute couture, meanwhile, the significance of the wedding dress was also growing. By 1957 it had become traditional to close a couture show with a white wedding gown, albeit unconventional "showstoppers" such as Yves Saint Laurent's cocoon dress from 1965.⁵ Nevertheless, the fact that the departing image was a bridal gown is illustrative of its increasing significance in high fashion. Into the 1960s, designs from "Paris, London and New York" were further linked to youthful modishness, leaving—as *The Australian Women's Weekly* put it in 1966—"sentimentalists" to sew their own dresses at home.⁶

As mentioned in the previous chapter, the Association of Bridal Manufacturers in the USA won an exemption on rationing of bridal silk on the grounds that the war was being fought to maintain American institutions such as marriage. As one member remembers explaining during lobbying, "American boys are going off to war and what are they fighting for except the privilege of getting married in a traditional way?"⁷ From the Association's point of view, this victory made it incumbent on bridal manufacturers to maintain the symbolism of the long, flowing wedding gown, with all the trappings of the white wedding. Nevertheless, our prevailing image of the 1950s bride is that of the starched, tea-length, "Rockabilly" dress worn

LEFT
A church wedding in Newport, Wales, 1950.

with a short peppy veil and flat ballet pumps. As Jellison explains, the bridal industry actively fought this fashionable silhouette, hoping to create a long-lasting style synonymous with the young American postwar bride.[8] Although the supremacy of Dior's silhouette was powerful, so were the bridal retailers. Early in the decade, when a bride chose a "ballerina length" gown it, or she, were still usually described as "modern" and remarked upon accordingly. "The modern bride," wrote one Australian fashion column in 1953, "to be fashionable, wears

162 How to Read a Wedding Dress

coloured gowns, wears them ballerina length and does not add the lucky orange blossom to her headdress."[9] This implication of being "fashionable" or "bridal" as a binary choice surfaces often in 1950s commentary, until later in the decade where the dialogue becomes more open. This is represented in a fashion column from 1958, which showcases seven looks "for the girl who wishes to dress as a bride on her wedding day." All include a wide-skirted silhouette of satin, faille, or sheer fabric with a tulle veil. Prominent among them is a "sweetly pretty" ankle-length and "chic" ballerina length design, with the long variants described conversely as "regal" and "romantic."[10] This suggests that by the end of the decade, as the shorter wedding dress prepared to take center stage in the 1960s, either style was viewed as conventional, with the floor-length skirt having a stately and sophisticated edge.

Elsewhere in the world, navigating the cost of the white wedding and speedily growing popularity of the white dress often meant hiring a gown. This was notable particularly in countries where a foreign power, with its own habits and customs that infiltrated society, had retreated. Such was the case in Taiwan, where, after Japan relinquished colonial control in 1945, the bridal kimono was no longer in favor. For many reasons elite Chinese Mainlanders had preferred the white bridal gown since the turn of the century, and this began to influence Taiwanese preferences away from the ancient tradition of wearing red. Crucially in this context, the positive influence of US political and military support during this period perhaps inevitably led to an adoption of some cultural customs. Gowns to rent, or on occasion to purchase, were widely available and as Bonnie Adrian has pointed out, family and studio photographs during the 1950s rarely show brides wearing anything other than a white Western wedding dress.[11] Similarly, from the late 1950s wedding and engagement photography in many East African countries was dominated by white bridal dress, particularly in urban centers such as Mombasa. Brides might "appear Swahili" by maintaining small elements such as henna tattoos in their photographs, whereas grooms (who would often appear alone in additional portraits) asserted their heritage through wearing a suit jacket with *kikoi* (cloth) instead of trousers.[12]

The dresses in this chapter range from mass-produced designs to couture, to homemade gowns that evoke a particular theme or emphasize a favorite detail. It also showcases two examples of well-known celebrity weddings, the dresses from which made a permanent mark on bridal dreams for years to come. Another dress, hailing from a small rural town in Western Australia, demonstrates the reach and influence of Hollywood, with a gown worn by a fictional on-screen heroine garnering almost as much admiration as that of Grace Kelly or Jacqueline Kennedy.

Wedding dress,

c.1947, Author's collection

This dress was made the same year as Princess Elizabeth's wedding gown, a silk-satin, pearl-encrusted design by Norman Hartnell. The designer of this gown is unknown, and it is far less lavish, but similarities can nevertheless be seen, emphasizing both the impact of the future Queen's choice, and the prevalence of a particular silhouette in the immediate post-war years.

The bodice fastens at one side with a metal zip: this row of dainty artificial pearl buttons is purely decorative. "Button-down-the-front" designs were known to give a "long slim line," as one fashion column described it in 1947, and the detail is here picked up on the sleeve cuffs.[13] This elegant style mimics a far more every day one, the shirtwaist, which buttoned up the front and usually featured a small, pointed collar. Here, the masculine-influenced design is softened by the use of lace and a striking wired collar.

This lightly wired collar can be worn flat or standing. The feature was commonly used and seen elsewhere in this book, with some arrangements more elaborate than others. One bride in 1942 chose a dress with a collar "wired into the shape of a lace lily leaf."[15]

The gently V-shaped neckline flows down to a waistline which, as with Elizabeth II's wedding dress (below), is pointed at center front and back.

The skirt is softly gathered at the sides and across the back, creating gentle movement as the bride walked down the aisle.

The dress is made from an artificial silk, probably rayon, with a floral brocade effect. Given the continuation of rationing, rayon was a popular choice, and brocaded versions were frequently recommended for both the bride and bridal party. Small touches of lace in lieu of an all-lace gown were also common at a time when restrictions persisted. "These days when a bride wears all lace," one Australian newspaper commented in 1945, "it is a fair guess that the dress comes under the luck bringer of 'something lent,' though no doubt there are a few homes where there is a length of 'off white' lace just waiting to be made up for such an event."[16]

Long lace cuffs finish at a point towards the knuckles. A BBC North American "Guest Night" talk in 1942 described one poignant story of a bride who, due to badly scarred hands following war work, "had a dress made with special lace cuffs to drape over her hands ... she didn't want [her scars] to be seen when the ring was slipped on."[14]

Full skirts leading into modest trains were common in the immediate postwar period, a way of incorporating some traditional excess within the confines of continuing clothes rationing.

Wedding dress,

1949, Claremont, Claremont Museum, Western Australia

This wedding dress was worn by Thelma Barton (née Mercer) when she married Dudley Barton in Claremont, a suburb near Perth, Western Australia in 1949. Its patterned silver lamé ("novelty" lamé) shows an embossed abstracted floral design, illustrating a popular trend for metallic fabrics. For her high-profile wedding in 1946, Patricia Mountbatten wore a very similar dress, described as "silver and gold brocade cut on classical lines, with a square neck, a tight bodice, long, tight sleeves and a full skirt trailing behind to form a train."[17]

These pleated, gathered bands of fabric are arranged vertically from shoulder to natural waistline, mimicking the shape of a bow. Their placement brings to mind the false bolero effects of late 1930s dress, which continued to be popular well into the '40s. They were also a common accesory for brides in straitened wartime and post-war circumstances, opting for a day dress rather than traditional wedding gown.

At the back, these swagged sections are gathered over each hip to create a soft, low bustle effect. "Hip treatment is carried out with bows and frills," wrote Perth's *Daily News* in March 1949, "and the bustle effect is ... almost universal."[19]

There is no additional surface decoration on this dress, with the dramatic drapery—leading into an exuberant train—speaking for itself. Other silver-clad brides of the era, however, opted for more. In 1946 an English woman chose a train "decorated with pearl butterflies," and others, light lace overlays.[21]

These long, close-fitting sleeves continue bridal trends from the war years, in which sleeves featuring little ornamentation or gathering were a necessity.

Sections of fabric are artfully draped over each hip, caught at the front with the ends free to fall down the skirt. This clever manipulation echoes fashionable trends from the mid-1940s onwards, with an accentuation of the hips through—most commonly—the addition of a peplum. It also looks to the past, emulating the robes of ancient Greece and Rome. Assuming that the majority of brides would want a historical silhouette, one Australian fashion column advised choosing from medieval, Renaissance, Elizabethan, the "crinoline" era, or "the Grecian type, with lovely draperies trailing on the ground at the back and with lines of classic purity that accentuate youth."[18]

The bride wore a two-tiered floor length veil and small coronet of flowers.

The long train is a clear indicator that clothing rationing had at last ended, the year before Mercer's wedding. It would not have been possible for many brides at the start of the conflict, when a long dress with a train of 2+ yards would have used 24 precious clothing coupons.[20]

Chapter 9: 1947–1959 165

Rayon satin and lace wedding dress,

1952, USA, Author's collection

◆

This dress by designer Priscilla of Boston was purchased at Garfinckel's department store in Washington, D.C. This design house was established in 1945 by Massachusetts-born Priscilla Kidder, who opened her first shop in Boston that year,[22] and the franchise swiftly grew, leading to Kidder being described as the "Dior of bridal design" and "queen of the aisle" for her relatively unique ready-to-wear status in the industry.[23] Her elaborate, comparatively conservative dresses gained even more attention when Grace Kelly chose Priscilla of Boston as the designer for her bridesmaids' dresses in 1956. This gown, worn by schoolteacher Nancy Herring Stuart in December 1951, when she was married to United State Marine Corps lieutenant Thomas R. Stuart at the United States Naval Academy Chapel in Annapolis, MD.

As seen in this portrait, the bride wore a "finger-tip" length veil with fitted Juliet cap. This veil length was frequently referenced as a desirable style during the decade, along with blusher and elbow length. In this case, the relatively short veil ensured that the elaborate lace train would not be obscured.

This small standing lace collar sits above the hugely popular sweetheart neckline, described in one fashion column as "among the most attractive for you to wear." Necklines took a plunge in the early years of the decade, and so important was this feature that one retailer commented "fifty percent of customers [buy] their dresses ... on the strength of the neckline."[24]

An off-the-shoulder neckline would have been considered daring for a wedding. In January 1952, a bride planning to wear a "brocade wedding gown [which looks] rather hard with a high neckline" asked *The Australian Woman's Weekly* "Dress Sense" column whether it would be "permissible" to wear an "off shoulder style." "You could achieve an off shoulder look," came the reply, "with a flesh toned net yoke. For a wedding gown this would be more appropriate than bare shoulders."[26]

This dress is cut without a waist seam or darts, fitted to the body through long seams that run the length of the garment. This makes it a princess line cut, a style much discussed in the early 1950s due to Queen Elizabeth's fondness for this molded feminine silhouette.[25]

The gown is made from rayon bridal satin, a cheaper, easily washable and storable alternative to silk satin. Use of artificial silk such as rayon was heightened during the war years, and in 1939 a touch of glamour was given to the fabric after its on-screen appearance as Scarlett O'Hara's bridal gown in MGM's *Gone with the Wind*.

The amount of lace on this gown illustrates a move away from the fashionable simplicity of wedding dresses. Significant ornamentation set Priscilla of Boston apart from its competitors, reflecting Kidder's wish to focus on New England's "morality" and "family atmosphere" through maintaining a sense of timelessness and tradition.[28]

This is a formal cathedral-length train, typically measuring 6–7 feet from the waistline down. These were often described as "extravagant" or "full" finishes to a gown in the 1950s, but newspaper wedding reports often seemed hesitant to definitively define the length, citing "cathedral-like" to describe a moderate to full-length train.

Film replica wedding dress,

1953, Western Australia, Author's collection

◆

This Australian-made dress is a direct replica of the gown designed by Helen Rose and worn by Elizabeth Taylor for the 1950 comedy Father of the Bride, in which she starred alongside Spencer Tracey. That a bride should choose to model her wedding aesthetic so closely on popular culture demonstrates the huge importance of Hollywood, and its associated glamour, in the lives of ordinary women. This bride was married in church, which required the modesty of long sleeves and a high neckline—so Taylor's costume provided the perfect mix of luxury, modernity, and respectability.

The bride, Pat Currie, is pictured above in the dress. Pat was by no means the only Australian bride to take inspiration from the film: a Wollongong newspaper in January 1951 described a wedding dress of "white waterwave taffeta and lace ... a replica of the wedding gown worn by Elizabeth Taylor in the film *Father of the Bride.*"[29]

By the mid-1950s, many evening gowns featured deep V-necks at both front and back. Taylor's dress was therefore somewhat ahead of its time. Beneath the double-layered satin V the bodice is a sweetheart, accentuated by the tiny waist and voluminous skirt.

Peter Pan collars were a common addition, described by designer Helen Rose as "inevitable." The style was often referenced in contemporary descriptions of bridal ensembles as being a neat finish to a lace yoke—seen here. The film version is held up and shaped by a wire insert.[31]

As with Taylor's ivory satin gown, the short row of covered buttons at center front are purely decorative. They are echoed on the sleeves and at the back of the dress, where they are functional.

Cascading folds of fabric hold the skirt open to reveal a delicate lace overlay (matching that on shoulders and neck). This added textual interest aligns with the fashion for layered and tiered skirts in bridal wear. Between 1950–1955, descriptions of society weddings included mentions of skirts with "draped apron effects," "full bouffant ... of sheer organdy," "cascading ruffles," "a half overskirt ..." and so on. Although slimmer styles were certainly in vogue, the prevalence and range of wide, extravagant designs demonstrates the continued influence of Dior's 1947 New Look.

Elizabeth Taylor in *Father of the Bride.*

This train is cathedral length, extending approximately three yards from the natural waistline. Trains remained popular throughout the 1950s and into the 1960s; nevertheless, by the middle of the 1950s there was a shift in perspective. Renowned Hollywood costume designer Edith Head remarked in 1954 that "the new point of view is entirely practical ... I don't think it spoils the sentiment. You still have your veil to hand down to posterity!"[30]

Jacqueline Kennedy's wedding dress by Ann Lowe,

1953, John F. Kennedy Presidential Library and Museum, Boston

The wedding dress worn by future First Lady Jacqueline Bouvier was created by Ann Lowe, the first noted African American fashion designer. It is a beautiful example of the American Dream; of early 1950s elite styling but also representing a far humbler story of racial inequality and intense personal and professional stress for Lowe. Her commission to produce fifteen outfits for the bridal party, including the wedding gown and mother-of-the-bride dress, struck disaster when a pipe burst in her studio. This gave Lowe and her team just ten days to recreate eight weeks' worth of painstaking work. Her efforts were met with financial hardship (a $700 profit turned into a $2,200 loss), discrimination and an almost complete lack of credit for her work, with even the bride neglecting to name Lowe for reporters.[32] While the two women repaired their relationship and Lowe has since received full recognition, this story is an important reminder of the battle faced by so many people of color to make a name and a living in the fashion industry.

The bride wore a rose-point lace wedding veil; a family heirloom that had been worn by her maternal grandmother. This was apparently to please her father, who had asked her to wear something "traditional and old-fashioned."[33]

The gown features the sewing technique known as *trapunto*, from the Italian "to quilt." It creates a 3D effect in fabric; here, layered designs produce ruffles and concentric circles. Other reports of weddings during the decade explicitly mention the use of this method, including "trapunto embroidery outlining [a] sheer yoke" (1950)[34] and "silk ribbon trapunto embroidery" (1953).[35]

Tiny wax orange blossoms nestle in the center of each skirt rosette. This tradition was carried into the 1950s, although a 1953 fashion column proposed that: "The modern bride, to be fashionable ... does not add the lucky orange blossom to her headdress."[36]

This extravagant "bouffant" skirt (which took fifty yards of French silk chiffon taffeta to create) was not to the bride's taste: she even compared it to a lampshade. She apparently felt particularly anxious about how she would appear in photographs published by *LIFE* magazine, preferring to show her famously favored straight lines and minimal ornamentation.[37] The choice of something more traditional is said to have been pushed on the couple by Jackie's in-laws, though she reportedly told designer Caroline Herrera that "It was the dress that my mother wanted me to wear and I hated it."[38] The bouffant skirt however was an extremely popular bridal choice, whether it was made floor or calf-length.

The flattering portrait neckline was a popular cut on bridal gowns. It was frequently mentioned throughout the decade in reports of weddings, maintaining equal popularity from the start to the end of the 1950s. "The portrait neckline finished with folds of silk illusion" wrote *Desert Sun* on January 4, 1954, describing a dress made with some inspiration from this iconic design.[39]

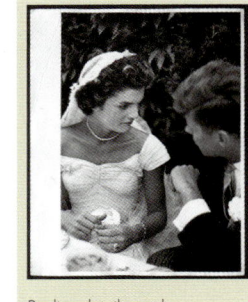

Bodice details can be seen in this candid portrait of Jacqueline Bouvier Kennedy and John Kennedy talking at their wedding reception, Newport, Rhode Island. (Library of Congress)

Wedding dress by Alfred Angelo,

1955–57. USA, Author's collection

◆

For nearly 30 years, Alfred Angelo (1933–2017) was one of the most popular and well-respected bridal companies. This dress represents the creative output of the company's founders, Philadelphia-based Alfred Angelo and his wife Edythe Piccione (1921–2012, known as Edythe Vincent). The latter was chief designer, and her dresses combined up-to-the-minute trends with the company's signature styling. She was also the author of *Facts and Fashions for the Bride-to-be* (1964), which offered tips relating to a bride's entire experience, as well as the business of choosing (and wearing) her dress. "Keep pinching yourself," she wrote, "it really is YOU for whom the Wedding March is being played."[40]

....

A fitted or "molded" bodice with lace overlay emphasizes fashionably cone-shaped breasts. "The desire of every woman is to have a firm, uplifted bosom" fashion writer Edyth Thornton McLeod commented in 1956.[41]

A curved lace peplum with scalloped edging complements the design on the bodice. A peplum was a popular way of creating or emphasizing an hourglass silhouette.

The "ballerina-length" skirt, its hem stopping just above the ankle, was instigated by Dior's "New Look" in 1947. Its popularity became ingrained during the 1950s, partly due to Audrey Hepburn's influence, and was an acceptable option for more formal wear such as bridal and debutante dresses.

Discussing such formal styles in 1950, one fashion column advised that "there must be at least six or seven overskirts to give the right ballerina impression, and there must be a very slim little waist above them all."[42] For brides with budget concerns, "street-length" (slightly shorter than ballerina) or ankle-length dresses were popular and practical choices, since—as another fashion advice column pointed out—such a dress would be "an extremely useful addition to your wardrobe for any festive occasion."[43]

The formality of the high collar is offset by a soft curved opening at center front. Another hugely popular neckline at this date, and worn with this style of gown, was the 'Queen Anne', which sat high at the back of the neck, taking its inspiration from open ruffs of the early seventeenth century.

Long sleeves with pointed cuffs, sometimes finishing over the knuckles, were extremely common, ideally, as one fashion writer put it, when "taper[ing] over slender wrists."[44]

The original owner of the dress, bride Betty, with groom John Gillis from Greensburg, Pennsylvania. Their wedding took place on May 19, 1957.

There is a panel of matching lace at the rear over nylon tulle, its design mirroring the scalloped edging at the peplum and bust. A 1958 advertisement for Alfred Angelo described a popular combination of lace and tulle: "Lace shares honors with frothy nylon tulle. Fashioned with a jeweled lace applique neckline."[46] Similar styles retailed from $55.95, equaling roughly $916.18 in 2021.

To create the desired flared shape, dresses like this with a "ballerina-length" skirt would have been worn over layers of stiffened petticoats. So popular was this silhouette, that by 1954 petticoat sales made up half of lingerie sales in the U.S.[45]

Grace Kelly's wedding dress and accessories designed by Helen Rose,

1956, USA, Philadelphia Museum of Art, Philadelphia

◆

The dress worn by Grace Kelly for her wedding to Prince Rainier of Monaco remains one of the most famous and influential bridal gowns of the twentieth century. Created by Metro-Goldwyn-Mayer costume designer Helen Rose, it was a gift to the actress from MGM Studios and was worn for the formal religious ceremony on April 19, 1956. Speaking of the experience the following year, Rose expressed her apprehension at creating the entire trousseau, commenting that "I've never seen a movie with my work in it that I didn't want to rework many of the ... details. When it came to Grace Kelly's trousseau ... I hoped I wouldn't have that same frustrated feeling." When Kelly completed her final fitting, however, she turned to the designer and declared: "Helen ... this is absolutely ideal."[47]

The focal point of the bodice is its use of antique rose point lace, a delicate Brussels needle lace featuring floral motifs. These motifs were enhanced and elevated by a raised outline (cordonnet) painstakingly detached from their original mesh ground and pieced together to follow the silhouette of the dress, obscuring any seams. From the late nineteenth century, technology advanced to allow the attachment of additional floral details, such as petals, enhancing the 3D appearance.[48]

Its frequent use of a rose pattern inspired the name, and it has been a popular bridal choice for generations.

Kelly wore this "Juliet" cap, decorated with lace and seed pearls and a wreath of paper orange blossoms. Inspired by Renaissance styles—and consequently by the type of headgear often worn on stage by the female protagonist in *Romeo and Juliet*—the look was incredibly popular during the 1950s and 1960s. It was widely hailed as practical as well as beautiful for its role in keeping the veil "in place," or even, as one 1950 newspaper report put it, of "confining" it.[50]

The circular veil was designed to keep her face as visible as possible to the 600 guests and 30 million viewers. At ninety yards long, it was a "chapel" length, decorated with pearls. Circular veils have no gathers and attach to the head with a flat comb.

In April 2011, Kate Middleton wore a Sarah Burton for Alexander McQueen design for her wedding to Prince William. With its handmade lace and long sleeves, it had distinct echoes of Kelly's style.

Touches of the same lace adorn the rest of the gown, as well as Kelly's accessories. The veil is accented with thousands of seed pearls, one of the smallest natural pearls usually measuring no more than 2mm in diameter.[49] Artificial varieties were composed of coated glass, and their tiny dimensions allowed for the most intricate of embroidery.

Helen Rose returned to a controversial idea used for a character she dressed in the film *Invitation* (1952), whereby the lace blouse of the bridal gown is made separate to the skirt. The wide sash, or cummerbund, "welds" them together and provides flexibility after the wedding, allowing the blouse to be worn with dinner suits, and the skirt with other formal blouses.[51]

At the rear of the skirt, three flat bows hold two sides together. Bow detailing became a particular feature of bridal gowns in the 1960s, often contributing the only decoration in an era when wedding dresses were becoming increasingly minimalist. Beneath the dress, Kelly wore a blue petticoat embellished with matching satin bows.

Silk taffeta, paired with one hundred yards of silk net, create this bell-shaped skirt, its shape enhanced by heavy pleats at the front and back.

Two petticoats are attached to the skirt by the waistband; a foundation petticoat of non-woven interfacing with ruffles of nylon net attached, and a petticoat of silk taffeta. This latter piece helped to create a smoothing layer between faille skirt and foundation petticoat. Skirt support was provided by use of a fourteen-inch-long silk taffeta base, with nylon net and lace ruffles supported by metal synthetic boning.[52]

170 How to Read a Wedding Dress

Wedding dress by Arnold Scaasi,

1958, USA, Chicago History Museum

◆

The final dress of this chapter is a notable departure from the rest, largely due to its bold orange color scheme. Its ingenious cut echoes Christobal Balenciaga's groundbreaking sack design, inspired by Norman Norell's earlier chemise, and has been imbued with Scaasi's favorite evening wear aesthetic. The dress was worn by Harriet Levy on Monday October 6, 1958 for her marriage to Kenneth Hirsch.

....

These short magyar or "kimono" sleeves are cut as one with the bodice, leading into a soft crossover neckline. The same cut was described as a "MUST" for the young bride, being a glamorous yet easy-to-make addition to the trousseau.[53]

Whilst the back of this dress drapes into a hanging "sack" style, the front offers what one fashion column called a "break" in the sack silhouette through the use of a "torso band of self material." This was recommended as the most wearable way of sporting the sack style, and *Punch* declared in 1959 that the sack, by "removing the waist altogether," paved the way for new possibilities in its placement.[54] Therefore, a design like this offered the "best of both worlds": the traditional, fashionable hourglass silhouette twinned with avant-garde uniqueness.[55]

The skirt ends at mid-calf, a length recommended as "correct" for eveningwear in particular. It remained popular throughout the decade for bridal, despite the industry's attempts to maximize profits by heavily promoting floor-length gowns.[56]

Shades of orange in general — ranging from the deep tone seen here to light apricot — were fashionable during the fall of 1958. For weddings, however, a white dress worn with train and veil was still the oft-stated ideal. This dress is made from silk taffeta, a fabric that became accessible to more brides after imitations were successfully produced. These were often composed of a mixture of silk with rayon, which provided the same crisp texture and finish.

From the middle of the decade, "back interest" through the use of buttons, bands of fabric, as well as bows and deep V-necklines (seen here) were all the rage. A British newspaper noted in 1959 that this trend was to the great benefit of the wedding guests, who "see the back of [the bride] most of the time."[57]

Both the under and over skirt are interfaced with organza and tulle and worn over a petticoat of gathered tulle. Despite a lack of traditional white, the opulent effect of this arrangement tied directly into the romanticism of the bouffant skirt and yards of fabric as dictated by Dior's New Look in 1947. The sloping, rounded shoulders and small waist seen here are also testament to that enduring silhouette.

… Chapter 10

1960–1979

At the start of the 1960s, the fashionable bridal silhouette did not differ greatly from what had gone before, and it was relatively easy to predict what a bride might wear. The fitted bodice and flared skirts of the New Look continued to hold sway after more than a decade, although the late 1950s empire line revival would gradually influence the dominant shift shape that characterized 1960s fashion. It was not until youth culture and fashion exploded and the counterculture developed that weddings became far less formal, and dresses took inspiration from more diverse sources, including politics and music. "Flower power," which developed as part of a peaceful protest to the Vietnam War, was shown both subtly and overtly in bridal wear, which has long integrated floral emblems and interpretations. The daisy-festooned ensemble within this chapter illustrates how a bride could maintain elements of convention, while boldly proclaiming her personal and social principles.

Gender politics during the decade were fraught and complex, represented in various ways through clothes. Many brides chose a minidress not only as a fashion statement, but also as a proclamation of emancipation in the face of an ancient institution. Across the world, modern cities—including, at that time, Kabul and Tehran—saw brides take their vows in a mini-dress. By the end of the 1960s, Lebanese brides, too, were generally wearing sleeveless versions for their big day, along with most of the female guests.[554] Calls for social equality also incited new feelings and fashions regarding wedding attire. The Black Power movement, a counterculture within the broader civil rights movement in America, saw an increase in use of the *dashiki*, a colorful, upper-body garment common in West African countries. Originally worn by the groom, it was marketed to both men and women in late 1960s Harlem, made in brightly colored fabrics with "modern patterns framing the neckline."[1] These designs, or ones made along similar lines, were also adopted by some white Americans without, Edward J. Reilly points out, "much attention to the heritage, giving birth to a new radical chic" (the term given to the upper-class associating with politically radical causes; an anxiety to be publicly and fashionably rebellious).[2]

The end of the decade witnessed the "Summer of Love" in 1967, resulting in an even more relaxed and carefree approach that often featured bare feet and unisex styles of dress. Those rejecting the industrial capitalist system would certainly not indulge in an expensive, single-use, mass-produced wedding dress. In keeping with the cultural and political mood, these "alternative" or "new" weddings would rather incorporate symbols of resistance and rebellion—making the ceremony about more than the union of a couple. In this way, although the bridal industry was not seriously threatened by shifts in convention and gender roles, for many young people weddings themselves (and the clothing chosen to partake in them) no longer represented the same values. Meanwhile, second-wave feminists were making their feelings about the wedding industry known by staging protests at bridal fairs. One particularly prominent event took place at Madison Square Garden in February 1969 by W.I.T.C.H. (Women's International Terrorists Conspiracy from Hell), who, attired in black veils, sang "here come the slaves, off to their graves" (*Confront the Whoremakers*, 1969).[3] For them, bridal gowns represented the "dehumanizing institution" and "legal whoredom" of marriage, undeniably radical beliefs, but ones that echoed the more moderate concerns expressed by other feminist groups, particularly around the symbolism of the white wedding dress and its insinuation that a woman should be "pure" on her wedding day. Simultaneously, and perhaps fittingly, the "little girl" trend—consisting of loose, A-line dresses or pinafores with headbands and flat shoes—carried over into bridal wear. An edition of popular *Brides* magazine in 1969 promoted "young at heart" styles, most notably frilly pinafore floor-length gowns accessorized with ruffled parasols. The look was deemed "enchantingly nostalgic for a grown-up bride," but ultimately infantilized adult bodies in a manner that feels at odds with the decidedly grown-up business of a wedding.[4]

RIGHT
Nostalgic details on a very contemporary wedding dress, 1979.

These debates continued into the 1970s, although ironically, the end of that decade was dominated by sartorial nostalgia for the early 1900s: an era in which marriage was still the only ultimate (and realistic) goal for many women. "Victorian" and "Edwardian" detailing, such as high necklines, frilly yokes, bishop sleeves, and long, flounced skirts were the height of fashion, building on the popularity of a rustic, "back-to-nature" aesthetic prompted by designers like Laura Ashley and Catherine Buckley. At the same time, the influence of disco saw brides clad in shimmering polyester which was often accented with historical details; medieval and Tudor as well as that of the early twentieth century. As Daniel Milford-Cottam put it, in this landscape bridalwear "often followed its own rules," which perhaps reflected a broader trend in society.[5] Rather than wedding gowns "standing out" as such, bridal sophistication should be "just about the newest look" (*Brides* magazine, 1977), which provided infinite possibilities and a solid excuse to move away from tradition.[6]

LEFT
George Harrison and Pattie Boyd pictured on their wedding day in 1966.

The influence of celebrities was just as strong as it had ever been, from Yoko Ono's white miniskirt in 1969 to the wedding of "rock n' roll" bride Bianca Pérez-Mora de Macias and Mick Jagger in 1971, both of which set a new trend for minimalism as well as championing the idea that a wedding outfit should reflect personality. For the first time it was becoming more common to cohabit before marriage, an attractive option for the young and unconventional since, unlike marriage, cohabitation was not socially sanctioned and did not involve legal obligations.[7] This corresponded with the advent of punk and its associated style, pioneered and widespread in Britain by Vivienne Westwood and Malcolm McLaren. This anti-authoritarian movement was not conducive to the convention of marriage, and many punk couples resisted taking that step. Those that did frequently embraced the "D.I.Y" slogan of the movement, which included home dressmaking and recycling. Meanwhile, celebrated designer Zandra Rhodes introduced a sanitized version of the punk aesthetic with a "punk" wedding dress, the finale of her "Conceptual Chic" collection show in 1977. This dress, with its safety pins, sink chains, and holes, juxtaposed with a large bow and a halter neck was never worn by a real bride. Rhodes was also far from embraced by bona fide punks, for whom the concept of couture was an antithesis to their values. Much subsequent "punk" styled bridal wear is therefore based on staples of early punk fashion that became mainstream thanks to designers like Rhodes: safety pins, rips, metal studs, and Dr. Martens boots.

By the end of the 1970s, American media was proclaiming that brides and grooms were inching back toward a traditional model. However, although the less conventional, socially uncomfortable trends of the counterculture were widely reported, the white wedding never truly disappeared during this period: evidenced by the high-profile marriages of Farrah Fawcett (1973), Aretha Franklin (1978), and Alana Stewart (1979). As Karen M. Durak observes, it was only once alternative ceremonies had become commonplace that the media declared tradition was "in," prompting the re-opening of bridal salons that had lost business earlier in the decade.[8] As has been seen in other transitional periods throughout this book, the 1960s and 1970s witnessed massive social and cultural shifts in a very short time span, making that escape to the past understandable and almost inevitable.

Studio portrait of a female fashion model dressed in bridal wear, England,

1961, Photo by Popperfoto via Getty Images

◆

The bridal gown in this fashion photograph does not stray far from the hourglass silhouette of the 1950s bride, with its full skirt and fitted bodice maintaining tradition. It starts to veer from convention mainly in terms of details and styling, moving slowly towards the minimalism that characterized fashion from the mid-1960s onwards.

By the early 1960s, voluminous shoulder-length veils were becoming the fashionable norm, but many brides still chose the longer, more traditional variety. The use of very long veils was noted, however, when they caused difficulties for the bride: as in the case of 23-year-old dancer Felicity Wright, whose floor-length veil caught in a bush during a "wayward wind," suggesting the impracticality of such a traditional choice.[9] The example shown here is light and airy, made from an open weave net and topped with a small pillbox hat featuring a spray of flowers to match the bouquet.

This plain rounded neckline speaks for itself, allowing attention to be focused on the bride's face and hairstyle. As designer Norman Norell described his more minimal approach from the 1940s onwards, "Just a plain round neckline, no crap on it ... I do think it changed the look of clothes."[10]

The slim sash is accentuated by a wide, flat bow in the front. This was a popular effect in the earliest years of the decade, and bows were popular in general, sometimes used to emphasize the placement of a developing empire line. Also seen here, whether present on the dress or not, veils and headpieces often featured bows either at the back or center.

Bodices were more commonly shaped with princess seams rather than darts, which created a softer, looser feel and appearance. Their use initially helped to mark the "gradual loosening" of the New Look silhouette, but soon became an accepted part of dress construction.[11]

Tapered sleeves remained a common feature until the end of the decade, and were often described as a "traditional" design choice, as were white gloves. One 1960s bride remembered "cutting the seam of the left ring finger on the glove, so my finger was ready for the ring."[12]

Moving on from the layers of stiff petticoats that characterized the 1950s, gowns of the early 1960s maintained skirt volume using pleats or gathers.[13]

Although the mini dress undoubtedly took center stage by the middle of the decade, some brides preferred to retain the floor-length skirt, and it waxed and waned in popularity. In 1965 an Australian fashion columnist advised brides that "the formal wedding dress is in fashion ... I have featured two beautiful floor-length designs."[14] The example shown in *The Australian Women's Weekly* is almost identical but features a slimmer skirt and the minimalism that was so in vogue by that date: principally, no lace or applique embellishment.

Wedding dress,

1964, Brighton Historical Society, Melbourne, Australia

◆

Rayleen Janetzki married Donald Haig in Geelong, Melbourne, on August 15, 1964. This dress was made for her by Deon's of Melbourne, a store specializing in bridalwear. Although the 1960s ushered in more daring styles such as the minidress, for weddings a degree of conservatism still reigned—particularly in the early years of the decade. Indeed, even by 1968, industry reports stated that the majority of 1.5 million first marriages were celebrated with traditional long dresses, made in white or ivory, worn with a train and veil. This dress carries on that neutral color scheme, retaining the fitted bodice and gathered skirt popular during the 1950s, but introducing some subtle changes in cut and decoration that provide a light, youthful feel to the gown.[15]

....

The boat or "bateau" neckline was typically cut wide, exposing all or most of the collarbone. It was especially in vogue from the 1950s onwards, when Audrey Hepburn popularized the style in her 1954 hit *Sabrina*.

A wide, slightly scooped neckline was a popular choice for brides wishing to later convert their gown into an evening or ball dress. An Australian fashion advice column advised one concerned bride-to-be in 1964 that "it is perfectly correct to have a ... décolleté neckline" that would also fit into fashionable evening styles after the wedding.[17]

Later, in 1957, Hepburn wore a Givenchy dress with similar neckline in the film *Funny Face* with Fred Astaire (above).

The use of darts, rather than softer princess seams, to shape the bodice recalls the sharper, more pointed bust silhouette of the previous decade.

Rather than the stiff petticoats and skirt supports of 1950s bridal gowns, this example uses side gathers to add volume.

Guipure lace flowers adorn the cuffs and center front of the dress. Guipure is made of a continuous bobbin lace without a mesh backing, and presented a suitable choice for popular applique ornamentation. This style of decoration continued to be popular into the end of the decade and the early 1970s, when "flower power" and an interest in natural motifs had become both fashionable and political. Brides could purchase their own lace trimmings to apply to a plainer dress; in Australia in 1966 applique guipure "which is most effective as a trim" was available from haberdashers for $21–$53 AUD a yard.[16]

The lustrous surface of silk dupioni provides additional textural interest to a simple design. Dupioni, along with lace, taffeta, brocade, satin, and bombazine were suggested by one bridal authority as "popular autumn bridal fabrics" in 1965.[18] On the bride's wedding day, August 15, 1964, the high in Melbourne was 22c and the low was 10c. This relatively cool range would have made silk an appropriate choice.[19]

Lace wedding dress,

mid-1960s, probably England, Fashion Museum Riga, Latvia

This mid-decade wedding dress is a good example of the popular blending of traditional and new. Its floor length, all-over lace and long sleeves maintain bridal consistency, while the empire line, bow ornamentation and short, voluminous veil speaks to fresh, youthful interpretations of what it meant to be a bride.

The artificial silk flowers seen on the veil were originally made as a corsage, intended to be worn around the wrist. The veil itself is a short, "bouffant" style popular in the early to middle years of the decade. These were sometimes attached to pillbox-style headdresses or ornamented with a large bow in the center.

High, rounded necklines were fashionable for both day and evening/occasion wear.

The empire line was introduced to bridal wear in the late 1950s and would become a staple of 1960s weddings from the middle of the decade onwards. As early as 1960, descriptions exist of dresses that were not cut with a true empire line, but employed other techniques to create that effect, including "a band of satin across the bodice."[20] Along with the high waistline came a slim, columnar skirt, and many dresses sported either this or a modest A-line.

Simple embellishments, such as this single bow, were often all that adorned the back of a dress.

This flat silk bow also serves to highlight the deep inverted pleat at the center of the train, which adds volume and drama as the wearer moves. This "Watteau" train, loosely based on its eighteenth-century predecessor, would often be made as a removeable accessory.

Evening gowns were worn widely during the 1960s, and the practice of re-using a bridal gown for that purpose continued.[22]

The train is attached at the waist, echoing a design described in one 1966 fashion column as a "very full scalloped-edged chapel train of lace [set into] the high waistline."[21] Although the 1960s empire line revival was far from a copy of its early nineteenth-century counterpart, details from the era did sometimes carry over. Here, scalloped edging provides the chief ornamentation and is arranged in a similar way to the 1819 example shown to the right. It was also a feature on the gown of Queen Adelaide of Great Britain when she married William IV in 1818. While later Regency garments were interspersed with tucking and piping and puffs, though, the 1960s iteration relies on a simple, uncomplicated aesthetic. Though mass-produced, such inspiration harks back to the "natural" pre-industrial age of textiles which would go on to influence late 1960s and 1970s design.

Fashion plate from 1819, showing similar scalloped edging.

180 How to Read a Wedding Dress

Wedding outfit worn by Pattie Boyd for her marriage to George Harrison,

1966, UK, photo by PA Images via Getty Images

◆

On Friday January 21, 1966, George Harrison married model and actress Pattie Boyd, whom he met two years previously on the set of the Beatles' first film A Hard Day's Night. "It was not the wedding I had dreamt of," Boyd later remembered. "I had always thought I'd have a big white wedding, as all little girls do."[23] The band's manager, Brian Epstein, suggested a secret registry office wedding to ensure as little press attention as possible, although, as Boyd recalled, "I naively thought the press wouldn't find out we were getting married. [But] we came out into the street to find dozens of press photographers lined up outside." Instead of a traditional white dress, Boyd chose a pink-red shot-silk dress by designer queen Mary Quant (for whom she had modelled) and a red fox-fur coat (also by Quant), a gift from the groom. Mary Quant, Boyd comments, was the only person the bride was allowed to tell about her impending wedding.[24]

The decade's fur fantasies, described by Jonathan Faiers as the reflection of a "native, skin-wearing, primeval aesthetic" seen in 1960s cinema is also embodied in the black Mongolian lamb coat worn by Harrison.[25]

Boyd's silk minidress was patterned with deep pink and red stripes. The popularity of stripes was partly inspired by the Op Art movement, leading into broader youthful assertions of boldness and independence, and here represented the epitome of "mod" style. "I loved that dark red color for winter," says Boyd. "Combined with the Mary Quant fox fur I thought it looked quite cool."[26] The year before, one fashion column agreed with the chosen color scheme, recommending pink and red together for bridesmaids: "Pink combined with dark red would look wonderful for a winter wedding."[27]

Boyd paired her coat and dress with "creamy stockings and pointy red shoes."[29] "In [fashion]," said one American newspaper in May 1966, "[are] pointy slip-ons or booties, even if you have to cut off your little toes to get into them."[30]

Because, Boyd recalls, she never had a clear or specific "white wedding dress dream," options were relatively unlimited and allowed for a dress based solely on what felt right at the time. Nevertheless, although the result was not a traditional wedding gown, she records that she did not wear it again after the event.[28]

So ingrained did the minidress become, that by the end of the decade it was readily suggested as a bridal option. "[It is] quite correct", wrote the *Australian Women Weekly*'s Betty Keep in 1968. "Numbers of modern brides wear a short skirted wedding dress and a to-the-floor-length tulle wedding veil."[31] The accessory of the bridal veil was frequently mentioned in fashion columns as a must alongside the most outré of gown choices. The lack of a veil here suggests the difference in expectation, at least in England, of appropriate wear for a registry office versus a church wedding.

Actress Raquel Welch wore a bridal mini dress in 1967 "a full nine inches above her knees."[32]

The bride's fox fur coat was chosen primarily for practical reasons in a cold British January. However, winter weddings were popular during the decade, and helped to promote a medieval aesthetic through fur, which was a favored garment trimming and lining for the elite in the fifteenth and sixteenth centuries.[33] The huge success of David Lean's *Doctor Zhivago* in 1965 also contributed to a winter aesthetic, conjuring romantic images of passionate sleigh rides through the snow, and, as one American newspaper put it in 1967, "an era of elegance that is really not lost but is here with us again"—in fashion at least.[34]

Studio portrait of D'Anna Thornton Wakefield in a wedding dress,

1967, Tallahassee, Florida, State Library and Archives of Florida

This youthful dress was chosen by D'Anna Thornton Wakefield for her wedding, and she is posing here for a formal bridal photograph to show off her gown and veil. With its empire waist and cascade of daisies, this dress epitomizes late 1960s optimism and activism.

This veil is in a mantilla style, derived from Spanish Catholic veils worn by women during a Mass. They were traditionally circular with a lace trim around the edge, a design that is reflected here, but with the addition of a floor-length train. Here, the lack of a popular headpiece or pillbox hat allows a full view of scattered lace daisies across the bride's hair.

This guipure-encrusted bodice highlights the placement of the waist, emphasizing a move away from the "traditional" natural waistlines and wide, A-line skirts that had dominated for so long. In March 1967, a British fashion column described "fashions for the Easter bride" as comprising "the latest in fashion dictates—full length dress and coat ensembles, empire-line [and] straight cut dresses."[35]

This slim, tubular skirt is gently gathered at the waistline, which—combined with its bishop sleeves and a high, round neckline—creates a softness and ease of wearing that is reminiscent of popular "babydoll" styles.

Plain white pumps were a classic shoe choice. As in the twenty-first century, some stores during the 1960s offered a shoe dying service, allowing brides to have their white "Shantung, peau de soie, smooth and brocade satin" shoes dyed to a more practical and long-lasting color after the wedding. This service was also available for bridesmaids, so that their pumps would exactly match the shade of their dresses.[36]

The daisy is a potent, instantly recognizable symbol of late 1960s and early 1970s "Flower Power." Mary Quant also trademarked the bloom as her official symbol in 1966, linking it to mod fashion as well as the hippie subculture. Daisies were mentioned constantly in newspaper descriptions of weddings and wedding dresses, and, in 1967, one Australian bride went to great lengths to show her love of the emblem. Her hand-crocheted train, composed of 4500 daisies, was 10 ft long and took 750 hours to complete. Further daisies made an appearance on her headdress, bouquet, and on the couple's wedding cake. Other brides chose to incorporate the flower only into their bouquet or as is also seen here, as a part of their veil.[37]

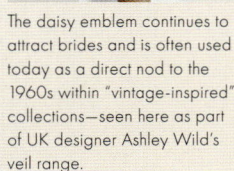

The daisy emblem continues to attract brides and is often used today as a direct nod to the 1960s within "vintage-inspired" collections—seen here as part of UK designer Ashley Wild's veil range.

Thai silk embroidered wedding dress,

1968, Auckland, New Zealand Fashion Museum

This striking dark teal mini dress was worn by Enid Eiriksson at her registry office wedding in Christchurch. She commissioned designer Annie Bonza to make the dress, which was constructed from a vibrant blue Thai silk and incorporates varied cultural references. The 1950s and 60s were a heyday for the Thai silk industry; the well-known Thai Silk Company having representatives in over 35 countries. From early in the decade, fashion pages were raving about this fabric's "look of luxury at within-reach prices"[38] which made it perfect for a young, fashion-conscious bride.

This standing, so-called "mandarin" collar was highly fashionable from the mid-1960s onwards, partly inspired by the jackets of Indian Prime Minister Jawaharlal Nehru. For brides wearing a more traditional white dress, an option was to feature a mandarin collar atop a sheer or lace yoke, often accented with a row of pearls, beads, or lace in a different design.

The sleeves are flared from the elbow down and the extra fabric caught at a point, creating the appearance of a split opening and separate sleeve beneath.

The bride wore a white fedora-style hat with a wide silk ribbon band. This was an unconventional choice, but fedoras were fashionable in general at the close of the decade. Due to a "resurgence in hat interest" from c.1967 onwards, American hat makers introduced a greater variety of women's sizes to cater to demand.[39]

The following year, Yoko Ono would popularize this bridal look when she married John Lennon in a floppy white sun hat. The wearing of a hat was often described as a bride "going mod" ("modern"), moving away from traditional features like veils, floor-length skirts, trains, and bouquets.

Maori Designs II, Horatio Robley, 1860s, Hawkes Bay Art Gallery & Museum

This ornate braid decoration was part of Annie Bonza's signature style. She was drawn to the technique through witnessing the creation of cornelli embroidery at an early design job. However, "I could never get the hang of doing cornelli," Bonza remembers, "so I substituted with braid."[40] Her application of braid was in many instances influenced by Austrian design, but here it has strong leanings to South Asian and specifically Indian clothing, which was a fixture of late 1960s fashion. A further influence, that of Māori design, can also be seen in the intricate spiraled and looped sections.

White was still far and away the most popular bridal shade, but if other colors were chosen, the aim was always to use the most fashionable. New Zealand fashion columns from 1966 to 1968 mention the popularity of "the newest teal shades,"[41] "fashionable aqua,"[42] and "lovely fashionable colours of navy, teal, green, turquoise or beige."[43]

Tones of teal, aqua blue, and turquoise were also popular for bridesmaids and mother-of-the-bride and groom. In one Australian instance, this included the groom too: "A young fashion photographer ... wore a white linen suit ... with an aqua shirt and pocket handkerchief [for his "something blue"]. His bride ... wore an aqua veil and a matching velvet waistband and rose ... and aqua shoes."[44]

Chapter 10: 1960–1979

Wedding dress,

1969, Brisbane, Queensland Museum

This ensemble was created for bride Clare Dempsey by the designer Gwen Gillam, "Brisbane's number one dressmaker."[45] It was worn at a July wedding ceremony, providing warmth against a chilly Australian winter. That same year, high fashion made a hooded statement in the form of Cristóbal Belanciaga's "monastic" wedding ensemble. This trapezoidal robe, topped with a conical hood in place of a veil, cut a sleek, architectural, and at the same time ghostly figure. It was not what was expected from bridal fashion, and it would be the designer's swansong.

Arctic fox fur trims the hood and matches the muff that the bride carried.

The dress is made from wool crepe. In 1965 Australian model Raelene Orr (following her work for the Wool Board) chose this fabric for herself and for her bridesmaids, partly due to her pessimism about the "Melbourne winter." Her entire trousseau was wool-based, with a going-away outfit comprising a wool crepe coat with "a luxurious Arctic fox collar, which can be removed for a plainer look."[47]

As seen in Pattie Boyd's wedding ensemble analysis, this use of fur was heavily influenced by hit film Doctor Zhivago (David Lean, 1965), a sweeping historical romance set in Russia during World War One and the Russian Civil War.
So impactful was the film that as late as 1971 it was still being referenced in fashion columns and wedding reports: "The bride ... wore a most attractive *Dr. Zhivago* style fur-lined maxi coat over a dress with fur-lined, round collar, cuffs and hem."[46]

Instead of a bouquet, brides sometimes wore muffs decorated with flowers or could take this idea a step further and carry a muff made entirely of flowers. A florist's manual from 1960 suggested using gardenias and lilies of the valley, which would be affixed to a ""heavy paper ... and white satin" frame.[48] Like many other style trends of the decade, this was a revival of a 1920s fashion accessory.

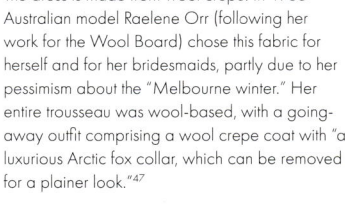

Another filmic influence was Joshua Logan's *Camelot* of 1967, which featured a fur-clad Vanessa Redgrave as Guinevere.

This is a kaftan (or *caftan*) style; a long, loose-fitting gown with ancient origins in Persia. Later popular in Morocco, kaftans were quickly adopted by hippies passing through North Africa in the late 1960s.[49] However, by the end of the decade it had taken on a more formal identity as eveningwear "made in some lush fabric, and worn after 5 p.m."[50] The style was greatly diversified when it came to weddings, with reports of brides choosing kaftans with guipure lace, high and turtleneck collars, pin tucks, crystal embroidery, and detachable trains.

Satin wedding dress,

c.1970, United Kingdom, Author's collection

This dress was made by Lillian Canter, a Liverpool-based bridal designer. Gowns from this establishment generally cost around £40, which equates to roughly $800 USD in 2022. "All brides are beautiful of course," read an advertisement from March 1971, "but Lillian Canter brides, like you, are very, very special."[51]

More conservative details such as this high collar are illustrative of the "granny" dress; a trend that incorporated historical "Victorian" designs and which first surfaced during the late 1960s. Throughout the 1970s, a dress was frequently described as "Victorian" when it featured a high neck, long sleeves, lace trim, and a train.

In the bridal world, the "granny" style coincided with a comforting link to traditionalism. A fashion advice column reader in 1971 remarked that she liked the look of a "cover-up wedding style,"[52] and in 1977 a British newspaper remarked more generally of "modest" bridal choices: "When a modern bride goes shopping for her wedding dress she doesn't want anything casual, anything gimmicky, anything at all trendy. It's reassuring how traditional this particular field of women's fashion stays."[53]

Similarly dressed brides in long, "heavy satin" with lace trim in 1969 and 1970 were recorded carrying "cascades" of flowers such as gardenias, hyacinths, ivy, and orchids. Their bridesmaids often dressed in olive green, ivory, yellow, and brown, carrying small bouquets with one type of flower.

The dress is trimmed with guipure lace appliques. These add definition to the waist and provide simple, yet effective elaboration.

A flat satin bow at center back frames the opening, leading to a mid-length train.

This dress displays a similar design but made in a cheaper crepe fabric. It evidences demand for the style to suit different prices and budgets. A dress like this, by "leading London designer" Emenson, would have cost anywhere between £15 and £45 in the early 1970s.[54]

Film tie-ins included costly replicas of this outfit, designed by Marjorie Cornelius for the franchise. Brides with smaller budgets could capitalize on this look by incorporating small amounts of flower-shaped guipure, as seen in the dress discussed here. *On Her Majesty's Secret Service* (1969) fueled a popularity for this type of lace after its female protagonist Tracy (Diana Rigg) wore an all-in-one pantsuit made entirely of guipure for her wedding to James Bond.

Bridal gown by Carven,

1973, France, Keystone Press/Alamy Stock Photo

◆

Carmen de Tomasso (1909–2015) founded her "Carven" fashion house in 1945. The designer drew great inspiration from global travel for her collections, and this led to her becoming one of the most successful young, female designers to license and sell their work overseas.[55] Regarding bridal wear, while her designs were often viewed as modern and fresh, Carven also took advantage of the decade's penchant for "Edwardian" style and incorporated it into her oeuvre. One such ensemble in 1971 was described as encompassing "coat and skirt and high-necked blouse [with] an Edwardian look, and the tailored design is softened by a feminine white fox fur hat and scarf."[56]

....

A contrasting yoke sits above a straight décolletage, terminating in a high oval-shaped neckline. The neck is edged in self-fabric, creating a simple effect that contrasts with the popularity for lace finishing.

This "monastic" headpiece takes the place of a traditional veil, and is strongly influenced by Cristóbal Balenciaga's conical headdress designed alongside his iconic, single-seamed bridal gown in 1967. Its use of tulle, however, provides a softer and more traditionally "bridal" alternative to Balenciaga's solid silk-satin. Brides could make their own versions at home with patterns by Vogue, which included a design for a "monastic" dress with long, straight skirt, slightly flared sleeves, and floor-length knotted girdle.

These sleeves flare from the elbow into circular bell cuffs, shaped with the same rounded edge as the skirt hem to create an abstracted floral design.

This distinctive skirt is made with organ or "projected" pleats, which are constructed by lifting folds from the fabric surface and rolling them into the desired shape. They bear some similarity to cartridge pleats but are generally much wider, approximately 4-5 inches. This results in bold, cylindrical gathers that stand proud, enhanced by scalloped edges on each section to give a petal-like appearance.

The dress is made from silk gabardine, a sturdy, tightly woven ribbed fabric. It is a far cry from the most popular soft and sheer bridal fabrics of the decade, but is necessary in order to achieve the strong, solid silhouette seen here. In the early 1970s it was also a popular fabric for tailored "going away" outfits, with yellow, pink, and light blue as favored hues.

Piping on hem and cuffs solidifies the curved outline. Brides sometimes chose colored piping to further highlight the contours of the dress, for example at one Australian wedding in 1979, the dress was "chiffon piped in blue ribbon."[57] Likewise, bridesmaids' dresses could be piped at the seams and hem in a different color to the body of the garment, i.e., "lemon with brown piping" (1979)[58] and "multicoloured ... with mauve piping" (1973).[59] Frequent mentions of this trimming call attention to its prevalence and popularity in the bridal world.

Polyester wedding dress,

1973, Fashion Archives and Museum, Shippensburg University, Pennsylvania

Nicole Klocek wore this gown at her wedding in 1973. Its design takes inspiration from the long, slinky dresses of the 1930s, which were extremely popular and effective on the dance floor during this "disco" era. Purely by virtue of having an empire waist, similar dresses were also labelled as "Regency" and, stemming from this inspiration, Grecian.

The 1940s was a key influence for 1970s bridal designers. A particularly close—and very poignant—similarity can be seen in this 1945 bridal gown made for a Holocaust survivor at a displaced persons camp. The dress was worn by other brides, too, and demonstrates the lengths people will go to obtain such a garment in the most difficult of circumstances. So strong was the 1940s' influence that, when designs for Yves Saint Laurent's *Libération* collection were presented in 1971, middle-aged audience members found themselves transported back to their wartime years, and many did not appreciate the reminder.[60]

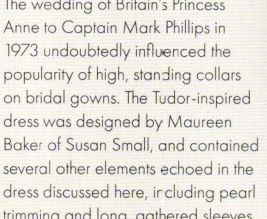

The wedding of Britain's Princess Anne to Captain Mark Phillips in 1973 undoubtedly influenced the popularity of high, standing collars on bridal gowns. The Tudor-inspired dress was designed by Maureen Baker of Susan Small, and contained several other elements echoed in the dress discussed here, including pearl trimming and long, gathered sleeves.

Gathering at neckline and bust helps to highlight the waistline.

This waistband forms an empire line, with the top seam cut in an inverted "V." It is trimmed with rows of white pearl plastic braid, on which larger oval and circular plastic pearls are edged with tiny clear ones.

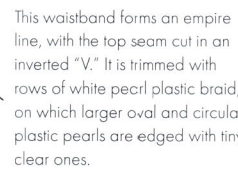

Waistband detail

Bishop sleeves, often described at the time as "Victorian sleeves," are gathered into broad cuffs.

In 1970, *It's Your Wedding* guide recommended that the length of a bride's train should be dictated by "the type of veil she wears ... the size of the church or other place of worship where she is going to be married."[61]

Consequently, a small chapel necessitated a chapel-length train, as seen here.

By mid-1972, an increasing "omission of veils and long trains so that all gowns are suitable for bride or bridesmaid" was reported.[62]

Wedding dress by Guy Laroche,

mid-late 1970s, Fashion Museum Riga, Latvia

◆

French-born Guy Laroche (1923–1989) set up his own couture house in 1957. Known for his emphasis on practicality as well as haute couture, he was credited with the reintroduction of a palette of bold, bright colors in the 1950s, and for his acclaimed perfume ranges from the 1960s onwards. Laroche's bridal wear was eclectic, ranging from, in 1972, "a sort of souffle of white and shocking pink,"[63] as one reporter described it, to mini dresses, to Victoriana-inspired, waterfall bustle gowns in the 1990s. This diversity is represented in the dress shown here, with its mix of tradition and forward-thinking couture.

....

This floral spray is styled to resemble begonias or roses, the latter being a favorite emblem in Laroche's pieces.

Deep necklines were a feature of Laroche's work, though this plunging "V" vies for attention with the sculptural, imposing trim that extends vertically down the front and back of the bodice. In lieu of sleeves, this broad, double layered "collar" paves the way for the larger-than-life gigot styles and padded shoulders of the following decade.

The 1960s saw a growing popularity for bridal dresses without sleeves, though for religious ceremonies bare arms were still frowned upon by some. By the early 1980s, long puffed sleeves were the epitome of bridal style, and late 1970s trends were heading this way. Brides who chose sleeveless dresses more often than not teamed them with a coat (sometimes with sheer lace sleeves), cape, or shawl.

Double layered "collar" detail.

The collar clearly mirrors the current fashion for deep frills around the neckline that were often worn off-the-shoulder. The style aligns with a prominent ruffled collar seen in Laroche's own late 1970s collections, particularly this shirt and blouse from his Autumn/Winter 1977–78 catwalk show.

The more traditional, floor-length, floral lace body of this dress is somewhat at odds with its striking collar. However, lace styles were popular during the 1970s (aligning with the vintage "granny" trend) and is here visually broken by a solid band at the hem. Other designers, including Jessica McClintock (of Gunne Sax) chose to trim wedding gowns lavishly with lace and leave the body plain, but in either case lace was often a dominant feature. McClintock even combined it with denim in her non-bridal ranges.[64]

Cotton printed wedding dress,

1977, England, Private collection

◆

This dress was purchased from Penny Plain, a small shop in Newcastle, UK, that the owner described as "not mod or trendy ... it is more than that. What we have tried to do is to provide the kind of merchandise that formerly we and our friends had to go to London to get."[65] The shop stocked homewares by Elizabeth David as well as "handwoven clothes" and garments sourced from cottage industries across the country.[66] This natural, homemade approach perfectly suited the suburban garden wedding of bride, Julia Hogg, and groom Christopher Edwards on September 17, 1977.

....

"It may have seemed strange to wear brown ... but this was the 'brown decade,'" the bride remembers. Her dress, however, presents a broad color spectrum, with four different printed cottons making up the body, sleeves, and panel inserts. The fabric is sprigged with floral and geometric shapes in blue, red, green, and orange. Such broad pattern combinations, including the use of differing panels of fabric to make up a single garment, were seen throughout the 1970s, with designers like Bill Gibb especially keen to capitalize on the trend.

This plastron was part of a nineteenth-century Tunisian tunic and illustrates a similar shape and placement.

The fabric that makes up this central bodice panel is also used to insert a flare into the sleeves. Traditional "ethnic, natural, or exotic" components were a huge part of European and American 1970s fashion, and aspects of that influence can be seen in this panel.[67]

The high waist and square neckline are seen in this Nativity by the workshop of Sienese artist Francesco di Giorgio Martini, c.1470.

The dress was worn with a cream crochet, fringed shawl, and drawstring cap. Shawls in general were fashionable from mid-decade onwards, closely aligned with the era's well-known "granny" style. Described as "luxurious" and "graceful" in fashion columns, magazines strongly encouraged brides to make their own with extensive instructions and patterns available.

Daniel Milford-Cottam describes 1970s design as being full of "unabashed historicism,"[68] and there are strong historical influences at play here. Newspaper descriptions of weddings frequently described sleeves flared from the elbow as "renaissance," and other elements also point to a filtered "Medieval" or, in particular, Italian Renaissance inspiration.

There is no train, which was not uncommon for many brides during the decade. Some bridal magazines and fashion columns injected a note of realism, recommending that "circumstances may alter [...] preconceived notions. The girl who pictured herself gliding down the aisle ... [with] a lengthy train may settle [with a dress that] will do little more than hint at a train."[69]

Polyester wedding dress, 1973. (detail) Fashion Archives and Museum, Shippensburg University

Lace wedding dress, 1960s, Fashion Museum Riga (front view).

Chapter 11
1980–1999

Although the contemporary era stresses that "anything goes" regarding bridal fashion, for many, a strong level of expectation (and comfort) in habit remains. This was especially true in the 1980s, in which tradition was deemed chic in the face of a rapidly changing political, social, and cultural landscape.[1] This was demonstrated strongly through the feminization of bridal fashion, hugely fueled by the "fairy tale" wedding of Charles and Diana in 1981. At the same time, a focus on the "executive bride" recognized that decisions around the wedding were increasingly being paid for—not just made—by bride as well as groom. "Busy, career-minded, and independent, the executive bride has a lot more on her mind than choosing doilies and flowers," *The Executive Bride: A Ten-week Wedding Planner* declared in 1985.[2] The 1980s subsequently witnessed an explosion of the wedding industry, aptly described in 2017 as "romanticized consumption."[3] The seriousness of this financial outlay was demonstrated through the most popular way of shopping for a dress: rather than visit a department store, brides-to-be could take advantage of specialized shops staffed by professional bridal consultants. They were able to choose a wedding dress that fit within their budget, but it was becoming more generally accepted that weddings should be scaled up, not down. Bridal magazines could be purchased alongside additional guides and booklets that aided brides in identifying "silhouettes, sleeves, necklines … A big help when you shop around for your wedding gown."[4]

Amid all this there still existed a strong market for the home dressmaker bride; manuals such as *Sew a Beautiful Wedding* (1980) reaching out to a continuing generation of women who sewed most of their own clothing. Even here, however, the authors acknowledged that the bridal industry could serve a valuable purpose for those creating their own gown. "Start trying on ready-made dresses," they advised, "to determine the most flattering style and color."[5] Although a large factor of this was cost (sewing a dress at home could save a bride up to 80 percent in the early 1980s),[6] a wish for authenticity was also paramount, and a desire to veer away from the "cookie cutter" off-the-rack styles. By this point bridal fashion was therefore very much in its own sphere; largely unrelated to clothes that a woman would wear on any other day.

The emergence of the goth subculture in the early 1980s, born from post-punk gothic rock, presented a somber bridal mood amid frilly white excess. This look became especially connected with Japanese street fashion and the "Gothic Lolita" (a variant of this aesthetic is seen in a "Sweet Lolita" wedding dress in the following chapter). In the early days of this counterculture, wedding dresses themselves formed an important part of the look, whether worn for that purpose or not. The "wedding dress look" featured ribbons, lace, and gloves, and was strongly influenced by bands including Christian Death, Strawberry Switchblade and The Bags. This was viewed by some goth afficionados as a "kind of virgin-whore aesthetic," a dichotomy that harks back to the Gothic representation of women in English literature.[7] This demonstrates the multilayered, postpunk elements of the scene that, initially, did not necessarily involve the wearing of purely black clothing and makeup.

The most fashionable "meringue" dresses had a relatively short shelf-life, however, with a high-profile denouement in *Four Weddings and a Funeral* (1994), in which Charles (Hugh Grant) compliments Carrie (Andie McDowell) at her wedding: "You look beautiful. Not a meringue in sight."[8] This ushered in the minimalist phase; a mid-1990s turning point in which wedding dresses became sleek and, thanks to designers like Vera Wang, "hip again."[9] The high-profile wedding of John F. Kennedy Jr. and Carolyn Bessette in 1996 also contributed to this phase, with the bride's stunningly simple slip dress marking a major turning point in bridal fashion. As fashion journalist Zanna Roberts Rassi put it, the dress "was the epitome of 90s minimalism. [It broke] all bridal rules in the most elegant way possible . . . a bold move in an era of froufrou."[10] This gown was, naturally, something of an outlier, though it was certainly reflected widely in more subtle ways.

RIGHT
Clean lines and soft color are seen in this 1996 ensemble.

The aforementioned "hipness" instigated by Wang included the introduction of color to bridal couture. Although, she stated, white "is hopeful and it's positive and clean, and most women look incredible in [it]," the designer's main aim was to offer options. She created whole lines in which each dress was a soft shade of blue, pink, or green, and others that featured white dresses with colored trim.[11] She was also a champion for the strapless dress, which since the 1950s had been widely decried as a respectable bridal cut.[12] Nevertheless, Vera Wang gowns were not within reach of every bride and, in America, chains like David's Bridal provided heavily discounted, synthetic gowns from 1990 onwards. This saw the beginning of large-scale off-the-rack bridal purchases, a gamechanger for the industry. While brides on a budget were still encouraged to buy off-the-rack from department stores, the stock levels and specialism of a bridal store proved far more alluring.

The westernized wedding dress continued to see adoption in all corners of the world, including within marginalized and diaspora groups. A particularly well-documented example from the late 1980s–1990s concerns Muslim women in the Hui Quarter in Xi'an, northwestern China. Brides here often wore white gowns (known as *hunsha*) for their weddings mainly because bridal fashion is not necessarily codified as religious. Within the complex history of Islam in China, wedding dresses allow, as Yang Yang explains, "the expression of individuals' faith in Islam to appear to be apolitical"[13] thereby using an ideological association with the West to resist negative government classification. It also, by the mid-1990s, allowed Hui women to dress "immodestly" for their weddings, backed up by female elders and marking a difference in male and female religiosity within their communities.[14]

In 1997, Ofra Goldstein-Gidoni described the West that was imagined by the Japanese wedding industry as a "Disney World West," part of the "Cinderella dream" that was first widely marketed to young couples in the 1980s and 1990s.[15] The nuptials of Charles and Diana are often cited as the catalyst of desire for a white (read Christian) Western wedding—despite only 1 percent of the Japanese population identifying as Christian. Nonetheless, commercial packages became available that offered a hotel lobby or chapel-style venue, cake, dress, and all the accoutrements necessary to stage a ceremony that, paradoxically, represented the country's gradual adoption of secular values. As Jeremy Lefebvre puts it, "the Christian wedding ceremonies of contemporary Japan are frequently discussed as unequivocally secular, mere scenery, or evidence of the Japanese obsession with fashion and conspicuous consumption."[16] By the mid-1990s, some brides interviewed at their "Western" weddings described feeling lighter and "more themselves" in their Western bridal gown than their traditional *uchikake* kimono, largely because they were by now so used to wearing *yōfuku* (Western clothes) on an everyday basis.[17]

Goldstein-Gidoni's reference to Disney World in relation to weddings is apt, in Japan or anywhere else, during this period. In 1991, Disney World began offering a wedding "service"

which, in response to requests from fans, took place in sight of Cinderella's Castle at the park in Orlando, Florida. Four years later, an exclusive wedding pavilion was established on the shores of man-made Seven Seas Lagoon, also part of a package that included ceremony, reception, and honeymoon in one "fairy tale" location. Disney World brides could either emulate a Disney princess (the late 1980s and early 1990s were, after all, widely regarded as the company's "Renaissance" with such titles as *The Little Mermaid*, *Beauty and the Beast*, and *Aladdin*) or select their own princess-style gown to fit the surroundings. This popularity has only increased, with the Disney Company releasing a range of bridal gowns in 2007 inspired by the characters of Ariel, Cinderella, and Snow White. These were originally produced by Alfred Angelo and continue to be manufactured by Allure featuring the inspiration of a wide array of heroines.[18]

At the other end of the spectrum of 1990s fashion is grunge, emanating from a genre of rock music that emerged in late 1980s Seattle. This label was given to various "alternative" acts and extended to clothing, incorporating Dr. Martens boots, checked flannel shirts, torn jeans, and oversized sweaters. Although this was a key look of the decade, it did not routinely make its way into bridal wear, since—being largely casual—it was difficult to integrate successfully. Rather, it has emerged in the twenty-first century as a nostalgic throwback to another time, adopted by brides wanting an unconventional appearance. "Glamorous Grunge," "Grungy Twist" and "Grunge Meets Disney" are three categories displayed on the website "Rock N Roll Bride—the ultimate guide for alternative brides."[19] These include tulle dresses worn with punky, studded leather jackets, combat boots, dyed pink hair, and checked flannel or tartan sashes.

Wedding dress,

1981, Brisbane, Queensland Museum

◆

This silk organza dress was designed by Brisbane-based Sue Spork (founder of Ceams Designs) for bride Felicity Harslett. Her wedding to Rowan Carr took place in the rural town of Stanthorpe, Queensland, on August 15, 1981. The dress was a finalist in the inaugural Retail Association Queensland Fashion Design Awards and exemplifies some prominent bridal trends of the previous and new decade. At the same time its ballerina length skirt and cream-colored, hand-appliqued silk flowers give the dress a practical adaptability.

The pie crust collar, popularized by Princess Diana, was a small standing band edged with an even ruffle. Here, a silk band in the same color as the applique and buttons creates synthesis with the whole design.

A row of covered buttons terminates in a small, narrow white bow. This is far more restrained than the trend for oversized bows that would follow Diana's wedding in July 1981.

The high neckline, long, puffy sleeves, and ruffles recall the hugely popular "prairie dress" style, which was a feature of 1970s dress and became globally recognized through British brand Laura Ashley. The trend was extended into the 1980s with the continuing success of *Little House on the Prairie*, an NBC TV adaptation of the books by Laura Ingalls Wilder. In Australia, where this dress was made and worn, the look was often referred to as "Edwardian," and the word was used very liberally to describe a wide range of floaty, "sedate" styles.[20]

These hand-appliqued silk flowers form shapes reminiscent of both ginkgo and poppies, in a soft peach shade. Along with "apricot and bone," this was a fashionable color for occasion wear in 1981 Australia.[22]

The success of the 1974 film *Picnic at Hanging Rock* also helped to solidify the fashion in Australia, and towards the end of the decade the aesthetic could still be seen in bridalwear. Designer Hilde Heim commented in 1987 that her "Victorian or Edwardian" designs were individual and special due to their fine attention to detail, comprising "pintucking, rouching and draping."[21]

A below-knee length hem was described variously as ballerina, tea-length, street-length or, in some fashion columns, "restaurant length," which was deemed appropriate for an informal wedding in 1981.[23] The length remained a popular alternative to the long, voluminous skirts that embodied the "more is more" bridal aesthetic of the decade.

198 How to Read a Wedding Dress

Wedding dress,

c.1980s, Brisbane, Western Australian Academy of Performing Arts, Perth

When Lady Diana Spencer married Charles, Prince of Wales in 1981, her dress—designed by David and Elizabeth Emmanuel—became the most copied bridal design in history. As David Emmanuel commented of Diana's dress, it was "very pretty and slightly old-fashioned"—[24] and the same aesthetic can be seen in this Australian dress. However, although the similarities are clear, they do not overwhelm an otherwise unique design. It was made by Deon's Bridal, a leading Brisbane wedding dress manufacturer. It is made from synthetic organza with an inbuilt net petticoat, acetate lining and synthetic lace.

Curator Anthea Jarvis reflected in 1983 that "a series of romantic influences [set] the popular style of today [which is a] pseudo-Edwardian image, with lace-encrusted bodice, long full sleeves and a flowing skirt."[25] All these aspects can be seen in this wedding dress. Alongside the prominently childish early-twentieth-century influences discussed here, there is certainly an adult Edwardian aesthetic derived from lacy "lingerie" turn-of-the-century dresses.

Australian designer Anthea Crawford commented in 1982 that: "Girls are girls again in soft sheer fabrics, frills, scallops, waists, and puffed sleeves."[27] Some of the design elements in this dress quite literally mimic the clothing of young girls, most pertinently in these shoulders resemblance to a pinafore. The influence of artists like Kate Greenaway and Beatrix Potter, who had so inspired designer Laura Ashley the previous decade, now took a central place in bridal wear.

This open work synthetic lace panel reveals the outline of a bodice with sweetheart neckline beneath, which provides shape and structure.

The same floral motif from the lace is picked up in these individual skirt appliques.

Synthetic organza provided the desired sheen at a lower cost. Not only that, it was also highly durable and praised by the likes of Queensland Ballet designer Desmond Heeley in 1986. He described synthetic organza as giving an illusion of delicacy: "I love genuine silk organza [but] technology's been very good."[26]

Puffed, frilled sleeves have several historical precedents, including (especially obvious on Diana's design) eighteenth-century frilled *engageantes* cuffs. Additionally, mid-1890s evening and wedding dresses come into play, with similar volume and a gathered cuff seen on this 1894 fashion plate (Metropolitan Museum of Art).

Satin wedding dress,

c.1989–1990, USA, Author's collection

◆

This late 1980s gown carries an "ILGWU" label—the International Ladies' Garment Workers' Union, which during the 1900s was one of the largest labor unions in the United States. A dress with this affiliation represented equality and solidarity with working women, and no compromise on quality: as ILGWU workers Carmen Natalio and Nellie Miranda expressed in 1991, "no gown will leave [the factory] until it's passed muster—no little threads hanging, no spots, no uneven hems or marks." They recognized that "this is the dress a bride has dreamed about all her life. She has put more than just money and emotion into it—she's put her hopes in too. So it has to be perfect."[28]

The ornate traditionalism of the 1980s wedding is certainly seen in this design, with its pearl-studded appliqué, embroidered net, and substantial train. However, the presence of a sculptural peplum reminds us of the conflict professional women faced. "Even if you find it hard to picture yourself," *Executive Bride* told readers in 1985, "a hard-driving professional woman, in something as traditional, as corny, as, yes, romantic as a wedding, you know you want one."[29] "Executive" women were no stranger to the ubiquitous power suit, which often featured a peplum around the waist. It enhanced a woman's curves but also added a masculine feel by equaling the width of strong, padded shoulders. Earlier in the decade bridal suits were often made with "a short peplum jacket and maybe some lace ... some bridesmaids were confused about whether they were attending a wedding [or] job interview."[30]

However, by the date of this late 1980s example, the career vibe was fading, and the peplum emphasized the gown's femininity, eschewing the earlier trend for oversized details and accessories. By the close of 1986, an anti-conservative look was being described as: "featuring lace, applique and beading in silks, satins, taffetas."[31] Peplums were also a fashionable feature of the late 1940s, and there are many reports of 1980s brides wearing their mother's dresses. Some small dressmaking enterprises also offered services including the creation of gowns "from old ... photographs ... and girls have brought us lace from their mother's wedding dress to make their own out of."[32]

"Dresses with plunging necklines look best with long-flowing hairstyles," advised award-winning Australian hairdresser Richard Fielder in 1989, "while high-necked gowns look best with the hair up"[33] In an era where the choice of neckline was purely the bride's (except for strictly religious ceremonies), both low and high were equally fashionable, and the choice could be made based on a favorite hairstyle alone.

The bride wore this curled-brim hat with feathers and faux pearl trimming.

Chapel length trains were long enough for drama, yet short enough to be manageable. Nevertheless, despite the fact that bridal gowns were now not expected to be worn more than once, detachable trains were a popular option. Nevertheless, in a period when the bridal shop, and advice of bridal consultants, was becoming ever more mainstream, brides were advised to use this service to find custom solutions. "Don't let concern about dancing and maneuverability at the reception worry you when selecting your dress," advised *Modern Bride Guide to Your Wedding and Marriage* in 1987. "At your final fitting, ask your bridal consultant to show you how to bustle your train so the detail will be visible, but so you can also be comfortable."[34] This skirt also has an inbuilt ribbon loop which a bride could use to hold up her train while dancing.

Wedding dress designed by Riitta Immonen, Finland,
c.1990, The Finnish Heritage Agency

◆

Riitta Immonen (1918–2008) was a fashion designer, artist, and entrepreneur. She was the co-founder of Marimekko along with Armi Ratia and opened her first boutique in Helsinki in 1942. This elegant silk satin bridal gown reflects Immonen's aesthetic and that of Marimekko, embodying a restrained approach with as few seams and darts as possible.[35] However, simple, clean lines did not necessarily cost any less than the yards of froth and frills of the previous decade. One fashion journalist, writing in 1994 about the popularity of bridal "giveaways" and special offers, nevertheless conceded that "It sounds as though weddings '90s style are one big freebie. They're not. If wedding dresses and crystal tiaras cost $1000 a throw ... the cost of the entire event should match the price of a small island."[36]

This cascading corsage features lilies, a flower heartily recommended by Letitia Baldrige's 1990 etiquette guide: "[The bride should carry] an armful of calla lilies. This is the time for her to have the loveliest flowers in the world—her own fantasy fulfilled."[37]

This squared shoulder line, leading into straight, slim-fitting sleeves, represents the transition between 1980s width and the pared down, slender look of later 1990s minimalism. This gradual change is illustrated by the fact that by the turn of the decade, the pads were usually removeable rather than sewn-in.

This "Watteau" train, attached at the edge of each shoulder, falls dramatically to the floor. These were not seen much on bridal wear until the late 1980s; earlier in the decade, *Bride's* and *Modern Bride's* magazines only reported five mentions of the style between 1984 and 1988. Immonen is, therefore, somewhat ahead of the trends.[38]

By the late 1990s the style was often marketed as removeable, and in 1997 the *Bridal Gown Guide* recommended variants made from tulle, accented with bows or looped spaghetti streamers, or edged with cording to match waistline and waistline.[39]

This satin head covering presents a distinct substitute to the veil, described in a 1990 wedding planner as a turban: "A long scarf of fine linen, silk or other fabric draped or preconstructed in soft folds around the head; often decorated with jewels."[40]

Previously popular in the 1970s, a headscarf variant of the design can be seen in this 1974 portrait of Finnish bride Pipsa Kaihua. Twenty years later, at her high-profile wedding to René Angélil, Celine Dion covered her hair behind a crystal headpiece, presenting an alternative to the conventionally popular combination of bridal updo with slim headband tiara.

Pipsa Kaihua at her wedding to Vesa Pallasvesa, Helsinki, 1974. (Finnish Heritage Agency)

These satin cuffs create a subtle variation and are echoed in the turned up "hem cuff" at the bottom of the skirt.

Cut without a waist seam this dress presents a meticulous fit that is shaped by darts elsewhere on the garment. The designer acknowledged the necessary symbiosis or, as she expressed it, "the same spirituality of the designer and the cutter" which "is fundamentally important to the process."[41]

Wedding dress,

1992, Philadelphia, Author's collection

◆

The word "minimalism" is often associated with nineties fashion, but it did not immediately apply to wedding dresses. For at least the first half of the decade those puffs, frills, swags, and trim so synonymous with the eighties bride reigned supreme. At the same time, however, seeds of change can be seen in this gown. Despite its elaborate ornamentation, the silhouette of this gown is noticeably slimmer than its 1980s predecessors, and the midi-length skirt with dropped waistline rejects the requisite voluminous skirt.

....

This fascinator-style cap created a base for an elaborately arranged veil, which was caught up in a fashionable froth at the back of the head. "Your bridal veil is going to be your crowning glory," wrote one guide in 1990, "so make sure it enhances your face and complements your gown."[42]

Shimmering sequins catch the light to display a range of colors, picking up on cream, pink and white shades across the entire gown.

Two layers of folded net create "shoulder pads." The resulting shape is rounder and softer than the excessive volume of 1980s examples.

The sweetheart neckline was a mainstay of 1980s bridal fashion. As previously mentioned, this was a clear nod to 1940s and 50s trends, fitting with a 1990 declaration that "The mother's dress is making a comeback. Brides love the nostalgia of it."[43]

"The dropped waist ... and off the shoulder sleeves are in vogue," wrote *Cincinnati Magazine* in January 1990. "Ivory is now the dominant color, holding a slight edge over white."[44]

This curving lace trim features deep points, from which double rows of pearl beads are caught up in swags. Tiny buds of pale pink silk roses anchor each swag (incidentally, it was not until the late 1990s that bridal flowers in general became bright colored). Such details were often rendered in icing during the late 1980s and early 1990s, as the book *Bridal Bargains* described in 1990: "Today's wedding cakes feature delicate detailing that even copies the lace motif of the bride's dress."[45]

An etiquette guide to "new manners for the Nineties" recommended that a midi or "street-length" dress (i.e., just below the knee) should be worn for "a very informal daytime wedding, any length you desire" for a formal afternoon wedding, and strictly a "long evening gown" for any ceremony and reception being held after six o'clock at night.[46] Regardless, up to the late 1990s most brides still chose a long, light-colored dress with veil.

Hot pink wedding dress by Victor Costa, Dallas, Texas,

1992, UNT College of Visual Arts + Design

◆

This glittering dress was made by Victor Costa, a significant American designer who created French haute-couture style gowns for the US market. His exuberant, feminine designs aimed to, in his words, "translate [a bride's] personality ... Even if it is her second or third wedding, every bride wants a special look. Usually, it is more fashion-oriented—a mirror of the times." This quote is particularly pertinent to the story of this particular dress, which was worn for a fifth marriage on February 1, 1992.[47]

Lavish surface embellishment mirrors that seen on fashionable white bridal gowns of the era. Such opulence was broadly considered "youthful," a problematic consequence of an industry that did little to appeal to the older bride. The 1990s saw a rapid number of "upwardly mobile professional women" who were delaying marriage, many of them preferring understated, so-called "age appropriate" options that were hard to come by in traditional bridal salons.[48]

Net was not seen as an especially "bridal" outer fabric until the influence of Vera Wang in the early 1990s. Here it is used as an overlay and for volume, but some designers used net in a far more risqué way, including Israeli designer Tamar Mendelbrod in 1992: "The traditional flowing veil and long satin gloves are designed to complement the daring net bodice, which is decorated with strategically placed beads and sequins."[49]

Rhinestones and sequins are used to great effect in Costa's design, too—despite a consensus among many fashion writers that "Simple elegance reigns ... Rhinestones, baguettes and other jewel treatments are used sparingly as trim to light up the new classic lines."[50]

The round neckline and flat ribbons on the shoulder detailing recall those on the wedding dress of Sarah Ferguson, Duchess of York, in 1986. A bow sat at the back of Ferguson's waist, anchoring the train and providing a similar aesthetic to the flowers used here.

Sarah Ferguson's marriage to Prince Andrew, 1986.

67-year-old bride Doris Dixon certainly eschewed tradition with her choice, embracing Costa's declaration that every bride wants a "special look." The designer's "look" was heavily inspired by that of other prominent designers, earning him the nickname of "knockoff king." These were created with cheaper materials, but still encompassed the drama and daring of designs such as Christian Lacroix's bustled (known as the "pouf" or "bubble") cocktail dress, c. 1986. The influence can be clearly seen in Costa's low back and voluminous bustle edged with silk flowers. Its chic evening elegance made it perfectly suited to the bride's exclusive venue, Brook Hollow Golf Club in Dallas.

This Jean Patou by Christian Lacroix gown, c. 1986–1987, shows a similar bustle caught up with a spray of silk flowers

Wedding ensemble by Frans Hoogendoorn, The Hague,

1994, Kunstmuseum, The Hague

◆

Frans Hoogendoorn, based in The Hague, is a household name in the Netherlands. Famous for dressing some of the best-known women in Dutch society, his designs are imbued with a classic and chic elegance inspired by Parisian fashion. However, despite its many historical influences, his design subverts all traditional associations and offers instead a striking ensemble that blurs gender distinctions, combining influences from both masculine and feminine ideals to create a truly unique "wedding dress." The date of this piece, 1994, is significant, as this was the year that the phrase "metrosexual" was first acknowledged. This gradually prompted a more widespread acceptance that gender might not, after all, be a purely binary concept and this allowed designers to experiment more openly.[51]

This striking hat is reminiscent in shape of 1820s top hats, which could also be made from straw for wear in lighter summer months. Although traditionally a very male accessory, it is softened here by the addition of a floor-length chiffon veil tied around the brim in an elaborate bow. The shape and height of this arrangement recall contemporaneous 1980s and 1990s bridal veils.

Straw top hat, 1820s, Metropolitan Museum of Art

A bridal headdress with veil arrangement, c. 1980–90 (Library of Congress)

Frivolous, oversized bows are a trademark of the designer. They were used too by Vivienne Westwood in the 1990s, who also took inspiration from history—in her case, the 1890s and 1910s.[52]

This bejeweled brooch on the neckerchief is mimicked on the sleeve cuffs, creating an additional pop of "bling."

The skirt of the jacket becomes a long, luxuriant silk train. This is one of the most "traditionally" bridal aspects of the whole ensemble, and recalls the trend of bridal overskirts, open in front to reveal either a sheath or miniskirt. It also mirrors the highly contemporary "offbeat" fashion for bridal jumpsuits, worn with an overskirt to allow a peep at the trousers beneath.

This imposing, diaphanous neckwear has many historical influences based in both male and female dress, from the women's puffed fichu of the late eighteenth century to the tall, artfully arranged neckcloths of the Regency dandy.

Redingote (detail), 1790, Los Angeles Country Museum of Art

Very wide, continuous lapels broaden the shoulders and their exaggerated points are reminiscent of 1970s unisex tailoring. They also evoke more ancient associations with late eighteenth century redingotes, which were inspired by men's riding coats and featured exaggerated lapels.

The waistline has a narrow cutaway at the front, similar in style to late-eighteenth-century men's coats. The two broad, rectangular pocket flaps are also eighteenth century in shape. Their placing, right at the edges of the coat, is a much more modern feature, and they serve to emphasize the wearer's hips.

204 How to Read a Wedding Dress

Silk wedding dress by Vivienne Westwood,

1999, National Gallery of Victoria, Melbourne

Vivienne Westwood, known for so long as the edgy "Queen of Punk," did not make her first serious foray into the romantic world of bridal wear until 1993. This sensuous and elegant gown incorporates some of the designer's trademark looks, as well as illustrating some very typical late 1990s bridal trends.

In 1995 the fashion editor of *Brides* magazine, Rachel Leonard, commented that there was, at that time, more variety than ever in bridal clothing. "One direction for the upcoming spring and summer season," she said, "emphasizes the wedding dress as a costume. It could be the slinky body-hugging style, à la Hollywood of the 1930s, or an 18th-century ballgown with a voluminous skirt and a tightly fitted top known as a bustier."[53] Both these inspirations can be seen here, with the corset based on Westwood's own eighteenth-century interpretation. Her 1990 "Portrait" and 1994 "On Liberty" collections showcased a flat-fronted bustier that, in Westwood's own words, "lift[ed] the breasts up" to create a "really, really sexy" effect.[54]

This draped neckline creates a cowl-neck effect, one that was often seen at both the front and back of bridal bodices during the decade.

1990s wedding dresses were often made and worn as two pieces, or as a single dress with the appearance of a separate bodice and skirt. The former is seen here and mirrors a celebrity wedding from the same year: Spice Girl Victoria Adams to footballer David Beckham. Her Vera Wang gown, also in a soft gold, featured a corseted strapless bodice and billowing trained skirt.

The train can be caught up in a "bustle," which simply meant the use of ribbons that held the train away from the ground after the ceremony. It could be attractively arranged, sometimes at a jaunty angle at the top of the thigh.

Metallic and high-shine fabrics were fashionable in general towards the end of the 1990s and into the millennium, promoting a futuristic aesthetic. Here, gold continues this theme and recalls a historical alternative to white.

After Gaultier, Westwood was one of the first designers to widely promote the daring "underwear-as-outerwear" look. The bustier takes its inspiration from eighteenth-century stays, such as those shown here. It was during this period, too, that bridal magazines and designers started to openly reassure brides that it was "okay to look sexy on your wedding day."[55]

1770s stays, Italy, Metropolitan Museum of Art

As this wedding dress from 1996 demonstrates, gold and other metallic hues were also very popular in the form of lace. "The radiance of gold in bridal lace has been popular [across Europe]," said Evelyn Bloom, an Australian lace buyer, in June 1996.[56]

Chapter 12

2000–2023

At the turn of the new millennium, strapless dresses were by far the most popular choice, sometimes worn with a stole or bolero. Skirt shapes were more varied, ranging from a clinging sheath style to a full-on "princess" style with layers of tulle. Shiny fabrics like satin and taffeta gave a subtle nod to the tech obsession that was manifested in fashion through metallic textiles. Other features seen in fashion more widely, such as layering, cowl necklines, spaghetti straps, and mesh fabric also found their way into some bridal designs. At the tail end of the 1990s, designers including Badgley Mischka anticipated the year 2000 by looking to previous decades, using lace (which generally made way for "bling" in this era) and beading to evoke nostalgic connotations.[1] The majority of brides continued to select a white or ivory gown, but the celebrity weddings of Gwen Stefani (2002), Portia de Rossi (2008), and Reese Witherspoon (2011) enhanced the popularity of blush and other pink tones.

Since then, a key priority of twenty-first-century bridal wear has been environmental sustainability. In the face of impending climate crisis, many brides feel that their wedding dress—perhaps more than any other clothing, with its wear-once tradition—should play a part in the fight toward carbon neutrality. Two ways of achieving this are to rent a dress, or choose a pre-owned or vintage gown, but this does not suit all tastes. Many designers are therefore paving the way for using recycled and plant-based textiles, along with compostable or recycled packaging. Silk, hemp, linen, and recycled polyester lining are popular options, but experimentation with fruit fibers including banana and pineapple (in which fibers are hand-extracted from the pineapple leaf, and the thread manually worked on a loom) is increasing. This is not a new technique, of course—Piña has been cultivated in the Philippines since the seventeenth century, used to create lustrous fabrics traditionally known as *nipis*. Likewise,

LEFT
Jusi fabric at a New York wedding, 2012.

banana (one of the strongest natural fibers) is used for silk-based *jusi* fabrics, thereby a popular bridal and occasion-wear alternative, and seen here worn by the mother of the bride at a wedding in New York, 2012 (see opposite).[2] A no-waste mentality has led many to re-think partaking in "trashing the dress," a post-wedding photography shoot in which the bride purposefully dirties, rips, cuts, or even sets fire to her dress. Also known as the "fearless bridal," this trend symbolizes the culmination of being a bride, but can also be viewed as feminist, destroying the patriarchal associations of a perfectly clean, crisp, white dress. A less wasteful alternative is recrafting the garment, either into a different dress or new textile piece altogether—this might involve quilting, upholstery, bag making, even Christmas ornaments.

Despite a wish to be mindful of the carbon footprint, gowns designed specifically for "destination weddings" became available from the early 2000s onwards. The concept of planning a wedding abroad became especially popular during the 1990s, and the need to choose an easily transportable, lightweight dress fit well with that decade's minimalist aesthetic (Cindy Crawford's 1998 lace slip wedding dress is a prime example). Since the early 2000s, though, designers such as Essence of Australia have marketed specific "beach wedding dresses" that exemplify a seaside aesthetic via effortless, "light as air" styles. These typically include low backs, lace or chiffon with exotic plant motifs, skirt slits, and blouson sleeves. Particularly popular during 2005–2010 for this purpose was the "Grecian" style, which was light, floaty, ethereal, and suggestive (especially to British brides) of an idealized sunny escape.

Elopement is now a far more accepted and popular choice, highlighting the romance of conducting a ceremony with just the couple and perhaps one or two close family members. Las Vegas remains one of the most popular locations for elopement and destination ceremonies. The Australian bride (see page 210) waited until she had arrived in the USA to purchase her dress, creating a chain of memories that culminated with a ceremony at an iconic chapel.

Together with environmental concerns comes ethical fashion, ensuring equitable wages and fair working conditions for the makers of mass-produced bridal pieces. Purchasing a gown made overseas also, naturally, contributes to carbon emissions as it makes the journey to its new owner. The moral cost of this is twofold when we consider the recent trend for unauthorized designer copies, made and sold at unfeasibly low prices. Global charities like Oxfam have taken steps to counter this, becoming the leader of bridal-specific charity retailing with up to 80 percent off new and pre-loved gowns. Some brides even re-donate once they have used their dress, continuing the altruistic and ethical cycle. "Don't expect dowdy cast-offs," wrote Tamsin Blanchard in 2013. "Only the finest donated dresses make it to their special shops … What could be better than knowing your bargain dress has helped people in the developing world?"[3]

LEFT
A Vegas wedding, 2013.

Since December 21, 2005, same-sex couples in Britain have been able to form a legal civil partnership. Across Europe, the same type of union was established from the late 1990s onwards, while some American states (including Vermont, New Hampshire, and Connecticut) legalized from 2000–2010.[4] Elsewhere in the world, the same has either been granted since the mid-2010s or continues to be under discussion. Civil unions grant many of the same rights as traditional marriages, and in some places are available to opposite-sex couples who want to make a legal and formal commitment, but who oppose the historical inegalitarian institution of marriage. Nevertheless, many people who identify as female and choose civil partnerships still wish to make a statement through ceremonial clothing, partaking in just the same landmark experiences as conventional brides. This demonstrates the symbolic and emotional power of the wedding dress, across cultures, genders, and legal recognition. The image opposite shows a civil partnership that took place in the Highlands of Scotland in 2011. Both brides wanted to express their commitment through dresses that complemented each other yet still reflected individual taste. Various elements, such as

RIGHT
A civil ceremony in 2011.

concentrated beading on the bodice and ruching at the waist, offset the gowns' differences (e.g., fabric type; straps vs. strapless) with ease.

When same-sex marriage was recognized in England, Wales, and Scotland in 2014, same-sex civil partners had the option to "convert" their union into a marriage. For many choosing to do so, the change in status did not necessarily require a second celebration and re-wear or renewal of outfits. For them, their first public declaration of commitment remained the most significant, while for others, the attainment of a right—for so long deemed heteronormative—more than warranted additional festivities.

Throughout this book, the concept of finding a "perfect" or "cream" wedding dress has surfaced time and again. It may be idealistic, but it is undoubtedly a key component of the modern wedding, and part of that "journey" marketed to engaged women. For transgender brides, however, having this "Cinderella moment" may be even more crucial and poignant than most. It represents perhaps the ultimate feminine garment, and a life event which, as transgender woman Precious Davis commented in 2017, "would be the ultimate catharsis for all the displaced longing of my childhood."[5] For women like Davis, the stakes are high, incorporating unfamiliar territory on a gargantuan scale. The novel act of shopping for a formal gown is intimidating in the first place, out of the realms of daily experience for most cis women. For transwomen, it means navigating the dimensions of a new body and working out what will both look and feel the best—and in some cases, coming to terms with a different sartorial reality than they might have imagined.

There are of course those who, in the words of designer Curtis Cassell, "don't even fit into the word 'bride,' which is why Queera [Cassell's brand] exists. 'It's individuality. It can't be simply men or women. It can be anything, anyone.'"[6] Cassell's wedding designs, which are explored in this chapter, offer a "mix and match" of shirt, shirtdress, pants, skirt and blazer, handing a wearer the autonomy to create their own signature look. Such designs demonstrate the sea change that is gradually encroaching on the strictly gendered history of the wedding dress. Since 2021 Christian Siriano (the designer responsible for Billy Porter's groundbreaking "tuxedo" Oscars gown) has turned his attention to producing "gender-bending" bridal fashion that is intended to suit anyone, no matter what body they were born with or transitioned into. His looks incorporate aspects of traditional menswear (such as the tuxedo jacket), pants-and-skirt combinations, and skirt layers of different lengths. This does not mean that we have reached a point where anyone of any gender would feel comfortable choosing a wedding dress, but it does imply that society is edging toward that goal.

We have seen how widely the white wedding dress and its accessories have been adopted and adapted since the nineteenth century. It seems to possess the ability to speak to brides across cultures, lending itself to the requirements of different societies and heritages. This chapter will explore how the bridal industry caters to women wishing to blend multiple facets of their background, and the ingenious professional and personal touches that make this possible. The common assumption that a bride will want to blend elements of her own culture with the western wedding aesthetic is expressed in manuals like *Wedding Feng Shui* (2010), which advises the bride to "start shopping for your qi pao or cheongsam" nine months before the wedding, and then "purchase or order veil, shoes, and other bridal accessories."[7]

As Wendy Leeds-Hurwitz points out, in theory all weddings are, to some extent, examples of intercultural communication "because all weddings effect the combination of individuals from different families … into a new whole, which will need to establish its own traditions."[8] For couples from entirely different cultural backgrounds, however, the distinctions are less subtle, and a bride may need to decide which aspects of each she wants her dress to display. For many couples, issues arise in trying to keep extended family happy, and these concerns can continue even after the wedding. An American wife of a Columbian man recalled with horror that her mother-in-law "tried to sell [my wedding dress] …without telling me. "What are you going to use it for?" [she asked] … she sort of didn't understand that that wasn't the point."[9] This scenario indicates generational as well as cultural dissimilarities, which brides across all countries and cultures must contend with.

2020 brought with it a global pandemic, and therefore, many disrupted or cancelled wedding plans. Nevertheless, it appears that even if dates, venues, and guest lists were curtailed or abandoned, the bride's choice of dress was not. Full bridal gowns purchased before the outbreak were still worn, even in hugely pared down ceremonies. Specially designed bridal face masks were worn—the selection of which, *Vogue* suggested in 2021, "is similar to choosing your wedding day accessories. Generally, it all starts with the dress."[10] In many places bridal boutiques were still open for business once they had established a health and safety plan. However, even with a COVID-safe dress appointment policy, shops had little control over the lead times for gowns to arrive in store. The shutdown of manufacturing facilities and disruption of normal operations meant that it could now take double the original lead time of 6–8 months. In such cases many brides turned away from tradition partly, according to events planner Lynn Easton, because "The more intimate feel of weddings during the pandemic has resulted in fewer rules, allowing brides to become more adventurous with fashion."[11] It is ironic that during a period in which "rules" of various kinds were legally enforced, couples should find freedom in their wedding choices. But, as a contributor to *Brides* magazine commented in 2021, the lack of imposed tradition meant that brides felt able to "throw expectations out of the window" and embrace patterned gowns, shorter hemlines, and "bold pops of color"—which, as Easton predicted, "are here to stay." The pandemic also did little to deter the producers of shows like *Say Yes to the Dress* (TLC), who steadfastly continued filming at various locations using social distancing and face masks. This demonstrated the continuing power of the bridal gown, perhaps even more fervent in times of international

RIGHT
A floral wedding dress in Perth, Australia, 2019.

crisis. The element of escapism that such reality shows provide was no doubt heightened during this time, too, bringing new viewers as well as retaining loyal fans.

As the 2020s continue, a key trend in bridalwear seems to be versatility. Increasingly, gowns are available with removeable trains, overskirts, even sleeves; as Monique Lhuillier put it in 2022, "brides not only want a statement look, but they also want multiple looks in one for their special day." [12] Many are also keen to create a personalized look via multiple suppliers, made simpler through one-of-a-kind pieces from vendors such as Etsy. Anything that is not white or "traditional" in flavor is still regarded in industry terms as "alternative," and brides who choose "ordinary" colored dresses are questioned more than others on their reasons.

The white wedding dress may have been a western innovation, but today it far transcends that history. This garment is perhaps unique in its ability to communicate so many of the facets that make us human, regardless of culture and background: commitment, desire, hope, beauty, fantasy, memory, and above all, love. It has been reimagined, rewritten, and reinvigorated to bring relevance to whoever chooses to wear it. This final chapter illustrates some of the ways this has been done, from Japan to South Korea to Nigeria, with a delicate synthesis and balance of culture, fashion, faith, and heritage.

Wedding dress,

2001, Sydney, Private collection

◆

This dress was worn by bride Lauren Levy for her wedding to Paul Joshua in Sydney, Australia, September 2, 2001. After seeing the style in a shop window, she knew that the gown's sophisticated "princess vibes" suited her vision. However, planning for an Orthodox Jewish wedding ceremony meant that the dress had to be made with certain considerations in mind, and the bride procured her dream style by commissioning custom details.

This style of tiara is known as a *diadem*, a "half crown" with curved scrollwork and crystals placed at intersections.

For modesty the bride's knees, shoulders, and arms must always be covered. This dress was strapless and sleeveless when purchased, so obvious amendments were needed. However, the bride was apprehensive that the sleeves might appear obviously "added"; wishing them to blend fluidly with the existing design. The resulting sleeves are made from sheer fabric that encases the upper back and shoulders in the manner of a classic "Queen Anne" neckline. A row of loops and buttons is incorporated from the original fitted bodice upwards, creating a smooth single fastening at the back.

The bride wore a veil partly in order to engage in the *bedeken*, a ceremony in which the groom covers his bride's face with a veil. This intimate moment before the vows (said under a *chuppah*) has several interpretations. One of the most prevalent pays homage to the Biblical story of Jacob, tricked into marrying the veiled Leah instead of the one he truly loved; her sister Rachel. As such, the ceremony allows the groom to formally "identify" his bride.

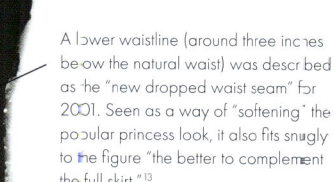

A lower waistline (around three inches below the natural waist) was described as the "new dropped waist seam" for 2001. Seen as a way of "softening" the popular princess look, it also fits snugly to the figure "the better to complement the full skirt."[13]

Traditionally, the wearing of white at a Jewish wedding is related more to spiritual purity than physical virginity. In some cases, it can indicate that the bride has visited the *mikveh* (ritual bath), marking a quiet transition from single to married life.

"Newest is the ball gown with a bustle in the back ... [and] a drop waist that is laced up in the back." The dress shown here is buttoned, but the rest of this description from *Cincinnati Wedding* magazine in spring/summer 2001 corresponds closely to the trends seen here.[14] The same publication recommended that "simplicity in details" was required in the new Millennium. "As opposed to lots of lace [or] heavy beading ... the details are understated: a touch of embroidery or beading, a smattering of pearls, a bit of lace." Subtle sparkle is seen here in a scattering of crystals across the bodice, with the same edging across neckline and sleeves.

Wedding gown worn with hijab,

2011, USA, Private collection

◆

This young bride had never had a definitive image of what she wanted for her wedding, but with a specific budget in mind, she "walked into David's Bridal and tried on some gowns, and the princess dress in all the photos is the one that jumped out to me. I put it on and just felt so magical. It fit me like a glove ... Done and done." Her wedding took place at the Al-Shareef Mosque in Long Beach, California, in December 2011, and this example illustrates a skillful blending of the white wedding tradition with the requirements of Islamic religious observance.

....

This scarf was a custom design by Vela (founded in 2009), and although the bride was "never fond of myself in a white scarf," she decided that "to keep with the white bride image I did need something to coordinate."

Dina Torkia, writing about Muslim bridal choices, comments that "when we think 'bridal' we often think diamonds, tulle, lace, or silk. For hijabis, they tend to incorporate these elements into their hijabs. Often it ends up being a little overboard, because ... we feel we have to make up for not having our hair out."[15] There is no such compromise or excess in this ensemble, since typically "bridal" elements are present on both bodice and skirt. The plain white scarf is ornamented only with soft ruffles, an especially fashionable look in 2011–2012. The ruffles' rolled edges subtly mirror those on the tulle hem, creating a delicate cohesion with the whole. This example demonstrates the variety and diversity present in contemporary Muslim weddings, as well as the creative ways that observant women can achieve a desired bridal look.

This beaded satin bodice, featuring a cuff neckline, was originally strapless. Since modesty was a key consideration, the bride commissioned a tailor-made bolero to cover her arms. Boleros have been a popular staple since the mid-nineteenth century, but seen prominently in bridal wear since the 1950s.

Layers of soft silk tulle make up this "princess" skirt, so-called because of its similarity to the costume associated with fairy-tale princesses. This is not based on any specific historical model, but has closest links to mid-nineteenth-century crinoline and earlier Romantic-era gowns—which, in turn, may relate to the period in which one of the greatest fairy tale authors, Hans Christian Andersen, was living and working. Dresses at this time were voluminous and took some inspiration from the full yet diaphanous costumes worn by ballet dancers like Marie Taglioni. Such elegant and romantic connotations provided the perfect silhouette for Walt Disney, whose princesses' gowns (particularly that of *Cinderella* in 1950) contribute hugely to their identity and narrative. It is not surprising that such vernacular pervades bridal shopping, with the aesthetic of a "modern fairy tale bride" exemplified through ethereal tulle, diamantes, and glistening white silk.

Scattered sequins across this expanse of tulle provide a touch of "bling." In 2011, one bridal guide warned against purchasing a dress using "Crystal Sparkle Chiffon," composed of "translucent flimsy fibers woven with polyester or nylon" to achieve the effect seen here at a lower cost.[16]

Representation of a "princess" style dress from the fairytale *Bluebeard*, 1921.

Gypsy wedding dress by Sondra Celli, Massachusetts, *2012*

This dress, priced at an incredible $20,000, is of a style that has become recognizable to legions of fans of the *Big Fat Gypsy Wedding* franchise, which premiered in the UK in 2010 and the USA in 2012. Elaborate weddings are an established part of Romany culture and history, but the series was criticized for exemplifying a "lack of understanding" of different (and distinct) Gypsy and Traveller communities; of undermining any progress that had been made to foster empowerment and inclusion in society.[17] Others have criticized this focus on "brash and bold" dresses as an "easy assertion of classism ... a metaphorical 'gate' separating 'us' from 'them'"[18] and of using extravagant dresses to mask real social problems. For others, though, the series affectionately shed light on intimate wedding preparations of a hidden community with a long history of discrimination, a humanizing lens that introduced the audience to a little-known face of bridal wear. It also shed light on exuberant "blinged" bridal wear, and designers such as Sondra Celli have achieved global fame for their inventive, one-of-a-kind creations that are custom-made to showcase the unique personality of the bride.

A one-shouldered effect is created through a continuous panel of decoration, which crosses the right shoulder to fasten in back. The look rose to particular prominence in 2011, with top designers including Vera Wang and Elie Saab releasing different takes on the style.

The weight of dresses like this can be staggering, with one example recorded at 75 pounds, necessitating the bride taping her hips with gauze to minimize scarring (others told of using disposable diapers for the same purpose).[19] One episode of the British TV show also featured a young bride fainting under her 140-pound gown. The bodice is decorated with illusion flowers, Swarovski crystal pins and flat-back crystals, which add to the garment's weight. Detailing continues onto the skirt on a separate panel, a feature also found in historical precedents (see the 1865 fashion plate opposite).

This sheer bodice with visible boning channels reflects a common trend since the early 2000s. It allows brides to show a small amount of skin, and is used frequently by designers including Pnina Tornai, who comments that "Sheer bodices are ideal for the daring bride looking for that extra va-va voom on her wedding day."[20]

Similar detailing, taken on to the skirt on a separate panel, is seen in this 1865 fashion plate.

Thelma Madine, the Liverpool-based dressmaker who shot to fame in the original UK version of *My Big Fat Gypsy Wedding*, describes the first commission she received from the traveller community. It was for a "*Gone with the Wind* dress," she remembers. "Oh, I loved the way you could hear the taffeta swish when Scarlett walked in the room. I adored these dresses."[21] That mid-twentieth century take on 1860s extravagance is taken to extremes here, as Madine's career saw the majority of traveller brides requesting the biggest skirts she could muster. These dresses, which physically distance the bride from her groom, mirror the propriety elicited by crinolined women in the 1860s. Gypsy brides are typically taught that their first kiss should be "at the altar," a promise that is made manifest through the barrier of a three-foot wide skirt.

Wedding dress by Carolina Herrera,

2012, Philadelphia Museum of Art

◆

Carolina Herrera is one of the best-known names in the modern, high-end bridal industry. However, her designs are certainly not consistently conventional. This dress bears several hallmarks of contemporary bridal couture, but Herrera's use of a single length of striped fabric, the tone of which changes from front to back, adds a bold twist. The gown was worn by bride Rachel Frishberg when she married her fiancé, Neil Press, at a Colorado ski resort in 2012. As a bride in her mid-30s, Frishberg was keen to choose a sophisticated yet recognizably "bridal" dress, and felt an instant connection when she saw this piece at a New York boutique. Despite a series of fitting disasters that almost made the dress unwearable, the wedding day was a success, and the gown is preserved for posterity at the Philadelphia Museum of Art.

....

The asymmetric bustle had its origins in the 1880s, when one-sided, off-center draperies were fashionable.

In many contemporary wedding dresses a makeshift, temporary "bustle" is created for practical reasons, mainly to keep the skirt away from the floor while dancing, but here it is an intended design feature. The bustle was a feature of Herrera's 2012 "Resort" collection, described by *Vogue* as "[likely] to find an Upper East Side audience."[22] However, the style itself was certainly popular across the board in bridal fashions, with integrated bustles seen in collections by Ronald Joyce, Paloma Blanca and Pronovias.

The bride wore her hair in an updo, foregoing a veil or other ornamentation such as a tiara. In 2012, bridal handbook *What's Your Bridal Style?* described such a choice as "modern or natural, without the virginal netting cover."[23]

Strapless dresses have long been a fashionable choice; described in 2002 as the "number one style" by an assistant bridal manager at Kleinfeld, New York.[24] A decade later, the *Bridal Bible* advised that "Strapless dresses are the new classics, and they're designed in every dress shape and style available ... Look for a version that flatters your particular build."[25] Brides often express concern that they will need to constantly pull up the dress to stop the bodice slipping; however, if fitted correctly the strapless dress should be snug and structured.

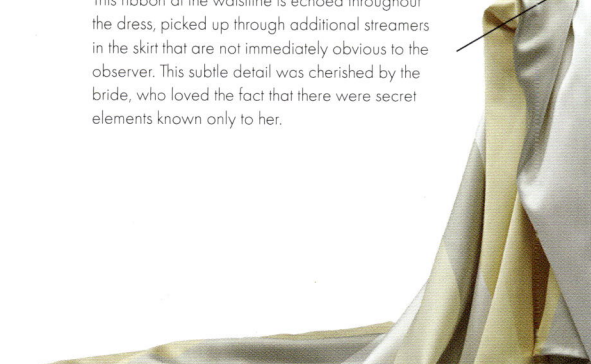

This ribbon at the waistline is echoed throughout the dress, picked up through additional streamers in the skirt that are not immediately obvious to the observer. This subtle detail was cherished by the bride, who loved the fact that there were secret elements known only to her.

The bride and groom on their wedding day. This shot illustrates the unique bustle positioning and effect when the train is held up from the floor. It also showcases the striking look of these silver, champagne, and off-white stripes.

The presence of a train and bustle made this dress suitably "bridal" to Frishberg, though at first she wondered whether the unusual striped fabric might offset that. This concern links to the perennial connection of white (and shades of white) as the only acceptable "bridal" color.

Wedding ensemble by Tubo Woman, Nigeria,

2017, Imageplotter News and Sports/Alamy Stock Photo

This two-tone ensemble (also available in pure white) is typical of designer Tubo's elegant luxury, and plays into global bridal trends for 2018 as well as featuring some characteristically Nigerian details. Founder Sandrah Tubobereni describes her approach as containing "A great deal of [Western] influence. TUBO is now an international brand. We have brides from across the globe, Nigerians and non-Nigerians." Known for her deft redesigning of traditional African bridalwear, Tuboberni launched her debut bridal collection, "Her Form," in 2018.

This bodice, named "Carine," can be paired with different skirt styles, contributing to the brand's goal of offering brides "stylish and easy to wear" options. It is made in an ivory shade, mirroring the traditional white of West African weddings.

Similar "balloon" sleeves are seen on this House of Worth ballgown from 1889, Metropolitan Museum of Art.

A strong western historical influence is seen in these voluminous, "balloon" elbow-length sleeves, which share characteristics of late 1880s- early 1890s ball gowns. An interpretation of this look could later be seen on 1980s bridal and other formal wear. It made a reappearance in the spring of 2018, and, as *Vogue* commented in 2022, "it's become more than just a fleeting style ... and has continually returned season after season."[26]

The model wears strappy high heeled sandals on the runway, which were also a popular bridal choice in 2017. Open toes and metallic shades were particularly widely put forward as a "must have."

In line with brands such as Viktor & Rolf and Marchesa, Tubo here offers a dress that goes beyond the actual ceremony. Marchesa's Fall 2018 "pouf-sleeved lace mini" would similarly, *Vogue* opined, be ideal for a rehearsal dinner or brunch.[27]

This plunge neckline is subtly supported by a sheer "illusion" panel, a highly fashionable feature by 2018.[28] Another illusory element is the lace effect, which is actually composed of embroidery and delicate appliques. Further appliques curve around the shoulders, standing proud of the sheer base to add texture. In July 2016, *Wedding Bells* magazine described this trend as "3D floral appliques that are just exploding off dresses and really transforming gowns into textual works of art."[29] The look was used by high-profile designers including Pronovics, Ramona Keveza and Monique Lhuillier.

This dramatic shade of gold creates links to traditional West African associations of power and prestige. The skirt is lined in a vibrant red, the use of which—along with the gold—was described by *Nigerian Entertainment Today* in 2017 as "Fierce red [and] gold," concluding that "Tubo wasn't afraid to play with all of it."[30] A slit at the left-hand side allows flashes of red to appear as the bride walks.

Chapter 12: 2000–2023

Wedding dress by Randy Fenoli, USA,

2019, Estrop/Getty Images

◆

Bridal designer Randy Fenoli is internationally known for his role as a consultant at New York's Kleinfeld Bridal, and consequently as a presenter for TLC's *Say Yes to the Dress*, filmed at Kleinfeld. In 2017, he launched his debut bridal range and, as a designer, draws on his personal interaction with thousands of brides. His mission is to "educate, elevate, and empower" a bride to choose "the most important dress in her life" and to recognize her "own personal beauty."[31] This dress is from "Silver Springs," Fenoli's Fall 2019 collection, which epitomizes the ethereal and dreamy aesthetic underpinning many designs that year.

....

These long sleeves are gathered into a cuff in the "bishop" style. When this became a popular bridal trend in 2019, they were often described as "bubble sleeves" to indicate the soft, curving volume from elbow down. Sleeves in general remained popular following the marriage of Prince William and Kate Middleton in 2011; however, adaptability is key in modern bridal design. Sleeves are often detachable, a feature shown in other designs by Fenoli the same year:

This design from the same collection includes removeable draped sleeves, described by *Harper's Bazaar* as "an eye-catching look that is upgraded and highly sophisticated" (Estrop/Getty Images).[32]

This sweetheart neckline plunges at the center, with an opening that finishes at waist level. Such designs are supported by a discreet band of fabric or flesh-colored modesty panel.

The dress is backless, dipping into a deep V that is met with a row of covered buttons. Backless designs were occasionally worn by bold brides in the 1930s, leading one Australian newspaper to report in 1934 that, in the eyes of the church, "backless and sleeveless wedding frocks seem to be the chief bone of contention."[33] Even today, backless wedding dresses are frequently described as a "risqué" choice, as *The Daily Telegraph* put it in 2017, particularly when combined with a form-fitting skirt.[34] In this example, the daring nature of the back of the gown is offset by the more full and traditional A-line skirt.

Ivory and silver floral appliqués embellish layers of Chantilly and *point d'Esprit* lace. The latter is composed of bobbinet covered with woven dots that scatter across the fabric. This creates a rich variation in texture, one that is not new in bridal wear. In 1907, a high society New York bride's dress, made from ivory satin "covered with fine point d'esprit of a creamy tint," was layered with appliques of "cream-colored Irish lace." This Paris-made gown was described as being of a style that "will set the fashion for other brides for some time to come."[35]

Wedding ensemble by QUEERA,
2021

◆

Queera Wang was established in 2020 by Curtis Cassell, a designer whose mission is to broaden sartorial options for LGBTQIA+ brides and grooms. The company's mission statement declares that its designs are about "fitting your body—not defining your gender,"[36] and Cassell's flexible mix-and-match, custom-style approach makes this ever more achievable. Although the label creates bridal wear, the aim remains to "transcend bridal" and embrace a glamour and element of fantasy that will suit all bodies and gender identities.

Constructing these eighteenth-century style Watteau pleats out of sheer fabric is a unique, contemporary spin on the look. Other bridal manufacturers including Marchesa, Claire Pettibone, and Jenny Packham have experimented with the design in lightweight fabrics, but this is usually incorporated as a detachable element. Furthermore, it is often constructed without such a direct nod to the layered box pleats seen during the eighteenth century.

Though a traditionally masculine design, this shirt collar does have bridal wear precedents. During the 1930s the "shirtwaist" style was very fashionable and extended to some bridal styles, such as this example worn by a Finnish bride, c. 1938.

This thick drawstring belt is practical, but also recalls a long tradition of decorative, waist-defining sashes and belts on wedding dresses.

These exaggerated bishop sleeves match the skirt volume and flow of its substantial train. The style was popular for both men and women in the nineteenth century, seen in this wedding shirt from the 1830s. It also enjoyed a revival in the 1970s as a fashionable bridal sleeve.

This ensemble is available as five separate components: shirt, shirtdress, pants, skirt, and a blazer. In this way, Cassell comments, "We're able to mix and match to our desired silhouette ... people could shop these same five items, and all come away with different looks that suit their gender identity."[37] An example of an alternative composition is seen below:

The sheer beaded shirt gown pays homage to *The Sound of Music*'s wedding scene, which Cassell "watched over and over as a young kid."

Kimono-inspired wedding dress by Eiko Ueda of Aliansa, Tokyo, Japan, 2022

Designer Eiko Ueda creates bridal and other occcsion gowns based on traditional uchikake kimono. She imbues a contemporary Western twist to create "new traditions" that prevent a bride having to compromise between the pull of different styles.

These distinctive gathers and folds at the top of a strapless bodice are often known colloquially as "crumb catcher" necklines. Not technically a "neckline," these fabric inserts or panels create a distinctly modern, architectural finish.

This wide sash is made entirely of *uchikake* fabric to mimic an obi and tied in a simple bow in the manner of the *Tsuke Obi*. Traditionally these sashes would not be worn over the *uchikake*, but on the long-sleeved *furisode* robe worn beneath.

The gown is accessorized with a sheer, flowing wrap featuring a floral design, the shape of which is reminiscent of *suisen* (Japanese bellflowers).

The fabric design includes cranes, which symbolize longevity in Japan, and often feature alongside pine (good fortune, longevity, and steadfastness), bamboo (good luck), and plum blossom (patience, hope, and vitality). In relation to weddings, cranes also offer the hope that conjugal happiness will be everlasting.

RIGHT

Traditional *uchikake* developed in the eighteenth century, used by high-ranking samurai women as a more substantial over-robe, which was usually worn open. By the nineteenth century, affluent urban women would wear *uchikake* for nearly all formal occasions.[38] Today, they are generally used only for bridalwear, but the importance of the garment to contemporary Japanese wearers cannot be overstated. Aside from being regarded as the most traditional form of bridal attire, it also generates strong nationalistic feelings. Today a bride will often change directly from her *uchikake* robe to a white Western gown, a switch that is rendered superfluous by Ueda's design.

This padded hem is known as *fuki*, an extension which adds weight to control the drape of the fabric. Historically, they were often made in a contrasting color (as seen above) and were more or less heavily padded to denote the wearer's age and status.[39] The use of white here is another twist to Ueda's "new tradition," but the *fuki* can be ordered in a variety of colors. Another approach, Ueda comments, is to base this hem on that of *Junihitoe*, a lavish kimono displaying many colored layers.

"Lolita" wedding ensemble, Japan,

2022, Oran Tantapakul/Alamy Stock Photo

◆

It is difficult to define "Japanese Lolita," which serves as an umbrella term for several subtly different looks—including goth, sweet, sailor, and princess. All of these, however, embody a self-consciously girlish aesthetic, with an abundance of flounces, ribbons, and lace. It holds conceptual connections to eighteenth- and nineteenth-century European dress—in particular the clothing used on dolls made by French company Jumeau. There is certainly a doll-like feel to the Lolita look, evolving from Otome-kei and then "doll kei" in the 1980s and 90s (especially the ultra girly "sweet Lolita," which is illustrated here). This is combined with Japanese "kawaii" features, a term which translates as a combination of "cute," "tiny," and "loveable," but that represents a large section of modern Japan, including cartoon culture. Characters across the Lolita spectrum appear in anime series and subsequently became part of urban street style, particularly in the Harajuku district of Tokyo.[40]

....

There is another bow at center front of the neckline, and another long, oversized tied ribbon hangs from the right hip. A padded heart-shaped applique sits in the middle of this bow, a clear homage to the romantic intent of the outfit.

Among the bricolage of Lolita style is the mid-nineteenth century, and 1850s and 1860s inspiration is clearly seen in this layered, structured skirt. Another Victorian influence lies in the short, layered, ruffled sleeves, reminiscent of evening and ball gowns. This abundance of ruffles also came from the "Victorian-meets-Little-House-on-the-Prairie" aesthetic of designer Isao Kaneko, who was responsible for the addition of "lace and ribbons. Lots of them" in order to find a strong brand identity for early Lolita supplier, "Baby, The Stars Shine Bright" (est. 1988 by Akinori Isobe).[41]

A similar voluminous tiered skirt can be seen in this nineteenth-century fashion plate from the Metropolitan Museum of Art.

An element of "princess Lolita" is illustrated here in the elaborate crown, worn at a jaunty angle.

Choker necklaces have been a part of Western fashion history for centuries, and their use in Lolita clothing recalls fashionable women of the Meiji and Taishō periods (1912–26), combining traditional kimono with imported accessories.[42] Featuring a bow at the front or side of the band is an especially prevalent Lolita staple.

Streamers hang from each shoulder, made from the same white ribbon that is used to create a faux corset effect at the sides of the bodice.

Frilled wrist cuffs are a fashion staple of the "Lolita" brand. Those shown here resemble traditional bridal garters, designed to be worn on the thigh. They are ornamented with bows that feature a white silk flower.

This long chiffon train extends from center back of the waistline, beneath a large ribbon bow. The combination of long train with short skirt was popular in the 1920s, though the train usually fell from the shoulders.

Thigh-high white stockings with lacy tops epitomize the "ideal": as a bridal guide from 2001 put it, "many brides-to-be envision themselves wearing flimsy corsets, thigh-high stockings, and frilly panties."[43] The author goes on to outline the realities of "being on your feet wearing a weighty gown for hours."[44] However, the "Lolita" bridal gown embodies a fantasy to some extent, though not in a sexualized way: rather, it symbolizes "a hyperstylized, lacy vision of femininity."

224 How to Read a Wedding Dress

Eco wedding dress,

2023, Miranda Bennett Studio, Austin, Texas

◆

Established in 2013, Miranda Bennett Studio was a woman-founded, eco-focused brand that prioritized perennial design, zero waste, recycling, and non-toxic color. Its locally made bridal range aimed to provide brides with a garment that lasts far beyond the wedding day, and this "Everyday" dress is a key example of that philosophy. Described as a style that will "weave seamlessly into anyone's wardrobe as an ethically made clothing staple," it represents a new, thoughtful, versatile juncture in bridalwear.[45]

The style of this dress takes its cue from Balenciaga's gamechanger: the chemise or "sack" of the late 1950s. This loose-fitting design was the polar opposite of the fashionable New Look silhouette, but it struck a chord with women looking for something new. By the 1960s it had evolved into the hugely popular shift, which was increasingly chosen by brides—as The Australian *Women's Weekly* reported in July 1966, "In general, American bridal dresses are short-short ... with the shift ... taking over from ballerina and Empire lines."[46]

Cap sleeves are a perennially popular option, and one that fit perfectly into the "Everyday" label of this dress. *Brides* magazine ran a feature on the cap sleeve in January 2023, pointing out that "cap sleeve gowns are not only comfortable, but odds are you're already wearing them. Many [clothes] come with this classic sleeve length."[47]

Silk noil (raw silk) is a sustainable option since it is made from the shorter "waste" fibers from inside a cocoon. The final fabric resembles linen, being slightly rough to the touch.[48] Historically the cloth was used by the military for "the making of the aeroplane and cartridge bag cloth," which "made practical the use of by-products of silk manufacture."[49]

Cristóbal Balenciaga, Chemise dress, c.1957, Rhode Island School of Design Museum

Tea-length or 'midi' dresses remain a popular choice for bridalwear. Typically, the definition of 'midi' is broad, often suggestive of a hem that ends at a point in between the knee and ankle.

A similar shift-style dress worn by a bride, England, 2017.

Cheongsam-inspired wedding gown by Wai-Ching Studio, Seattle,

2023

◆

Cheongsam (also known in Mandarin as qipao) emerged as a garment associated with female students in the early twentieth century, inspired by the long male changshan robe. Eliminating the trousers beneath, this interpretation gradually became a tight-fitting dress with side slits, a mandarin collar, and asymmetrical closure fastened with knotted buttons. Originally a symbol of urban modernity in the Republic of China, the garment fell in and out of favor there and within Taiwan, Malaysia, Singapore, and Hong Kong. While it was adapted for brides during this time, today its most common use is as a wedding dress. This design by Chrissy Wai-Ching draws on her global aesthetic and fusion of "Asian flair [with] contemporary textile design," seamlessly incorporating both Western and Chinese elements to create a unique wedding gown.

....

The handmade nature of this dress, and all of Wai-Ching's pieces, can be seen as testament to the traditional Chinese dressmaking process. This involved the employment of a seamstress, a personal brief, and a laborious making and fitting process. The expectation, Jenny Lim contends, was that the finished garment would be bestowed "with the expectation that they'll wear it for the rest of their life and then maybe pass it down to generations to come."[50]

Since the start of the twenty-first century, it has been popular—both within China itself and the diaspora communities of Canada, the USA, Australia, and Britain—for brides to wear a separate white Western dress and cheongsam.[51] Some, indeed, choose to wear up to five gowns of varying styles and shades.

This design eliminates that need, incorporating various key elements of east and west. Some of its design choices, however, are inspired directly from ancient Chinese practices, including calligraphy, which is showcased via hand done freestyle embroidery on the bodice front.

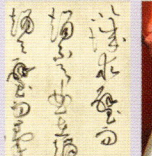 

Detail of calligraphy by Huang Tingjian, c. 1095, Metropolitan Museum of Art, New York

This train illustrates another Western wedding staple. It is not usually worn in conjunction with a cheongsam, but has become a prerequisite for those searching for an opulent white gown. In 2009, it was Chinese bride Lin Rong who set the world record for longest train, measuring almost 2.2 kilometers and decorated with 9,999 red silk roses.[53]

Postwar cheongsam incorporated many Western tailoring techniques, particularly in Singapore during the 1950s and 1960s, where cosmopolitan women preferred a tight-fitting silhouette.[52] These elements—most notably darts at bust and waist—are used here to create the three-dimensional Western bodice of contemporary cheongsam.

Two-tone gowns have long been a popular way of coordinating bridesmaids' outfits with that of the bride. They can also set the color scheme for other wedding details, including flowers and linen, to create a cohesive theme. Here, burgundy signifies the traditional Chinese association of the shade with good luck and happiness, offset with ivory panels that symbolize a more recent—but pervasive—Western wedding tradition.

White cheongsam has become another popular choice in recent years. An early example of the trend is seen in this image featuring actress Virginia Chang at her 1939 wedding in Washington D.C. Her white cheongsam is worn with a veil and sheer embroidered sleeves.

Modern bridal hanbok by House of Leehwa,

2023, Los Angeles, California

House of Leehwa (이화고전방), a family business based in Los Angeles, provides a range of Western and Korean bridal gowns. Their mission is to make hanbok "accessible to everyone of all backgrounds," whether of Korean descent or not, aiming to create dresses that "combine both Western and Korean elements for the modern bride who is in search of a unique wedding dress."[54] Hanbok (meaning "Korean clothing") is traditional national dress, now worn primarily for special occasions such as weddings. Its form and construction have remained largely unchanged over the centuries, but "modern hanbok"—shown here—is lighter and slimmer, thereby allowing increased ease of movement. This design is white and strapless, a diversion from Korean wedding tradition, and worn with a tiara

A traditional formal robe known as *hwarot*, late 19th–early 20th century. Today, it is often worn by brides at a *paebaek* following the main wedding ceremony. Minneapolis Institute of Art. Gift of Kang Collection, Korean Fine Art in honor of Dr. Matthew Welch.

Women's hanbok consist of the jeogori (top) and chima (skirt). The jeogori is typically short, sitting above the natural waistline, and closes with strips or strings of fabric known as goreum. This strapless bodice mirrors the high waist and close fit of traditional jeogori, and a decorative silver bow pays tribute to the goreum.[55]

Crowns and headdresses have been a part of Korean bridal dress for centuries. This narrow, tall tiara is reminiscent of shape to the jokduri, a traditional headpiece worn for weddings and other special occasions.[57]

Original chima were—as in this example—fairly full, worn over a petticoat (sokchima) and pleated all around the waist. Traditionally, a young bride would wear a bright green jeogori with crimson red chima.[58]

By the mid-1990s, fashion magazines were showing Western-inspired bridal hanbok in white, often sprinkled with a floral design to distinguish from traditional white mourning attire. In this example, stylized flowers adorn the silver bodice and trim. These floral shapes appear to take inspiration from a range of species including peonies (symbolizing royalty and wealth in Korea) and chrysanthemums (fidelity).

The double rows of decoration at the hem are geumbak, a traditional Korean goldleaf technique used on formal hanbok.[56] In the precolonial era, such ornate goldleaf imprint and embroidery featured only on the hanbok of aristocratic brides. A design featuring cranes is shown here; as in other East Asian countries, these birds represent longevity and are often shown on bridal kimono in Japan.

This design by Leehwa also utilizes a strapless bodice, and more closely mirrors the fit of Western examples with its longer waistline.

Glossary of Terms

áo dài Unisex Vietnamese formal wear consisting of a long, split tunic and trousers.

Bridal Crown A circular headdress originally worn in Central and Northern Europe. It would act as a symbol of both status and purity, decorated with fresh flowers and herbs or, for those who could afford it, precious metals, pearls, and mirrors.

Bridal Consultant Fashion expert employed by a bridal dress salon. These professionals help brides choose their dress, those of their bridesmaids, and advise on other aesthetic aspects of the wedding.

Bridal Salon A specialized store or boutique where brides can try and buy from a selection of wedding dresses. The word "salon" suggests an elegant, fashionable, artistic establishment.

Bridesmaid Dress A dress worn by the bride's attendants. These are usually made in colors and styles that match or complement the bridal gown. The tradition has become more mainstream since the mid-nineteenth century, when maids usually wore white dresses and veils on their heads along with the bride.

Cheongsam Chinese female dress inspired by clothing of the Manchu people. It is long, form-fitting and features a standing collar, closed with frog fastenings.

Clandestine Wedding Also known as a Fleet Marriage, this was a wedding with no public notification, and which took place outside the bride and groom's neighborhood. Until the Marriage Act of 1754, such ceremonies were legal in England.

Corset (nineteenth century onwards) An undergarment stiffened with whalebone, worn on the torso and shaped to compress the waist. Used to enable the fit of fashionable dresses. In the twenty-first century, many designer dresses are made with internal boning to ensure a smooth and flattering fit.

Eco clothing Clothes that are made in consideration of the environmental and social impact of textile production. They are usually made from recycled or organic materials, an approach that is being seen far more frequently for bridal and other formal occasion wear.

Elopement Any marriage performed swiftly and privately (often in secret), traditionally in order to wed without parental approval.

Garter A piece of lingerie worn around one thigh, usually embellished with lace and ribbons. While once a practical accessory, they are now purely decorative and sometimes used for a "garter toss" at the wedding reception.

Girdle Also known as bridal "shapewear," contemporary girdles are worn under the wedding dress to achieve a streamlined silhouette.

Going-Away/Honeymoon Dress A formal outfit, sometimes a travelling suit, which the bride would change into immediately following the wedding.

Hanbok Traditional Korean formalwear which for brides includes a *jeogori* (upper garment) and *chima* (skirt), typically in red.

Kawaii Refers to the "culture of cuteness" in Japan, often suggesting a childlike and innocent aesthetic that also appears in "Lolita" bridalwear.

Kimono Traditional robe that is also the national dress of Japan. For bridalwear, it comprises a T-shaped wraparound garment tied with a sash (*obi*), made from elaborately decorated silk in black, red, or white.

Lingerie The concept of lingerie as a visually appealing garment became standard from the late nineteenth century onwards. The market for specifically bridal lingerie, purchased for the wedding night and beyond, corresponded with this broader development in underwear.

Mini dress A very short dress, its hemline sitting well above the knee. Usually cut straight in the form of a shift dress, it could be sleeved or sleeveless and was first chosen for bridal wear from the mid-late 1960s.

Mod 1960s term meaning "modern," "in fashion"— particularly in relation to clothes.

Penny Wedding A Scottish marriage ceremony in which guests each paid a penny towards the expenses (eighteenth/nineteenth centuries).

Petticoat (sixteenth–twenty-first centuries) Skirts were referred to as *petticoats* throughout the eighteenth century. Into the nineteenth century, the term came to mean only a skirt worn as a foundational garment. In the twenty-first century, many women choosing a "ballgown" or "princess" style wedding gown will wear a stiffened petticoat to maintain the skirt shape.

Robe à l'anglaise (eighteenth century) Gown with close-fitted torso with a long, full skirt, usually worn without paniers. The skirts were often worn draped *à la polonaise*. Also sometimes known as an English bed gown, nightgown, or close-bodied gown.

***Robe à la française* (eighteenth century)** A one-piece gown, usually open-fronted, worn with a stomacher and decorated petticoat. Worn over a corset and paniers to hold out the sides of the skirt.

Robe de style An alternative to the low-waisted flapper style, of the 1920s, made with wide panier skirts that loosely mimicked the eighteenth-century fashionable silhouette.

Sari/Saree Hailing from the Indian subcontinent, this is a stretch of fabric that is attached to the waist and shoulder, worn over a fitted bodice and petticoat. Its traditional bridal color is red, worn with rich gold jewelry.

Second-day wedding A gathering on the day following the ceremony and reception. In Europe and America, it would usually take place at the home of the groom's parents or other relatives, perhaps welcoming a larger number of guests who had not attended the wedding itself. The occasion sometimes necessitated an additional formal garment for the bride.

***Sinsik* (1930s onwards)** The name given in South Korea to "new style" weddings based on Christian traditions, as opposed to traditional *kusik* (old style).

Tiara An ornamental, normally jeweled band worn at the front of the head.

Train (Dress) The trailing back portion of a skirt, extended to various lengths depending on the occasion and style of dress. Sometimes detachable. Where possible, bridal gowns traditionally featured long trains to impress guests, but on contemporary styles are generally chosen according to the bride's aesthetic preference.

Travelling Dress A practical ensemble, often tailored and made from wool, worn for long periods of travel. Some brides chose to wear a smart travelling suit as their wedding dress so that they could leave immediately for their honeymoon after the ceremony/reception.

Trousseau The collection of clothes, linen and other household textiles to be used by a woman in her early married life. Trousseaux (a diminutive of *trousse* meaning bundle) were often used as a signal of the family's wealth, and became particularly commonplace from the mid-nineteenth century onwards.

Veil A sheer fabric head and face covering that has been associated with brides since antiquity. Originally worn for religious and spiritual reasons, veils are often a purely symbolic and decorative accessory.

White Wedding The term often used to describe a traditional Western (Christian) church wedding, featuring a white dress, white flowers, and other white accessories to symbolize purity.

Notes

Introduction

[1] Dyer, Richard. *White: Essays on Race and Culture*, Oxford: Taylor & Francis, 2013.

[2] Otnes, Cele C., et al. *Cinderella Dreams: The Allure of the Lavish Wedding*, Oakland: University of California Press, 2003, p.31.

[3] Bennett Kinnon, Joy. "New And Glamorous Styles For Season's Brides," *Ebony Magazine*, June 2003, p.66.

[4] Monger, George. *Marriage Customs of the World: From Henna to Honeymoons*, London: Bloomsbury Academic, 2004, p.174.

[5] Dalby, Liza Crihfield. *Kimono: Fashioning Culture*, London: Vintage, 2001, p.115.

[6] Ramdya, Kavita. *Bollywood Weddings: Dating, Engagement, and Marriage in Hindu America*, New York: Lexington Books, 2010, pp.39-43.

[7] Lahiri, Jhumpa. *The Namesake*, Boston: Mariner Books, 2004, p.213.

[8] Yue, Daiyun. *China and the West at the Crossroads: Essays on Comparative Literature and Culture*, Singapore: Springer Nature Singapore, p.127.

[9] de Mooij, Marieke. *Consumer Behavior and Culture: Consequences for Global Marketing and Advertising*, New York: SAGE Publications, 2019.

[10] Scharff, David E. *Psychoanalysis and Psychotherapy in China: Volume 1*, Oxford: Taylor & Francis, 2018.

[11] Kim, Chil-Soon. "Analysis of Wedding Behavior of Chinese Women in their 20s to 30s in Shanghai and Neighboring Cities," *Fashion & Textile Research Journal*, no.2 (2012), pp.251–260.

[12] Xinhua, "From Cheongsam to Western Wedding Gown," *China Daily*, October 16, 2011, https://www.chinadaily.com.cn/china/2011-10/16/content_13907881.htm

[13] Lennon, Rachael. *Wedded Wife: A Feminist History of Marriage*, London: Aurum, 2023, p.105.

[14] "Bridal Gowns Market Size & Share to Surpass $73.2 Billion by 2030, Growing at a CAGR of 6.5%," Zion Market Research, June 6, 2023, https://www.globenewswire.com/news-release/2023/06/06/2682526/0/en/Bridal-Gowns-Market-Size-Share-to-Surpass-73-2-Billion-by-2030-Growing-at-a-CAGR-of-6-5-Zion-Market-Research.html

[15] Prince, Althea and Silva-Wayne, Susan, *Feminisms and Womanisms: A Women's Studies Reader*, London: Women's Press, 2004, p.221.

Chapter 1

[1] Guth, Tracy. *Dresses*, Laguna Beach: Friedman/Fairfax, 2000, p.8.

[2] Gilchrist, Roberta. *Medieval Life: Archaeology and the Life Course*, Martlesham: Boydell Press, 2012, p.94.

[3] O'Hara, Diana. *Courtship and Constraint: Rethinking the Making of Marriage in Tudor England*, Manchester: Manchester University Press, 2002, p.68.

[4] Amt, Emilie. *Women's Lives in Medieval Europe: A Sourcebook*, Oxford: Taylor & Francis, 2013, p.75.

[5] Diamant, Anita. *The Jewish Wedding Now*, New York: Scribner, 2017, p.42.

[6] Fenn, Violet. *Sex and Sexuality in Victorian Britain*, Barnsley: Pen and Sword Books, 2020, p.3.

[7] *Catholic Telegraph*, Vol.3, 1844, p.218.

[8] Deloney, Thomas. *The History of John Winchcomb, Usually Called Jack of Newbury*, Anatiposi Verlag, 2023, p.40.

[9] Mikhaila, Ninya, and Malcolm-Davies, Jane. *The Tudor Tailor: Reconstructing Sixteenth-Century Dress*, London: Batsford Books, 2006, p.44.

[10] Oliver, K. *Samuel Richardson, Dress, and Discourse*, London: Palgrave Macmillan, 2008, p.189.

[11] Fehrman, Kenneth, and Fehrman, Cherie. *Color The Secret Influence*, Hoboken: Prentice Hall, 2000, p.160.

[12] Leland, John, and Hearne, Thomas. *Joannis Lelandi Antiquarii de rebus britannicis collectanea*, Impensis Gul. & Jo. Richardson, 1770, p.343.

[13] "The Wedding dress from the Palmwood Wreck," Museum Kaap Skil, accessed 25 June 2025, https://kaapskil.nl/en/discover/collection-highlights/the-wedding-dress-from-the-palmwood-wreck/

[14] Mays, Dorothy A. *Women in Early America: Struggle, Survival, and Freedom in a New World*, New York: Bloomsbury Academic, 2004, p.248.

[15] Salih, Sarah. *Versions of Virginity in Late Medieval England*, Martlesham: D.S. Brewer, 2001, p.220.

[16] Frick, Carole Collier. *Dressing Renaissance Florence: Families, Fortunes, and Fine Clothing*, Baltimore: Johns Hopkins University Press, 2005, p.107.

[17] Ibid, p.288.

[18] Brucker, Gene A. *Florence: The Golden Age 1138–1737*, Oakland: University of California Press, 1998, p.43.

[19] Cronin, Vincent. *The Florentine Renaissance*, London: Random House, 2011.

[20] Webster, John, and Dyce, Alexander. *The Works of John Webster: With Some Account of the Author, and Notes*, London: G. Routledge and Sons, 1877, p.27.

[21] Gibson, Wendy, and Lam, Kevin D., *Women in 17th Century France*, London: Palgrave Macmillan UK, 1989, p.56.

[22] Ibid.

[23] Cressy, David. *Birth, Marriage, and Death: Ritual, Religion, and the Life-Cycle in Tudor and Stuart England*, Oxford: Oxford University Press, 1997, p.362.

[24] Pepys, Samuel. *Diary and Correspondence*, London: Bell & Daldy, 1867, p.12.

[25] *Encyclopedia of Soviet Law*, Belgium, Springer Netherlands, 1985, p.455.

[26] Greene, Frederick Davis. *Armenian Massacres and Turkish Tyranny*, American Oxford Publishing Company, 1896, p.455.

[27] Montagu, Mary Wortley, and Fluegel, Johann Gottfried. *The Letters of Lady M. W. Montagu, During the Embassy to Constantinople 1716–18*, F. Volckmar, 1835, p.133.

[28] Ells, Benjamin Franklin, *The Western Miscellany*, Harvard: B.F. Ells, 1778, p.118.

[29] *BETWEEN: The Culture of Dress Between East and West: Proceedings of the 64th Annual Conference*, September 25–30, 2011, Serbia, Ethnographic Museum, 2012, p.145.

Chapter 2

[1] Behrend-Martinez, Edward, ed. *A Cultural History of Marriage in the Age of Enlightenment*, London: Bloomsbury Publishing, 2021, p.3.

[2] O'Hara, Diana. *Courtship and Constraint: Rethinking the Making of Marriage in Tudor England*, Manchester: Manchester University Press, 2002, p.64.

[3] Haywood, Eliza Fowler. *The Female Spectator*, Eastbourne: T. Gardner, 1745, p.105.

[4] Olsen, Kirstin. *Daily Life in 18th-Century England*, London: Bloomsbury Publishing, 2017, p.225.

[5] Anishanslin, Zara. *Portrait of a Woman in Silk: Hidden Histories of the British Atlantic World*, New Haven: Yale University Press, 2016, p.90.

[6] Engel, 2004

[7] Richardson, Samuel. *Clarissa Harlowe: Volume III*, Outlook Verlag, 2018, p.51.

[8] Phegley, Jennifer. *Courtship and Marriage in Victorian England*, Santa Barbara: ABC-CLIO, 2012, p.111.

[9] Baetjer, Katharine. *British Paintings in the Metropolitan Museum of Art, 1575–1875*, New York: Metropolitan Museum of Art, 2009, p.43.

[10] Olsen, 2017, p.108.

[11] Baumgarten, Linda. *What Clothes Reveal: The Language of Clothing in Colonial and Federal America: The Colonial Williamsburg Collection*, Williamsburg: Colonial Williamsburg Foundation, 2002, p.144.

[12] White, Carolyn L. *American Artifacts of Personal Adornment, 1680–1820: A Guide to Identification and Interpretation*, Walnut Creek: AltaMira Press, 2005, p.98.

[13] *Popular Antiques Yearbook: Volume 2: Trends and Prices of Everyday Antiques for 1987*, London: Phaidon Christie's, 1987, p.130.

[14] Radclyffe-Thomas, Babette, "Gilded Age beauties: Sargent's American Heiresses at Kenwood," The Costume Society, June 3 2025, https://costumesociety.org.uk/blog/post/guest-blog-month2021tracking-elizabeth-bullswedding-dress-across-time-and-place-atlanticcrossings-1731-1910

[15] Object Record, "Wedding Dress of Miss Elizabeth Bull (Mrs Roger Price)," Revolutionary Spaces, accessed June 25, 2025, https://revolutionaryspaces.catalogaccess.com/objects/813

[16] Radclyffe-Thomas, Babette, "Gilded Age beauties: Sargent's American Heiresses at Kenwood," The Costume Society, June 3 2025, https://costumesociety.org.uk/blog/post/guest-blog-month2021tracking-elizabeth-bullswedding-dress-across-time-and-place-atlanticcrossings-1731-1910

[17] Apostolos-Cappadona, Diane. *A Guide to Christian Art*, London: Bloomsbury Publishing, 2020, p.211.

[18] Lee, Soyoung, "Goryeo Celadon," Metropolitan Museum of Art, October 1, 2003, https://www.metmuseum.org/essays/goryeo-celadon

[19] *Clothing and Fashion: American Fashion from Head to Toe* [4 Volumes], Santa Barbara: ABC-CLIO, 2015, p.94.

[20] Seleshanko, Kristina. *Carry Me Over the Threshold*, Grand Rapids: Zondervan, 2009, p.79.

[21] Carlisle, Elizabeth Pendergast. *Earthbound and Heavenbent: Elizabeth Porter Phelps and Life at Forty Acres 1747-1817*, New York: Scribner, 2004, p.9.

[22] Object page, "Robe à l'anglaise," Metropolitan Museum of Art, accessed June 25, 2025, https://www.metmuseum.org/art/collection/search/642392

[23] Waugh, Norah. *The Cut of Women's Clothes: 1600–1930*, Oxford: Taylor & Francis, 2013, p.20.

[24] Chrisman-Campbell, Kimberly. *Worn on This Day: The Clothes That Made History*, Philadelphia: Running Press, 2019.

[25] de Goncourt, Edmond, and de Goncourt, Jules. *The Woman of the Eighteenth Century: Her Life, from Birth to Death, Her Love and Her Philosophy in the Worlds of Salon, Shop and Street*, Oxford: Taylor & Francis, 2013, p.20.

[26] Majer, Michele. "1750-1759," Fashion History Timeline, July 28 2021, https://fashionhistory.fitnyc.edu/1750-1759/

[27] Ripley, Georgina. "14 rarely seen fashions from the National Museum of Scotland archives," CNN, April 20, 2016, https://edition.cnn.com/style/article/national-museum-of-scotland-archives

[28] Object page, "Women's dress; second-day wedding dress; bridesmaid dress,", Finna.fi, accessed June 25, 2025, https://www.finna.fi/Record/museovirasto.719271470A4E34D9612D3F01CA394FBB?sid=3094272081

[29] ed. Harvey, Karen, ed. *History and Material Culture: A Student's Guide to Approaching Alternative Sources*, Oxford: Taylor & Francis, 2013, p.96.

[30] Lemire, B., *Dress, Culture and Commerce: The English Clothing Trade Before the Factory, 1660–1800*, London: Palgrave Macmillan, 1997, p.66.

[31] Bettini, Maurizio. *Women and Weasels: Mythologies of Birth in Ancient Greece and Rome* Chicago: University of Chicago Press, 2013, p. 99.

[32] Object page, "The Dress of all Dresses," Livrustkammaren, 2021, accessed June 25, 2025, https://livrustkammaren.se/en/royal-history/royal-histories/dresses-and-jewellery/the-dress-of-all-dresses/

[33] Delpierre, Madeleine. *Dress in France in the eighteenth century*, New Haven: Yale University Press, 1997, p.54.

[34] Object page, "The Dress of all Dresses," Livrustkammaren, 2021, accessed June 25, 2025, https://livrustkammaren.se/en/royal-history/royal-histories/dresses-and-jewellery/the-dress-of-all-dresses/

[35] Baumgarten, 1986, p.25.

[36] Object page, "Robe à la française," Metropolitan Museum of Art, accessed June 25, 2025, https://www.metmuseum.org/art/collection/search/86881

[37] Robinson, Mary. *Memoirs of the Late Mrs. Mary Robinson, 2: Written by Herself, in Two Volumes*, Richard Phillips, 1803, p.71.

[38] Gernerd, Elisabeth. *Material Literacy in 18th-Century Britain: A Nation of Makers*, London: Bloomsbury Publishing, 2020, p.199.

[39] "I do!" Hampshire Cultural Trust, accessed June 25, 2025, https://www.cultureoncall.com/i-do/

[40] *Clothing and Fashion: American Fashion from Head to Toe* [4 Volumes], Santa Barbara, ABC-CLIO, 2015, p.261.

[41] *Tronderoser 5 - Fornuft og folelser*. Norway. Vigmostad & Bjorke/Bladkompaniet AS, 2021.

[42] Crowston, Clare Haru. *Fabricating Women: The Seamstresses of Old Regime France, 1675–1791*, Durham NC, Duke University Press, 2001, p.150.

[43] Tveite, Stein. "The Norwegian textile market in the 18th century," *Scandinavian Economic History Review* 17, no.2, 1969, p.162.

[44] Smith, John Thomas. *Nollekens and His Times: Comprehending a Life of that Celebrated Sculptor; and Memoirs of Several Contemporary Artists, from the Time of Roubiliac, Hogarth, and Reynolds, to that of Fuseli, Flaxman, and Blake*, Henry Colburn, 1828, p.42.

[45] Mann, Herman, and Sampson, afterwards Gannett. *The Female Review: Or, Memoirs of an American Young Lady (Deborah Sampson), Whose Life and Character are Peculiarly Distinguished, Being a Continental Soldier for Nearly Three Years, in the Late American War*, 1797, p.238.

[46] Object page, "Gown," Historic New England, accessed June 25, 2025, https://www.historicnewengland.org/explore/collections-access/gusn/189811/

[47] Bogansky, Amy Elizabeth. *Interwoven Globe: The Worldwide Textile Trade, 1500–1800*, Norway, Metropolitan Museum of Art, 2013, p.99.

[48] Hill, Georgiana. *A History of English Dress from the Saxon Period to the Present Day*, Kirkwood: Putnam, 1893, p.147.

[49] Smith, John Thomas, and Nollekens, Joseph. *Nollekens and His Times*, Second Edition. Henry Colburn, 1829, p.17.

[50] https://www.christies.com/en/lot/lot-5211255.

Chapter 3

[1] Yarwood, Doreen. *Illustrated Encyclopedia of World Costume*, New York: Dover Publications, 2011, p.440.

[2] Zieseniss, Charles Otto, and Le Bourhis, Katell. *The Age of Napoleon: Costume from Revolution to Empire, 1789–1815*, New York: Metropolitan Museum of Art, 1989, p.89.

[3] Challamel, Augustin, et al. *The History of Fashion in France: Or, The Dress of Women from the Gallo-Roman Period to the Present Time*, Low, Marston, Searle, & Rivington, 1882, p.187.

[4] Austen, Jane. *Emma: An Annotated Edition*, Cambridge: Harvard University Press, 2012, p.342.

[5] Tevis, Julia Ann, and Tevis, John. *Sixty Years in a School-Room: An Autobiography of Mrs. Julia A. Tevis*, Hansebooks GmbH, 2017, p.259.

[6] *Weekly Intelligence*, London, August 16, 1818.

[7] Austen, Jane. *Pride and Prejudice: An Annotated Edition*, London: Harvard University Press, 2010, p.329.

[8] "The Selector," *The Sydney Gazette and New South Wales Advertiser* (NSW: 1803–1842), February 4, 1826, http://nla.gov.au/nla.news-article2185180

[9] *Redmond's Bride, a fragment, and other poems*, 1824, p.44.

[10] *La Belle Assemblee 7*, 1828, p.258.

[11] Juhasz, Esther. In Simon, Reeva S., et al. eds. *The Jews of the Middle East and North Africa in Modern Times*, New York: Columbia University Press, 2003, p.214.

[12] Horne, Alistair. *Friend Or Foe: A History of France*, London: Orion, 2012.

[13] Stevenson, Pauline. *Bridal Fashions*, Middlesex: Ian Allan, 1978.

[14] Gomme, George Laurence. *Manners and Customs*, Stock, 1890, p.61.

[15] Southey, Robert. *Southey's Common-place Book*, Longman, Brown, Green and Longmans, 1850, p.326.

[16] Franck, Robert R., ed. *Bast and Other Plant Fibres*, Oxford: Taylor & Francis, 2005, p.332 / Darwin, Tess. *The Scots Herbal: The Plant Lore of Scotland*, Mercat Press, 1996, p.173.

[17] Houck, Carter, ed. *White Work: Techniques and 188 Designs*, New York: Dover Publications, 2013, p.4.

[18] Mathiassen, Tove Engelhardt, Nosch, Marie-Louise, and Ringgaard, Maj, eds. *Fashionable Encounters: Perspectives and Trends in Textile and Dress in the Early Modern Nordic World*, Oxford: Oxbow Books, 2014, p.182.

[19] Smith, H. W. *Life and Correspondence of the Rev. William Smith*, 1880, p.350.

[20] *The Lady's Magazine, Or, Entertaining Companion for the Fair Sex, Appropriated Solely to Their Use and Amusement*, London: Robinson and Roberts, 1793, p.76.

[21] Austen, Jane. *Selected Letters*, Oxford: Oxford University Press, 2004, p.23.

[22] Emery, Sarah Smith. *Reminiscences of a Nonagenarian*, W.H. Huse & Company, 1879, p.30.

[23] Wright, Merideth. *Everyday Dress of Rural America, 1783–1800: With Instructions and Patterns*, New York: Dover Publications, 1992, p.40.

[24] *Sun*, December 5, 1806, p.4, via https://www.britishnewspaperarchive.co.uk

[25] *Morning Post*, June 30, 1801, p.4, via https://www.britishnewspaperarchive.co.uk

[26] Wright, 1992, p.48.

[27] Buck, Anne. *Thomas Lester, His Lace and the East Midlands Industry, 1820-1905*, Ruth Bean, 1981, p.2.

[28] Vidi. *Mr. Frank: The Underground Mail-agent*, Philadelphia: Lippincott, Grambo & Company, 1853, p.18.

[29] *Philadelphia, Three Centuries of American Art: Bicentennial Exhibition, April 11–October 10, 1976*: [catalogue], Philadelphia: Philadelphia Museum of Art, 1976, p.211.

[30] Object page, "Wedding Gown with Train and Rosettes," Rijksmuseum, accessed June 25, 2025, https://www.rijksmuseum.nl/en/collection/object/Wedding-Gown-with-Train-and-Rosettes--da0feac27775f742f7c0b5e2e2cbf965?query=margaretha&collectionSearchContext=Art&page=1&sortingType=Popularity

[31] Mackrell, Alice. *Shawls, Stoles and Scarves*, London: Batsford, 1986, p.92.

[32] de la Haye, Amy. *Ravishing: The Rose in Fashion*, New Haven: Yale University Press, 2020, p.118.

[33] *Westmorland Advertiser and Kendal Chronicle*, February 8, 1812, via https://www.britishnewspaperarchive.co.uk

[34] Staniland, Kay. *In royal fashion: the clothes of Princess Charlotte of Wales & Queen Victoria 1796–1901*, London: Museum of London, 1997, p.62.

[35] Hone, William. *Hone's authentic account of the Royal Marriage, consisting of original memoirs of Prince Leopold and Princess Charlotte, ... a variety of anecdotes of his Serene Highness hitherto unknown ... details of the marriage ceremonial, and description of the dresses, equipages, etc.*, 1816, p.38.

[36] Niles, Hezekiah. *Niles' Weekly Register*, Baltimore: Hezekiah Niles, 1816, p.383.

[37] Jones, C. Rachel. *The Princess Charlotte of Wales: An Illustrated Monograph*, London: B. Quaritch, 1885, p.142.

[38] Staniland, Kay. *In Royal Fashion: The Clothes of Princess Charlotte of Wales and Queen Victoria, 1796–1901*, London: Museum of London, 1997, p.185.

[39] *The Repository of Arts, Literature, Fashions, Manufactures, &c.* London: Ackermann, 1816, p.55.

[40] Byron, George Gordon. *Poetry of Byron: Chosen and Arranged*, London: Macmillan and Company, 1892, p.46.

[41] *The Literary Panorama*, 1812, p.757.

[42] Object page, "Pair of wedding shoes," V&A, accessed June 25, 2025, https://collections.vam.ac.uk/item/O75615/pair-ofwedding-unknown/

[43] https://blog.nls.uk/a-scottish-penny-wedding/

[44] Dunbar, John Telfer. *The Costume of Scotland*, London: Batsford, 1989, p.155.

[45] Clevenger, Jennifer Lynn. *Poetry as a Source of Knowledge on Historic Dress in a Social, Political, and Economic Context: The Scottish Highlanders from 1603 through 1830 as an Example*, Diss. Virginia Tech, 2004, p.282.

[46] Houston, R. A. *Bride Ales and Penny Weddings: Recreations, Reciprocity, and Regions in Britain from the Sixteenth to the Nineteenth Centuries*, Oxford, Oxford University Press, 2014, p.113.

[47] Clevenger, 2004, p.286.

[48] Wood, Edward J., *The Wedding Day in All Ages and Countries*, New York: Harper & Bros., 1869, p.74.

[49] Elliott, Maude Howe ed. *Art and Handicraft in the Woman's Building of the World's Columbian Exposition, Chicago, 1893*, Paris: Boussod, Valadon & Company, 1893, p.189.

[50] *The Australian* (Sydney, NSW: 1824–1848), December 12, 1829, http://nla.gov.au/nla.news-article36866522

[51] Bohleke, Karin J. *Nineteenth-century Costume Treasures of the Fashion Archives and Museum: 1800–1900*, Shippensburg: Shippensburg University Fashion Archives and Museum, 2010, p.14.

[52] Cumming, Valerie, et al. *The Dictionary of Fashion History*, London: Bloomsbury Publishing, 2017.

[53] "Female Fashions for August," *The Sydney Monitor*, December 14, 1829, p.2. http://nla.gov.au/nla.news-article32072924

[54] Mrs Gore. *The Rose Fancier's Manual*, London: H. Colburn, 1838, p.27.

[55] Loudon, Jane. *Stories of a Bride: by the Author of The Mummy*, London: H. Colburn and R. Bentley, 1829, p.161.

[56] Toplis, Alison. *The Clothing Trade in Provincial England, 1800–1850*, Oxford: Taylor & Francis, 2015, p.140.

[57] Hill, Georgiana. *A History of English Dress from the Saxon Period to the Present Day*, London: R. Bentley, 1893, p.243.

[58] Ibid.

[59] "London and Parisian Fashions", *The Hobart Town Courier* (Tas. : 1827–1839), January 13, 1837, http://nla.gov.au/nla.news-article4173978

[60] "Newest London Fashions for April," *The Sydney Monitor* (NSW: 1828–1838), August 20, 1834, http://nla.gov.au/nla.news-article32146990

[61] *The Young Lady's Book: A Manual of Elegant Recreations, Exercises, and Pursuits*, Boston: Carter, Hendee and Babcock, and Abel Bowen, 1829, p.311.

Chapter 4

[1] Kha, Henry. *A History of Divorce Law: Reform in England from the Victorian to Interwar Years*, Oxford: Taylor & Francis, 2020, p.2.

[2] Sherr, Lynn, and Kazickas, Jurate. *The American woman's gazetteer*, New York: Bantam Books, 1976, p.165.

[3] Bischoff, Gottlieb-Wilhelm. *Lehrbuch der botanik: bd., 1.-2. th. Specielle botanik I-II*, 1840. Germany, E. Schweizerbart's, 1840, p.200.

[4] *The Etiquette of Love, Courtship, and Marriage. To which is Added, the Etiquette of Politeness*, Milner & Sowerby, 1859, p.106.

[5] Ibid, p.104.

[6] Chesnut, Mary Boykin. *Mary Chesnut's Diary*, London: Penguin Publishing Group, 2011.

[7] Ibid.

[8] "The Paris Fashions," *The Age* (Melbourne, Vic.: 1854–1954), July 24, 1867, http://nla.gov.au/nla.news-article185505190

[9] "The Ladies' Column," *Adelaide Observer* (SA: 1843–1904), July 17, 1869, http://nla.gov.au/nla.news-article159464099

[10] *The Court Magazine and Monthly Critic, and Lady's Magazine and Museum: A Family Journal of the Belles Lettres, Music, Fine Arts, Drama, Fashion, Etc.*, London: Dobbs, 1838, p.328.

[11] "Newest London Fashions for April," *The Sydney Monitor* (NSW: 1828–1838), August 20, 1834, http://nla.gov.au/nla.news-article32146990

[12] "Fashions," *The Sydney Herald* (NSW: 1831–1842), October 19, 1837, http://nla.gov.au/nla.news-article12858513

[13] Unknown author. *The Grove Encyclopedia of Materials and Techniques in Art*, Oxford: Oxford University Press, 2008, p.317.

[14] *The Ladies' Work-table Book: Containing Clear and Practical Instructions in Plain and Fancy Needlework, Embroidery, Knitting, Netting, Crochet, and Tatting: with Numerous Engravings, Illustrative of the Various Stitches in Those Useful and Fashionable Employments*, London: H.G. Clarke, 1843, p.164.

[15] Ramsay, L.G.G., and Edwards, Ralph, eds. *The Connoisseur Period Guides to the Houses, Decoration, Furnishing, and Chattels of the Classic Periods*. New York: Reynal, 1958, p.133.

[16] Warner, Frank. *The Silk Industry of the United Kingdom: Its Origin and Development*, London: Drane's, 1921, p.285.

[17] Knowles, Katie. "Consumerism and Curation: Sarah Tate's Resistance," Black Perspectives, June 25, 2021, https://www.aaihs.org/consumerism-and-curation-sarah-tates-resistance/

[18] Jenkins, Wilbert L., *Seizing the New Day: African Americans in Post-Civil War Charleston*, Bloomington, Indiana University Press, 2003, p.7.

[19] Schwalm, Leslie A. *A Hard Fight for We: Women's Transition from Slavery to Freedom in South Carolina*, Champaigne, University of Illinois Press, 2023, pp.53–54.

[20] *Blackwood's Edinburgh Magazine*, Magazine 57, No. 355, May 1845. Russia, ЛитРес, 2021.

[21] Hall, Allen A., ed. *The Politician*, Nashville: B.R. McKennie, 1846, p.478.

[22] Richardson, Frances. *Rural change in north Wales during the period of the industrial revolution: Livelihoods, poverty and welfare in Nantconwy, 1750–1860*, Oxford: University of Oxford, 2015, p.48.

[23] Mitchell, Sally. *Daily Life in Victorian England*, Santa Barbara: ABC-CLIO, 2008, p.163.

[24] *The New Monthly Belle Assemblee*, 1857, vol. 46–47, p.333.

[25] Braddon, Mary Elizabeth. *The Doctor's Wife: A Novel* (Classic Reprint), London: FB&C Limited, 2016, p.154.

[26] "Fashions for December," *The Melbourne Daily News* (Vic.: 1848–1851), April 30, 1849, http://nla.gov.au/nla.news-article226472389

[27] Lemire, Beverly and Riello, Giorgio, eds. *Dressing Global Bodies: The Political Power of Dress in World History*, Oxford: Taylor & Francis, 2019.

[28] Clark, Rowena. *Hatches, Matches and Dispatches: Christening, Bridal & Mourning Fashions*, Melbourne: National Gallery of Victoria, 1987, p.57.

[29] *The Keepsake*, London: Bogue, 1850, p.16.

[30] *Blackwood's Lady's Magazine and Gazette of the Fashionable World, Or, St. James's Court-register of Belles Lettres, Fine Arts, Music, Drama, Fashions, &c.* A.H. Blackwood, G. Simpkin, and J. Page, 1850, p.85.

[31] "Paris Fashions for December," *Adelaide Times* (SA: 1848–1858), April 29, 1851, http://nla.gov.au/nla.newsarticle207068946

[32] Knight, Charles. *Knight's Cyclopadia of the Industry of All Nations: 1851*, London: C. Knight, 1851.

[33] *Court Etiquette; a guide to intercourse with royal or titled persons, to drawing rooms, levees, courts and audiences, the usages of social life. By a Man of the World*, London: Charles Mitchell, 1849, p.93.

[34] Phegley, Jennifer. *Courtship and Marriage in Victorian England*, Santa Barbara: ABC-CLIO, 2012, p.124.

[35] *The New York Journal: An Illustrated Literary Periodical*, New York: P. D. Orvis, 1854, p.53.

[36] "The Royal Wedding," *The Cornwall Chronicle* (Launceston, Tas.: 1835–1880), March 20, 1858, http://nla.gov.au/nla.news-article65731575

[37] "The Mystery of a Lady's Dress," *South Australian Weekly Chronicle* (Adelaide, SA: 1858–1867), September 10, 1859, http://nla.gov.au/nla.newsarticle96491914

[38] Quirindi & District Historical Society, New South Wales, Australia.

[39] Blaszczyk, Regina Lee. *The Color Revolution*, Cambridge MA, MIT Press, 2012, p.21.

[40] Janvrin, Mary, W. "Squire Holman's Wooing," *Peterson's Magazine*, 1858, p.325.

[41] "Fashions for April," *The Courier* (Hobart, Tas.: 1840–1859), July 13, 1855, http://nla.gov.au/nla.newsarticle2486922

[42] "Dress and Fashion," *South London Observer*, March 23, 1881, p.7.

[43] *Gossip*, London, June 6, 1885, p.131.

[44] Manning Valley Historical Society, New South Wales, Australia.

[45] Lean, Vincent Stuckey, et al. *Lean's Collectanea*, Bristol: J. W. Arrowsmith, 1902, p.90.

[46] *Sacramento Daily Union 10*, no. 1441, November 7, 1855.

[47] "Fashions for March," *The Hobart Town Advertiser* (Tas.: 1839–1861), June 2, 1860, http://nla.gov.au/nla.newsarticle264688522

[48] "Fashions for November," *Colonist*, February 12, 1861, https://paperspast.natlib.govt.nz/newspapers/TC18610212.2.21

[49] "Fashions, Gossip, etc." *The Queenslander* (Brisbane, Qld.: 1866–1939), October 27, 1866, http://nla.gov.au/nla.newsarticle20310114

[50] "Fashions for February," *New Peterson Magazine*, 1860, p.175.

[51] Hale, Sarah J. and Godey, L. A. eds. *Godey's Lady's Book*, 1870, p.397.

[52] Probert, Rebecca. *Tying the Knot*, Cambridge: Cambridge University Press, 2021, p.104.

[53] Alcott, Louisa May. *The Complete Works of Louisa May Alcott*, DigiCat, 2022.

[54] Groves, Nancy Alice. *A Study of Quaker Costume*, Madison: University of Wisconsin–Madison, 1951, p.85.

[55] *The Habits of Good Society: A Handbook for Ladies and Gentlemen*, New York: Carleton, 1863, p.425.

[56] https://samlingar.shm.se.

[57] "English Fashions for March," *The South Australian Advertiser* (Adelaide, SA: 1858–1889), June, 1868, http://nla.gov.au/nla.news-article31978898

[58] *Marysville Daily Appeal*, December 5, 1869.

[59] "Hints on Buying a Trousseau," *The Goulburn Herald and Chronicle* (NSW: 1864–1881), September 19, 1868, http://nla.gov.au/nla.news-article101476934

[60] "Hints on Buying a Trousseau," *Daily Southern Cross*, October 29, 1868, https://paperspast.natlib.govt.nz/newspapers/DSC18681029.2.32

[61] Bishop, John Leander, et al. *A History of American Manufactures from 1608 to 1860*, London: E. Young, 1868, p.113.

[62] Object page, "Wedding ensemble," Metropolitan Museum of Art, accessed June 25 2025, https://www.metmuseum.org/art/collection/search/107837

[63] Volo, Dorothy, and Volo, James M. *Daily Life in Civil War America*, Santa Barbara: ABC-CLIO, 2009, p.335.

[64] Hartley, Florence. *Ladies' Book of Etiquette, and Manual of Politeness*, Boston: G.W. Cottrell, 1860. p.33.

[65] Hale, Sarah Josepha Buell. *Manners: Or, Happy Homes and Good Society All the Year Round*, Boston: J. E. Tilton, 1868, p.128.

[66] *Bazaar Exchange and Mart, and Journal of the Household*, 1891, p.1026.

Chapter 5

[1] Cunningham, Patricia Anne and Voso Lab, Susan, eds. *Dress and Popular Culture*, Bowling Green: Bowling Green State University Popular Press, 1991, p.101.

[2] Lansdell, Avril. *Wedding Fashions, 1860–1980*, Princes Risborough: Shire Publications, 1983, p.25.

[3] *Arthur's Illustrated Home Magazine*, 1878, p.395.

[4] *Sun & Central Press*, April 20, 1871, p.11.

[5] Backett-Milburn, K. & McKie, L., eds. *Constructing Gendered Bodies*, London: Palgrave Macmillan, 2001, p.129.

[6] Howe, Irving. *World of Our Fathers: The Journey of the East European Jews to America and the Life They Found and Made*, New York: Open Road Media, 2017.

[7] Howard, Vicki. *Brides, Inc.: American Weddings and the Business of Tradition*, Philadelphia: University of Pennsylvania Press, 2008, p.100.

[8] *Public Opinion*, 1871, p.363.

[9] Doake, Margaret. *May Darling*, London: Literary Production Committee, 1881, p.68.

[10] "Girls' Gossip," *The Ballarat Star* (Vic.: 1865–1924), December 2, 1882, http://nla.gov.au/nla.news-article202700243

[11] Howard, 2008, p.170.

[12] "Broadbrim's New York Letters," *Bendigo Advertiser* (Vic.: 1855–1918), June 24, 1882, http://nla.gov.au/nla.newsarticle88627533

[13] *Tunbridge Wells Journal*, September 2, 1886.

[14] "Ladies" *The Sydney Mail and New South Wales Advertiser* (NSW: 1871–1912), April 3, 1880, p.636. http://nla.gov.au/nla.newsarticle161879970

[15] *Ladies' Home Journal*, 1889, p.24.

[16] *The Delineator*, 1880, p.317.

[17] Lansdell, Avril. *Wedding Fashions 1860–1980*, Princes Risborough: Shire Publications, 1983, p.25.

[18] Hill, Kate. *Britain and the Narration of Travel in the Nineteenth Century: Texts, Images, Objects*, Oxfordshire: Taylor & Francis, 2017.

[19] "A Wedding Wardrobe," *Weekly Times* (Melbourne, Vic.: 1869–1954), February 15, 1873, http://nla.gov.au/nla.news-article220454510

[20] *Arthur's Home Magazine*, 1872, p.134

[21] Cheadle, Eliza. *Manners of Modern Society: Being a Book of Etiquette*, London: Cassell, Petter & Galpin, 1872, p.82.

[22] *North Devon Journal*, September 29, 1870, p.6.

[23] MacKay, M. Elaine. *Beyond the Silhouette: Fashion and the Women of Historic Kingston*, Kingston Ontario: Agnes Etherington Art Centre, 2007, p.41.

[24] *The Young Ladies' Journal*, 1873, p.15.

[25] Gardner, Sue, ed. *A to Z of Crochet*, Bothell: Martingale, 2010, p.4.

[26] *Placer Herald*, September 22, 1877, p.6.

[27] Bohleke, 2010. p.48.

[28] Riley, Glenda. *The female frontier: a comparative view of women on the prairie and the plains*, Lawrence: University Press of Kansas, 1988, p.49.

[29] Hepworth, George Hughes. *Rocks and Shoals: Lectures to Young Men*, Boston: American Unitarian Association, 1870, pp.31–32.

[30] "Our Lady's Letter," *The Capricornian* (Rockhampton, Qld.: 1875–1929), December 11, 1875 http://nla.gov.au/nla.news-article65738236

[31] *Demorests' Monthly Magazine*, 1878, p.552.

[32] "The Lady's Column," *The Australasian* (Melbourne, Vic.: 1864–1946), October 26, 1872, http://nla.gov.au/nla.newsarticle137575272

[33] *Townsend's monthly selection of Parisian costumes*, 1877.

[34] Fry, Herbert. *London in 1880: Illustrated with Bird's-eye Views of the Principal Streets*, London: D. Bogue, 1880, p.117.

[35] Anlağan, Cetin, and Bragner, Robert. *Turkish Tiles and Ceramics*, Istanbul: Sadberk Hanim Museum, 1995, p.143.

[36] *Petaluma Argus Courier*, December 6, 1943.

[37] Hartley, Florence. *Ladies' Book of Etiquette, and Manual of Politeness*, Boston: G.W. Cottrell, 1860, p.261.

[38] "Home Interests," *The Queenslander* (Brisbane, Qld.: 1866–1939), December 6, 1873, http://nla.gov.au/nla.newsarticle27278756

[39] "The Ladies' Column," *The Albury Banner and Wodonga Express* (NSW: 1860–1927; 1929–1931; 1933–1938), January 2, 1875, http://nla.gov.au/nla.newsarticle257944746

[40] Aindow, Rosy. *Dress and Identity in British Literary Culture, 1870–1914*, Oxford: Taylor & Francis, 2016.

[41] *Lakes Chronicle and Reporter*, May 12, 1877.

[42] "The Fashions of the Month," *The Sydney Mail and New South Wales Advertiser* (NSW: 1871–1912), May 17, 1879 http://nla.gov.au/nla.news-article162809305

[43] "The Ladies' Column," *The Albury Banner and Wodonga Express* (NSW: 1860–1927; 1929–1931; 1933–1938), February 15, 1879: http://nla.gov.au/nla.newsarticle257953650

[44] Frost, S.A. *The Art of Dressing Well. A Complete Guide to Economy, Style and Propriety of Costume ... To which are Added One Hundred Hints for Dressing Well*, New York: Dick & Fitzgerald, 1870. p.108.

[45] *Demorest's Monthly Magazine*, 1880, p.131

[46] *San Jose Mercury-news*, November 27, 1881.

[47] "Coquille Ruche," *The Australasian* (Melbourne, Vic.: 1864–1946), November 25, 1882, http://nla.gov.au/nla.newsarticle138646001

[48] Shippensburg University Fashion Archives and Museum.

[49] *New Peterson Magazine*, 1888, p.576.

[50] *Sacramento Daily Union*, January, 1882.

[51] "The New Trimmings of the Season," *The Brisbane Courier* (Qld.: 1864–1933), June 2, 1883 http://nla.gov.au/nla.news-article3418680

[52] "Feminine Fashions and Fancies," *The Express and Telegraph* (Adelaide, SA: 1867–1922), November 11, 1888, http://nla.gov.au/nla.news-article208196740

[53] "Feminine Fashions and Fancies," *The Express and Telegraph* (Adelaide, SA: 1867–1922), November 5 1879, http://nla.gov.au/nla.news-article207656929

[54] Symonds, John Addington. *New Italian Sketches*, Leipzig: Bernhard Tauchnitz, 1884, p.217.

[55] Olson, Greg. *Voodoo Priests, Noble Savages, and Ozark Gypsies: The Life of Folklorist Mary Alicia Owen*, Columbia: University of Missouri Press, 2012, p.44.

[56] Eliot, George. *Silas Marner, and Scenes of Clerical Life*, Boston: Fields, Osgood & Co., 1869, p.108.

[57] *Daily Alta California*, December 23, 1887.

[58] *Good Housekeeping*, 1887, p.ii.

[59] *The Delineator*, 1880, p.99.

[60] "Orange blossoms, a marriage chronicle," 1884, p.18.

[61] *Arthur's Home Magazine*, 1884, p.663.

[62] *The Bulletin*, April 12, 1884, p.16.

[63] Sarkar, Ajoy K., et al. *The Fairchild Books Dictionary of Textiles*, New York: Bloomsbury Publishing, 2021, p.37.

[64] "Fashions," *The Colac Herald* (Vic.: 1875–1918), December 13, 1889: http://nla.gov.au/nla.news-article87350193

[65] "Orange Blossoms," *Queensland Figaro and Punch* (Brisbane, Qld.: 1885–1889), December 31, 1887, http://nla.gov.au/nla.news-article84114504

[66] *Daily Alta California*, February 19, 1888.

[67] *Placer Herald*, July 16, 1887.

[68] "Dress Worn at Weddings," *Adelaide Observer* (SA: 1843–1904), May 5, 1888, http://nla.gov.au/nla.newsa-rticle160776747

[69] "New Fashion Notes," *Melbourne Punch* (Vic.: 1855–1900), December 29, 1887, http://nla.gov.au/nla.newsarticle174573218

[70] "An Aboriginal Wedding," *Queensland Figaro and Punch* (Brisbane, Qld.: 1885–1889), January 28, 1888, http://nla.gov.au/nla.newsarticle84108511

[71] "The Ladies' Page," *Leader* (Melbourne, Vic.: 1862–1918, 1935) August 10, 1889, http://nla.gov.au/nla.newsarticle198057049

[72] *Peterson's Magazine*, 1885, p.467.

[73] *Tenbury Wells Advertiser*, November 13, 1888, p.5.

[74] https://milingimbiart.com/yolngu-namesochre/.

[75] https://www.alrc.gov.au/publication/recognition-of-aboriginal-customary-laws-alrcreport-31/12-aboriginal-marriages-and-familystructures/marriage-in-traditional-aboriginalsocieties

[76] "Wedding Ceremony at the Aboriginal Station, Coranderrk," *Illustrated Australian News for Home Readers* (Melbourne, Vic. : 1867–1875), April 25, 1868, http://nla.gov.au/nla.newsarticle60449278

[77] *Table Talk*, 1889, p.9.

[78] *Frank Leslie's Illustrated Newspaper*, November 7, 1889, p.323.

[79] *Elgin Courant, and Morayshire Advertiser*, July 26, 1889.

[80] "Sho," *The Gippsland Farmers' Journal and Traralgon, Heyfield and Rosedale News* (Vic.: 1887–1893), November 26, 1889 http://nla.gov.au/nla.newsarticle227352496

[81] *The Delineator*, 1889, p.399.

[82] Ibid, p.383.

[83] *The Australian Journal: A Weekly Record of Literature, Science, and Art*, 1889, p.518.

[84] "Wedding Favours," *The Armidale Express and New England General Advertiser* (NSW: 1856–1861; 1863–1889; 1891–1954), June 7, 1887, http://nla.gov.au/nla.newsarticle192881423

[85] "A Bride's Shoes," *Newcastle Morning Herald and Miners' Advocate* (NSW: 1876–1954), June 27, 1885, http://nla.gov.au/nla.news-article139076511

Chapter 6

[1] *Ladies' Home Journal*, 1889, p.25.

[2] "Bridal Fashions," *Marysville Daily Appeal*, March 10, 1899, p.3.

[3] Montemurro, Beth. *Something Old, Something Bold: Bridal Showers and Bachelorette Parties*, New Brunswick: Rutgers University Press, 2006, p.135.

[4] Ed. Ganong, L.H. & Coleman, M.J., *The Social History of the American Family: An Encyclopedia* Thousand Oaks: SAGE Publications, 2014, p.1438.

[5] Charsley, Simon. *Wedding Cakes and Cultural History*, Oxford: Taylor & Francis, 2022, p.131.

Notes 235

[6] Shrimpton, Jayne. *Tracing Your Ancestors Through Family Photographs: A Complete Guide for Family and Local Historians*, Barnsley: Pen & Sword Books Limited, 2014, p.128.

[7] *Bazaar Exchange and Mart, and Journal of the Household*, 1893, p.460.

[8] Abelson, Elaine S. *When Ladies Go A-thieving: Middle-class Shoplifters in the Victorian Department Store*, Oxford: Oxford University Press, 1992, p.25.

[9] Lomax in Ugolini, Laura. *Cultures of Selling:Perspectives on Consumption and Society Since 1700*, Oxford: Taylor & Francis, 2018, p.273.

[10] Crossick, G. & Jaumain, S., eds. *Cathedrals of Consumption: European Department Stores, 1850-1939*, Oxford: Taylor & Francis, 2019.

[11] Eluwawalage, Damayanthie ed. *Fashion: Tyranny and Revelation*, Leiden: Brill, 2019, p3.

[12] Bagnall, Kate and Martinez, Julia T., *Locating Chinese Women: Historical Mobility Between China and Australia*, Hong Kong: Hong Kong University Press, 2021, p.47.

[13] "The Latest Fashions," *Australian Town and Country Journal* (Sydney, NSW: 1870–1919), September 14, 1904, http://nla.gov.au/nla.news-article71514305>.

[14] *The Museum Journal*. Lubbock: West Texas Museum Association, 1973, p.61.

[15] Ibid.

[16] Haakenson, Bergine & Fairbanks, Carol, eds. *Writings of Farm Women, 1840–1940: An Anthology*, Oxford: Taylor & Francis, 2017.

[17] Edwards, Nina. *Dressed for War: Uniform, Civilian Clothing and Trappings, 1914 to 1918*, London: I.B.Tauris, 2014, p.164.

[18] *Vanity Fair*, 1966, p.110.

[19] Weber, Eugen. *Peasants Into Frenchmen: The Modernization of Rural France, 1870–1914*, Redwood City: Stanford University Press, 1976, p.228.

[20] "What It Was," *Australian Town and Country Journal* (Sydney, NSW: 1870–1919), April 9, 1892, http://nla.gov.au/nla.newsarticle71236372

[21] "Wedding Dresses," *The Cumberland Free Press* (Parramatta, NSW: 1895–1897), August 10, 1895, http://nla.gov.au/nla.news-article144435309

[22] *The Florists' Exchange*, Florists' Exchange Publishing Company, 1890, p.71.

[23] Cole, George S. *A Complete Dictionary of Dry Goods and History of Silk, Cotton, Linen, Wool and Other Fibrous Substances*, Chicago: W. B. Conkey Company, 1892, p.128.

[24] *The Australian Journal: A Weekly Record of Literature, Science, and Art* 1891, p.118.

[25] "Weddings," Leader (Melbourne, Vic. : 1862–1918, 1935), December 23, 1899, http://nla.gov.au/nla.newsarticle198073511

[26] Hernandez, P. Grace "Near Neighbors: Brooklyn Dressmakers in the Brooklyn Museum Costume Collection at The Metropolitan Museum of Art," Metropolitan Museum of Art, accessed June 25, 2025: https://www.metmuseum.org/blogs/now-atthe-met/features/2013/near-neighbors

[27] Wells, Richard A., *Manners, Culture and Dress of the Best American Society*, Springfield MA: King Richardson & Co., 1891, p.346.

[28] *The Ladies' Home Journal*, 1893, p.29.

[29] *Brooklyn Blue Book*, 1896, p.ix.

[30] *Mariposa Gazette*, January 26, 1895, p.4.

[31] *San Francisco Call*, June 7, 1899.

[32] Klug, Sophie. *The Art of Dressmaking*, London: J.T. Miller, 1895 p.36.

[33] *The Ladies' Home Journal*, 1894, p.35.

[34] *The Ladies' Home Journal*, 1891, p.33.

[35] *Auckland Star*, Issue 76, April 1, 1899, p.6.

[36] *Daily Telegraph*, Issue 7125, July 28, 1894, p.6

[37] *San Diego Union and Daily Bee*, May 2, 1892.

[38] *Pacific Rural Press*, December 12, 1896.

[39] *Morning Tribune*, June 3, 1894.

[40] "Women's Chats," *The West Australian* (Perth, WA: 1879–1954), December 25, 1896, http://nla.gov.au/nla.article3104575

[41] *Good Housekeeping Magazine*, 1890, p.i.

[42] Cooke, Maud C. *Social Life Or the Manners and Customs of Polite Society*, CreateSpace Independent Publishing Platform, 2015, p.157.

[43] "Short Story," *The Cumberland Argus and Fruitgrowers Advocate* (Parramatta, NSW: 1888–1950), September 29, 1894, http://nla.gov.au/nla.news-article85652153

[44] Hazelius-Berg, Gunnel, *Draktreformer under 1800-talet, Fataburen Nordiska Museets och Skansens Arsbok*, 1949, pp.127–156.

[45] Object page. "Reformkjole, 1904," Musems and Palaces website, Denmark, accessed June 25, 2025, https://natmus.dk/historisk-viden/temaer/modens-historie/1890-1920/reformkjole/

[46] "Something About Dress Reform," *Morning Tribune*, January 10, 1884, p.4.

[47] "A Remarkable Wedding," *Poverty Bay Herald*, March 16, 1894, p4.

[48] "Yokes and Sleeves," May 28, 1904, *Bromsgrove & Droitwich Messenger*, p.8.

[49] *Santa Barbara Weekly Press*, May 28, 1903.

[50] Seleshanko, Kristina. *Edwardian Fashions: A Snapshot in Time from Harper's Bazar 1906*, New York: Dover Publications, 2019, p.vi.

[51] "The Ladies," *The Express and Telegraph* (Adelaide, SA : 1867–1922), March 3, 1906, http://nla.gov.au/nla.newsarticle208798445

[52] Nunn, Joan. *Fashion in Costume, 1200-200*, New York: New Amsterdam Books, 2000, p.185.

[53] *Chico Record*, May 21, 1905.

[54] *Los Angeles Herald*, March 15, 1908.

[55] *San Bernardino Sun*, November 20, 1907.

[56] La Barre, Kathleen Mabel, and La Barre, Kay D., *Reference Book of Women's Vintage Clothing, 1900-1909*, Portland: La Barre Books, 2003, p.326.

[57] *Stockton Independent*, September 22, 1905.

[58] Smiley, James Bethuel. *Modern Manners and Social Forms: A Manual of the Manners and Customs of the Best Modern Society, Comp. from the Latest Authorities*, James B. Smiley, 1890, p112.

[59] Miller, Janet E., and Barbara M. Reagan. "Degradation in weighted and unweighted historic silks," *Journal of the American Institute for Conservation*, 1989, 97–115.

[60] *San Francisco Call*, May 8, 1904.

[61] "Again Adopt Men's Fashions: Suspender Effects for Women Now In Vogue-Taffeta and Surah Costumes," *Morning Press*, May 14, 1905, p.3.

[62] Lee, Elizabeth Batts, *Talks On Successful Gowning*, 1910, p.178.

[63] "Wedding Bells," *The Kadina and Wallaroo Times* (SA: 1888–1954), July 13, 1910, http://nla.gov.au/nla.newsarticle109117470

[64] *San Luis Obispo Daily Telegram*, August 27, 1909, p.8.

[65] "Wedding," *The Inverell Times* (NSW: 1899–1907, 1909–1954), April 1, 1913, http://nla.gov.au/nla.newsarticle185936596

[66] *South Bucks Standard*, August 21, 1908, p.5.

[67] Ritter, Thomas Jefferson. *Mother's Remedies: Over One Thousand Tried and Tested Remedies from Mothers of the United States and Canada*, Project Gutenberg, 2010, p.735.

[68] Allinson, May. *Dressmaking as a Trade for Women in Massachusetts*, United States Bureau of Labor Statistics, 1916, p.84.

[69] York, Kathleen. *Bridal Fashion 1900–1950*, London: Bloomsbury Publishing, 2012, p.10.

[70] "Suggestions for the June Bride," *Dundee Evening Telegraph*, May 31, 1909, p.6.

[71] *Derbyshire Advertiser and Journal*, November 5, 1909.

[72] Tebbs, Louisa Augusta, and Tebbs, Rosa. *The Art of Bobbin Lace: a Practical Text Book of Workmanship*, 1907.

[73] *Los Angeles Herald*, June 4, 1911.

[74] Lee, 1910, p.177.

[75] *Placer Herald*, August 3, 1912.

[76] Lee, 1910, p.178.

[77] "Wade—Tickle," *Northern Star* (Lismore, NSW: 1876–1954), January 6, 1914, http://nla.gov.au/nla.newsarticle72285250

[78] "The Marriage of the Hon. Mary Bruce," *Dundee Courier*, April 27, 1910, p.7.

[79] "Social Happening of Interest," *San Bernardino Sun*, June 25, 1911, p.8.

[80] *San Luis Obispo Daily Telegram*, May 18, 1916, p.4.

[81] Ibid.

[82] *Telephone Review*, New York Telephone Company, 1915, p.243.

[83] *The Delineator*, 1919. p.29.

[84] *United States Economist, and Dry Goods Reporter*, 1916, p.103.

[85] *Sacramento Daily Union*, August 27, 1916, p.19.

[86] "The Wardrobe," *The Argus* (Melbourne, Vic.: 1848–1957), August 25, 1915, http://nla.gov.au/nla.newsarticle1552654

[87] "A Hundred Years of Funny Fashions: How a Modern Student of 'Clothes Lines' Traces the Astonishing Variations in Feminine Garb from Early in the Last Century to the Present Perplexing Fascinating 'Hobble.'" *San Diego Union and Daily Bee*, July 20, 1919, p.4.

[88] Adler, David. *David Adler, Architect: The Elements of Style*, Chicago: Art Institute of Chicago, 2002, p.56.

[89] *San Francisco Call*, June 17, 1914.

Chapter 7

[1] "Pre-War and Post-War Brides," *Hull Daily Mail*, September 26, 1919, p.6.

[2] *The Delineator*, 1919, p.83.

[3] Hill, Daniel Delis. *Advertising to the American Woman, 1900–1999*, Columbus: Ohio State University Press, 2002, p.71.

[4] "Woman's World," *Circular Head Chronicle* (Stanley, Tas.: 1906–1954), March 9, 1927, http://nla.gov.au/nla.newsarticle169011872

[5] "Bare Arms," *Cowra Free Press* (NSW: 1911–1937), March 1, 1927, http://nla.gov.au/nla.news-article262040759

[6] "Sleeveless Frocks," *The Herald* (Melbourne, Vic.: 1861–1954), February 24, 1927, http://nla.gov.au/nla.newsarticle243609089

[7] King, John Alexander. *Weddings: Modes, Manners & Customs of Weddings*, New York: Delineator, 1927, p.28.

[8] *The Sphere: An Illustrated Newspaper for the Home*, 1922, p.282.

[9] Eluwawalage, ed. 2019, p.5.

[10] "Woman's Interests," *The West Australian* (Perth, WA: 1879–1954), March 26, 1929, http://nla.gov.au/nla.newsarticle32268429

[11] Object page, "Refugee bride and groom separated at time of enemy's invasion of Udine, finally united at Rome," Library of Congress, accessed June 25, 2025, https://www.loc.gov/item/2017672741/.

[12] "Autumn Hats," *Sunday Times* (Perth, WA: 1902–1954), March 25, 1917, http://nla.gov.au/nla.newsarticle58023961

[13] *Sacramento Daily Union*, January 30, 1914.

[14] Ritter, 2010.

[15] https://collections.tepapa.govt.nz/object/54177.

[16] "Paris Fashions," *The Sun* (Sydney, NSW: 1910–1954), April 5, 1920, http://nla.gov.au/nla.newsarticle222410888

[17] "Too-gauzy Frocks," *Daily Herald* (Adelaide, SA: 1910–1924), August 9, 1920, http://nla.gov.au/nla.newsarticle106550764

[18] "Paris Fashions," *The Sun* (Sydney, NSW: 1910–1954), April 5, 1920, http://nla.gov.au/nla.newsarticle222410888

[19] *Otago Witness*, June 15, 1920, p.54.

[20] *Greymouth Evening Star*, March 22, 1920, p.8.

[21] "Family Notices," *Table Talk* (Melbourne, Vic.: 1885–1939), September 29, 1921, http://nla.gov.au/nla.newsarticle146317648

[22] Emery, Joy Spanabel. *A History of the Paper Pattern Industry: The Home Dressmaking Fashion Revolution*, London: Bloomsbury Publishing, 2014, p.242.

[23] Eichler, Lillian. *Book of Etiquette*, 2013, p.79.

[24] "Family Notices," 1921, p.14.

[25] "The Popular Bow," *Sydney Mail* (NSW: 1912–1938), November 7, 1923, http://nla.gov.au/nla.news-article159035806

[26] "The Wardrobe," *The Argus* (Melbourne, Vic.: 1848–1957), August 24, 1921, http://nla.gov.au/nla.newsarticle4668441

[27] Object record, "Dress," Chicago History Museum, accessed June 25, 2025, https://images.chicagohistory.org/asset/28922/

[28] *Good Housekeeping*, 1924, p.68.

[29] "The Bridal Gown," *Sunday Times* (Perth WA: 1902–1954), August 26, 1928 http://nla.gov.au/nla.news-article58362593

[30] *Tatler*, 1929, p.52.

[31] *Healdsburg Tribune*, August 30, 1926.

[32] "Tea Table Gossip," *The Daily Telegraph* (Sydney, NSW: 1883–1930), January 10, 1929 http://nla.gov.au/nla.newsarticle246391775

[33] *Coronado Eagle and Journal*, December 21, 1926.

[34] "A Bridal Dress," *Chronicle* (Adelaide, SA: 1895–1954), July 21, 1928, http://nla.gov.au/nla.news-article90046650

[35] King, John Alexander. *Weddings: Modes, Manners & Customs of Weddings*, New York: Delineator, 1927, p.26.

[36] Ibid, p.69.

[37] "Armand's Bride," *The Mail* (Adelaide, SA: 1912–1954), October 19, 1929 http://nla.gov.au/nla.news-article63435482

[38] *McCall's*, New York: McCall Publishing Company, 1926, p.8.

[39] *Tatler*, 1927

[40] King, 1927, p.70.

[41] Object page, "Wedding dress worn by Margaret Elizabeth Cowled (nee Hamilton)," Powerhouse Collection, access June 25, 2025, https://collection.powerhouse.com.au/object/169115

[42] *The Ladies' Home Journal*, July 1920, p.60.

[43] "Woman's Interests," *The West Australian* (Perth, WA: 1879–1954), August 21, 1928, http://nla.gov.au/nla.newsarticle32216988

[44] "Fancy Dress Weddings," *Chronicle* (Adelaide, SA: 1895–1954), August 27, 1927, http://nla.gov.au/nla.newsarticle90082404

[45] "Wedding," *Cootamundra Herald* (NSW: 1877–1954), February 29, 1928, http://nla.gov.au/nla.news-article143572405

Chapter 8

[1] Anderson, Cinda. *Voices of the Great Depression: The 1930s*, Bloomington: Author House, 2002, p.57.

[2] Endres, Kathleen L., and Lueck, Therese. *Women's Periodicals in the United States: Consumer Magazines*, Santa Barbara: ABC-CLIO, 1995, p.39.

[3] Kendall, Laurel. *Getting Married in Korea: Of Gender, Morality, and Modernity*, Oakland: University of California Press, 1996, p.65.

[4] Kim, Hong-gi. *K-fashion: Wearing a New Future*, Sejong-si: Korean Culture and Information Service, 2012, p.31.

[5] Finnane, Antonia. *Changing Clothes in China: Fashion, History, Nation*, New York: Columbia University Press, 2008.

[6] Shaw, Scott, and Olsen, Kim. *Your Wedding, Your Way: The Modern Couple's Guide to Destination Elopements, Courthouse Ceremonies, Intimate Dinner Parties, and Other Nontraditional Nuptials*, San Francisco: Chronicle Books LLC, 2022, p.220.

[7] "What to Wear to a Wartime Wedding," Imperial War Museum, accessed June 25, 2025, https://www.iwm.org.uk/history/what-to-wear-to-a-wartime-wedding

[8] "War Wedding," *Manchester Evening News*, December 2, 1942, p.2.

[9] Object page, "Lace & Celanese Boudoir Cap With Floral Trims," The Underpinnings Museum, accessed June 25, 2025, https://underpinningsmuseum.com/museumcollections/lace-celanese-boudoir-cap-with-floral-trims/

[10] Phipps, Ciara, and Reed, Claire. *Making Vintage Wedding Dresses: Inspiring Timeless Style*, Ramsbury: Crowood, 2017.

[11] "'Loop Line' New Skirts," *Liverpool Echo*, June 24, 1949, p.5.

[12] *Army, Navy, Air Force Journal & Register*, Army and Navy Journal, Incorporated, 1947, p.1196.

[13] *The Australian woman's mirror* (Sydney: The Bulletin Newspaper), 1924, http://nla.gov.au/nla.obj-407259832

[14] "Wedding," *The Forbes Advocate* (NSW: 1911–1954), September 13, 1929, http://nla.gov.au/nla.newsarticle218368872

[15] "Shades of 2010," *Ballidu-Wongan Budget* (WA: 1927–1941), November 1, 1930 http://nla.gov.au/nla.newsarticle253568635

[16] Farrell-Beck, Jane, and Parsons, Jean. *20th-Century Dress in the United States*, London: Bloomsbury Academic, 2007, p.98.

[17] Shippensburg University Fashion Archives and Museum

[18] Howard, 2008, p.215.

[19] "Famous Wedding Dresses," *Chronicle* (Adelaide, SA: 1895–1954), January 18, 1934, http://nla.gov.au/nla.newsarticle92359318

[20] *San Pedro News Pilot*, August 14, 1934.

[21] "Yellow Satin for Bride," *The Age* (Melbourne, Vic.: 1854–1954), May 17, 1937, http://nla.gov.au/nla.news-article203883374

[22] *Petaluma Argus Courier*, June 24, 1939, p.2.

[23] MacDonald, Anne L. *No Idle Hands: The Social History of American Knitting*, London: Random House Publishing Group, 2010.

[24] *Blue Lake Advocate*, June 22, 1935, p.2.

[25] "Shirtwaist Wedding Gown Is Chic," *Indian Valley Record*, May 30, 1935, p.4.

[26] Sterling, Robin. *Newspaper Clippings from the Cullman, Alabama, Democrat 1930–1934*, Lulu.com, 2019, p.135.

[27] "Choosing a Wedding Dress," *The Week* (Brisbane, Qld.: 1876–1934) May 2, 1934, http://nla.gov.au/nla.newsarticle182611764

[28] "The New Sleeves," *Musselburgh News*, October 2, 1936, p.14.

[29] Shrimpton, 2014, p.114.

[30] *Judische Rundschau*, August 14, 1936, p.9.

[31] *The Mood Guide to Fabric and Fashion: The Essential Guide from the World's Most Famous Fabric Store*, New York: ABRAMS, 2015.

[32] *Dundee Courier*, May 19, 1938, p.5.

[33] "Instalment Six," *Sunday Times* (Perth, WA: 1902–1954) August 9, 1931, http://nla.gov.au/nla.newsarticle58683835

[34] *The South Eastern Times* (Millicent, SA: 1906–1954), April 16, 1948, http://nla.gov.au/nla.news-page22458798

[35] "Chute Gown," *Healdsburg Tribune*, August 11, 1941, p.1.

[36] "White Net Gown Worn by Hobart Bride," *Examiner* (Launceston, Tas.: 1900–1954), September 19, 1946, http://nla.gov.au/nla.news-article96468393

[37] Object page, "Evening dress," Metropolitan Museum of Art, accessed June 25, 2025, https://www.metmuseum.org/art/collection/search/159412.

[38] English, Bonnie, and Munroe, Nazanin Hedayat. *A Cultural History of Western Fashion: From Haute Couture to Virtual Couture*, London: Bloomsbury Publishing, 2022, p.88.

[39] "Brides' Problems," *The Courier-Mail* (Brisbane, Qld.: 1933–1954), March 22, 1945, http://nla.gov.au/nla.newsarticle48975353

[40] "Yarrawonga Bride," *Border Morning Mail* (Albury, NSW: 1934–1935; 1938–1952), October 8, 1949, http://nla.gov.au/nla.news-article264038433

[41] "Tiny Laced Waists and Blossoming Hips," *Advocate* (Burnie, Tas.:1890–1954) January 26, 1946, http://nla.gov.au/nla.news-article68959985

[42] *Calexico Chronicle*, September 5, 1946.

[43] "Dress Sense," *The Australian Women's Weekly* (1933–1982), April 24, 1948, http://nla.gov.au/nla.news-article51200013

Chapter 9

[1] Hatherley, Owen. "The Ministry of Nostalgia," *Bradford Observer*, August 26, 1949, p.3.

[2] Rouhier-Willoughby, Jeanmarie. *Village Values: Negotiating identity, gender, and resistance in rural Russian life-cycle rituals*, Bloomington: Slavica, 2008, p.129.

[3] *Oakland Tribune*, June 5, 1952, p.12.

[4] *LIFE*, 1952, p.119.

[5] Bass-Krueger, Maude. "Everything You Ever Wanted To Know About The White Wedding Dress," *British Vogue*, accessed June 25, 2025, https://www.vogue.co.uk/gallery/history-of-the-white-wedding-dress

[6] "Bridal Fashions," *The Australian Women's Weekly* (1933–1982), November 9, 1966, http://nla.gov.au/nla.news-article51973046

[7] Jellison, 2008, p.68.

[8] Ibid, p.73.

[9] "Choice of the bride," *The Daily News* (Perth, WA: 1882–1955), December 28, 1953 http://nla.gov.au/nla.newsarticle266140954

[10] "The Summer Bride Dressed In White," *The Australian Women's Weekly* (1933–1982), October 22, 1958, http://nla.gov.au/nla.news-article47814556

[11] Adrian, Bonnie. *Framing the Bride: Globalizing Beauty and Romance in Taiwan's Bridal Industry*, Oakland: University of California Press, 2003, pp46-47.

[12] Cameron, Elisabeth and Peffer, John eds. *Portraiture and Photography in Africa*, Bloomington: Indiana University Press, 2013, p.273.

[13] "Dress Sense…" *The Australian Women's Weekly* (1933–1982), December 6, 1947, http://nla.gov.au/nla.newsarticle46945445

[14] "A Bride's Lace Cuffs," *The Riverine Herald* (Echuca, Vic.: Moama, NSW: 1869–1954; 1998–2002), October 17, 1942, http://nla.gov.au/nla.news-article116309846

[15] "Beston-Hargraves Wedding," *Examiner* (Launceston, Tas.: 1900–1954), February 2, 1942, http://nla.gov.au/nla.news-article91503112

[16] "'Dream' Frock for Bride is Promise of Things to Come," *The Telegraph* (Brisbane, Qld.: 1872–1947), March 12, 1945, http://nla.gov.au/nla.newsarticle186330286

[17] "Society Wedding," *Kalgoorlie Miner* (WA: 1895–1954), October 28, 1946, http://nla.gov.au/nla.newsarticle95557847

[18] "Wedding Frocks Vie in Contrast," *The Telegraph* (Brisbane, Qld.: 1872–1947), February 5, 1947, http://nla.gov.au/nla.newsarticle186690547

[19] "Easter Bride," *The Daily News* (Perth, WA: 1882–1955), March 26, 1949, http://nla.gov.au/nla.newsarticle79823122

[20] "Cannot Buy Wedding Dress," *The Daily Telegraph* (Sydney, NSW: 1931–1954), June 19, 1942, http://nla.gov.au/nla.news-article247999470

[21] *Tonbridge Free Press*, July 15, 1949, p.5.

[22] Sletcher, Michael ed. *New England: The Greenwood Encyclopedia of American Regional Cultures*, London: Bloomsbury Academic, 2004, p.156.

[23] Phipps & Reed, 2017, np.

[24] "A Page for Women," *The Central Queensland Herald* (Rockhampton, Qld.: 1930–1956) October 2, 1952, http://nla.gov.au/nla.news-article75826305

[25] "Queen May Favour a 'Princess' Line," *The West Australian* (Perth, WA: 1879–1954), September 10, 1953, http://nla.gov.au/nla.news-article49231616

[26] "Dress Sense," *The Australian Women's Weekly* (1933–1982), January 2, 1952, http://nla.gov.au/nla.news-article44558502

[27] Howard, 2008, p.165.

[28] Priscilla of Boston Collection, 1940-1994, Archives Center, National Museum of American History.

[29] "News for Women," *South Coast Times and Wollongong Argus* (NSW: 1900–1954), January 22, http://nla.gov.au/nla.news-article143043988

[30] Rose, Helen. *"Just Make Them Beautiful": The Many Worlds of a Designing Woman*, London: Dennis-Landman Publishers, 1976, p.70.

[31] "Film star's wardrobe," *The Australian Women's Weekly* (1933–1982), November 3, 1954, http://nla.gov.au/nla.newsarticle47400545

[32] Soo Hoo, Fawnia. "The Powerful Story Behind Jackie Kennedy's Wedding Dress," *Vanity Fair*, 2023, accessed June 25, 2025, https://www.vanityfair.com/style/2023/01/jackie-kennedy-wedding-dress

[33] Hunt, Amber, and Batcher, David. *The Kennedy Wives: Triumph and Tragedy in America's Most Public Family*, Guilford: Lyons Press, 2014, p.151.

[34] *San Bernardino Sun*, October 1, 1950, p.48.

[35] "Dona Jean Butler Says Vows with Lorne Geib," *San Bernardino Sun*, December 6, 1953, p.13.

[36] *The Daily News* (Perth, WA: 1882–1955), December 28, 1953, http://nla.gov.au/nla.news-page29737763

[37] Leaming, Barbara. *Jacqueline Bouvier Kennedy Onassis: The Untold Story*, New York: St. Martin's Publishing Group, 2014, p.46.

[38] Mulvaney, Jay. *Jackie: The Clothes of Camelot*, New York: St. Martin's Publishing Group, 2014.

[39] *Desert Sun*, January 4, 1954, p.1b.

[40] *Santa Cruz Sentinel*, May 16, 1965, p.24.

[41] Thornton McLeod, Edyth, "Beauty After 40," *San Bernardino Sun*, January 17, 1956, p.11.

[42] "Eve Gilbert's London Fashion Feature," *Examiner* (Launceston, Tas.: 1900–1954), April 18, 1950, http://nla.gov.au/nla.newsarticle52713971

[43] *The Australian Women's Weekly* (1933–1982), March 18, 1950, http://nla.gov.au/nla.news-page4307364

[44] *Advocate* (Burnie, Tas.: 1890–1954), February 15, 1951, http://nla.gov.au/nla.news-page5955722

[45] Voss, Kimberly Wilmot. *Newspaper Fashion Editors in the 1950s and 60s: Women Writers of the Runway*, Cham: Springer International Publishing, 2021, p.45.

[46] *San Bernardino Sun*, May 11, 1958, p.18.

[47] Rose, Helen, "Grace Kelly's bridal gown," *San Bernardino Sun*, May 19, 1957, p.38.

[48] Haugland, H. Kristina. *Grace Kelly: Icon of Style to Royal Bride*, Philadelphia: Philadelphia Museum of Art, 2006, p.46.

[49] Robinson, Jeffrey. *Grace of Monaco: The True Story*, New York: Hachette Books, 2015.

[50] "Juliet Cap Worn By Bride," *The Dandenong Journal* (Vic.: 1927–1954), August 30, 1950, http://nla.gov.au/nla.newsarticle219303659

[51] Haugland, 2006, p.33.

[52] Ed. Lennard, Frances & Ewer, Patricia. *Textile Conservation: Advances in Practice*, Amsterdam Elsevier, 2010, p.78.

[53] "Woman's Page," *The Argus* (Melbourne, Vic.: 1848–1957), February 28, 1956, http://nla.gov.au/nla.newsarticle72538321

[54] *Punch*, 1959, p.72.

[55] "Dress Sense," *The Australian Women's Weekly* (1933–1982), March 5, 1958, http://nla.gov.au/nla.news-article51599123

[56] Jellison, 2008, p.75.

[57] *Bognor Regis Observer*, June 5, 1959, p.6.

Chapter 10

[1] Peleikis, Anja. *Lebanese in Motion: Gender and the Making of a Translocal Village*, transcript, 2003, p.133.

[2] Rielly, Edward J. *The 1960s*, London: Bloomsbury Academic, 2003.

[3] Dow, Bonnie J. "The Movement Meets the Press: The 1968 Miss America Pageant Protest," *Watching Women's Liberation, 1970: Feminism's Pivotal Year on the Network News*, 2014, https://doi.org/10.5406/illinois/9780252038563.003.0002

[4] *Brides*, March 1969, p.82.

[5] Milford-Cottam, Daniel. *Fashion in the 1970s*, London: Bloomsbury Publishing, 2018, p.59.

[6] Wallace, Carol. *All Dressed in White: The Irresistible Rise of the American Wedding*, London: Penguin Books, 2004, p.225.

[7] Clayton, Richard R., and Harwin L. Voss. "Shacking up: Cohabitation in the 1970s," *Journal of Marriage and Family*, 1977, pp.273–83, https://doi.org/10.2307/351123

[8] Dunak, Karen M. *As Long as We Both Shall Love: The White Wedding in Postwar America*, New York: NYU Press, 2013, p. 9 *Daily Mirror*, August 31, 1964, p.3.

[10] Polan, Brenda, and Tredre, Roger. *The Great Fashion Designers: From Chanel to McQueen, the Names that Made Fashion History*, London: Bloomsbury Publishing, 2020.

[11] Vaughan et al., 2015, p.312.

[12] Cavazos, Linda Q. *One Dark Morning: The True Story of Surviving a Fallen Trooper*, Lulu Press, Incorporated, 2020, p.32.

[13] Vaughan et al., 2015, p.312.

[14] "Wedding Dress Sense," *The Australian Women's Weekly* (1933–1982), January 13, 1965, http://nla.gov.au/nla.newsarticle51384308

[15] Howard, 2008, p.174.

[16] "Types of lace you can buy," *The Australian Women's Weekly* (1933–1982), June 29, 1966, http://nla.gov.au/nla.news-article44523819

[17] "Dress Sense," *The Australian Women's Weekly* (1933–1982), May 20, 1964, http://nla.gov.au/nla.news-article51779822

[18] *Santa Cruz Sentinel*, May 16, 1965.

[19] "Weather map, forecast," *The Canberra Times* (ACT: 1926–1995), August 15, 1964, http://nla.gov.au/nla.newsarticle105838575

[20] "Empire Line Effect in Bridal Gown," *The Canberra Times* (ACT: 1926–1995), May 30, 1960, http://nla.gov.au/nla.news-article103080994

[21] "Empire Line Gown for June Bride," *King Island News* (Currie, King Island: 1912–1986), July 6, 1966, http://nla.gov.au/nla.newsarticle264711397

[22] "Dress Sense," *The Australian Women's Weekly* (1933–1982), May 4, 1966, http://nla.gov.au/nla.news-article44024313

[23] Interview with Pattie Boyd, September 2021.

[24] Ibid.

[25] Faiers, Jonathan. *Fur: A Sensitive History*, New Haven: Yale University Press, 2020, p.86.

[26] Interview with Pattie Boyd, September 2021.

[27] "Dress Sense," *The Australian Women's Weekly* (1933–1982), April 14, 1965, http://nla.gov.au/nla.news-article46932445

[28] Interview with Pattie Boyd, September 2023.

[29] Boyd, Pattie, and Junor, Penny. *Wonderful Tonight: George Harrison, Eric Clapton, and Me*, New York: Crown, 2008.

[30] *Palos Verdes Peninsula News*, May 5, 1966.

[31] "Dress Sense," *The Australian Women's Weekly* (1933–1982), September 25, 1968, http://nla.gov.au/nla.newsarticle51976311

[32] "Mini-Wedding," *The Canberra Times* (ACT: 1926–1995), February 16, 1967, http://nla.gov.au/nla.newsarticle106962563

[33] Faiers, 2020, p.93.

[34] *Desert Sun*, September 1, 1967.

[35] "Fashions for the Easter Bride," *Drogheda Independent*, March 10, 1967, p.9.

[36] *Herts and Essex Observer*, January 27, 1961, p.10.

[37] *Sausalito News*, April 3, 1963, p.7.

[38] "A compact look at two weddings… She said 'I will' with daisies," *The Australian Women's Weekly* (1933–1982), February 22, 1967, http://nla.gov.au/nla.newsarticle44797012

[39] "Spring Fashions in Thai Silk," *The Australian Women's Weekly* (1933–1982), July 10, 1963, http://nla.gov.au/nla.news-article47510578

[40] *San Bernardino Sun*, July 23, 1967, p.34.

[41] Jennings, Shona. "Annie Bonza," New Zealand Fashion Museum, 2013, accessed June 25, 2025, https://nzfashionmuseum.org.nz/annie-bonza/

[42] *Press*, May 7, 1968, p.13.

[43] *Press*, January 3, 1968, p.11.

[44] *Press*, August 16, 1966, p.8.

[45] "The Groom Wore 'Something Blue' Too," *The Australian Women's Weekly* (1933–1982), May 1, 1968, http://nla.gov.au/nla.news-article44559629

[46] English, Bonnie, and Pomazan, Liliana. *Australian Fashion Unstitched: The Last 60 Years*, Cambridge: Cambridge University Press, 2010, p.32.

[47] "Folk Mass At Wedding," *The Coromandel Times* (Blackwood, SA: 1970–1976), August 5, 1971, http://nla.gov.au/nla.newsarticle261090296

[48] "All-wool Wedding," *The Australian Women's Weekly* (1933–1982) April 28, 1965, http://nla.gov.au/nla.newsarticle51396068

[49] *Florist's Manual of Modern Design: Volume II*, 1960, p.24.

[50] Rhodes, Chloe. *A Certain Je Ne Sais Quoi: Words We Pinched From Other Languages*, London: Michael O'Mara, 2009.

[51] "Dress Sense," *The Australian Women's Weekly* (1933–1982), January 1, 1969, http://nla.gov.au/nla.newsarticle43202299

[52] *Runcorn Weekly News*, March 18, 1971, p.7.

[53] "Dress Sense," *The Australian Women's Weekly* (1933–1982), August 11, 1971, http://nla.gov.au/nla.newsarticle46452529

[54] *Crewe Chronicle*, August 25, 1977, p.14.

[55] *Liverpool Echo*, February 7, 1973, p.7.

[56] https://vintagefashionguild.org/fashionhistory/carven-of-paris/

[57] "Edwardian Bridal Look," *Papua New Guinea Post-Courier* (Port Moresby: 1969–1981), September 3, 1971, http://nla.gov.au/nla.news-article250200792

[58] "Yesterday's Weddings," *The Canberra Times* (ACT: 1926–1995), January 21, 1979, http://nla.gov.au/nla.newsarticle136976089

[59] "Wedding," *King Island News* (Currie, King Island: 1912–1986), July 18, 1979, http://nla.gov.au/nla.news-article264832088

[60] "Married by Bride's Father," *The Coromandel Times* (Blackwood, SA: 1970–1976), January 25, 1973, http://nla.gov.au/nla.news-article261115600

[61] Milford-Cottam, 2018, np.

[62] Bryant, Flora F. T., and Bryant, Kendall S., *It's Your Wedding: A Complete Wedding Guide for Making the Most Important Day of Your Life the Most Beautiful and Memorable*, Cowles Book Company, 1970, p.69.

[63] "For '72 Brides…and Maids," *The Australian Women's Weekly* (1933–1982), June 7, 1972, http://nla.gov.au/nla.newsarticle51274147

[64] "Laroche's hotch-potch of heavy looks," *Birmingham Daily Post*, January 27, 1972, p.23.

[65] Martin, Richard ed. *Contemporary Fashion*, London: St. James Press, 1995, p.354.

[66] "Tastes," *Newcastle Journal*, October 15, 1971, p.5.

[67] Ibid.

[68] Vaughan Lee, H. et al, 2015, p.243.

[69] Milford-Cottam, 2018, np.

Chapter 11

[1] "Choosing the bridal gown," *The Canberra Times* (ACT: 1926–1995), June 18, 1976: http://nla.gov.au/nla.newsarticle131823609

[2] Freudenheim, Ellen. *The Executive Bride: A Ten-week Wedding Planner*, New York: Bantam Books, 1985, p.1.

[3] Carter, Julia, and Duncan, Simon. *Reinventing Couples: Tradition, Agency and Bricolage*, London: Palgrave Macmillan UK, 2017, p.186.

[4] *Ideas for Brides*, 1983.

[5] Brown, Gail and Dillon, Karen. *Sew A Beautiful Wedding*, Oregon: Palmer/Pletsch Associates, 1980, p.10.

[6] Ibid, p.6.

[7] Harriman, Andi, and Bontje, Marloes. *Some Wear Leather, Some Wear Lace: The Worldwide Compendium of Postpunk and Goth in the 1980s*, Norway, Intellect Books, 2014, p.82.

[8] Newell, Mike. 1994.

[9] *Far Eastern Economic Review*, 2003, p.48.

[10] Burchfield, Rachel. "25 Years Later, Carolyn Bessette-Kennedy's Wedding Dress Still Stuns," *Vanity Fair*, 2021, accessed June 25, 2025, https://www.vanityfair.com/style/2021/09/25-years-later-carolyn-bessette-kennedys-wedding-dress-still-stuns

[11] Krohn, Katherine E., *Vera Wang: Enduring Style*, Minneapolis: Twenty-First Century Books, 2009, pp.42-3.

[12] Chrisman-Campbell, Kimberly. *Skirts: Fashioning Modern Femininity in the Twentieth Century*, New York: St. Martin's Publishing Group, 2022.

[13] Ha, Guangtian, Jaschok, Maria and Harris, Rachel, eds. *Ethnographies of Islam in China*, Honolulu: University of Hawaii Press, 2021, p.98.

[14] Davis, Deborah, ed. *The Consumer Revolution in Urban China*, Oakland: University of California Press, 2000, p.105.

[15] Goldstein-Gidoni, Ofra. *Packaged Japaneseness: Weddings, Business and Brides*, Honolulu: University of Hawaii Press, 1997, p.133.

[16] LeFebvre, Jesse R. "Christian wedding ceremonies: 'Nonreligiousness' in contemporary Japan," *Japanese Journal of Religious Studies*, 2015, pp.185-203.

[17] Goldstein-Gidoni, 1997, p.124.

[18] Zemler, Emily. *Disney Princess: Beyond the Tiara: The Stories. The Influence. The Legacy*, New York: Epic Ink, 2022.n

[19] Object page. "Rock n Roll Bride Magazine Issue 52," *Rock n Roll Bride*, accessed June 25, 2025, https://www.rocknrollbride.com/shop/?item=RNRMAG_0052

[20] "Fancy Dress: A new way to beat the blues," *The Australian Women's Weekly* (1933–1982), December 15, 1932, http://nla.gov.au/nla.news-article57125829

[21] "Dressing up for a quiet revolution in fashion," *The Canberra Times* (ACT: 1926–1995), June 25, 1987, http://nla.gov.au/nla.news-article118299973

[22] "Belconnen Mall Fashion," *The Canberra Times* (ACT: 1925–1995), August 13, 1981, http://nla.gov.au/nla.news-article127063919

[23] "Brides 81," *The Canberra Times* (ACT: 1926–1995), August 20, 1981, http://nla.gov.au/nla.news-article127067560

[24] Emanuel, David, and Emanuel, Elizabeth. *A Dress for Diana*. London: Pavilion Books, 2006, p.104.

[25] Jarvis, Anthea. *Brides: Wedding Clothes and Customs, 1850-1980*, Liverpool: Merseyside County Museums, 1983.

[26] *Danse Au Canada*, Issues 50-57, p.8.

[27] "Glad Rags," *The Canberra Times* (ACT: 1926–1995), July 1, 1982, http://nla.gov.au/nla.news-article126881932

[28] *The Laborer*, 1991, p.11.

[29] Freuder-Leim, Ellen. *The Executive Bride: A Ten-week Wedding Planner*, New York: Bantam Books, 1985.

[30] Fields, Denise, and Fields, Alan. *Bridal Gown Guide 1999: Discover the Dress of Your Dreams at a Price You Can Afford*, Boulder: Windsor Peak Press, 1998, p.343.

[31] "Designer Labels – Half Price," *The Australian Jewish News* (Melbourne, Vic.: 1935–1999), November 28, 1986, http://nla.gov.au/nla.news-article261640487

[32] "Special service for a special day," *Fenland Citizen*, March 9, 1983, p.8.

[33] "Prize winning style," *The Australian Jewish News* (Melbourne, Vic.: 1935–1999), August 18, 1989, http://nla.gov.au/nla.newsarticle261913935

[34] Dahl, Stephanie H. *The Modern Bride Guide to Your Wedding and Marriage*, New York: Random House Publishing Group, 1987, p.114.

[35] Aav, Marianne. *Marimekko: Fabrics, Fashion, Architecture*, Bard Graduate Center for Studies in the Decorative Arts, Design, and Culture, New York, and the Design Museum, Finland, 2003, p.91.

[36] "More to Life: Not for me those Wedding Bills," *The Canberra Times* (ACT: 1926–1995), July 19, 1994, http://nla.gov.au/nla.news-article118191593

[37] Baldrige, Letitia. *Letitia Baldrige's complete guide to the new manners for the '90s*, New York: Rawson Associates, 1990, p.255.

[38] Harmel, Melissa. *The fashion cycles of bridal gown styles from 1969-1988: predicting future trends*, Texas Tech University, 1990, p.161.

[39] Fields, Denise. *Bridal Gown Guide: Discover the Dress of Your Dreams at a Price You Can Afford*, Boulder: Windsor Peak Press, 1997, pp.214–328.

[40] *Bride's Wedding Planner*, New York: Fawcett Columbine, 1990, p.111.

[41] Oksala, Pauliina. *Pukusuunnittelijan ja toteuttajan yhteistyo nayttamopuvun valmistusprosessissa*, 2020, p.7.

[42] Moreno, J, et al. *Kasalan*. Cambridge: J. Moreno, 1990, p.202.

[43] *Cincinnati Magazine*, January 1990, p.83.

[44] Ibid.

[45] Fields, Alan S., and Fields, Denise. *Bridal Bargains: Secrets to Throwing a Fantastic Wedding on a Realistic Budget*, Boulder: Windsor Peak Press, 1990, p.142.

[46] Baldrige, 1990, p.315.

[47] *Dressing the Bride*, New York: Crown Publishers, 1993, p.61.

[48] Jellison, 2008, p.50.

[49] "What you need for your simcha," *The Australian Jewish News* (Melbourne, Vic.: 1935–1999), July 31, 1992, http://nla.gov.au/nla.news-article261484736

[50] *Milwaukee Magazine*, 1990, p.11.

[51] Exhibition page, "Frans Hoogendoorn," Kunst Museum Den Haag, accessed June 25, 2025, https://www.kunstmuseum.nl/en/exhibitions/frans-hoogendoorn

[52] Fiore, Ann Marie. *Understanding Aesthetics for the Merchandising and Design Professional*, London: Bloomsbury Academic, 2010, p.390.

[53] *Santa Cruz Sentinel*, January 19, 1995.

[54] Kelly, Ian, and Westwood, Vivienne. *Vivienne Westwood*, London: Pan Macmillan UK, 2014.

[55] "Present trends at a grassroots level," *The Canberra Times* (ACT: 1926–1995), July 18, 1995, http://nla.gov.au/nla.newsarticle128288083

[56] "Bridal laces spun with gold," *The Australian Jewish News* (Melbourne, Vic. : 1935–1999), June 28, 1996, http://nla.gov.au/nla.news-article260901969

Chapter 12

[1] Gardetti, Miguel; Angel, Muthu, and Subramanian Senthilkannan, eds. *Handbook of Sustainable Luxury Textiles and Fashion: Volume 1*, Singapore: Springer Nature Singapore, 2015, p.35.

[2] Blanchard, Tamsin. *Green is the New Black: How to Save the World in Style*, London: Hodder & Stoughton, 2013.

[3] "Factbox: List of states that legalized gay marriage," Reuters, 2013, accessed June 25, 20255, https://www.reuters.com/article/us-usa-courtgaymarriage-states-idUSBRE95P07A20130626

[4] Davis, Precious. "I'm a Trans Bride—Here's How I Found My Dream Wedding Dress," Wedding Wire, 2017, accessed June 25, 2025, https://www.weddingwire.com/wedding-ideas/transgender-woman-bride-wedding-dress

[5] Davidson, Annie. "7 LGBTQ+ Wedding Dress Designers to Have on Your Radar," *Brides*, 2024 accessed June 25, 2025, https://www.brides.com/lgbtq-wedding-dressdesigners-5189139

[6] Lau, Laura, and Lau, Theodora. *Wedding Feng Shui: The Chinese Horoscopes Guide to Planning Your Wedding*, New York: HarperCollins, 2010, p.6.

[7] Leeds-Hurwitz, Wendy. *Wedding as Text: Communicating Cultural Identities Through Ritual*, Oxford: Taylor & Francis, 2002, p.21.

[8] Ibid, p.45.

[9] "The Ultimate Guide to Bridal Accessories," *Brides*, 2021, accessed June 25, 2025, https://www.brides.com/bridal-accessoriesguide-5205388

[10] Kaupke, Laura Lajiness. "42 Beautiful Bridal Face Masks For Every Wedding Style," *Vogue*, 2021, accessed June 25, 2025, https://www.vogue.com/article/bridal-face-masks

[11] Manners, Ivy. "'Epic' Dresses and Maximalist Cakes: These '80s Wedding Trends Are Back'," *New York Times*, March 23, 2022.

[12] Diamant, Anita. *The New Jewish Wedding, Revised*. New York: Scribner, 2001, p.40.

[13] Kooler, Donna. *Elegant Wedding Ceremonies*, Little Rock: Leisure Arts Incorporated, 2001, p.65.

[14] *Cincinnati Wedding*, Spring/Summer 2001, p.36.

[15] Torkia, Dina. *Modestly*, London: Ebury Publishing, 2018.

[16] Jones, G L. *Book Wedding Dress The Do's and Don'ts of Buying a Wedding Dress Guide and Planner*, Lulu.com, 2011. p.15.

[17] James, Zoe. *The Harms of Hate for Gypsies and Travellers: A Critical Hate Studies Perspective*, Cham: Springer International Publishing, 2020, p.29.

[18] Davis, Mark ed. *Liquid Sociology: Metaphor in Zygmunt Bauman's Analysis of Modernity*, Oxford: Taylor & Francis, 2016.

[19] Slade, Alison; Narro, Amber J. and Buchanan, Burton P. eds. *Reality Television: Oddities of Culture*, New York: Lexington Books, 2014, p.127.

[20] Pnina Tornai, accessed June 25, 2025, https://www.pninatornai.com/

[21] Madine, Thelma. *Tales of the Gypsy Dressmaker*, London: HarperCollins Publishers, 2012.

[22] Schneier, Matthew. "Carolina Herrera Resort 2012," Vogue Runway, 2011, accessed June 25, 2025, https://www.vogue.com/fashion-shows/resort-2012/carolina-herrera

[23] Cooper, Casey, and Naylor, Sharon. *What's Your Bridal Style?* New York: Citadel Press, 2012.

[24] Rothstein, Ronald, et al. *How to Buy Your Perfect Wedding Dress*, Guildford: Touchstone, 2002, p.59.

[25] Naylor, Sharon, et al. *Bridal Bible: Inspiration for Planning Your Perfect Wedding*, Guilford: Lyons Press, 2012, p.46.

[26] "Sandrah Tubobereni – Giving traditional wedding attires global appeal," *Allure Magazine*, 2018, accessed June 25, 2025, https://allure.vanguardngr.com/2018/06/sandrah-tubobereni-giving-traditional-wedding-attires-global-appeal/

[27] Fass, Madeline. "The Puff-Sleeve Trend is Here to Stay," *Vogue*, July 19, 2022.

[28] Farra, Emily. "The 6 Major Trends of Fall '18 Bridal Fashion Week," *Vogue*, October 10, 2017.

[29] Dela Rosa, Roseanne. "2017 Wedding Dress Trends You Need To Know About: 3D Floral Details," *Wedding Bells Magazine*, July 5, 2016.

[30] Akabogu, Njideka, "Lookbook Review: TUBO's debut bridal collection, 'Her Form' is as pleasing as they come," *Nigerian Entertainment Today*, August 23, 2017.

[31] "Meet Randy," Randy Fenoli Bridal, accessed June 25, 2025, https://randyfenoli.com/about/

[32] Hall, Heather and Goldberg, Carrie. "These Are The It Bridal Trends of 2019," *Harper's Bazaar*, February 21, 2019.

[33] "Women's Column," *The Mercury* (Hobart, Tas.: 1860–1954), October 13, 1934, http://nla.gov.au/nla.newsarticle29162634

[34] Rutherford, Karlie. "'I can see your underwear': Brides choosing backless, high split wedding dresses over traditional gowns," *The Daily Telegraph*, June 7, 2017.

[35] "A New York Marriage," *The Express and Telegraph* (Adelaide, SA: 1867–1922), May 6, 1899, http://nla.gov.au/nla.newsarticle209567547

[36] "Mission," Queera, accessed June 25, 2025, https://www.queerawarg.com/mission

[37] Interview with Curtis Cassell, August 2023.

[38] Gluckman, Dale Carolyn ed. *Kimono as Art: The Landscapes of Itchiku Kubota*, London: Thames & Hudson, 2008, p.23.

[39] Dalby, 2001, p.102.

[40] Monden, Masafumi. *Japanese Fashion Cultures: Dress and Gender in Contemporary Japan*, London: Bloomsbury Publishing, 2014, p.114.

[41] Godoy, Tiffany. *Style Deficit Disorder: Harajuku Street Fashion–Tokyo*, San Francisco: Chronicle Books, 2007, p.142.

[42] Irvine, Greg, ed. *Japanese Art and Design*. New York: Harry N. Abrams, 2016, p.241.

[43] Hagen, Shelley. *I Do*, New York: Simon and Schuster, 2001, p.176.

[44] Godoy, 2007, p.160.

[45] Miranda Bennett Studios, 2022/3.

[46] "Orange blossoms are OUT," *The Australian Women's Weekly* (1933–1982), July 6, 1966, http://nla.gov.au/nla.newsarticle44024729

[47] Varina, Rachel and Caldwell, Chloe. "16 Cap Sleeve Wedding Dresses for a Classic Bridal Look," *Brides*, June 15, 2023.

[48] Poe Durbin, Holly. *The Costume Designer's Toolkit: The Process of Creating Effective Design*, Oxford: Taylor & Francis, 2022.

[49] *Dry Goods Guide*, Black Publishing Company, 1918, p.19.

[50] "Our Story," Wai Ching, accessed June 25, 2025, https://wai-ching.com/our-story/

[51] https://china.usc.edu/say-yes-westglobalization-qipao

[52] Sim, Cheryl. *Wearing the Cheongsam: Dress and Culture in a Chinese Diaspora*, London: Bloomsbury Publishing, 2019, p.153.

[53] Segre-Reinach, Simona and Ling, Wessie, eds. *Fashion in Multiple Chinas: Chinese Styles in the Transglobal Landscape*, London: Bloomsbury Publishing, 2018, p.184.

[54] "Chinese bride trains eye on wedding dress record," Reuters, 2007, accessed June 25, 2025, https://www.reuters.com/article/us-chinawedding-idUSTRE5751VE20090806

[55] "Bridal Hanbok," Leehwa Wedding & Hanbok, accessed June 25, 2025, https://www.leehwawedding.com/pages/bridal-hanbok

[56] Lee, Samuel Songhoon. *Hanbok: Timeless Fashion Tradition*, Seoul: Seoul Selection, 2015.

[57] Lee, Jin-hyuk, ed. *Korean Handicrafts: Art in Everyday Life*. Korea Foundation, 2014.

[58] *Korean-English Dictionary of Korean Historical Terms*, Volume 28 [Jok ~ Ji]. iBook., 2020.

Bibliography

Author of The Mummy. *Stories of a Bride*. United Kingdom, H. Colburn and R. Bentley, 1829.

Adrian, Bonnie. *Framing the Bride: Globalizing Beauty and Romance in Taiwan's Bridal Industry*. University of California Press, 2003.

Alexander, Kimberly S. *Treasures Afoot: Shoe Stories from the Georgian Era*. United States, Johns Hopkins University Press, 2018.

Anderson, Cinda. *Voices of the Great Depression--The 1930's*. United States, Author House, 2001.

Anishanslin, Zara. *Portrait of a Woman in Silk: Hidden Histories of the British Atlantic World*. United Kingdom, Yale University Press, 2016.

Bagnall, Kate and Julia T. Martinez. *Locating Chinese Women: Historical Mobility Between China and Australia*. Hong Kong, Hong Kong University Press, 2021.

Baumgarten, Linda. *Eighteenth-century Clothing at Williamsburg*. United States, Colonial Williamsburg Foundation, 1986.

Bettini, Maurizio. *Women and Weasels: Mythologies of Birth in Ancient Greece and Rome*. United Kingdom, University of Chicago Press, 2013.

Blanchard, Tamsin. *Green is the New Black: How to Save the World in Style*. United Kingdom, Hodder & Stoughton, 2013.

Blanco F., José, Mary D. Doering, Patricia Hunt-Hurst, and Heather Vaughan Lee. *Clothing and Fashion: American Fashion from Head to Toe [4 Volumes]*. United States, ABC-CLIO, 2015.

Brucker, Gene A. *Florence: The Golden Age 1138–1737*. Berkeley, University of California Press, 1998.

Cameron, Elisabeth L. and John Peffer, eds. *Portraiture and Photography in Africa*. Indiana University Press, 2013.

Challelmel, M. Augustin. *The History of Fashion in France: Or, The Dress of Women From the Gallo-Roman Period to the Present Time*. United States, Westphalia Press, 2018.

Chrisman-Campbell, Kimberly. *Skirts: Fashioning Modern Femininity in the Twentieth Century*. United States, St. Martin's Publishing Group, 2022.

Clark, Rowena. *Hatches, Matches and Dispatches: Christening, Bridal & Mourning Fashions*. Australia, National Gallery of Victoria, 1987.

Cronin, Vincent. *The Florentine Renaissance*. United Kingdom, Random House, 2011.

Crowston, Clare Haru. *Fabricating women: the seamstresses of Old Regime France, 1675–1791*. United Kingdom, Duke University Press, 2001.

Cunningham, Patricia Anne and Susan Voso Lab, eds. *Dress in American Culture*. Bowling Green State University Popular Press, 1993.

Dalby, Liza Crihfield. *Kimono: Fashioning Culture*. United Kingdom, Vintage, 2001.

Darwin, Tess. *Edinburgh Scots Herbal: The Plant Lore of Scotland*. United Kingdom, Mercat Press, 1996.

Davis, Deborah, *The Consumer Revolution in Urban China*. United Kingdom, University of California Press, 2000.

Davis, Mark, ed. *Liquid Sociology: Metaphor in Zygmunt Bauman's Analysis of Modernity*. United Kingdom, Taylor & Francis, 2016.

de la Haye, Amy. *Ravishing: The Rose in Fashion*. United Kingdom, Yale University Press, 2020.

Diamant, Anita. *The Jewish Wedding Now*. United Kingdom, Scribner, 2017.

Doake, Margaret. *May Darling*. The Literary Production Committee, 1881.

Dunak, Karen M. *As Long as We Both Shall Love: The White Wedding in Postwar America*. United States, NYU Press, 2013.

Edwards, Nina. *Dressed for War: Uniform, Civilian Clothing and Trappings, 1914 to 1918*. United Kingdom, I.B.Tauris, 2014.

Eluwawalage, Damayanthie, ed. *Fashion: Tyranny and Revelation*. Netherlands, Brill, 2019.

Ehrman, Edwina. *The Wedding Dress: 300 Years of Bridal Fashions*. United Kingdom, V&A Pub., 2014.

Eluwawalage, Damayanthie. *Fashion: Tyranny and Revelation*. Netherlands, Brill, 2019.

Engel, Barbara Alpern. *Women in Russia: 1700–2000*. Cambridge University Press, 2004.

Frank, Robert R. *Bast and Other Plant Fibres*. United Kingdom, Taylor & Francis, 2005.

Far Eastern Economic Review – 166, no. 13–25 (2003).

Freudenheim, Ellen. *The Executive Bride: A Ten-week Wedding Planner*. United States, Bantam Books, 1985.

Frick, Carole Collier. *Dressing Renaissance Florence: Families, Fortunes, and Fine Clothing*. United Kingdom, Johns Hopkins University Press, 2005.

Ganong, Lawrence H. and Marilyn Coleman. *Remarried Family Relationships*. India, SAGE Publications, 1994.

Godoy, Tiffany. *Style Deficit Disorder: Harajuku Street Fashion—Tokyo*. United States, Chronicle Books, 2007.

Goldstein-Gidoni, Ofra. *Packaged Japaneseness: Weddings, Business and Brides*. United States, University of Hawaii Press, 1997.

Goodall-Cristante, Hollis. *Kimono as Art: The Landscapes of Itchiku Kubota*. United Kingdom Thames & Hudson, 2008.

Haakenson, Bergine and Carol Fairbanks, eds. *Writings of Farm Women, 1840–1940: An Anthology*. United Kingdom, Taylor & Francis, 2017.

Harriman, Andi, and Marloes Bontje. *Some Wear Leather, Some Wear Lace: The Worldwide Compendium of Postpunk and Goth in the 1980s*. Norway, Intellect Books, 2014.

Harris, Rachel, Guangtian Ha, and Maria Jaschok, eds. *Ethnographies of Islam in China*. United States, University of Hawaii Press, 2021.

Harrison, Richard. *Contemporary Fashion*. United Kingdom, St. James Press, 1995.

Harvey, Karen, ed. *History and Material Culture: A Student's Guide to Approaching Alternative Sources*. United Kingdom, Taylor & Francis, 2013.

Haugland, H. Kristina. *Grace Kelly: Icon of Style to Royal Bride*. United Kingdom, Philadelphia Museum of Art, 2006.

Hill, Daniel Delis. *Advertising to the American Woman, 1900–1999*. United States, Ohio State University Press, 2002.

Horne, Alistair. *Friend Or Foe: A History of France*. United Kingdom, Orion, 2012.

Howard, Vicki. *Brides, Inc.: American Weddings and the Business of Tradition*. United States, University of Pennsylvania Press, Incorporated, 2008.

Howe Elliott, Maud, ed. *Art and Handicraft in the Woman's Building of the World's Columbian Exposition, Chicago, 1893*. France, Boussod, Valadon & Company, 1893.

Howe, Irving. *World of Our Fathers: The Journey of the East European Jews to America and the Life They Found and Made*. United States, Open Road Media, 2017.

James, Zoë. *The Harms of Hate for Gypsies and Travellers: A Critical Hate Studies Perspective*. Germany, Springer International Publishing, 2020.

Jarvis, Anthea. *Brides: Wedding Clothes and Customs, 1850–1980*. Merseyside County Museums, 1983.

Judd, Mary Catherine. *Classic Myths*. United States, Rand-McNally & Company, 1901.

Kendall, Laura. *Getting Married in Korea: Of Gender, Morality, and Modernity*. University of California Press, 1996.

Kim, Chil-Soon. "Analysis of Wedding Behavior of Chinese Women in their 20's to 30's in Shanghai and Neighboring Cities." *Fashion & Textile Research Journal* 14, no. 2 (2012): 251–260.

Kim, Hong-gi. *K-fashion: Wearing a New Future*. South Korea, Korean Culture and Information Service Ministry of Culture, Sports and Tourism, 2012.

Krohn, Katherine E. *Vera Wang: Enduring Style*. United States, Twenty-First Century Books, 2009.

Lahiri, Jhumpa. *The Namesake*. United Kingdom, Mariner Books, 2004.

Leeds-Hurwitz, Wendy. *Wedding as Text: Communicating Cultural Identities Through Ritual*. United Kingdom, Taylor & Francis, 2002.

LeFebvre, Jesse R. "The Rise of Wedding Churches: The Nonreligious Transformation of Japanese Christianity." *Journal of Religion in Japan* 1.aop (2022): 1–32.

Lemire, Beverly, and Giorgio Riello, eds. *Dressing Global Bodies: The Political Power of Dress in World History*. United Kingdom, Taylor & Francis, 2019.

Lemire, B. *Dress, Culture and Commerce: The English Clothing Trade Before the Factory, 1660–1800*. United Kingdom, Palgrave Macmillan UK, 1997.

Lennon, Rachael. *Wedded Wife: A Feminist History of Marriage*. United Kingdom, Aurum, 2023.

Lilleenget By, Tone. *Trønderroser 5 – Fornuft og følelser*. Norway, Bladkompaniet AS, 2021.

Lomax, Susan, "The View from the Shop: Window Display, the Shopper and the Formulation of Theory." In *Cultures of Selling: Perspectives on Consumption and Society Since 1700*, edited by John Benson and Laura Ugolini, Ashgate, 2006.

Lueck, Therese, and Kathleen L. Endres. *Women's Periodicals in the United States: Consumer Magazines*. United Kingdom, ABC-CLIO, 1995.

MacDonald, Anne L. *No Idle Hands: The Social History of American Knitting*. United Kingdom, Random House Publishing Group, 2010.

Madine, Thelma. *Tales of the Gypsy Dressmaker*. United Kingdom, HarperCollins Publishers, 2012.

Mann, Herman. *The Female Review: Or, Memoirs of an American Young Lady (Deborah Sampson), Whose Life and Character are Peculiarly Distinguished, Being a Continental Soldier for Nearly Three Years, in the Late American War. ... With an Appendix. ... By a Citizen of Massachusetts*. Massachusetts, Dedham, 1797.

Mays, Dorothy A. *Women in Early America: Struggle, Survival, and Freedom in a New World*. United States, Bloomsbury Academic, 2004.

Mikhaila, Ninya, and Jane Malcolm-Davies. *The Tudor Tailor: Reconstructing Sixteenth-Century Dress*. Batsford, 2006.

Milford-Cottam, Daniel. *Fashion in the 1970s*. United Kingdom, Bloomsbury Publishing, 2018.

Monger, George. *Marriage Customs of the World: From Henna to Honeymoons*. United States, Bloomsbury Academic, 2004.

Monden, Masafumi. *Japanese Fashion Cultures: Dress and Gender in Contemporary Japan*. United Kingdom, Bloomsbury Publishing, 2014.

Montemurro, Beth. *Something Old, Something Bold: Bridal Showers and Bachelorette Parties*. United Kingdom, Rutgers University Press, 2006.

Munroe, Nazanin Hedayat, and Bonnie English. *A Cultural History of Western Fashion: From Haute Couture to Virtual Couture*. United Kingdom, Bloomsbury Publishing, 2022.

Oliver, K. *Samuel Richardson, Dress, and Discourse*. United Kingdom, Palgrave Macmillan UK, 2008.

Otnes, Cele C., and Elizabeth Pleck, eds. *Cinderella Dreams: The Allure of the Lavish Wedding*. University of California Press, 2003.

Peleikis, Anja. *Lebanese in Motion: Gender and the Making of a Translocal Village*. Germany, transcript Verlag, 2015.

Phegley, Jennifer. *Courtship and Marriage in Victorian England*. Ukraine, ABC-CLIO, 2012.

Phipps, Ciara. *Making Vintage 1930s Clothes for Women*. United Kingdom, Crowood Press, 2019.

Piljac, Pamela A. *Bride-To-Bride Book: A Complete Wedding Planner for the Bride Revised Edition*. United States, Bryce-Waterton Publications, 1990.

Poe Durbin, Holly. *The Costume Designer's Toolkit: The Process of Creating Effective Design*. United Kingdom, Taylor & Francis, 2022.

Probert, Rebecca. *Marriage Law and Practice in the Long Eighteenth Century: A Reassessment*. Cambridge University Press, 2009.

Ramdya, Kavita. *Bollywood Weddings: Dating, Engagement, and Marriage in Hindu America*. United States, Lexington Books, 2010.

Riley, Glenda. *The female frontier: a comparative view of women on the prairie and the plains*. United Kingdom, University Press of Lawrence, Kansas, 1988.

Robinson, Mary. *Memoirs of the Late Mrs. Mary Robinson, 2: Written by Herself, in Two Volumes*. Richard Phillips, 1803.

Rouhier-Willoughby, Jeanmarie. *Village values: negotiating identity, gender, and resistance in urban Russian life-cycle rituals*. Bloomington, Slavica, 2008.

Shaw, Scott, and Kim Olsen. *Your Wedding, Your Way: The Modern Couple's Guide to Destination Elopements, Courthouse Ceremonies, Intimate Dinner Parties, and Other Nontraditional Nuptials*. United States, Chronicle Books LLC, 2022.

Sim, Cheryl. *Wearing the Cheongsam: Dress and Culture in a Chinese Diaspora*. United Kingdom, Bloomsbury Publishing, 2019.

Slade, Alison F., Amber J. Narro, and Burton P. Buchanan, eds. *Reality Television: Oddities of Culture*. United States, Lexington Books, 2014.

Smith, John Thomas. *Nollekens and His Times: Comprehending a Life of that Celebrated Sculptor; and Memoirs of Several Contemporary Artists, from the Time of Roubiliac, Hogarth, and Reynolds, to that of Fuseli, Flaxman, and Blake*. United Kingdom, Henry Colburn, 1828.

Staniland, Kay. *In royal fashion: the clothes of Princess Charlotte of Wales & Queen Victoria 1796–1901*. London, Museum of London, 1997.

Stevenson, Pauline. *Bridal Fashions*. United Kingdom, Ian Allan, 1978.

Toplis, Alison. *The Clothing Trade in Provincial England, 1800–1850*. United Kingdom, Taylor & Francis, 2015.

Tveite, Stein. "The Norwegian textile market in the 18th century." *Scandinavian Economic History Review* 17, no. 2 (1969): 161–178.

Volo, Dorothy, and James M. Volo. *Daily Life in Civil War America*. United States, ABC-CLIO, 2009.

Wallace, Carol. *All Dressed in White: The Irresistible Rise of the American Wedding*. United Kingdom, Penguin Books, 2004.

Wigston-Smith, Chloe, and Serena Dyer, eds. *Material Literacy in 18th-Century Britain: A Nation of Makers*. United Kingdom, Bloomsbury Publishing, 2020.

Wood, Edward J. *The Wedding Day in All Ages and Countries*. United Kingdom, Bentley, 1869.

Wright, Merideth. *Everyday Dress of Rural America, 1783–1800: With Instructions and Patterns*. United Kingdom, Dover Publications, 1992.

Wynne, Elizabeth, and Eugenia Wynne Campbell. *The Wynne Diaries, 1789–1820*. Oxford, Oxford University Press, 1982.

Yue, Daiyun. *China and the West at the Crossroads: Essays on Comparative Literature and Culture*. Singapore, Springer Nature Singapore, 2016.

Image Credits

Introduction

Page 6 Apple and Cheese Photography, California.

Page 9 A fashionable wedding in Kamerun, Schomburg Center for Research in Black Culture, Jean Blackwell Hutson Research and Reference Division, The New York Public Library. *The New York Public Library Digital Collections*. 1912. https://digitalcollections.nypl.org/items/510d47de-1027-a3d9-e040-e00a18064a99

Page 10 A bride emerging from a sedan chair assisted by two women, set in a palatial residence. Colour woodcut by Kuniyoshi, 1847/1850. Wellcome Collection. Public Domain Mark. Source: Wellcome Collection.

Page 11 A model presents a creation of Taiwanese designer Tsai Meiyue's 2011 spring/summer wedding dress collection at China Fashion Week in Beijing on October 29, 2010. LILIAN WU/AFP via Getty Images.

Page 13 Wedding in Scotland, 2012. Image by Caro Weiss Photography, courtesy of Emilie Maguin and Ewan Cameron.

Chapter 1

Page 19 *William II, Prince of Orange, and his Bride, Mary Stuart*, Anthony van Dyck, 1641, Rijksmuseum, Amsterdam.

Page 20 (main image) *The Story of Esther*, Marco del Buono Giamberti (Italian, Florence 1402–1489 Florence) and Apollonio di Giovanni di Tomaso (Italian, Florence ca. 1416–1465 Florence), Metropolitan Museum of Art, New York, Rogers Fund, 1918.

Page 20 (top right) *Portrait of a Woman*, Master of the Castello Nativity, probably 1450s, Metropolitan Museum of Art, New York, The Jules Bache Collection, 1949.

Page 21 Jerome Robbins Dance Division, The New York Public Library. "[Branle]" *The New York Public Library Digital Collections*. 1650 - 1659. https://digitalcollections.nypl.org/items/ab2a2dc0-1ea0-0133-9c8c-58d385a7bbd0

Page 22 (main image) *Fille Armenienne, que l'on conduit à l'Eglise pour la marier*, plate 87 from "Recueil de cent estampes représentent differentes nations du Levant", After Jean Baptiste Vanmour (French, Valenciennes 1671–1737 Istanbul (Constantinople)), 1714-15, Metropolitan Museum of Art, New York, Bequest of Mrs. Charles Wrightsman, 2019.

Page 22 (left) *Armenian Wedding*, Jean Baptiste Vanmour, 1720–1737, Rijksmuseum, Amsterdam.

Page 22 (right) The Miriam and Ira D. Wallach Division of Art, Prints and Photographs: Picture Collection, The New York Public Library. "A Turkish lady in her wedding dress" *The New York Public Library Digital Collections*. 1802-01-01. https://digitalcollections.nypl.org/items/510d47e2-d15d-a3d9-e040-e00a18064a99.

Page 23 *Wedding Feast of Saint Elizabeth of Hungary and Louis of Thuringia in the Wartburg*, inner left wing of an altarpiece made for the Grote Kerk in Dordrecht, c.1490–1495. Meester van de Heilige Elisabeth-Panelen. Rijksmuseum, Amsterdam. Purchased with the support of the Vereeniging Rembrandt.

Pages 24–25 Marco del Buono Giamberti and Apollonio di Giovanni di Tomasco, The Story of Esther, c.1460-70, Metropolitan Museum of Art, New York. Rogers Fund, 1918.

Chapter 2

Page 28 A nobleman and an alderman sit at a table negotiating a marriage settlement between the son of the former and the daughter of the latter. Engraving by Louis Gérard Scotin after William Hogarth, April 1st, 1745. Wellcome Collection 38350i.

Page 31 (main image) William Hogarth, *The Wedding of Stephen Beckingham and Mary Cox*, 1729, Metropolitan Museum of Art, New York, Marquand Fund, 1936.

Page 31 (left) Dress, British, c.1725, Metropolitan Museum of Art, New York. Purchase, Irene Lewisohn Bequest, 1964.

Page 31 (right) Wedding or betrothal fan, German, c.1770–90, Metropolitan Museum of Art, New York, The Moses Lazarus Collection, Gift of Josephine and Sarah Lazarus, in memory of their father, 1888–95.

Page 32 (main image) Elizabeth Bull's wedding dress, 1735, Revolutionary Spaces, Boston, MA. Courtesy of Revolutionary Spaces.

Page 32 (left) Elizabeth Bull's wedding dress, 1735 (detail) Revolutionary Spaces, Boston, MA. Courtesy of Revolutionary Spaces.

Page 32 (inset, left) Wedding dress with extremely wide, puffed sleeves, c.1835, Rijksmuseum, Amsterdam. Gift of Jonkvrouw C.I. Six, 's-Graveland.

Page 32 (inset, right) Dress, Italian, 1725-40, Metropolitan Museum of Art, New York. Purchase, Irene Lewisohn Bequest, 1993.

Page 33 (main image) Wedding dress 1742, Hulton Fine Art Collection. "Dress of Spitalfields silk, with pink satin quilted petticoat. Second half of eighteenth century," 18th century. From Georgian Art (1760–1820)   Burlington Magazine Monograph III, by [B. T. Batsford, London, 1929] Artist Unknown. (Photo by The Print Collector/Getty Images).

Page 33 (left) *Marriage A-la-Mode, Plate IV*, April 1, 1745. Simon Francis Ravenet, the elder after William Hogarth, Metropolitan Museum of Art, New York. Gift of Sarah Lazarus, 1891.

Page 34 (main image) Robe à l'Anglaise, ca.1747; altered 1770s (front view), British, Metropolitan Museum of Art, New York. Purchase, Friends of The Costume Institute Gifts, 2014. **Back view and detail** as above.

Page 34 (top left) *Pamela is married* (1745); published 1762 from a series of twelve illustrations to Pamela by Samuel Richardson, 1745, 2nd edition, published by John Boydell, London, 1762. Antoine BENOIST (engraver), Joseph HIGHMORE (after). National Gallery of Victoria, Melbourne Felton Bequest, 1921. This digital record has been made available on NGV Collection Online through the generous support of the Joe White Bequest.

Page 34 (bottom right) Length of silk by Anna Maria Garthwaite (detail), 1748, woven by Thomas Brant. Metropolitan Museum of Art, New York. Rogers Fund, 1962.

Page 35 (main image) Dress (Mantua) with Train, anonymous, c. 1750–c. 1760 (front view), Rijksmuseum, Amsterdam. Gift of Jonkvrouw C.I. Six, 's-Graveland, 1978. **Back view and page 42** as above.

Page 36 (main image) "Second day wedding dress" (front view), 1765, Historical Collections, The National Museum of Finland, Helsinki. **Back view** as above.

Page 36 (left) Petticoat, maker unknown, Southeastern Connecticut or Rhode Island, circa 1750. Historic Deerfield, gift of Helen Geier Flynt, F.122. Photo by Penny Leveritt.

Page 36 (top left) Wedding dress, British or French, c.1760 (detail), Metropolitan Museum of Art, New York. Gift of Mary Eastwood and Gertrude Knevels, 1940.

Page 36 (top right) "The pleasures of the married state," W. Proud del. et sculp, [between 1770 and 1789], Library of Congress, LC-USZ62-59621 (detail). Library of Congress Prints and Photographs Division Washington, D.C. 20540 USA.

Page 37 (main image) Wedding Dress of Princess Sofia Magdalena, 1766, Royal Armoury, Stockholm (front view). Bonnevier, Helena, Livrustkammaren/ SHM (CC BY 4.0). **Back view and bodice detail** as above.

Page 38 (main image) Wedding dress, c.1760s, England (front view). Collection of Mary D. Doering. **Back view** as above.

Image Credits   **245**

Page 38 (left) Dress, French, c.1775 (detail), Metropolitan Museum of Art, New York. Isabel Shults Fund, 2005.

Page 38 (bottom right) *Mrs. Robinson as Perdita*, Richard Cosway, ca. 1779, Metropolitan Museum of Art, New York. Bequest of Alexandrine Sinsheimer, 1958.

Page 39 (main image) Sack-back open robe and petticoat, c.1770–75 (front view), England, Hampshire Cultural Trust. © Hampshire County Council. Provided by the Hampshire Cultural Trust, 2025. **Back view** as above.

Page 40 (main image) Wedding dress, c.1779–1780 (front view), Stiftelsen Kunstindustrimuseet, The Design Collections. Nasjonalmuseet, Oslo, Norway. **Back view** as above.

Page 40 (inset), and page 43 Robe à la Française (detail), French, 1760–70, Metropolitan Museum of Art, New York. Brooklyn Museum Costume Collection at The Metropolitan Museum of Art, New York. Gift of the Brooklyn Museum, 2009; H. Randolph Lever Fund, 1966.

Page 40 (right) Wedding crown, Norway, 19th century. Metropolitan Museum of Art, New York. Gift of Mrs. Mansfield Ferry, 1955.

Page 41 (main image) Deborah Sampson bridal gown, 1760, Historic New England. **Detail** as above.

Page 41 (right) Women's & Children's fashion plates, 18th century. Plate 037 (detail), Metropolitan Museum of Art, New York. Gift of Woodman Thompson.

Chapter 3

Page 46 *Country Wedding*, Unidentified Artist after John Lewis Krimmel, early 19th century, Pennsylvania Academy of the Fine Arts. John S. Phillips Collection.

Page 49 *Saada, the Wife of Abraham Ben-Chimol, and Préciada, One of Their Daughters*, Eugène Delacroix, 1832, Metropolitan Museum of Art, New York. Gift of Paul Beck, Jnr.

Page 50 (main image) *Mariage républicain*. (IFF 31), Legrand, Pierre François, Graveur. Legrand, Pierre François, Editeur, 1794. Museo Carnavalet - Historia de París.

Page 50 (left) *Journal de la Mode et du Goût*, 20 juillet 1792, 15e cahier, pl. 2, A.B. Duhamel (probably), 1792. Gift of P.L.M. Verhaak.

Page 50 (right) Woman's Dress, France or England, Textile: c. 1770; Dress: 1785–1790. Los Angeles County Museum of Art. Gift of the J. Paul Getty Museum (M.86.238).

Page 51 Bridal gown, c.1797, National Museum of Denmark, Copenhagen (front view). Photography by Peter Danstrøm & Roberto Fortuna. **Back view** as above.

Page 52 (main image) Wedding dress, American, c.1799, Museum of Fine Arts, Boston. Gift of Mrs. Ward Thoron.

Page 52 (inset, left) *Young woman with ribbed headpiece, Chapeau a Côtes*, 1799–1801 (detail), Rijksmuseum, Amsterdam. Purchased with the support of the Flora Fonds / Rijksmuseum Fonds.

Page 52 (inset, right) *Journal des Dames et des Modes*, Costume Parisien, 19 mai 1798, An 6, (20.): Coiffure négligée en fichu (...), anoniem, 1798 (detail), Rijksmuseum, Amsterdam. Purchase from the F.G. Waller Fund.

Page 52 (bottom right) Woman's Dress (Robe à la française), Netherlands, Amsterdam, 1740–1760 (detail), Los Angeles County Museum of Art. Purchased with funds provided by Suzanne A. Saperstein and Michael and Ellen Michelson, with additional funding from the Costume Council, the Edgerton Foundation, Gail and Gerald Oppenheimer, Maureen H Shapiro, Grace Tsao, and Lenore and Richard Wayne (M.2007.211.928).

Page 53 (main image) Indian muslin wedding dress, c.1806, England, Manchester Art Gallery (front view). © Manchester Art Gallery. **Side view** as above.

Page 53 (bottom right) Friedrich Carl Gröger: wedding portrait of Emilie and Johann Philipp Petersen, Hamburg 1806; now in the collection of Deutsches Historisches Museum Berlin, Inventory number Gm 92/52. 1806. GroegerPetersen. The Picture Art Collection / Alamy Stock Photo.

Page 54 (main image) Quaker Wedding dress, 1809, worn by Lydia Poultney (American, Philadelphia, 1788–1871), Philadelphia Museum of Art. Bequest of Lydia Thompson Morris, 1932.

Page 54 (left) Ensemble for a Quaker Woman: Two Kerchiefs, Bonnet, Cap, Cape, Dress, and Shawl, c.1830. Artist/maker unknown, American, Philadelphia Museum of Art. Gift of Margaret J. Hall in memory of Abigail B. Massey, 1983.

Page 54 (right) Evening dress, French, c.1809, Metropolitan Museum of Art, New York (detail). Brooklyn Museum Costume Collection at The Metropolitan Museum of Art. Gift of the Brooklyn Museum, 2009; Gift of Theodora Wilbour, 1947.

Page 55 (main image) Wedding Gown with Train and Rosettes, anonymous, 1812 (front view), Rijksmuseum, Amsterdam Gift of Jonkvrouw C.I. Six, 's-Graveland. **Back view** as above.

Page 55 (left) Fashion Plate, 'Parisian Ball Dress' for 'La Belle Assemblée', John Bell (England, 1745–1831), Los Angeles County Museum of Art. Gift of Dr. and Mrs. Gerald Labiner (M.86.266.292).

Page 55 (right) Wedding dress, American, 1812 (detail). Gift of Prudence S. Regan, in memory of Prudence Rindell Sanford, 1980.

Page 56 (main image), and page 64 Princess Charlotte's wedding dress, 1816. White silk net embroidered in silver strip with a spotted ground and borders. (Photo by Museum of London/Heritage Images/Getty Images).

Page 56 (left) Marie Antoinette: The Queen of Fashion: Court Lady in a Robe de cour, Pietro Antonio Martini, after Jean Michel Moreau, 1789 (detail), Rijksmuseum, Amsterdam. http://hdl.handle.net/10934/RM0001.COLLECT.150193

Page 56 (right) The Princess Charlotte of Wales and Prince Leopold of Cobourg, The New York Public Library Digital Collections. https://digitalcollections.nypl.org/items/510d47e2-ebb2-a3d9-e040-e00a18064a99

Page 57 (main image) Woman's Wedding Dress, c. 1818. Artist/maker unknown, American, Philadelphia Museum of Art. Gift of Mrs. Paul Reid Tait, 1965.

Page 57 (left) Wedding slippers, American, 1810–19, Brooklyn Museum Costume Collection at The Metropolitan Museum of Art, New York. Gift of the Brooklyn Museum, 2009. Gift of J. Ethel Brown, 1956.

Page 57 (top right) Women 1800-1819 Part 1, Plate 115, 1814, Gift of Woodman Thompson, Costume Institute Fashion Plates, Metropolitan Museum of Art, New York.

Page 57 (right) Observateur des Modes, 1818, No. 2 : Capote de gaz (...), Rijksmuseum, Amsterdam. Purchased with the support of the F.G. Waller-Fonds.

Page 58 Jerome Robbins Dance Division, The New York Public Library. "The penny wedding," *The New York Public Library Digital Collections*. 1848. https://digitalcollections.nypl.org/items/50f9c000-8cb8-0134-43b3-00505686a51c. Gift of Lincoln Kirstein.

Page 59 (main image) Fashion plates (Weddings 1820-1869), Plate 001 (detail), Costume Parisien, 1820, Metropolitan Museum of Art, New York. Gift of Woodman Thompson.

Page 59 (left), and page 65 Edging, late 18th century, Flemish (detail), Metropolitan Museum of Art, New York. Rogers Fund, 1906.

Page 60 (main image) Batiste Wedding Dress, 1825, Philadelphia, Fashion Archives and Museum, Shippensburg University, Pennsylvania. **Detail (bottom right)** as above.

Page 60 (bottom left) Wedding dress, American, 1824. Brooklyn Museum Costume Collection at The Metropolitan Museum of Art. Gift of the Brooklyn Museum, 2009; Gift of the Jason and Peggy Westerfield Collection, 1969.

Page 60 (top left) Couple in Wedding Dress, Edme Jean Pigal, 1823 (detail), Rijksmuseum. Gift from the heirs of P. van Eeghen, Amsterdam.

Page 61 (main image, right) Wedding dress, silk, 1829, Collections of Maine Historical Society, A86-27.

Page 61 (main image, left) Fashion plates (Weddings 1820–1869), Plate 004, Metropolitan Museum of Art, New York. Gift of Woodman Thompson.

Page 61 (far left) Petit Courrier des Dames, 25 avril 1828, No. 549: Costume de Mariée..., anonymous, 1828, Rijksmuseum, Amsterdam. Purchased with the support of the F.G. Waller-Fonds.

Page 61 (bottom left) Rosa Canina, Lawrance, Mary, d. 1830 (Etcher), NYPL. New York Public Library Digital Collections.

Page 62 (main image) Mary Bufton's Wedding dress, 1834, (front view). Hereford Museum & Gallery, Herefordshire Museum Service. **Rear view** as above.

Page 62 (left) Fashion plates (Women 1830-1831), Plate 070, *Petit Courrier des Dames* (detail), Metropolitan Museum of Art, New York. Gift of Woodman Thompson.

Page 62 (right) Pelerine, American, ca. 1835, Brooklyn Museum Costume Collection at The Metropolitan Museum of Art, New York. Gift of the Brooklyn Museum, 2009; Gift of the National Society of Colonial Dames in the State of New York, 1978.

Page 63 (main image) Wedding dress with extremely wide, puffed sleeves, anonymous, in or before 1835, Rijksmuseum, Amsterdam. Gift of Jonkvrouw C.I. Six, 's-Graveland.

Page 63 (left) Fashion plates (Women 1820-1869), Plate 006, 1832, Metropolitan Museum of Art, New York. Gift of Woodman Thompson.

Page 63 (right) "The queen of the Belgians in her wedding dress," Hopwood, William, *The New York Public Library Digital Collections*. https://digitalcollections.nypl.org/items/510d47e0-f27c-a3d9-e040-e00a18064a99

Chapter 4

Page 69 *Portrait of a bride*, c.1860s. Collection of Drs. K. and B. Bohleke.

Page 70 Wedding stereoview, c.1857. Collection of Drs. K. and B. Bohleke.

Page 72 (main image center and right), and page 87 Wedding dress, 1837, front view. Indianapolis Museum of Art at Newfields, Purchased with funds provided by The National Society of the Colonial Dames of America in the State of Indiana, 2003.81. **Rear view and detail** as above.

Page 72 (main image left) Wedding dress worn by Amanda Grim, 1839, Pennsylvania. Fashion Archives and Museum, Shippensburg University, Pennsylvania.

Page 72 (top left) Portrait of Amanda Grim, c.1839. Fashion Archives and Museum, Shippensburg University, Pennsylvania.

Page 73 (main image) Wedding dress, c.1844, (front view) Metropolitan Museum of Art, New York. Gift of Mrs. Osborne Howes, 1950. **Detail** as above.

Page 73 (top left) Evening dress, American, 1840–42. Brooklyn Museum Costume Collection at The Metropolitan Museum of Art, New York. Gift of the Brooklyn Museum, 2009; Gift of Claire Lorraine Wilson, 1942.

Page 73 (right) Fashion plates (Weddings 1820–1869). Plate 038 (detail), "El Correo de Altramar," Metropolitan Museum of Art, New York. Gift of Mary P. Hayden.

Page 74 (main image) Sarah Tate's wedding dress, c.1845, Witte Museum, San Antonio, Texas.

Page 74 (left), and pages 84–85 Slave Marriage Ceremony. A wedding ceremony. Woodcut, 19th century. Getty Images UK: Bettmann / Contributor.

Page 74 (right) Fashion plates (Weddings 1820-1869), *Le Moniteur de la Mode*, 1845. Metropolitan Museum of Art, New York. Gift of Woodman Thompson.

Page 75 (main image) Wedding dress, 1848, front view. © National Museum of Wales. **Side view** as above.

Page 75 (right) *Magasin des Demoiselles*, March 1849, Metropolitan Museum of Art, New York. Gift of Woodman Thompson.

Page 75 (left) Le Moniteur de la Mode, 1849 (detail), Metropolitan Museum of Art, New York. Gift of Woodman Thompson.

Page 76 (main image) Wedding dress, 1850, England. National Gallery of Victoria, Melbourne. Gift of Mrs Betty Blunden, 1979. This digital record has been made available on NGV Collection Online through the generous support of Professor AGL Shaw AO Bequest.

Page 76 (left) Fashion plates (Weddings 1820-1869), Le Moniteur de la Mode, 1849. Metropolitan Museum of Art, New York. Gift of Woodman Thompson.

Page 76 (right) Wedding Waistcoat, 1860, Metropolitan Museum of Art, New York. Gift of The Misses Mary L. and Katherine Gardner, 1958.

Page 77 (main image) Tarlatan wedding dress, 1854, Nordiska Museet/DigitaltMuseum. Photograph by Mats Landin. **Rear view** as above.

Page 77 (top center) Bridal crown, Sweden, 1854, Nordiska Museet/DigitaltMuseum. Photograph by Frida Lönnberg.

Page 78 (main image) 1850s wedding dress, front view, c.1855-1905, Quirindi & District Historical Society, NSW.

Page 78 (left) Newspaper image of descendant wearing the dress, 1970s. Quirindi & District Historical Society.

Page 78 (top center) Albert Sands Southworth and Josiah Johnson Hawes, *A Bride and Her Bridesmaids*, Smithsonian American Art Museum. Museum purchase made possible by Walter Beck.

Page 79 (main image) Wedding dress, c.1860, front view, Manning Valley Historical Society, New South Wales. **Rear view, bonnet, and detail** as above.

Page 79 (left) Dress, American, 1860-3, Metropolitan Museum of Art. Gift of Mrs. Charles D. Dickey, Mrs. Louis Curtis Jr., and Mr. S. Sloan Colt, 1957.

Page 80 (main image), and page 86 Dress, Wedding; c.1860; 948/23.1-3, South Canterbury Museum, New Zealand. **Rear view and evening bodice detail** as above.

Page 80 (left) Fashion plates (Wedding 1820-1869), Plate 085, (detail), *Beilage zur allgerneinen Musterzeitung*, May 1861. Metropolitan Museum of Art, New York. Gift of Lee Simonson.

Page 80 (inset right below) Wedding dress, American, 1858–59 (detail), Metropolitan Museum of Art, New York. Gift of Miss Frances Williams, 1957.

Page 81 (main image) Quaker wedding dress, 1863 (front view), Fashion Archives and Museum, Shippensburg University, Pennsylvania. **Rear view** as above.

Page 81 (below) Woman's Quaker Bonnet, United States, 1860, Los Angeles County Museum of Art. Mrs. Alice F. Schott Bequest.

Page 82 (main image) Wedding dress, 1865, The Hallwyl Museum, Stockholm, Sweden. Photo: Landin, Mats/Nordiska Museet.

Page 82 (left) Wedding dress, c.1867, England. National Gallery of Victoria, Melbourne. The Schofield Collection. Purchased with the assistance of a special grant from the Government of Victoria, 1974. This digital record has been made available on NGV Collection Online through the generous support of Professor AGL Shaw AO Bequest.

Page 82 (right) Portrait of Wilhelmina von Hallwyl, Jens Mohr, the Hallwyl Museum, Stockholm, Sweden.

Page 83 (main image) Wedding ensemble, American, 1868 (front view). Metropolitan Museum of Art, New York. Gift of Mrs. Francis Howard and Mrs. Avery Robinson, 1953. **Side view and detail** as above.

Page 83 (right) Fashion plates (Weddings 1820–1869), Plate 006 (detail), *Les Modes Parisiennes*, Peterson's Magazine, October 1867. Gift of Woodman Thompson.

Chapter 5

Page 90 Bridal couple, late 1870s, USA. Collection of Drs. K. and B. Bohleke.

Page 92 Satin wedding dress with orange blossom, 1879. Courtesy XIXGallery, Poland.

Page 95 Wedding ensemble by Herman Rossberg, 1887, Metropolitan Museum of Art, New York. Gift of Mrs. James G. Flockhart, 1968.

Page 96 (main image) Wedding dress, 1872. Courtesy of the Essex Peabody Museum. Photo by Dennis Helmar. Gift of Miss Annie L. Cutts, 1958. 129156.1A-D.

Page 96 (right above) "Bridal-dress; Bonnets," 1872 (detail), *The Peterson Magazine*. Wallach Division Picture Collection, New York Public Library Digital Collections.

Page 96 (right below) "1872, 'engageantes' and peplum." Collection of Drs. K. and B. Bohleke.

Page 97 (main image) Wedding Dress, Unknown maker, 1872–1876, Agnes Etherington Art Centre, Queen's University, Ontario, Canada. Gift to Queen's Drama Club from an unknown donor, before 1948. **Side view** as above.

Page 97 (right) *Sir Richard Pearson* mezzotint (detail), Unknown, after Grignion (Jnr) 1780. National Gallery of Victoria, Melbourne. Felton Bequest, 1926. This digital record has been made available on NGV Collection Online through the generous support of the Joe White Bequest.

Page 97 (left) Elisabeth Louise Vigée Le Brun, *Marie Antoinette in a Park*, c.1780–81, Metropolitan Museum of Art, New York. Bequest of Mrs. Charles Wrightsman, 2019.

Page 98 (main image) Plaid wedding dress, 1873 (front view), New York. Fashion Archives and Museum, Shippensburg University, Pennsylvania. **Rear view** as above.

Page 98 (left) Fashion plates (Wedding 1870–1929), Plate 003 (detail), *Peterson's Magazine*, November 1870 (detail), Metropolitan Museum of Art, New York. Gift of Woodman Thompson.

Page 98 (top center) André Adolphe-Eugène Disdéri (French, 1819–1889). *Princess de Metternich*, 1864. Albumen print. Los Angeles: The J. Paul Getty Museum, 84.XD.379.169. J. Paul Getty Museum.

Page 98 (right) *Journal des Dames et des Demoiselles*, 15 November 1872, No. 1085B, Jules David (1808–1892), 1872 (detail), Rijksmuseum, Amsterdam. Purchased with the support of the F.G. Waller-Fonds.

Page 99 (main image) Wedding dress, 1878 (front view), England. Fashion Archives and Museum, Shippensburg University, Pennsylvania. **Side view and detail** as above.

Page 99 (left) Bridal portrait, 1948. Fashion Archives and Museum, Shippensburg University, Pennsylvania.

Page 99 (right) Photograph of woman wearing dress with 'crenelated' hemline, c.1870s. Collection of Drs. K. and B. Bohleke.

Page 100 (main image) Silk and swansdown wedding dress, 1879, England. © Hampshire County Council. Provided by the Hampshire Cultural Trust, 2025.

Page 100 (right) *Illustrirte Frauen-Zeitung*, 14 April 1879, Pl. 394, Rijksmuseum, Amsterdam. Gift of the M.A. Ghering-van Ierlant Collection.

Page 101 (main image) Silk wedding dress, 1880 (front view), USA, Metropolitan Museum of Art, New York. Gift of Mrs. Robert C. Booth, 1934. **Rear view and detail** as above.

Page 101 (above right) Fashion plates (Wedding 1870–1929), Plate 025 (detail), "Les Modes Parisiennes," *Peterson's Magazine*, September 1879, Metropolitan Museum of Art. Gift of Leo Van Witsen.

Page 102 (main image) Two-piece wedding dress, c.1882–85 (front view). Fashion Archives and Museum, Shippensburg University, Pennsylvania. **Rear view and details** as above.

Page 102 (right below) Wedding dress, 1885, unknown maker, Australia. National Gallery of Victoria, Melbourne, Gift of Mr. J. G. H. Sprigg, 1971. This digital record has been made available on NGV Collection Online through the generous support of Creative Victoria through Culture Victoria.

Page 103 (main image) Floral wedding dress, c.1875–85, The Queensland Women's Historical Association.

Page 103 (right) Fashion plates (Wedding 1870–1929), Plate 037 (detail), *Modes Vraies*, April 1882, Metropolitan Museum of Art, New York. Gift of Woodman Thompson.

Page 103 (far right) Sprigged dress, 1866 © Manchester Art Gallery.

Page 103 (left) Portrait of a bride wearing floral-sprigged silk brocade, late 1880s. Collection of Drs. K. and B. Bohleke.

Page 104 (main image) "Mrs. Daniel Reese Wolfe in her Wedding Dress," 188–, J.C Strauss Studio. Courtesy of the Missouri Historical Society, St. Louis.

Page 104 (left) "Revue de la Mode," *Gazette de la Famille*, Sunday 18 October 1885, 14e Année, No. 720: Toilettes de M.elle Thirion. Rijksmuseum, Amsterdam.

Page 104 (right) Wedding gloves, c.1887, America, Metropolitan Museum of Art, New York. Gift of Miss Constance P. Brown, 1955.

Page 104 (left below), and page 108 Woman's Dress, England, c.1885 (rear view), Los Angeles County Museum of Art. Purchased with funds provided by Suzanne A. Saperstein and Michael and Ellen Michelson, with additional funding from the Costume Council, the Edgerton Foundation, Gail and Gerald Oppenheimer, Maureen H. Shapiro, Grace Tsao, and Lenore and Richard Wayne (M.2007.211.781a-b).

Page 105 (main image) Cotton batiste and lace wedding dress, late 1880s, Fashion Archives and Museum, Shippensburg University, Pennsylvania. **Rear view detail** as above.

Page 105 (left) *Revue de la Mode, Gazette de la Famille*, 1882, 11e année, No. 575: Jupons & Corsets (...), E. Cheffer, 1882 (detail), Rijksmuseum, Amsterdam.

Page 106 (main image) Wedding dress, silk taffeta/beads/braid, worn by Janet McDonald, Australia, c.1887, Powerhouse Museum, Sydney. Powerhouse Collection. Gift of Lorrie Cowled, 1984. Photographer Marinco Kojdanovski.

Page 106 (right) "Marriage of Aboriginal natives," Corranderk c.1873? National Library of Australia, 1311389.

Page 106 (left) "New style for bridal dress," 1880s, *Peterson Magazine*. Collection of Drs. K. and B. Bohleke.

Page 107 (main image) Wedding dress, 1889, Museum of Fine Arts, Boston. Gift of Mr. Henry S. Hall, Jr.

Page 107 (left), and page 109 Wedding dress, Department Store Fox, 1892 (detail), Metropolitan Museum of Art. Gift of William Kelly Simpson, Helen-Louise K. Simpson Seggerman, Elizabeth Simpson Bennett and Sarah P. F. Simpson French, in memory of their parents, Mr. and Mrs., Kenneth F. Simpson, 1983.

Page 107 (right) Fashion plates (Wedding 1870–1929), Plate 053, July 1889 (detail), Metropolitan Museum of Art, New York. Gift of Woodman Thompson.

Chapter 6

Page 113 Chinese bridal party, Rockhampton, Queensland, c.1900. State Library of Queensland.

Page 116 (main image) Ribbed silk wedding dress, 1890 (front view), USA. Fashion Archives and Museum, Shippensburg University, Pennsylvania. **Rear view** as above.

Page 116 (bottom) "Wedding dresses," *The Peterson Magazine*, July 1890. Wallach Division Picture Collection, New York Public Library Digital Collections.

Page 117 (main image) Wedding dress, 1893, by A.C Coady, New York. Brooklyn Museum Costume Collection at The Metropolitan Museum of Art, New York. Gift of the Brooklyn Museum, 2009; Gift of Mrs. James Pensa, 1967.

Page 117 (right) Day dress, c.1895 by Jean-Philippe Worth. National Gallery of Victoria, Melbourne. Purchased with funds donated by Mrs. Krystyna

Campbell-Pretty in memory of Mr. Harold Campbell-Pretty, 2015. This digital record has been made available on NGV Collection Online through the generous support of Professor AGL Shaw AO Bequest.

Page 118 Wedding dress, 1894 (front view), Tepapa Tongarewa Museum of New Zealand. Gift of Miss C Rothwell, 1982. **Rear view** as above.

Page 119 (main image) Wedding and graduation gown, 1894, Pennsylvania. Daughters of the American Revolution, Washington D.C.

Page 119 (right) Portrait of the bride, 1894, Pennsylvania. Daughters of the American Revolution, Washington D.C.

Page 120 (main image) Reform Wedding Dress, c.1900-04, National Museum Denmark, Copenhagen. Photography by Peter Danstrøm & Roberto Fortuna.

Page 120 (right) Photograph of a "reform" wedding party, 1894, *New Zealand Graphic and Ladies' Journal*, 3 March 1894. Sir George Grey Special Collections, Auckland City Libraries - Tāmaki Pātaka Kōrero.

Page 120 (left) Dante Gabriel Rossetti, *The Salutation of Beatrice*, 1880–02, oil on canvas, 60 ¾ x 36 in. (154.3 x 91.4 cm), Toledo Museum of Art, Ohio. Purchased with funds from the Libbey Endowment, Gift of Edward Drummond Libbey, 1960.8.

Page 121 (main image) Two-piece wedding dress, 1903, American (front view). Author's collection/photo by Aaron Robotham. **Rear view** as above.

Page 121 (left) The Miriam and Ira D. Wallach Division of Art, Prints and Photographs: Picture Collection, The New York Public Library. "Another get-rich-quick swindle" *The New York Public Library Digital Collections*. 1903. https://digitalcollections.nypl.org/items/510d47e2-d190-a3d9-e040-e00a18064a99.

Page 122 Wool wedding dress, c.1906, USA (front view). Fashion Archives and Museum, Shippensburg University, Pennsylvania. **Rear view** as above.

Page 123 (main image) Black wedding dress, 1906, USA (front view). Fashion Archives and Museum, Shippensburg University, Pennsylvania. **Rear view** as above.

Page 123 (inset, left) White wedding gown worn by Lydia Cann, 1893, USA. Fashion Archives and Museum, Shippensburg University, Pennsylvania.

Page 123 (inset, right) Portrait of the bride, 1907, USA. Fashion Archives and Museum, Shippensburg University, Pennsylvania.

Page 124 (main image) Cotton wedding dress, Waltham Forest, London, c.1910. © London Museum.

Page 124 (right) "De Gracieuse" by Doucet, 1908, Metropolitan Museum of Art, New York. Gift of Woodman Thompson.

Page 125 (main image) "Lingerie" wedding dress with sash, USA, 1910s (front view). Author's collection/photo by Aaron Robotham. **Rear view** as above.

Page 125 (left) The Miriam and Ira D. Wallach Division of Art, Prints and Photographs: Picture Collection, The New York Public Library. "Woman in bridal gown" *The New York Public Library Digital Collections*. 1912. https://digitalcollections.nypl.org/items/510d47e0-f294-a3d9-e040-e00a18064a99.

Page 126 (main image) Wedding dress, c.1911–13, Scotland (front view). Author's collection/photo by Aaron Robotham. **Rear view and details** as above.

Page 126 (left) "Shoes worn by the bride, 1911–1913," Author's collection/photo by Aaron Robotham.

Page 126 (inset, bottom, far right) Embroidered cotton dress (sleeve detail), c.1910–15, USA. Author's collection/photo by Aaron Robotham.

Page 127 (main image) Portrait of the bride, 1915, USA. Fashion Archives and Museum, Shippensburg University, Pennsylvania.

Page 127 (left) Cotton batiste wedding dress, 1915, USA. Fashion Archives and Museum, Shippensburg University, Pennsylvania.

Page 127 (right), and page 129 Wedding dress with standing collar (detail), Hirsch Department Store, Amsterdam, 1915, Rijksmuseum, Amsterdam. Gift of the heirs of Van Reenen.

Page 128 (main image, left) Wedding dress, 1916. Silk satin, lace, silk flowers. Lucile, Chicago. Gift of the Art Institute of Chicago.

Page 128 (main image, right) Wedding dress and petticoat, 1791, England, Maker Unknown. National Gallery of Victoria, Melbourne. Purchased, 1970. This digital record has been made available on NGV Collection Online through the generous support of Professor AGL Shaw AO Bequest.

Page 128 (left) Elisabeth Louise Vigée Le Brun, *Comtesse de la Châtre*, 1789, Metropolitan Museum of Art, New York. Gift of Jessie Woolworth Donahue, 1954.

Chapter 7

Page 133 Wedding dress detail, 1926, Wales. Private collection.

Page 135 (main image) *Refugee bride and groom separated at time of enemy's invasion of Udine, finally united at Rome, 1918*, Library of Congress, Washington D.C. (detail). American National Red Cross photograph collection. **Colorized version** as above.

Page 135 (left) Detail from a 1917 edition of *The Delineator*, USA. Courtesy of Susan Grote.

Page 136 Wedding dress, 1920 (front view) by Drapery Supply Association, Dunedin, New Zealand. Te Papa Tongarewa. Gift of Mrs. Tui Preston, 1984. **Rear view** as above.

Page 137 Wedding Dress, 1921 (front view), Liverpool, England. Brighton Historical Society, Victoria, Australia. Victorian Collections: https://victoriancollections.net.au/items/5b4bff9621ea670f281c7d08. **Rear view** as above.

Page 138 Wedding dress by Jeanne Lanvin, 1924 (front view), Paris, Chicago History Museum. Gift of Mrs. Robert McCormick Adams.

Page 139 (main image) Bridal ensemble, c.1926. Daughters of the American Revolution, Washington D.C.

Page 139 (left) Portrait of the bride, 1926. Daughters of the American Revolution, Washington D.C.

Page 139 (right) Image detail from *Le Petit Echo de la Mode*, December 1926. Author's collection.

Page 140 (main image) Silk crepe wedding dress, 1928 (front view), Pennsylvania, USA. Author's collection. **Rear view** as above.

Page 140 (right) Bridal portrait, 1928, Pennsylvania, USA. Author's collection.

Page 141 (main image) Silver tissue wedding dress worn by Margaret Elizabeth Cowled (nee Hamilton), 1928, Powerhouse Museum, Sydney. Powerhouse Collection. Gift of Lorrie Cowled, 1934. Photographer Marinco Kojdanovski.

Page 141 (right) Paniers, British, c.1750, Metropolitan Museum of Art. Purchase, Irene Lewisohn Bequest, 1973.

Chapter 8

Page 144 Wedding portrait of Lollaretta Pemberton and Grover Allen, 1939. Collection of the Smithsonian National Museum of African American History and Culture, Gift of Rita C. Organ and Pemberton Family.

Page 145 Matson Photo Service, photographer. *Wedding at St. George's Cathedral on June 3rd*. Bride & groom, close-up. Jun 3. Photograph. Retrieved from the Library of Congress, www.loc.gov/item/2019704500/.

Page 147 Unattributed bridal portrait, July 10 1936. Toronto, Canada. Collection of Drs. K. and B. Bohleke.

Page 148 (main image) Wedding Dress, 1930, Perth, Western Australia. Author's collection. **Collar detail** as above.

Image Credits 249

Page 148 (right) "Woman wearing green evening gown, front and back views." The Miriam and Ira D. Wallach Division of Art, Prints and Photographs: Picture Collection, The New York Public Library. *The New York Public Library Digital Collections.* 1930–1939. https://digitalcollections.nypl.org/items/510d47e3-f7f6-a3d9-e040-e00a18064a99.

Page 149 (main image) Elopement outfit, 1935, Pennsylvania. Fashion Archives and Museum, Shippensburg University, Pennsylvania. **Detail** as above.

Page 149 (right) "Knits and Listens. Washington, D.C., Dec. 2. 1938. Without dropping a stitch, Mrs. Leon Henderson, wife of the Secretary of the Monopoly Committee, nonchalantly continues her knitting as she listened to testimony at the Committee hearing today". Harris & Ewing photograph collection Repository. Library of Congress Prints and Photographs Division Washington, D.C. 20540 USA.

Page 150 (main image) Satin and lace wedding dress, 1936 (front view), Pennsylvania. Author's collection/photo by Aaron Robotham. **Rear view** as above.

Page 150 (left) Bridal portrait, 1936, Pennsylvania. Author's collection.

Page 151 (main image) Wedding dress shipped to the United States by a German Jewish woman murdered at Riga, 1936 (front view). United States Holocaust Memorial Museum Collection, Gift of Bernard Lubran. **Sleeve detail, and page 156** as above.

Page 152 (main image) Wedding Outfit, 1937, UK, John Bright Collection (front view with cloak). **Rear view, and front view without cloak** as above.

Page 152 (right) Back view of green evening dress, 1934. The Miriam and Ira D. Wallach Division of Art, Prints and Photographs: Picture Collection, The New York Public Library. "Back view of green evening dress." The New York Public Library Digital Collections. 1934. https://digitalcollections.nypl.org/items/510d47e3-f7f7-a3d9-e040-e00a18064a99

Page 153 (main image) Parachute silk wedding dress, c.1945, UK (front view). Author's collection/photo by Aaron Robotham. **Rear view** as above.

Page 153 (right) Finnish bridal portrait, early-mid 1940s, Valokuvaaja. Photographer: Isak Paavalniemi, 1920–1949.

Page 154 (main image) Wedding dress by Norman Norell, 1946, Indianapolis Museum of Art at Newfields (front view). Gift of Bonnie Birnbaum. © *Norman Norell.* **Rear view, and page 157** as above.

Page 154 (left) "In printed crepe-de-chine—powderblue scattered with flowers—this afternoon dress, with its little velvet bolero and corselet to match, and its 1830 sleeves, strikes an original note." Evening Post, Volume CXII, Issue 58, 5 September 1931, page 9. National Library of New Zealand/Stuff Ltd.

Page 154 (right) Corselet, American or European, 1860s. Metropolitan Museum of Art, New York. Gift of Miss Margaret Brown, 1943.

Page 155 Woman's Wedding Gown with Veil, United States, 1830-1833 LACMA. Gift of Mrs. James Bishop.

Chapter 9

Page 160 Couple at their wedding reception, 1947, UK. Private collection.

Page 162 Church wedding in Newport, Wales, 1950. Private collection.

Page 164 (main image) Brocade wedding dress, 1947 (front view). Author's collection/photo by Aaron Robotham. **Rear view** as above.

Page 164 (left) The wedding dress worn by Princess Elizabeth, later Queen Elizabeth II, in 1947, on display at a new exhibition, UK, 2nd June 1973. Photo by Evening Standard/Hulton Archive/Getty Images.

Page 165 (main image) Silver wedding dress, 1949, Claremont Museum (front view). Claremont Museum, Western Australia. **Rear view** as above.

Page 165 (right) Portrait of the bride, 1949, Claremont Museum. Claremont Museum, Western Australia.

Page 166 (main image) Wedding dress 1952 by Priscilla of Boston, front view. Author's collection/photo by Aaron Robotham. **Rear view** as above.

Page 166 (left) Portrait of the bride and groom, 1952, author's collection.

Page 166 (right) Vivien Leigh (1913–1967), British actress, wearing a wedding dress, and Thomas Mitchell (1892–1962), US actor, in uniform, in a publicity still issued for the film, *Gone with the Wind*, 1939. The drama, directed by Victor Fleming (1889–1949), starred Leigh as "Scarlett O'Hara", and Mitchell as "Gerald O'Hara". (Photo by Silver Screen Collection/Getty Images).

Page 167 (main image) Film replica wedding dress, 1953, Perth, Western Australia (front view). Author's collection/photo by Aaron Robotham. **Rear view** as above.

Page 167 (right) UNITED STATES - 1950: Elizabeth Taylor dressed for her role in the film *Father of the Bride*, Hollywood, 1950. Photo by Transcendental Graphics/Getty Images.

Page 167 (left) Portrait of the bride.

Page 168 (main image) Jacqueline Bouvier Kennedy's wedding dress on display at John F. Kennedy Presidential Library and Museum, Boston, MA. Chuck Pefley / Alamy Stock Photo.

Page 168 (right) Jacqueline Bouvier Kennedy and John Kennedy talking at their wedding reception, Newport, Rhode Island] / Toni Frissell. Retrieved from the Library of Congress, www.loc.gov/item/2016647755/.

Page 169 (main image) Alfred Angelo Wedding dress, USA, 1955 (front view). Author's collection/photo by Aaron Robotham. **Rear view** as above.

Page 169 (right) Portrait of the bride and groom, 1955. Author's collection.

Page 170 (main image) Grace Kelly's Wedding Dress and Accessories. Designed by Helen Rose, American, 1904–1985. Made by the wardrobe department of Metro-Goldwyn-Mayer, Culver City, California, founded 1924. Philadelphia Museum of Art (front view). Gift of Her Serene Highness, the Princesse Grace de Monaco, 1956, 1956-51-1a--d--4b. **Rear view** as above.

Page 170 (right) Catherine Middleton arrives to attend her Royal Wedding to Prince William at Westminster Abbey on April 29, 2011 in London, England. Getty UK. Samir Hussein / Contributor.

Page 171 Wedding dress, 1958. Silk taffeta (front view). Scaasi, New York, Chicago History Museum. Gift of Mrs. Kenneth Hirsch. **Rear view** as above.

Chapter 10

Page 175 Bridal portrait, England, 1979. Author's collection.

Page 176 Beatle George Harrison, at his wedding to model Pattie Boyd at Epsom, Surrey, UK, 1966 (detail). File Reference #1013 123 THA. © JRC / The Hollywood Archive – All Rights Reserved. PictureLux / The Hollywood Archive / Alamy Stock Photo.

Page 178 Model wearing a wedding dress on a stage, photo John French. UK, 1961. V&A Images / Alamy Stock Photo.

Page 179 (main image) Wedding dress, 1964 (front view). Brighton Historical Society, Victoria, Australia. **Side view** as above.

Page 179 (left) LOS ANGELES - 1957: Actress Audrey Hepburn poses for a publicity still for the Paramount Pictures film *Funny Face* in 1957 in Los Angeles, California. Photo by Donaldson Collection/Michael Ochs Archives/Getty Images.

Page 180 (main image) Lace wedding dress, 1960s, Fashion Museum Riga (front view). Photograph by Maris Morkans. **Rear view, and page 191** as above.

Page 180 (right) Fashion plates (Women 1800–1819), Plate 051, *Costumes allemand et francois*, 1819 (detail), Metropolitan Museum of Art, New York. Gift of Woodman Thompson.

Page 181 (main image) Beatle George Harrison, at his wedding to model Pattie Boyd at Epsom, Surrey, UK, 1966 (detail). File Reference #1013 123

THA. © JRC / The Hollywood Archive – All Rights Reserved. PictureLux / The Hollywood Archive / Alamy Stock Photo.

Page 181 (left) George Harrison and Patti Boyd Harrison Cut Their Wedding Cake. Bettmann / Contributor.

Page 181 (right) Wedding of Raquel Welch and Patrick Curtis, Paris, 14th February, 1967. (Photo by KEYSTONE-FRANCE/Gamma-Rapho via Getty Images).

Page 182 (main image) Studio portrait of D'Anna Thornton Wakefield in a wedding dress – Tallahassee, Florida, 1967, Florida Memory. Richard Parks collection. N2008- 5, Photographic collection, ca 1962–1974; Box 6.

Page 182 (right) Daisy bridal veil by Ashley Wild, 2021. Ashley Wild Designs, photography by Lydia Stamps https://www.lydiastampsphotography.com/.

Page 183 (main image) Thai silk wedding mini dress, 1968, New Zealand, loan courtesy of Enid Eiriksson. **Detail** as above.

Page 183 (right) Horatio, Robley, Three watercolor on paper studies of Māori rafters. Each is a different design in white, black and red, c.1860s, Signed. Undated (detail), gifted by Lady Florence Maclean.

Page 183 (left) Portrait of the bride and groom. Loan courtesy of Enid Eiriksson.

Page 184 (main image) Wedding dress, 1969 (front side view), Brisbane, Queensland Museum. Queensland Museum Network, H48204.

Page 184 (left, above) Headshot of American actor Geraldine Chaplin, wearing a large fur hat and collar, looking straight ahead in a scene from director David Lean's film, *Doctor Zhivago*, 1965. Photo by Hulton Archive/Getty Images.

Page 184 (left, below) Kino. Camelot, (CAMELOT) USA, 1967, Regie: Joshua Logan, VANESSA REDGRAVE. Photo by FilmPublicityArchive/United Archives via Getty Images.

Page 185 (main image) Wedding dress by Lillian Canter, c.1970 (front view). Author's collection/ photo by Aaron Robotham. **Rear view** as above.

Page 185 (left) Wedding dress by Emenson, c.1970, Author's collection.

Page 185 (right) English actress Diana Rigg wearing a lace outfit in a promotional portrait for *On Her Majesty's Secret Service*, directed by Peter R. Hunt, 1969. Rigg plays Contessa Teresa di Vicenzo/Tracy Bond in the film. Photo by Silver Screen Collection/ Getty Images.

Page 186 Wedding dress in gabardine silk paired with nun's headpiece in tulle, from Carven's winter collection. Keystone Press / Alamy Stock Photo.

Page 187 (main image) Polyester wedding dress, 1973, Fashion Archives and Museum, Shippensburg University (front view). **Detail, and page 190** as above.

Page 187 (top right) Princess Anne and Mark Phillips pose on the balcony of Buckingham Palace in London after their wedding, UK, 14th November 1973. (Photo by Evening Standard/ Hulton Archive/Getty Images). Evening Standard / Stringer.

Page 187 (left) Parachute silk wedding dress worn in a displaced persons camp, 1940s. US Holocaust Memorial Museum, courtesy of Lilly Lax Friedman.

Page 188 (main image) Wedding dress by Guy Laroche, late 1970s, Fashion Museum Riga (front view). Photograph by Maris Morkans. **Rear view and detail** as above.

Page 188 (right) Guy Laroche Fall-Winter runway collection 1977-78 (Photo by Pierre Vauthey/ Sygma/Sygma via Getty Images).

Page 189 (main image) Wedding dress, 1977, Newcastle, private collection (front view). Photograph by Aaron Robotham. **Rear view** as above.

Page 189 (left, above) Plastron (Collar) from a Tunic, Metal wrapped thread, wool, glass; embroidered, Metropolitan Museum of Art, New York. Gift of Mrs. Ormond Riblet, 1948.

Page 189 (right) Wedding portrait, 1977, private collection.

Page 189 (left, below) Francesco di Giorgio Martini, *The Nativity* (detail), mid 1400s. The Metropolitan Museum of Art, New York. Gift of George Blumenthal, 1941. 41.100.2; National Gallery of Art, Washington, D.C. Samuel H. Kress Collection, 1952.5.8.

Chapter 11

Page 195 Bride and groom, 1996, England. Private collection.

Page 198 Wedding dress, 1981, Brisbane, Queensland Museum (front side view). Queensland Museum Network. Rear view, as above.

Page 199 (main image) Wedding dress, 1981, Brisbane (front view). Western Australian Academy of Performing Arts. **Rear view** as above.

Page 199 (above, center) The New York Public Library. "Joan Ponsonby, 1891" *The New York Public Library Digital Collections*. 1905. https:// digitalcollections.nypl.org/items/510d47e0-eb5b-a3d9-e040-e00a18064a99.

Page 199 (right) Fashion plates (Women 1890–1896) Plate 031 (detail), Journal Demoiselle, 1894, Metropolitan Museum of Art, New York. Gift of Woodman Thompson.

Page 200 (main image) Wedding dress, International Ladies' Garment Workers' Union (ILGWU) 1989–90 (front view). Author's collection/photo by Aaron Robotham. **Rear view** as above,

Page 200 (top right) Hat worn with ILGWU dress, 1989-90. Author's collection.

Page 201 (main image) Wedding dress designed by Riitta Immonen, Finland, 1990. The Finnish Heritage Agency. Photograph by Seppo Konstig.

Page 201 (right) Pipsa Kaihua at her wedding to Vesa Pallasvesa, Helsinki, 1974. The Finnish Heritage Agency. Photograph by *Kari Rainer Pulkkinen*.

Page 202 (main image) Wedding dress, 1992, Philadelphia (front view). Author's collection/ photo by Aaron Robotham. **Rear view and detail** as above.

Page 203 (main image) Wedding dress by Victor Costa, 1992 (front view). Courtesy of Texas Fashion Collection, University of North Texas College of Visual Arts & Design, photographer Andrew Jones. Gift of the Estate of Doris I. Dixon, 1996.016.002. **Rear view** as above.

Page 203 (above center) Close-up view of just-married couple Sarah, Duchess of York and Prince Andrew, Duke of York as they kiss on kiss the balcony of Buckingham Palace, London, England, July 23, 1986 (detail). Photo by Derek Hudson/ Getty Images.

Page 203 (right) PARIS, FRANCE - OCTOBER 12: Haute Couture designs are exhibited from Jean Patou par Christian Lacroix (L) Thierry Mugler (R) during the press preview of The Collection of Danielle Luquet De Saint Germain on display at Drouot on October 12, 2013 in Paris, France. Photo by Kristy Sparow/Getty Images.

Page 204 (main image) Wedding ensemble by Frans Hoogendoorn, The Hague, 1994 (front view). Kunstmuseum Den Haag. **Side view and bow detail** as above.

Page 204 (inset far left) Raffia top hat, French, c.1820, Metropolitan Museum of Art, New York. Gift of Michael E. Lane, 1984.

Page 204 (inset left) Bride and groom kneeling at altar during wedding ceremony with wedding party, minister, and guests looking on], c.1980–90 (detail). Library of Congress, Prints & Photographs Division, Visual Materials from the Rosa Parks Papers, [reproduction number, e.g., LC-DIG-ppmsca-38464].

Page 204 (right) Woman's Dress (Redingote) Europe, circa 1790 (detail). LACMA. Purchased with funds provided by Robert and Mary M. Looker (M.2009.120).

Image Credits **251**

Page 205 (main image) Wedding dress by Vivienne Westwood, 1999. National Gallery of Victoria, Melbourne. Purchased, 2001 © Public Domain. This digital record has been made available on NGV Collection Online through the generous support of Professor AGL Shaw AO Bequest.

Page 205 (left) 1770s Italian silk stays. Gift of The Metropolitan Museum of Art, New York, 1940.

Page 205 (right) Private collection.

Chapter 12

Page 208 Bride with her parents, Brooklyn, New York, 2012. Courtesy of Romanie Garcia-Lee.

Page 210 Vegas chapel wedding portrait, 2013. Courtesy of Kristy Juengling.

Page 211 A civil partnership celebrated on Loch Goil, Scotland, in February 2011. Courtesy of Drs. Chloe Goodall and Miriam Buncombe.

Page 213 Signing the register in a floral wedding dress, 2019, Western Australia. Courtesy of Dr. C. Lagos Urbina and R. Tobar.

Page 215 Wedding dress worn for an Orthodox Jewish ceremony. Courtesy of Lauren Joshua.

Page 216 (main image) Wedding dress worn with hijab, 2011, USA. Courtesy of Khadijah Abdul-Aleem.

Page 216 (left) *Fatima looking out over garden, with birds* (detail), 1921. The Miriam and Ira D. Wallach Division of Art, Prints and Photographs: Picture Collection, The New York Public Library. "Fatima looking out over garden, with birds" The New York Public Library Digital Collections.

Page 217 (main image) WALTHAM, MA - MAY 21: A gypsy wedding dress, priced at $20,000, with swarovski crystal pins and flat-back crystals. Dress designer Sondra Celli and her staff, including "The Blingettes," work on gypsy wedding party clothes, on Monday, May 21, 2012. Photo by Pat Greenhouse/The Boston Globe via Getty Images.

Page 217 (left) Pnina Tornai For Kleinfeld – Runway – New York Fashion Week: Bridal October 2016. Photo by Albert Urso/Getty Images.

Page 217 (right) Bridal fashion, *Englishwoman's Domestic Magazine*, April 1865, (detail), Metropolitan Museum of Art, New York. Gift of Woodman Thompson.

Page 218 (main image) Wedding dress Designed by Carolina Herrera; Worn by Rachel Frishberg Press, 2013. Philadelphia Museum of Art: Gift of Rachel Frishberg Press, 2013, 2013-12-1.

Page 218 (left) Dinner dress by Mme. Grapanche, 1884–86, Metropolitan Museum of Art, New York. Gift of Mrs. J. Randall Creel, 1963.

Page 218 (right) Portrait of the bride and groom, 2013. Courtesy of Rachel Frishberg Press.

Page 219 (main image) London, UK. 12th Aug, 2017. Day 2, Show 1. The Tubo designs are presented by models on the runway. This show features designs by Jutu, Becca Apparel, Luvita Creations, Abisola Akanri, Atelier Nsoromma, Trish O, Tubo. Valerie Azinge Atelier, Tobams Colours. Since debuting in 2011, the two day Africa Fashion Week London, AFWL, has grown into one of the largest Africa inspired fashion events in Europe. Imageplotter News and Sports/Alamy Live News.

Page 219 (left) Ballgown, House of Worth, 1889 (detail), Metropolitan Museum of Art, New York. Gift of Mrs. James G. Flockhart, 1968.

Page 220 (main image) BARCELONA, SPAIN – APRIL 26: A model walks the runway at Randy Fenoli fashion show during the Valmont Barcelona Bridal Fashion Week at Fira Barcelona Montjuic on April 26th, 2019 in Barcelona, Spain. Photo by Estrop/Getty Images.

Page 220 (left) Wedding dress by Randy Fenoli, 2019, Getty UK BARCELONA, SPAIN – APRIL 26: A model walks the runway at Randy Fenoli fashion show during the Valmont Barcelona Bridal Fashion Week at Fira Barcelona Montjuic on April 26th, 2019 in Barcelona, Spain. Photo by Estrop/Getty Images.

Page 221 (main image) Wedding dress by Queera, 2021. Courtesy of Curtis Cassell. **Rear view and details** as above.

Page 221 (right, center) Wedding shirt, 1830-70, Metropolitan Museum of Art, New York. Brooklyn Museum Costume Collection at The Metropolitan Museum of Art, New York. Gift of the Brooklyn Museum, 2009; Ella C. Woodward Memorial Fund, 1926.

Page 221 (right, below) Julie Andrews in *The Sound of Music*, 1965. Photo by RDB/ullstein bild via Getty Images.

Page 221 (right, above) Mr. and Mrs. Niemeläinen's wedding photo, 1938 (detail), Suomi, Helsinki, Finland Museovirasto (Museum Agency), History picture collection, Fotografiamo Pietinen's collection.

Page 222 (main image) Dress by Aliansa, Tokyo, 2022/23.

Page 222 (left) *Flower Arrangement of Suisen (Narcissus) in a Flat Green Dish* (detail) by Utagawa Toyohiro (Japanese, 1763–1828), Metropolitan Museum of Art, New York. Gift of Estate of Samuel Isham, 1914.

Page 223 Woman's Overrobe (Uchikake) with Books and Mandarin Orange Branches, Japan, first half of the 19th century. Metropolitan Museum of Art, New York. Gift of Mr. and Mrs. Earl Morse, 1972.

Page 224 (main image) Beautiful young woman with white lolita dress with European garden Japanese fashion, 2022. Oran Tantapakul / Alamy Stock Photo.

Page 224 (left) Fashion plate (Weddings, 1820–1869) Plate 047, *Godey's Lady's Book*, 1850. Metropolitan Museum of Art. Gift of Woodman Thompson.

Page 225 (main image) Eco Wedding Dress by Miranda Bennett Studios, 2023 (front view). Courtesy Miranda Bennett Studio.

Page 225 (left) Cristóbal Balenciaga, designer. Chemise dress, *c.* 1957, RISDM, 1997.83. Museum purchase with funds from the Fine Arts Committee and Mary B. Jackson Fund.

Page 225 (right) Wedding portrait, Bristol, UK, 2018, private collection.

Page 226 (main image) Wedding dress by Chrissy Wai-Ching, 2023. Photograph by Eva Blanchard. **Detail**, as above.

Page 226 (inset, far left) Biographies of Lian Po and Lin Xiangru. Calligrapher Huang Tingjian Chinese, *c.* 1095 (detail), Metropolitan Museum of Art, New York. Bequest of John M. Crawford Jr., 1988.

Page 226 (right) Art plus diplomacy. Washington, D.C., May 13. Miss Virginia Chang, star of the Chinese Cultural Theater, yesterday changed her role of Queen to the role of bride. She was married in the beautiful Gardens of Twin Oaks, the Chinese Embassy, to Kien-Wen Yu, second secretary of the embassy. The simple Chinese ceremony culminated a whirlwind romance and was performed by Chinese ambassador, Dr. Hu Shih. Left to right: Chinese ambassador Dr. Hu Shih, the bride, and Kien-Wen Yu (detail), Library of Congress. Harris & Ewing photograph collection.

Page 227 (main image) Modern bridal hanbok by Leehwa, 2023. Designed and handmade by Laura H. Park, founder of Leehwa Wedding & Hanbok, based in Los Angeles, California.

Page 227 (right) Modern bridal hanbok by Leehwa, 2023 (white and gold). Designed and handmade by Laura H. Park, founder of Leehwa Wedding & Hanbok, based in Los Angeles, California.

Page 227 (left) A traditional formal robe known as hwarot, late 19th–early 20th century. Minneapolis Institute of Art. Gift of Kang Collection, Korean Fine Art, in honor of Dr. Matthew Welch.

Index

A

Aboriginal Australian 106
African wedding dress (*see also* Nigerian wedding dress) 8–9, 48, 163, 174, 219
Alfred Angelo 161, 169, 197
A-line 8, 147, 175, 180, 182, 220
American Civil War 70–71, 81, 83
Anne, Princess Royal 187
Applique 96, 101, 106, 114, 121, 169, 178–179, 185, 198–200, 219–220, 224,
Armenian wedding 22
Austen, Jane 47, 52

B

Balenciaga, Christobal 171, 186, 225
Ballet 126, 162, 199, 216
"Ballgown" wedding dress (*see also* "Princess" wedding dress) 10, 197, 208, 215–217, 224, 228
Beading 21, 52, 55, 83, 101, 104, 106, 126, 139–140, 183, 200, 202–203, 208, 211, 215–216, 221
Beatles, The 181
Bouquet 33, 41, 50, 61, 75, 77, 82, 126, 127, 132, 137, 139, 141, 150, 178, 182–185
Bridal crown (*see also* Tiara) 77, 137, 224, 227
Bridal magazines/columns 47–48, 52, 59, 70, 83, 90–91, 96, 98, 102, 104, 107, 116, 121, 132, 134, 144, 160–161, 175–176, 189, 194, 201–202, 205, 213, 215, 219, 225, 227
Bridal salon 114, 177, 203, 228

Bridesmaids 33, 41, 48, 70–71, 74, 112, 116–118, 120, 123–124, 128, 133, 136, 166, 181–187, 200, 226, 228–229
Boyd, Pattie 181, 184
Bustle 71, 83, 96–98, 102, 104–108, 147, 165, 188, 200, 203, 205, 215, 218

C

Cape (*see also* Pelerine) 62, 188
Cap 31, 33, 58, 125, 127–128, 133, 146, 166, 170, 189, 202
Cassell, Curtis (QUEERA) 212, 221
Charlotte, Princess of Wales 56, 64
Cheongsam 10, 212, 226, 228
Chinese wedding (*see also* Cheongsam and Qi Pao) 10, 113, 163, 226, 228
Civil partnership (*see also* Same sex wedding, *see also* LGBTQIA+) 210–211, 221
Clandestine wedding 29, 228
Cloak 152
Coat 29, 82, 96–97, 120, 181–182, 184, 186, 188, 204
Collar 51, 75–76, 81, 83, 97, 101, 103, 105, 107, 117–118, 126–127, 129, 138, 148, 150–151, 164, 166–167, 169, 183–185, 187–188, 198, 221, 226, 228
Corsage 43, 160, 180, 201
Corset (*see also* Stays) 93, 154, 205, 224, 228
Crepe 52, 55, 117, 125–126, 138, 140, 145, 149, 184–185

Crinoline (skirt support) 76–83, 165, 216–217

D

Department stores 93, 112, 114, 117, 125–127, 136, 146, 166, 194, 196
Diamonds 56, 102, 117
Diana, Princess of Wales 194, 196, 198–199
Dior, Christian (*see also* New Look) 154, 160, 162, 166–167, 169, 171
Disney 196–197, 216
Don't Tell the Bride 12
Dress reform 69, 93, 120
Dropped waist 134, 138–141, 202, 215

E

Eliot, George 103
Elopement 29, 48, 149, 209, 228
Embroidery 16–18, 20–21, 29, 32, 35–36, 46, 50–53, 56, 59–60, 73, 97, 101, 107, 114, 124, 126–127, 135–136, 168, 170, 183–184, 200, 215, 219, 226–227
Empire line 50–64, 58, 120, 124, 128, 136, 153, 174, 178, 180, 182, 187, 189, 225, 227
Evening dress 47–48, 51, 54–55, 57, 63, 73, 80, 91, 107, 119, 133, 147–148, 150, 152, 167, 171, 179–180, 184, 202–203, 224

F

Fan 31, 107
Fascinator 202

Index 253

Fashion plate 47, 50, 52, 55, 57, 59, 61, 63, 73, 75–76, 80, 83, 96, 98, 100, 103–105, 107, 118, 124, 199, 217
Fenoli, Randy (see also *Say Yes to the Dress*, see also Kleinfeld bridal salon), 220
Fichu (see also Neckerchief) 35, 41, 50, 54, 58, 60, 62, 204
French Revolution 46, 50
Fur 37, 99, 135, 152, 181, 184, 186

G
Gaultier, Jean Paul 205
Garter 16, 21, 82, 161, 224, 228
Gibson, Charles Dana 121,
Gloves 59, 73, 104, 124, 178, 194, 203
"Granny" dress 185, 188–189
Going-away dress 152
Great Depression, The 144–145
Grecian 16, 36, 52, 57, 122, 165, 187
Groom's clothing 21–22, 29, 31, 35, 50, 76, 106, 132, 135, 146–147, 163, 174, 181, 183, 221
Grunge fashion 197
Gypsy (traveller) wedding 217

H
Hanbok 146, 227
Hat (bridal) 50, 114, 124, 127, 133, 135, 140, 144, 146, 178, 183, 186, 200, 204
Hepburn, Audrey 169, 179
Herrera, Carolina 168, 218
Hijab 216
Hogarth, William 31, 33
Holocaust 146, 151, 187
Honeymoon 94, 102, 161, 197, 228
Hoogendoorn, Frans 204

I
ILGWU (International Ladies' Garment Workers' Union) 200
Illusion neckline 219
Indian wedding 9, 229
Italian Renaissance 120, 189

J
Japanese Lolita 194, 224
Japanese wedding (see also Kimono) 9
Jewish wedding 16, 20, 48–49, 69, 151, 215

K
Katherine, Princess of Wales 10, 170, 220
Kelly, Grace 163, 170
Kennedy, Jacqueline 168
Keveza, Ramona 219
Kimono 9, 146, 163, 171, 196, 222, 224, 227–228
Kleinfeld bridal salon 218, 220
Knitwear 149, 160, 182, 189,
Korean wedding (see also Hanbok) 145–146, 227

L
Lace 31, 33, 37, 50–52, 63, 68, 70, 73, 76–79, 81–82, 90, 97–99, 101, 103–105, 107, 114, 117, 121, 123, 127, 133–134, 138, 141, 149–150, 164–167, 169, 178, 180, 183, 185–186, 188, 194, 199–200, 202–203, 205, 208–209, 215–216, 219, 224
Bobbin 53, 59–61, 118, 125, 179
Brussels 100
Chantilly 220
Crochet 97, 139
Guipure 179, 182, 184
Limerick 137
Point lace 56, 91, 148, 168, 170, 220
Swiss lace 60
Lanvin, Jean 133, 138
Las Vegas wedding 209–210
Laroche, Guy 188
LGBTQIA+ (see also Same-sex wedding, see also Civil partnership, see also Transgender) 210, 221
Lingerie 91, 169, 228
Lhuillier, Monique 214, 219
Lowe, Ann 168

M
Marchesa 221
Marie Antoinette 56, 97, 154
Mary, Princess Royal 134, 141
Mary, Queen of Scots 16
Mini dress 174, 178, 181, 183, 188, 228
Minimalist/ism 170, 177–178, 195, 202, 209
Mourning 9–10, 71, 81, 83, 93, 117, 123, 227
Muslim wedding (see also Hijab) 216
Muslin 46–47, 52

N
Neckerchief (see also Fichu) 50, 204
Neckline
Square 52–53, 101, 189, 201
Sweetheart 31, 166–167, 199, 202, 220
V-neck 105, 126, 153, 167, 171
New Look (see also Christian Dior) 147, 154, 167, 169, 171, 174, 178, 225,
Nigerian wedding dress (see also African wedding dress) 8, 48, 163, 174, 219
Norell, Norman 154, 157, 171, 178
Norwegian wedding 40

O

One-shouldered dress 217
Orange blossom 21, 35, 59, 70, 76, 90–92, 94, 96, 100, 102–103, 107, 123, 163, 168, 170

P

Packham, Jenny 221
Parachute Silk 153
Pearls 16, 18, 20, 31, 47–48, 52, 55–56, 96, 99, 101, 107, 117, 132, 138, 149–150, 164–165, 170, 183, 187, 200, 202, 215, 228
Pelerine (*see also* Cape) 62
Penny wedding 58, 228
Pettibone, Claire 221
Petticoat 28–29, 32–34, 36, 38–41, 52, 61, 93, 121, 128, 154, 169–171, 178–179, 199, 227, 228–229
Pleats
    Bodice 38–39, 40, 61, 72, 76, 105, 107, 116, 124, 165, 221
    Skirt 102, 116, 122, 140, 178, 186, 227
Philippines (fabric) 208
Polyester 176, 187, 208, 216
"Princess" or wedding dress (*see also* "ballgown" wedding dress) 10, 197, 208, 215–217, 217, 224, 228
Priscilla of Boston 161, 166
Print fabrics 41, 62–63, 123, 189,
Purse 135

Q

Qi pao (*see also* Chinese wedding) 146
Quaker wedding 18, 54, 69, 81
Queen Elizabeth 166
Queen Victoria 63, 68, 70, 73, 77–78, 90–91, 100, 102

R

Rationing 114, 146, 153, 160–161, 164–165, 114, 146, 153, 160–161, 164–165
Rayon (*see also* Synthetic fabrics) 117, 147, 164, 166, 171
Robe à la
    Française (*see also* Sack dress) 30–31, 34, 38–40, 229
    l'Anglaise 34, 38, 128, 228
    Polonaise 39, 97, 228
Robe de Style 128, 134, 141, 138

S

Sack dress (*see also* Robe à la Française) 39–40, 141
Sack dress (1950s) 171, 225
Same-sex wedding, (*see also* LGBTQIA+, *see also* Civil partnership) 210–211, 221–222,
Sash 77, 80, 82, 107, 119, 121, 125, 127–128, 136, 153, 170, 173, 197, 221, 228
Say Yes to the Dress (*see also* Fenoli, Randy, Tornai, Pnina, and Kleinfeld bridal salon) 12, 213, 220
Scaasi, Arnold 171
Second-day Wedding 36
Sequins 17, 56, 99, 202–203, 216
Shawl 53, 58, 188–189
Shell 41, 56, 72, 101, 150
Shirring 114, 123, 139, 141, 153,
Shoes 16, 58, 107, 126, 150, 175, 181–183, 212
Silver tissue (metallic fabric) 31, 56, 141
Sleeveless wedding dress 133, 139, 141, 150, 174, 188, 215, 220, 228
Sofia Magdalena, Princess of Denmark 37
"Something blue" 79, 96, 183
Stays (*see also* Corset) 37, 205
Stockings 50, 106, 181, 224

Strapless wedding dress 196, 205, 208, 211, 215–216, 218, 222, 227
Suit (for bride, *see also* Travelling suit) 94–95, 100, 102, 104, 118, 122, 135, 160, 185, 200, 204, 228
Swedish wedding 37, 77, 82
Synthetic fabrics (*see also* Rayon) 70, 147, 170, 196, 199

T

Taylor, Elizabeth 167
Tiara (*see also* Bridal crown) 133, 201, 215, 218, 227, 229
Tornai, Pnina 217
Train (skirt) 20, 37, 42, 52–56, 60, 69, 71, 91, 99–101, 104, 107, 112, 118, 120–122, 124, 126, 134, 137–140, 150–152, 160–161, 164–165, 171, 179–180, 182–183, 185, 187, 189, 201, 203–205, 214, 218, 221, 224, 226, 229
    Cathedral length 166–167
    Demi 96
    Detachable 35, 136, 184, 200
    Square 136, 139, 165
Transgender (*see also* LGBTQIA+) 211–212, 221
Travelling suit or dress (*see also* Suit) 47, 94–95, 100, 102, 104, 118, 122, 135, 228
Trousseau 16, 20, 46–47, 50, 70, 76, 82, 91, 93, 96, 107, 114, 120, 122, 128, 132, 150, 170–171, 184, 229
Tubobereni, Sandrah 219
Tulle 48, 55, 63, 78, 94, 125, 137, 140, 146, 163, 169, 171, 181, 186, 197, 201, 208, 216,

U

Ueda, Eiko 218

V

Veil, 16 21–22, 47–48, 51, 53–54, 59, 63, 73, 76, 82, 90, 94, 99–100, 103, 112–114, 123–125, 127, 133–135, 137, 140, 144, 146, 150, 152, 162–163, 168, 171, 175, 178–184, 186–187, 203–204, 212, 215, 218, 226, 228–229

Circular 170
    Finger-tip length 166
    Floor-length 139, 165, 204
    Mantilla 182
    Shoulder-length 180, 203
    Tiered 165

W

Wang, Vera 195, 203, 205, 217
Watteau pleats 39, 180, 201, 221

World War One 22, 135, 141, 184
World War Two 146, 153, 184

Z

Zips 158